International Law

Aspen Treatise Series

International Law

Ninth Edition

MARK WESTON JANIS
William F. Starr Professor of Law
University of Connecticut
Formerly Reader in Law and Fellow of Exeter College
University of Oxford

ASPEN
PUBLISHING

Cover image: iStock.com/Jitalia17

To contact Customer Service, e-mail customer.service@aspenpublishing.com, call 1-800-950-5259, or mail correspondence to:

Aspen Publishing
Attn: Order Department
1 Wall Street
Burlington, MA 01803

1 2 3 4 5 6 7 8 9 0

ISBN 979-8-8920-7538-1

Library of Congress Cataloging-in-Publication Data

Names: Janis, Mark W. author
Title: International law / Mark Weston Janis, William F. Starr Professor of Law, University of Connecticut, Formerly Reader in Law and Fellow of Exeter College, University of Oxford.
Description: Ninth edition. | Burlington : Aspen Publishing, 2026. | Includes index. | Summary: "Treatise on International Law for law students"—Provided by publisher.
Identifiers: LCCN 2026017744 | ISBN 9798892075381 hardcover | ISBN 9798892075404 ebook
Subjects: LCSH: International law | Conflict of laws | International economic relations | International courts | International agencies
Classification: LCC KZ3140.J36 A35 2026
LC record available at https://lccn.loc.gov/2026017744

ABOUT ASPEN PUBLISHING

Aspen Publishing is a leading provider of legal education content and digital learning solutions in the United States and globally. Our innovative products and platforms—designed based on best practices in learning science—engage students and enhance outcomes. From textbooks and audiobooks authored by renowned experts to digital platforms and products like LEAF, Connected eBooks, Connected Quizzing, PracticePerfect, and JD-Next, we empower the next generation of legal professionals with innovative, trusted, and accessible resources.

The Aspen Casebook Series, affectionately known as the "red and black" casebooks among law faculty and students, includes hundreds of highly regarded textbooks across more than 80 disciplines. These range from foundational courses like Torts and Contracts to emerging electives such as Sustainability and the Law of Policing. Our study aids, including the popular *Examples & Explanations* series, help law students master complex topics with clarity and confidence.

Aspen's expertise extends to undergraduate education with our Paralegal, Criminal Justice, and Business Law series, offering the same hallmark quality to a broader audience. JD-Next, our groundbreaking online law school prep course and admissions test, provides a realistic preview of law school, equips students with essential skills for academic success, and evaluates their readiness for legal studies.

Aspen Publishing Is Proud to Be a UWorld Company

Since 2003, UWorld has been a global leader in developing high-quality learning tools for students preparing for high-stakes exams. With a commitment to excellence, UWorld has helped millions of students in undergraduate, graduate, and professional programs in fields such as medicine, nursing, finance, and law achieve their academic and career goals.

Founded by Chandra S. Pemmasani, M.D., during his medical residency, UWorld began focusing on medical education and has since expanded into various academic fields, including law. In 2020, UWorld launched its Legal vertical, starting with its comprehensive Multistate Bar Exam (MBE®) Question Bank, followed by the acquisition of Themis Bar Review, which integrated resources to provide a complete bar exam preparation experience. In 2024, UWorld expanded its offerings by acquiring Aspen Publishing, enhancing its suite of legal education products.

Today, UWorld offers an unparalleled range of study materials that blend active learning methods with expert content, ensuring students and educators can access the most effective resources. From bar preparation to law school success, UWorld is committed to supporting the next generation of legal professionals. Learn more at uworld.com.

To Janet and the boys

Summary of Contents

Contents

Preface

This book endeavors to introduce the discipline of international law in such a way as to clarify and order a dauntingly complex and variegated subject. It is written with J.L. Brierly's English classic, *The Law of Nations*, in mind. It is my aim to provide a book, as Brierly did first in 1928 and last in 1955, "not intended as a substitute for the standard text-books on the subject, but as an introduction either for students who are beginning their law courses, or, I hope, for laymen who wish to form some idea of the part that law plays, or that we may reasonably hope that it will play, in the relation of states." Two important distinctions, besides the obvious one of relative modernity, distinguish Brierly's book and mine. First, Brierly's book drew heavily, though far from exclusively, on British practice in international law; mine emphasizes the international practice of the United States. Second, this book's ambit is somewhat broader than Brierly's in that I introduce international law not only in its traditional public or interstate sense, but also in its increasingly important private and commercial aspects.

Between this ninth edition and the earlier editions (1988, 1993, 1999, 2003, 2008, 2012, 2016, and 2021) more changes have been made to the substantive international law of the later chapters than to the early conceptual chapters that introduce international legal rules and process. Besides just keeping up to date, this new edition captures, I hope, the spirit of our transition to the post–Cold War era and the re-emergence of nationalism and the problems posed by American exceptionalism, both judicial and political to international law. Brierly's *The Law of Nations* faced similar transitional tasks: The first two editions of 1928 and 1936 were written amidst all the doubts about the viability of international law in the interwar period, the third edition of 1942 emerged in the carnage of World War II, and the fourth and fifth editions of 1949 and 1955 sought to capture the flavor of the Cold War and the new threat of nuclear annihilation. My book shares Brierly's view, expressed in his fourth edition, that international law "is neither a myth on the one hand, nor a panacea on the other, but just one institution among others which we can use for the building of a saner international order."

Three questions more or less structure the text: What are international legal rules? What is international legal process? What role does international law play in international relations? Answering the questions in order yields an unremarkable organization for an international law book except that the law of treaties is discussed alongside the topic of treaties as a source of international law, public international arbitration and the International Court follow immediately after the role of international law in the municipal courts, and, as aforementioned, the "private" as well as the "public" part of international law is introduced. The book is meant to reflect international law generally and should prove a useful read either on its own or as a supplement to any of the standard American legal or political casebooks on the subject. Except for a fuller rendering of some sources normally abbreviated, the standard forms of American legal citation have been followed in the footnotes.

Although the book and its faults are mine, I know that its perspectives have been shaped and sharpened by the able scholars who taught me, especially Thomas Kuhn and Joseph Strayer at Princeton, Brian Simpson and Humphrey Waldock at Oxford, and Louis Sohn and Henry Steiner at Harvard; to them I am particularly grateful. Three years in the Navy, three more practicing international law with Sullivan & Cromwell in New York and Paris, and now 45 years teaching in the United States, England, and continental Europe have given me certain insights but denied me others. Let me thank friends and colleagues who have helped along the way: Dapo Akende, William Alford, Nicholas Bamforth, David Bederman, Rudolf Bernhardt, Phillip Blumberg, Fernand Boulan, Tony Bradley, John Bridge, Ian Brownlie, Thomas Buergenthal, George Bustin, William Butler, Dan Caldwell, David Caron, Dominique Carreau, Fred Chapman, Frederick Chen, Sarah Cox, Paul Craig, James Crawford, Donald Daniel, Yves Daudet, Ruth Deech, Jozef Deelen, Laura Dickinson, Carolyn Evans, François Ewald, Tim Fisher, Francesco Francioni, James Friedberg, Jochen Frowein, Albert Gastmann, Martin Glassner, Edward Gordon, Richard Graving, Christine Gray, Keith Highet, Garfield Horn, James Hyde, Olimpiad Ioffe, Karel Jungwiert, Richard Kay, Benedict Kingsbury, Harold Koh, Hans Christian Krüger, Molly Land, Dominik Lasok, Herbert Lazerow, Detlef Leenen, Randall Lesaffer, Michel Lesage, Vaughan Lowe, Houston Lowry, Robert Lutz, Hugh Macgill, Daniel Magraw, Aleth and Phillipe Manin, Geoffrey Marshall, Myres McDougal, Willajeanne McLean, Thomas Morawetz, John Murphy, James Nafziger, Ved Nanda, Eboni Nelson, John Noyes, Daniel O'Connell, Mary Ellen O'Connell, William Park, Jeremy Paul, David Perrott, Ellen Peters, Istvan Pogany, David Pugsley, Michael Reisman, Eibe Riedel, Adam Roberts, Horace Robertson, Alfred Rubin, Leila Sadat, Dan Sarooshi, Henry Schermers, Stephen Schwebel, David Seymour, Anne-Marie Slaughter,

Ted Stein, Dennis Stone, Kurt Strasser, Stefan Talmon, Nicholas Triffin, Jean Van den Eynde, Willem Van Genugten, Carlos Vazquez, Brian Walsh, Wang Tieya, Ruth Wedgwood, Christopher Weeramantry, Carol Weisbrod, Luzius Wildhaber, Richard Wilson, Ineta Ziemele, and Elizabeth Zoller. Thanks are also due to my students at Connecticut, Cornell, UCLA, Oxford, Paris, Strasbourg, Tilburg, Münster, and Riga; to my research assistants over all the editions, James Streeto, Peter Morgan, John Fitzpatrick, Ricardo Sousa, Richard Wilde, Jennifer Glaudemans, Dora Ziamou, Woo Lee, Susanne Brose, Bridgett Sandusky, Michael Casey, Brent Houston, John Von Kohorn, Robert Menzel, Rytas Stankunas, Eric Hisey, Blake Ratcliff, Darcy Jones, Scott Schaeffer, Rebecca Ullman, Joanne Cossitt, Derek Ghan, Nancy Livak, Joanna Taatjes, David Woods, Kyle Zelazny, Adam Yagaloff, Lauren Birt, Michael Knortz, Hilary Polak, Cassidy Mills, Christian Burr, Christopher Gelino, Richard Joslyn, Christian Torres, and Ariana Monson; to my secretaries and typists, Kathe Kane, Sharon Lizak, Sandra Michalik, Delia Roy, Joan Wood, and Margaret Kent; to my publishers at Little Brown, Aspen, and Wolters Kluwer, Richard Heuser, Carol McGeehan, David Bemelmans, Elizabeth Kenny, Richard Kravitz, Dan Mangan, Jessica Barmack, Eric Holt, John Devins, Dena Kaufman, Tom Daughhetee, Eric Song, and Ameer Malik; and, of course, to Janet, and my sons Matthew, Robert, Philip, and Edward, and their families.

Mark Weston Janis

Hartford & Oxford
February 2026

International Law

CHAPTER 1

The Nature of International Law

A. THE HISTORY OF INTERNATIONAL LAW

The roots of international law run deep in history. In early religious and secular writings, there are many evidences of what we now know as international law; there are, for example, the detailed peace treaties and alliances concluded between the Jews and the Romans, Syrians, and Spartans.[1] The Romans knew of a *jus gentium*, a law of nations, which Gaius, in the second century, saw as a law "common to all men,"[2] a universal law that could be applied by Roman courts to foreigners when the specific law of their own nation was unknown and when Roman law was inapposite. In the seventeenth century, the Dutch jurist Hugo Grotius argued that the law of nations also established legal rules that bound the sovereign states of Europe, then just emerging from medieval society, in their relations with one another.[3] Grotius' classic of 1625, *The Law of War and Peace*, is widely acknowledged, more than any other work, as founding the modern discipline of the law of nations, a subject that, in 1789, the English philosopher Jeremy Bentham renamed and refashioned as "international law."[4]

[1] 1 Maccabees 8:17-32, 11:28-37, 12:1-23.

[2] The Four Commentaries of Gaius on the Institutes of the Civil Law, 1 *The Civil Law* 81 (Scott ed. 1973).

[3] H. Grotius, *De Jure Belli ac Pacis Libri Tres* (Kelsey trans. 1925).

[4] J. Bentham, *An Introduction to the Principles of Morals and Legislation* 296 (Burns and Hart eds. 1970).

Nowadays, the terms the *law of nations* and *international law* are often used interchangeably.

At least since the end of the Thirty Years' War in 1648, world politics has principally involved the relations of more or less independent sovereign states. An important part of international law has consequently had to do with the establishment of a set of mutually agreed-upon rules respecting the nature of these states and their fundamental rights and obligations *inter se* [see Chapter 6]. If there is a single international legal principle underlying the modern state system, it probably is the one neatly framed by Montesquieu in 1748[5] and offered to Napoleon in 1806 by Talleyrand: "that nations ought to do to one another in peace, the most good, and in war, the least evil possible."[6]

International law is sometimes conceived to be divided into public and private parts, the first concerning the legal relations of states, the second involving the law governing the foreign transactions of individuals and corporations. However, the public-private division of international law can be misleading. Many of the laws and processes traditionally within the ambit of public international law actually concern private, not public, parties, while much of the domain of private international law covers the transactions of public entities. Nonetheless, the terms *public* and *private* international law are highly popular and, in a rough kind of way, do compartmentalize legal rules addressing two problem areas: Public international law mostly concerns the political interactions of states [see Chapters 6 and 7]; private international law relates to legal aspects of the international economy and conflicts and cooperation among national legal systems [see Chapters 9 and 10].

Few deny that the rules of international law actually influence state behavior. Even international law's most famous jurisprudential critic, John Austin, acknowledged in 1832 that international legal rules were effective. At the same time, however, he argued that, because there was no international sovereign to enforce it, international law could not be the same sort of positive law as that enacted by sovereign states for internal application:

> [T]he law obtaining between nations is not positive law: for every positive law is set by a given sovereign to a person or persons in a state of

[5] Montesquieu, L'esprit des lois, *Oeuvres complètes* 527, 531 (Editions du Seuil 1964).

[6] T.D. Woolsey, *International Law* 306 (1st ed. 1860).

> subjection to its author. As I have already intimated, the law obtaining between nations is law (improperly so called) set by general opinion. The duties which it imposes are enforced by moral sanctions: by fear on the part of nations, or by fear on the part of sovereigns, of provoking general hostility, and incurring its probable evils, in case they shall violate maxims generally received and respected.[7]

Just a few years later, in 1836, the United States diplomat Henry Wheaton, in the first great English-language treatise on international law, was already grappling with Austin's characterization of the rules governing international politics as being a form of mere "morality."[8] Wheaton accepted Austin's view that international law's principal sanction was "the hazard of provoking the hostility of other communities," but contended that "[e]xperience shows that these motives, even in the worst times, do really afford a considerable security for the observance of justice between States, if they do not furnish the perfect sanction annexed by the lawgiver to the observance of the municipal code of any particular State."[9] Unlike Austin, Wheaton found international law sufficiently law-like to justify calling it "law,"[10] a definitional outcome reached by generations of subsequent international lawyers.[11]

Whether the international rules regulating interstate behavior are to be properly termed "legal" or "moral" is in truth a question that can only be answered after one has made more or less arbitrary definitions of what really constitutes "law" and "morality," a sometimes sterile exercise.[12] Suffice it to say at this early stage of our own discussion that there are a great many rules regulating international politics commonly referred to as "international law" and that these rules are usually, for one reason or another, observed in international practice. Moreover, there is no doubt that the norms of international law are frequently

[7] J. Austin, *The Province of Jurisprudence Determined* 208 (1st ed. 1832).

[8] H. Wheaton, *Elements of International Law with a Sketch of the History of the Science* 47 (1st ed. 1836).

[9] Id. at iii-iv.

[10] Id. at 47-50; see M.W. Janis, *America and the Law of Nations: 1776-1939* 61-69 (2010).

[11] See, e.g., L. Oppenheim, 1 *International Law* 3-15 (8th ed. Lauterpacht 1955).

[12] "The only intelligent way to deal with a verbal question like that concerning the definition of the word 'law' is to give up thinking and arguing about it." Williams, International Law and the Controversy Concerning the Word "Law," 22 *British Yearbook of International Law* 146, 163 (1945).

applied as rules of decision by law courts, domestic [see Chapters 4 and 10] as well as international [see Chapters 5, 7, 8, and 9].

B. THE RULES OF INTERNATIONAL LAW

We know reasonably well how to identify rules of "municipal law" (the term used by international lawyers to denote the internal laws of national legal systems). Municipal rules of law generally are thought to emanate from national constitutions, municipal statutes, executive regulations, and the decisions of municipal courts. Oftentimes the possible sources of municipal law include not only formal legislatures, but also other political structures when these institutions are accepted to actually generate rules of law. Of course, municipal legal systems differ among themselves, and what may be a source of legislation in one country may not be so in another. For example, law courts are thought to be makers of legal rules in the United States, but not in France.

In international law, the identification of legal rules is quite different than it is in most municipal legal systems. The reason for this is directly linked to international law's very nature. Given the international political system of nation-states and the idea of state sovereignty, the sources of international law cannot be equivalent to those of most domestic laws. There are only occasional international imitations of national constitutions, parliaments, executives, and courts. For example, the United Nations system offers only skeletal international governmental bodies that have just begun to be fleshed out in practice [see Chapter 7]. This is not to say that some international organizations, especially regional ones such as the European Union, have not come close to creating municipal-like sources of international law [see Chapter 9.B]. It is only to note that, on the whole, we must abandon most municipal-like sources when we look for the rules of international law.

Given the rarity of effective formal international legislative, executive, and judicial organs, some have said quite simply that international law does not or cannot exist and that the only real rules of law are those generated by sovereign states for their own internal consumption. The trouble with such a simplistic assertion is that it contradicts centuries of practice during which governments, courts, and others have, for one reason or another, found and applied rules of international law.

B. The Rules of International Law

Traditionally, rules of international law have been identified by looking to the various forms of rulemaking conduct of two or more states. Although these different forms of conduct tend to blend one into another, it is helpful at the outset to think of each form as a discrete source of a certain sort of international law.

The first and plainest source of international law is the explicit, usually written, agreements that states make among themselves. These agreements are often labeled treaties or conventions. A municipal law analogy to this source of international law is, of course, the idea of contract. Like contracts, treaties are capable of creating voluntary, though legally binding, relations. These are sometimes known as "conventional international law" [see Chapter 2].

A second source of international law is the customary practice, other than the making of treaties, of states among themselves. Such international customary practice has municipal analogies in commercial law notions such as "the course of dealing" and "the usage of trade," where practice creates justifiable expectations of future observance. International practice is thought capable of creating binding rules of law known as "customary international law" [see Chapter 3.A].

Rather different in conception from the international practice of states as a source of international law is the general municipal practice of states. The idea is that if most or all states observe certain rules as part of their domestic laws, then it may be presumed that these rules are so fundamental as to be more or less automatically a part of international law. Such rules deriving from or reflecting the common municipal laws of states are known as "general principles of law" [see Chapter 3.B.1].

Note how at least the first two sources of international law may be said to emanate from the consent of states. With conventional international law, the states that are parties to a treaty explicitly agree to be bound by certain rules. With customary international law, their consent is implicit, to be found in their international practice.

The consensual notion is, however, not the only possible justification for believing that treaties and custom are proper sources of international law. Some have said that these forms of state conduct are simply manifestations of rules that are bound to exist regardless of state consent and that, beyond general principles of law, there are other sorts of nonconsensual rules of international law, sometimes termed *jus cogens* or fundamental norms. Behind such nonconsensual ideas lie notions of natural law that have been more or less fashionable over time [see Chapter 3.B.2]. A debate between natural lawyers and positive lawyers (as those who insist on the posited rules of states are called) is longstanding in international law. At this juncture, it is more or less immaterial to decide whether positivist or naturalist notions better justify treating state agreements and practice as sources of international law; these sources, at least, being agreed to be sources all the same.

In practice, lawyers, whether positivist or naturalist by persuasion, look to a wide variety of evidences to find, apply, and develop rules of international law. In this search there is sometimes no bright line dividing the evidences of the different sources of international law. For example, a provision of a treaty may be an evidence of state custom in general as well as an evidence of a particular state agreement. It is usually true that the evidences of customary international law, general principles of law, and *jus cogens* are more diverse than those of conventional international law.

Some usual evidences of customary international law are, in no particular order, constitutional, legislative, and executive promulgations of states; proclamations; judicial decisions; arbitral awards; writings of specialists on international law; international agreements; and resolutions and recommendations of international conferences and organizations. Evidences of conventional international law include the written agreements themselves and, to a lesser degree, material related to the drafting and conclusion of the agreements. Furthermore, it may sometimes be necessary to interpret international agreements in the context of international custom, in which case the extensive body of evidences available in finding customary international law becomes relevant to the finding of conventional international law as well. Evidences of general principles of law include municipal laws, doctrines, and judicial decisions [see Chapter 3.A.3].

C. THE PROCESS OF INTERNATIONAL LAW

Just as the rules of international law are very different in kind from the rules of municipal law, so too is the process of international law quite different from that in a domestic legal system. Unlike most municipal legal systems where courts, agencies, and other formal organs of dispute settlement or rule application are all more or less coordinated in an integrated and hierarchical legal system, international legal process displays a complexity that may verge on anarchy. The different and sometimes uncoordinated ways in which matters are handled in international law often seem to defy the very idea of any international legal "system" at all.

The special character of international legal process, like the special nature of international legal rules, is explicable in terms of state sovereignty. Given the international political system, it should come as no surprise that a large part of formal legal procedural authority in the world today resides not in any formal supranational legal system but in the states themselves. It also should come as no surprise that, in most cases, neither states nor municipal legal systems defer, as a matter of course, to any legal authority outside the state, even in matters relating to international law or to foreign states. Indeed, the lion's share of disputes involving international law or touching international matters that actually go to formal legal adjudication is decided by municipal, not international, courts [see Chapters 4 and 10].

There are, of course, international courts established by treaty. The most influential of these are the International Court of Justice at The Hague [see Chapter 5], Western Europe's two regional international courts, the European Court of Human Rights at Strasbourg [see Chapter 8.B.2] and the European Court of Justice at Luxembourg [see Chapter 9.B], the International Tribunal for the Law of the Sea in Hamburg [see Chapter 7], and the International Criminal Court in The Hague [see Chapter 8]. Add to the municipal and international courts the many international arbitral tribunals, both public [see Chapter 5.A] and private [see Chapter 9.C].

Note that courts or arbitral tribunals can be "international" in at least three ways. First, they can be set up by international agreement. Second, they can apply international law. Third, they can deal with cases involving parties or transactions touching more than one country. Although municipal courts and many arbitral tribunals are not international in the first (constitutional) sense, they are often international in the second (rule) or third (transactional) sense.

To get a true picture of the complexity of international legal process, one must add to all these tribunals the normal and extraordinary diplomatic interactions of states, as well as the processes of municipal and international executive and administrative agencies. Unlike a domestic legal order, international law displays little procedural hierarchy. One or another court, one or another agency, one or another diplomatic settlement very often has no accepted primacy over another.

Given the complexity and uncertainty of much international legal process, why is it that states and courts, merchants and lawyers persist in finding and applying, developing, and reforming international law? The answer certainly lies not in any theoretical elaboration of the preferred place of international law in the modern world. Rather, international law's vitality rests in the continuing practical utility of international law in at least three circumstances. First, in a traditional Roman universal-law sense of the law of nations, it is sometimes useful for different states to follow similar rules or apply like standards in their domestic legal orders, for example, with respect to international commercial transactions [see Chapter 9.A.1]. Second, in a Grotian or Benthamite interstate sense of international law, it often makes sense for sovereign states to limit their own liberties in exchange for reciprocal limitations on the part of other states, for example, to protect diplomats [see Chapter 10.C.3] and human rights [see Chapter 8.B] or to limit weapons [see Chapter 6.C]. Third, and more important, states have found international law helpful as a means for achieving common international goals, such as the creation of international organizations and regimes [see Chapter 7], the promotion of economic well-being [see Chapter 9], and the facilitation of cooperation among national legal systems [see Chapter 10].

Although international law, like the law of any legal system, is not always respected, the fact is that there is more international law today than ever before. Moreover, the role it plays in world affairs—political, economic, social, and humanitarian—has never been greater. As trade, transport, culture, and communications link the peoples of the globe ever closer together, so are we likely to rely ever more upon international law in the future.

CHAPTER 2

Treaties

Most rules of international law find their source in the explicit, usually written, agreements of states. Such international agreements are commonly called treaties, although they may also be termed conventions, pacts, protocols, statutes, or accords. However they may be styled, treaties are essentially contracts between states.

A. TREATIES AS INTERNATIONAL LAW

International agreements, like private contracts, are something more than statements of expected future conduct. Treaties create legally obligatory rights and duties, and it is this obligatory aspect that makes them part of international law. International lawyers use the phrase *pacta sunt servanda* to express the fundamental principle that agreements between and among sovereign states must be respected [see Chapter 6.A.2].

In earlier centuries, the obligatory force of treaties could be attributed to religious solemnities. When properly and devoutly concluded, treaties were thought to be legally binding because the wrath of the gods would be visited on treaty violators.[1] Today we count on

[1] See A. Nussbaum, *A Concise History of the Law of Nations* 1-3 (rev. ed. 1954); Wehberg, Pacta Sunt Servanda, 53 *American Journal of International Law* 775 (1959); Janis, Religion and the Literature of International Law, *The Influence of Religion on International Law* 61 (M.W. Janis ed. 1991).

no such threat of supernatural force to cement the contracts between states. Sometimes it is said that treaties are legally binding because there is a natural law or a general principle of law that agreements, including international agreements, are to be obeyed. More usually, we turn to the authority of sovereign states to account for the mandatory character of treaties.

In terms of much international law theory, international agreements are thought to be legally binding because they have been concluded by sovereign states consenting to be bound. The idea is that states by virtue of their sovereignty may authoritatively regulate not only their own internal affairs, but also their international relations. As the Permanent Court of International Justice put it in the *Wimbledon* case:

> The Court declines to see in the conclusion of any Treaty by which a State undertakes to perform or refrain from performing a particular act an abandonment of its sovereignty. No doubt any convention creating an obligation of this kind places a restriction upon the exercise of the sovereign rights of the State, in that it requires them to be exercised in a certain way. But the right of entering into international engagements is an attribute of State sovereignty.[2]

In international practice states are usually the actors actually enforcing treaty obligations. Such enforcement may be international, for example, by the use of interstate persuasion or force, or by a decision of an international organization, court, or arbitral tribunal; or national, for example, by the application of rules drawn from international agreements to discrete cases by domestic courts [see Chapter 4.B].

In Article 38, the Statute of the International Court of Justice puts international conventions first in its list of the rules to be applied by the Court in deciding cases before it:

> 1. The Court, whose function is to decide in accordance with international law such disputes as are submitted to it, shall apply:
>
> (a) international conventions, whether general or particular, establishing rules expressly recognized by the contesting States;
>
> (b) international custom, as evidence of a general practice accepted as law;

[2] 1923 P.C.I.J. Reports, ser. A, no. 1, at 25.

> (c) the general principles of law recognized by civilized nations;
>
> (d) subject to the provisions of Article 59, judicial decisions and the teachings of the most highly qualified publicists of the various nations, as subsidiary means for the determination of rules of law.
>
> 2. This provision shall not prejudice the power of the Court to decide a case *ex aequo et bono*, if the parties agree thereto.

Article 59 reads:

> The decision of the Court has no binding force except between the parties and in respect of that particular case.[3]

Although the word *sources* does not appear in it, Article 38 is frequently employed as a listing of the sources of international law. An important itemization, Article 38 binds only the ICJ's judges, and never was and never will be an authoritative or comprehensive account of the sources of international law in general. Article 38's listing might be best understood as a paradigm, molding the common comprehension of the sources of international law.[4] For more on other varieties of international legal rules, see Chapter 3.

Many observers assign legal rules drawn from international agreements the highest rank among all the sources of international law. This status is justified because most treaties so plainly show both the terms of international legal rules and the consent of states to be bound by such rules. Indeed, every other sort of international law is usually much more troubled than are treaties by questions of rule specificity and state consent [see Chapter 3].

This does not mean that treaties are free of the concerns afflicting other sorts of international law. In practice, the fate of international agreements as a form of international law is inextricably linked to other varieties of international law. This is so, first of all, because the basic principle of treaty law, the norm that treaties are legally binding, *pacta sunt*

[3] Statute of the International Court of Justice, arts. 38, 59, as annexed to the Charter of the United Nations, 59 Stat. 1055, T.S. No. 993, 3 Bevans 1153, 1 U.N.T.S. (signed at San Francisco June 26, 1945; entered into force October 24, 1945).

[4] Janis, A Little Meta-Theory: Paradigms, Article 38, and the Sources of International Law, in *The Oxford Handbook of the Sources of International Law* 264 (S. Besson & J. d'Aspremont eds. 2017).

servanda, may be seen either as a fundamental norm or as a rule drawn from the customary practice of states. Even a provision in an international agreement that the agreement as a whole legally binds the parties is itself actually mandatory only if it can be supported by a fundamental norm or a rule of customary international law that makes treaties obligatory in general. Second, treaties must often be interpreted in the light of the rules of customary international law or of the nonconsensual sources. Like statutes in a common law context, treaties often presume and rely upon a preexisting set of legal rules. Third, international agreements may sometimes supersede or be superseded by other sorts of international law.

The sheer quantity of treaties demonstrates their continuing utility in the long course of international relations. Treaties concluded between 1648 and 1918 fill 243 thick books; between 1920 and 1946 some 205 more volumes; and there are more than 50,000 treaties between 1946 and 2017.[5]

In 1625, Grotius wrote words as true today as four centuries ago:

> [T]here is no state so powerful that it may not at some time need the help of others outside itself, either for purposes of trade, or even to ward off the forces of many foreign nations united against it. In consequence we see that even the most powerful peoples and sovereigns seek alliances, which are quite devoid of significance according to the point of view of those who confine law within the boundaries of states. Most true is the saying, that all things are uncertain the moment men depart from law.[6]

International agreements still promote trade and ward off foreign forces. For example, the Convention of Establishment Between the United States and France, like many other "friendship, commerce and navigation" treaties, facilitates "mutually advantageous investments and mutually beneficial commercial relations."[7] With respect to defense,

[5] 1 C.T.S. (1648-1649)–243 C.T.S. (1919); 1 L.N.T.S. (1920)–205 L.N.T.S. (1944-1946). Recording 4,834 treaties registered with the League of Nations; and United Nations, www.un.org (Mar. 31, 2023), listing more than 50,000 treaties registered since 1946. See Chapter 3.

[6] H. Grotius, *De Jure Belli ac Pacis Libri Tres* 17 (prolegomena sect. 22) (Kelsey trans. 1925). See M.W. Janis, Sovereignty and International Law: Hobbes and Grotius, *Essays in Honour of Wang Tieya* 391 (Macdonald ed. 1994).

[7] Preamble, 11 U.S.T. 2398, T.I.A.S. No. 4625, 401 U.N.T.S. 75 (signed at Paris November 25, 1959; entered into force December 21, 1960).

the clause below from the North Atlantic Treaty was invoked for the first time on the day after the September 11, 2001 terrorist attacks on New York and Washington:

> [A]n armed attack against one or more of them in Europe or North America shall be considered an attack against them all; and consequently they . . . will assist the Party or Parties so attacked by taking forthwith, individually and in concert with the other Parties, such action as it deems necessary, including the use of armed force, to restore and maintain the security of the North Atlantic area.[8]

In other aspects of practice, international agreements, *inter alia,* assure international postal services,[9] stabilize international monetary relations,[10] and set international standards for labor practices,[11] as well as protect patents,[12] fundamental rights,[13] fisheries,[14] diplomats,[15] and

[8] Art. 5, 63 Stat. 2241, T.I.A.S. No. 1964, 4 Bevans 828, 34 U.N.T.S. 243 (signed at Washington April 4, 1949; entered into force August 24, 1949). On NATO's decision of September 12, 2001 to invoke Article 5, see The Evolution of NATO, *Financial Times,* Sept. 24, 2001, at 23.

[9] Constitution of the Universal Postal Union, 16 U.S.T. 1291, T.I.A.S. No. 5881, 611 U.N.T.S. 7 (done at Vienna July 10, 1964; entered into force January 1, 1966).

[10] Articles of Agreement of the International Monetary Fund, 60 Stat. 1401, T.I.A.S. No. 1501, 3 Bevans 1351, 2 U.N.T.S. 39 (formulated at the Bretton Woods Conference July 1-22, 1944; entered into force December 27, 1945).

[11] Instrument for the Amendment of the Constitution of the International Labor Organization, 62 Stat. 3485, T.I.A.S. No. 1868, 4 Bevans 188, 15 U.N.T.S. 35 (dated at Montreal October 9, 1946; entered into force April 20, 1948; reentered into force for the United States February 18, 1980).

[12] Patent Cooperation Treaty, 28 U.S.T. 7645, T.I.A.S. No. 8733 (done at Washington June 19, 1970; entered into force January 24, 1978).

[13] European Convention for the Protection of Human Rights and Fundamental Freedoms, 213 U.N.T.S. 221, European T.S. 5 (signed at Rome November 4, 1950; entered into force September 3, 1953; not in force for the United States).

[14] Convention on Fishing and Conservation of the Living Resources of the High Seas, 17 U.S.T. 138, T.I.A.S. No. 5969, 559 U.N.T.S. 285 (done at Geneva April 29, 1958; entered into force March 20, 1966).

[15] Vienna Convention on Diplomatic Relations, 23 U.S.T. 3227, T.I.A.S. No. 7502, 500 U.N.T.S. 95 (done at Vienna April 18, 1961; entered into force April 24, 1964; for the United States November 13, 1972).

women.[16] Virtually every human activity is to some degree the object of some treaty.

With little international government to regulate international activities, the rules of international law, especially those drawn from treaties, provide an important measure of world order. International agreements often serve as a sort of international legislation where states explicitly agree to make rules to govern their own conduct, as well as the activities of their individual and corporate nationals. Though treaties are not usually enforced by executive machinery on the international plane comparable to that available on the national level, the fact is that treaty rules are generally well respected in practice. Their actual effectiveness is largely due to the mutual benefit that accrues to all sides from their reciprocal observance.[17]

Treaties may be thought of as contractual, legislative, constitutional, or aspirational. As international contract or *traité-contrat,* a treaty may simply accomplish some exchange or concession, for example, the treaty by which Russia ceded Alaska to the United States for $7.2 million in gold.[18] As a form of international legislation or *traité-loi,* a treaty may formulate rules pertaining to patterns of regular behavior among states, for example, the Convention on Consular Relations.[19] As a kind of international constitution, a treaty may set the legal foundation for an international body, as has the Charter of the United Nations.[20] Finally, in an aspirational mode, treaties may set goals for international society, for example, the Kellogg-Briand Pact of 1928, which renounced "war as an instrument of national policy."[21] Some argue that an aspirational treaty like Kellogg-Briand can sometimes have real-world efficacy.[22]

[16] Convention on the Political Rights of Women, 27 U.S.T. 1909, T.I.A.S. No. 8289, 193 U.N.T.S. 135 (done at New York March 31, 1953; entered into force July 7, 1954; for the United States, April 8, 1976).

[17] See T. Franck, *The Power of Legitimacy Among Nations* (1990).

[18] Convention Ceding Alaska, 15 Stat. 539, T.S. No. 301, 11 Bevans 1216 (signed at Washington March 30, 1867; entered into force June 20, 1867).

[19] 596 U.N.T.S. 261 (done at Vienna April 24, 1963).

[20] 59 Stat. 1031, T.S. No. 993, 3 Bevans 1153 (signed at San Francisco June 26, 1945; entered into force October 24, 1945) [hereinafter cited as "UN Charter"].

[21] 46 Stat. 2343, T.S. No. 796, 2 Bevans 732, 94 L.N.T.S. 57 (signed at Paris August 27, 1928; entered into force July 24, 1929).

[22] O.A. Hathaway & S.J. Shapiro, *The Internationalists: How a Radical Plan to Outlaw War Remade the World* (2017). Cf. Wertheim, The War Against War, *The Nation,* Dec. 3-10, 2018. Whatever the case, the norms in Kellogg-Briand figured in the prosecution of the war criminals at Nuremberg [see Chapter 8].

A. Treaties as International Law

International agreements need not necessarily establish new rules of international law. Often, treaties serve to codify rules already customary in international practice. Treaties that codify practice may sometimes clarify or modify preexisting customary rules. As we discuss below, one such mostly codifying treaty is the 1969 Vienna Convention on the Law of Treaties.[23] Compliance with treaties may vary according to their type. So, for example, aspirational treaties, like human rights conventions, may be more expressive of how a state chooses to be perceived than instrumental in assuring that state's actual compliance.[24]

States make a great many arrangements *inter se* and sometimes there will be a question about where to draw the line between international agreements that are legally binding treaties and so-called gentlemen's agreements and other varieties of "soft law" that may not be binding in law, though they may have some moral or political force.[25] Informal softer international agreements are increasingly common.[26] In the opinion of the International Court of Justice (ICJ), it may generally be assumed that international agreements are legally binding regardless of the intent of a state to view an accord as merely a moral or political engagement.[27] So for example, in 1994, the ICJ held that the signed minutes of a meeting among the foreign ministers of Bahrain, Qatar, and Saudi Arabia, recording an agreement to submit a maritime and territorial delimitation dispute to the Court if diplomatic negotiations were to fail, constituted a legally binding agreement regardless of the protest of the foreign minister of Bahrain that the minutes were simply "a statement recording a political understanding."[28]

[23] U.N. Doc. A/CONF.39/27 (1969), 1155 U.N.T.S. 331, reprinted in 63 *American Journal of International Law* 875 (1969) (signed at Vienna May 23, 1969; entered into force January 27, 1980; not in force for the United States) [hereinafter cited as "Vienna Convention"].

[24] Hathaway, Do Human Rights Treaties Make a Difference?, 111 *Yale Law Journal* 1935, 2002-2003 (2002).

[25] Bernhardt, Treaties, 7 *Encyclopedia of Public International Law* 459, 460-461 (1984); Nash, Contemporary Practice of the United States Relating to International Law: International Acts Not Constituting Agreements, 88 *American Journal of International Law* 515 (1994). A discussion of "soft law" is to be found in Chapter 3.

[26] Pauwelyn, When Structures Become Shackles: Stagnation and Dynamics in International Lawmaking, 25 *European Journal of International Law* 733 (2014).

[27] J. Klabbers, *The Concept of Treaty in International Law* 165-217 (1996).

[28] 1994 I.C.J. Reports 112, 116-122.

Treaties may be concluded between only two states and thus be bilateral, such as the many extradition treaties that the United States has entered into with other countries.[29] International agreements may also bind several or many states and so be multilateral, as, for example, is the General Agreement on Tariffs and Trade.[30] And, although a treaty must have at least two parties, it is sometimes possible for a unilateral declaration or act to have binding legal effect. For example, in the *Nuclear Tests* cases, the International Court of Justice decided that several public statements made by the French government that it no longer intended to conduct atmospheric nuclear tests in the South Pacific constituted "an undertaking to the international community": "declarations made by way of unilateral acts, concerning legal or factual situations, may have the effect of creating legal obligations."[31]

The word *treaty* in a general international law sense includes all the many different sorts of explicit international agreements. The term has, however, two other rather different and more particular definitions. First, the Vienna Convention on the Law of Treaties for its purposes defines a "treaty" to mean "an international agreement concluded between states in written form and governed by international law."[32] Thus, the Vienna Convention excludes from its ambit any agreement involving private parties or international organizations,[33] as well as unwritten international agreements. Second, the Constitution of the United States refers to "treaties" in Article II, where it provides that the President of the United States "shall have Power, by and with the Advice and Consent of the Senate, to make Treaties, provided two thirds of the

[29] See, e.g., Extradition Treaty Between the United States and Great Britain, TIAS No. 07-426 (signed at Washington, March 31, 2003; entered into force April 26, 2007).

[30] 61 Stat. (5), (6), T.I.A.S. No. 1700, 4 Bevans 639, 55-64 U.N.T.S. (concluded at Geneva October 30, 1947; entered into force January 1, 1948).

[31] 1974 I.C.J. Reports 253, at 269-270, 267.

[32] Vienna Convention, supra, art. 2(1)(a).

[33] In practice, international organizations, for example, the United Nations and the European Union, are increasingly making and bound by international agreements. Hollis, Why State Consent Still Matters—Non-State Actors, Treaties and the Changing Sources of International Law, 23 *Berkeley Journal of International Law* 137 (2005). The United Nations has prepared a second international agreement, not yet in force as of September 2025, viz., the 1986 Vienna Convention on the Law of Treaties Between States and International Organizations or Between International Organizations. U.N. Doc. A/CONF.129/15 (Mar. 21, 1986), reprinted in 25 *International Legal Materials* 543 (1986).

Senators present concur."[34] In the law of the United States, therefore, treaties are often distinguished from international agreements made without the Senate's formal advice and consent [see Chapter 4]. Since this book generally uses the word "treaty" and the term "international agreement" interchangeably, when Vienna-type and Article II-type treaties are discussed, they are differentiated.

B. THE LAW OF TREATIES

International agreements are not only a principal source of international legal rules, but also are themselves the subject of a considerable body of international law called the law of treaties. The law of treaties serves much the same function in international law as the law of contracts does in municipal law. It sets forth the accepted rules respecting, *inter alia*, the making, effect, amendment, invalidity, and termination of agreements among states.

Traditionally, the law of treaties was found in customary international law. However, beginning in 1949, the International Law Commission, a U.N. advisory group composed of jurists from around the world, set to work developing a draft code of the law of treaties. The Commission's consideration of the law of treaties lasted almost two decades and was directed by a Special Rapporteur, a position filled successively by four British academic lawyers: Professors Brierly, Lauterpacht, Fitzmaurice, and Waldock. In 1961, it was decided that the codification process should lead to the conclusion of an international agreement.[35] Finally, in 1966, a draft convention on the law of treaties was ready to be submitted to the U.N. General Assembly.[36] A Conference on the Law of Treaties was thereupon convened; it met in Vienna in 1968 and 1969 and adopted the Convention on the Law of Treaties.[37] The Vienna Convention, or the so-called Treaty on Treaties,

[34] U.S. Constitution, art. II, §2.

[35] I. Sinclair, *The Vienna Convention on the Law of Treaties* 1-5 (2d ed. 1984) [hereinafter cited as "Sinclair"].

[36] U.N. Doc. A/CONF.39/5, vol. I, at 7.

[37] Vienna Convention, supra.

came into force upon ratification by a thirty-fifth state on January 27, 1980.[38]

Since the Vienna Convention is largely, though not entirely, a codification of the existing customary international law of treaties,[39] it constitutes a useful depository of international legal rules even for countries, like the United States, which are not yet parties to it. So, for example, the U.S. Department of State has recognized the Vienna Convention as "the authoritative guide to current treaty law and practice," while the *Restatement (Fourth) of the Foreign Relations Law of the United States* notes that "the U.S. executive branch has accepted that many of the Convention's provisions reflect binding customary international law, and U.S. courts have often referred to the Convention."[40] The United States is not alone. Noting the "surprisingly low" number of parties to the Vienna Convention, Anthony Aust has commented that the "treaty is a victim of its own success"; even before the signatures to it "were dry, states were referring to the Convention as an authoritative statement on the law of treaties."[41]

1. The Making of Treaties

In looking at the law of treaties, we first consider the international law that has to do with the negotiation and form of treaties, the process of consent to treaties, the reservations to treaties, and the entry of treaties

[38] [1980] 1 *Yearbook of the International Law Commission* 5. As of September 2025, some 116 states were parties to the Vienna Convention.

[39] As the International Law Commission pointed out, its "work on the law of treaties constitutes both codification and progressive development of international law." [1966] 2 *Yearbook of the International Law Commission* 177. Similarly, the International Court of Justice has repeatedly held that the Vienna Convention "may in many respects be considered as a codification of existing customary law on the subject." Thirlway, The Law and Procedure of the International Court of Justice, 1960-1989 (Part Three), 62 *British Yearbook of International Law* 1, 3 (1991).

[40] S. Exec. Doc. L., 92d Cong., 1st Sess., at 1 (1971); American Law Institute, 1 *Restatement of the Law Fourth: The Foreign Relations Law of the United States: Selected Topics in Treaties, Jurisdiction, and Sovereign Immunity* 7 (2018) [hereinafter cited as "Restatement (Fourth)"].

[41] Aust, Limping Treaties: Lessons from Multilateral Treaty-Making, 50 *Netherlands International Law Review* 243, 250 (2003).

into force. All these topics concern the ways in which states make explicit and legally binding agreements among themselves.

Article 6 of the Vienna Convention provides that "[e]very State possesses capacity to conclude treaties."[42] As part of the exercise of its sovereign capacity, each state's own domestic constitutional law (and thus not rules of international law) determines which governmental organs have the power to conclude international agreements. In practice, it is usually the executive branch of government, sometimes the President or Prime Minister, but more usually the Department of State, Foreign Office, or Ministry of Foreign Affairs, that actually negotiates treaties. The U.S. Supreme Court held in the *Curtiss-Wright* case in 1936 that the power to make treaties is one of those powers "vested in the federal government as necessary concomitants of nationality."[43]

The circumstances in which treaties are negotiated can vary dramatically. In bilateral treaty negotiations, the proceedings may be subject to the play of personalities and be conducted quite privately. Consider, for example, the personal negotiation by U.S. President Franklin D. Roosevelt and British Prime Minister Winston Churchill of the agreement that in 1940 exchanged U.S. naval warships for British North American naval bases at a time when the United States was still neutral in the Second World War.[44] In stark contrast are gigantic and quite public multilateral treaty negotiations such as those leading to the 1982 United Nations Convention on the Law of the Sea (UNCLOS) [see Chapter 7]. The UNCLOS negotiations began in 1968 and stretched out for 15 years, involved thousands of delegates from more than 150 countries, and included hundreds of official meetings.[45]

It is generally agreed that states that are part of a federal union may in some circumstances have authority to make international agreements. There is much doctrinal disagreement, however, about whether such authority emanates from international law or from municipal

[42] Vienna Convention, supra.

[43] United States v. Curtiss-Wright, 299 U.S. 304, 318 (1936).

[44] See C. Hull, 1 *The Memoirs of Cordell Hull* 831-843 (1948).

[45] Wertenbaker, The Law of the Sea, *The New Yorker*, Aug. 1, 1983, at 38. The U.S. delegation alone often numbered more than 100 persons and "was usually the scene of more intense negotiations than was UNCLOS [the Third United Nations Conference on the Law of the Sea] itself." A.L. Hollick, *U.S. Foreign Policy and the Law of the Sea* 35 (1981).

constitutional law.[46] Whatever the source of such authority, it seems plain that, in practice, national constitutional law effectively limits component states with respect to their treaty-making powers. In some federations, such as Austria, Australia, and India, the component states are given virtually no treaty-making powers. In other unions, notably Canada, Germany, Switzerland, and the United States, there are at least a few limited treaty-making powers available to the component states.[47] So, for example, rather confusingly, in the United States, the Constitution in Article I, section 10 both prohibits the several states from entering "into any Treaty, Alliance or Confederation," and permits a state with "the consent of Congress" to "enter into [an] Agreement or Compact with another State, or with a foreign Power."[48] Moreover, the Supreme Court has permitted the states to enter into treaties not concerning political or security matters that do not "encroach upon or impair the supremacy of the United States."[49] Though there is no article in the Vienna Convention providing for component states in a federal union to make treaties, nothing in the Convention prohibits component states, if authorized by municipal constitutional law, from exercising such powers.

The international rules that pertain to the negotiation of treaties mostly have to do with the circumstances under which governments have a right to rely on certain individuals as the authorized representatives of foreign states. Such reliance is justified either if a person "produces appropriate full powers," that is, some form of official documentation attesting to a diplomat's authority to represent the state in treaty negotiations, or if "it appears from the practice of the states concerned or from other circumstances that their intention was to consider that person as representing the state for such purposes and to dispense with full powers."[50] Certain individuals, for example, heads of

[46] L. DiMarzo, *Component Units of Federal States and International Agreements* 1-4 (1980).

[47] Id. at 4-58.

[48] U.S. Constitution, art. I, §10(1), (3).

[49] Virginia v. Tennessee, 148 U.S. 503, 518 (1893). For recent examples, see Eight U.S. Great Lakes States, Ontario and Quebec Conclude New Agreements to Limit Diversions of Water from Great Lakes Basin, 100 *American Journal of International Law* 467 (2006); United Kingdom and California Conclude Agreement on Global Warming, 100 *American Journal of International Law* 933 (2006).

[50] Vienna Convention, supra, art. 7(1).

state and ministers of foreign affairs, are presumed to have authority to represent their states without having to produce full powers.[51]

Nowadays, there is usually little international concern about "full powers," since instantaneous communications make it possible for governments to control their representatives in even distant negotiations.[52] Much more important in practice is the determination, as a matter of domestic law, about who in the government is responsible for treaty negotiations. In the United States, the President is expressly granted the "Power, by and with the Advice and Consent of the Senate, to make Treaties, provided two thirds of the Senators present concur."[53] This is ordinarily taken to authorize the President to negotiate treaties or, more usually, to delegate the negotiating power to others, typically the Secretary of State, ambassadors, and diplomats.[54] We explore below other questions about the allocation of domestic powers to make treaties [see Chapter 4].

Unlike the making of contracts in municipal law, the signing of a treaty cannot usually be assumed to constitute an acceptance by a party that a treaty's provisions are to become legally binding obligations. Rather, in international law, signature is more frequently only that part of the negotiation process that involves the adoption and authentication of a treaty's text. "Adoption" is not formally defined in the Vienna Convention, but in international practice the term is normally taken to refer to that step of the treaty-making process wherein the states agree on the final form and content of the agreement.[55] In most cases, the text of a treaty must be satisfactory to all participating states before it can be adopted, although if the text emanates from the work of an international conference, a vote of two-thirds or another mutually agreed-upon fraction of the states present and voting may suffice.[56] This two-thirds vote rule seems to represent a "progressive development" of international law rather than a codification of customary international law.[57] After a treaty's text is adopted, a representative of a participating state may indeed sign or initial the treaty, but that act

[51] Id., art. 7(2).
[52] Sinclair, supra, at 30.
[53] U.S. Constitution, art. II, §2.
[54] Restatement (Fourth), supra, at 13-14.
[55] Sinclair, supra, at 33.
[56] Vienna Convention, supra, art. 9.
[57] Sinclair, supra, at 12-13, 33-39.

usually does not constitute an expression of consent by that state to be legally bound. Rather, it is only an indication that the state agrees that the text of the treaty is authentic and definitive.[58]

Like the civil law of contracts,[59] the international law of treaties looks primarily to consent and the wills of the parties to determine whether an agreement in law has been concluded. The emphasis of international law on the consent of the parties is due not only to the influence of the civil law, but also to the realities of the international legal system where state sovereignty and independence loom so large. Treaties are most likely to be legally binding instruments in fact as well as in theory when they are indeed voluntary and purposeful commitments of states. Consequently, international law is little bothered with nuances about the form of treaties, though it is much concerned to establish clearly whether states actually consent to be bound.

The Vienna Convention reads very broadly: "The consent of a state to be bound by a treaty may be expressed by signature, exchange of instruments constituting a treaty, ratification, acceptance, approval or accession, or by any other means if so agreed."[60] In all of these cases, states are permitted to specially agree as to the means to be used to establish consent. This may be done by the treaty itself or otherwise.[61] In most cases, treaties make explicit provision about how consent is to be formally registered.[62] Among all the many ways in which states may express their consent to be bound by treaty obligations, two methods stand out in practice: ratification and accession.

Ratification involves a state that has played a part in the negotiation of a treaty and has signed the text. Consent by ratification has both a domestic side, which is governed by municipal rules (such as the constitutional process in the United States involving a two-thirds vote of the Senate) [see Chapter 4], and an international side, which is usually set forth in the treaty itself (such as a requirement that there

[58] Vienna Convention, supra, art. 10.

[59] See O. Kahn-Freund, C. Lévy & B. Rudden, *A Source-Book on French Law* 315-348 (2d ed. 1979); J. Dupichot, *Le droit des obligations* 13-50 (1978).

[60] Vienna Convention, supra, art. 11.

[61] Id., arts. 12(1), 13, 14(1), 15.

[62] One study found that more than 90 percent of the post-World War II agreements examined explicitly provided how consent was to be registered. Frankowska, De la prétendue présomption en faveur de la ratification, 73 *Révue générale de droit international public* 62, 78 (1969).

be an exchange of instruments of ratification among the contracting states or a deposit of such instruments with a depositary).[63]

Accession is the route followed by a state that did not originally negotiate or sign a treaty, but that subsequently wishes to adhere to the agreement. A special form for accession is prescribed neither by the Vienna Convention nor by customary international law. Instead, individual treaties quite regularly detail the manner by which states may accede to the agreement. For example, the Antarctic Treaty provides that it is open for accession to any state that either is a member of the United Nations or is invited to accede to the Treaty by all of the contracting parties and that, in either case, then deposits an instrument of accession with the government of the United States, the depositary government.[64] Although treaties may otherwise provide, acceding states usually assume the same legal position vis-à-vis the treaty and other contracting states as is held by states that have ratified the agreement. Of course, acceding states will also have their own domestic constitutional rules about the process of accession.

Among the few formalities about consent that exist in the law of treaties is the rule of the Vienna Convention that treaties must be in writing.[65] However, in customary international law, it is possible for treaties to be in oral form. For example, in the *Eastern Greenland* case in 1933, the Permanent Court of International Justice held that an oral declaration by Nils Claus Ihlen, then the Norwegian Minister for Foreign Affairs, made in negotiations at the Paris Peace Conference in 1919, that "the Norwegian Government would not make any difficulty" with respect to Denmark's plans to obtain general recognition of Danish sovereignty over the whole of Greenland, constituted a legally binding obligation of Norway.[66] The lesson of the *Eastern Greenland* case discouraged U.S. Secretary of State Dean Rusk from tossing a coin, even in jest, with the Foreign Minister of Honduras for title to the Swan Islands in the Caribbean.[67]

[63]Vienna Convention, supra, art. 16.

[64]Art. XIII, 12 U.S.T. 794, T.I.A.S. No. 4780, 402 U.N.T.S. 71 (signed at Washington December 1, 1959; entered into force June 23, 1961).

[65]Vienna Convention, supra, art. 2(1)(a).

[66]1933 P.C.I.J. Reports, ser. A/B, no. 53, at 69-71.

[67]Rusk, The Role and Problems of Arbitration with Respect to Political Disputes, *Resolving Transnational Disputes Through International Arbitration* 15, 18 (Carbonneau ed. 1984).

Even though a state is not a party to a treaty, it may occasionally be bound by the treaty's terms. This may happen, for example, when the rules of a treaty pass into customary international law [see Chapter 3]. Or it may be that a state can be deemed by certain of its acts to have accepted a treaty's obligations. This latter case, however, is rare. As the International Court of Justice noted in 1969 in the *North Sea Continental Shelf* cases, "it is not lightly to be presumed that a State which has not carried out these formalities [of ratification or accession], though at all times fully able and entitled to do so, has nevertheless somehow become bound in another way."[68]

A treaty is fundamentally a contract between states and, as such, normally represents the express legal rights and obligations to which all the parties to the treaty have agreed. There may, however, be certain provisions of a treaty that one or more parties refuse to accept; such refusals are commonly called reservations. The Vienna Convention defines a reservation as "a unilateral statement, however phrased or named, made by a State, when signing, ratifying, accepting, approving or acceding to a treaty, whereby it purports to exclude or to modify the legal effect of certain provisions of the treaty in their application to that State."[69]

In the case of a bilateral treaty, a reservation is usually thought to represent a rejection of the treaty in its given form, and no legally binding agreement results until and unless the other party expressly accepts the reservation. The situation is more complicated, however, when there is a multilateral treaty, and the many problems relating to reservations really only date from the late nineteenth century when multilateral conventions became commonplace.[70] Although at first a unanimity rule prevailed for multilateral as well as for bilateral treaties, in time it became accepted practice for states to attach particular reservations to multilateral treaties to which they were nonetheless considered to be parties.[71] A survey of 1,164 multilateral treaties that entered into force between 1919 and 1971, for 17,438 parties, found that there were some

[68] 1969 I.C.J. Reports 4, 26.

[69] Vienna Convention, supra, art. 2(1)(d). On reservations in the Vienna Convention and as treated in the Restatement (Third), see Riesenfeld, International Agreements, 14 *Yale Journal of International Law* 455, 456-462 (1989).

[70] I. Detter, *Essays on the Law of Treaties* 47-48 (1967).

[71] See the 630-page study: International Law Commission, *Guide to Practice on Reservations to Treaties: Report of the International Law Commission on the Work of its Sixty-Third Session,* General Assembly Official Records, 66th Session, Supplement No. 10, U.N. Doc. A/66/10/Add.1 (2011).

691 reservations, indicating that reservations, while far from being regular practice, were certainly not unusual.[72] Treaties may also explicitly permit or prohibit reservations, albeit one study found that about half of all treaties had no language about reservations whatsoever.[73]

The Vienna Convention provides that "[a] State may, when signing, ratifying, accepting, approving or acceding to a treaty, formulate a reservation" unless the reservation is prohibited by the treaty, is not one of the specified permissible reservations, or "is incompatible with the object and purpose of the treaty."[74] In the *Belilos* case in 1988, the European Court of Human Rights found that an interpretative declaration made by Switzerland to the European Convention on Human Rights and Fundamental Freedoms constituted an invalid reservation to the Convention, and that Switzerland was still bound by the treaty terms.[75]

Even if a reservation is permissible, other states may still object. In some cases, actual acceptance of the reservation by other states may be required, for example, if there is a limited number of parties to the treaty and if "the application of the treaty in its entirety" is an "essential condition of the consent" of all parties. In other cases, acceptance may be assumed, for example, when the treaty expressly provides for a certain reservation or when a state raises no objection to the reservation after 12 months.[76]

If a state accepts a reservation made by another state, then the reservation modifies the treaty reciprocally for both states. However, a reservation made by one state and accepted by another state does not modify the treaty for other parties as among themselves. It may be possible in some circumstances for a state that objects to a certain reservation made by another state not to oppose the entry into force between itself and the other state of the other terms of the treaty.[77]

[72] Gamble, Reservations to Multilateral Treaties: A Macroscopic View of State Practice, 74 *American Journal of International Law* 372, 377 (1980).

[73] Galbraith, Treaty Options: Towards a Behavioral Understanding of Treaty Design, 53 *Virginia Journal of International Law* 309 (2013).

[74] Vienna Convention, supra, art. 19.

[75] European Court of Human Rights, Judgment of 29 April 1988, ser. A, no. 132. See Bourguignon, The *Belilos* Case: New Light on Reservations to Multilateral Treaties, 29 *Virginia Journal of International Law* 347 (1989); Edwards, Reservations to Treaties: The *Belilos* Case and the Work of the International Law Commission, 31 *University of Toledo Law Review* 195 (2000).

[76] Vienna Convention, supra, art. 20.

[77] Id., art. 21(3).

The complexity resulting from reservations to multilateral treaties is illustrated by the 1951 advisory opinion of the International Court of Justice in the *Reservations to the Convention on the Prevention and Punishment of the Crime of Genocide* case. The Court was asked by the U.N. General Assembly whether reserving states were parties to the Convention on the Prevention and Punishment of the Crime of Genocide when some, though not all, of the other negotiating states objected to the reservations made. The Court found that "[i]t is well established that in its treaty relations a State cannot be bound without its consent, and that consequently no reservation can be effective against any State without its agreement thereto," but that nonetheless the "object and purpose of the Genocide Convention imply that it was the intention of the General Assembly and of the States which adopted it that as many States as possible should participate."[78] Thus, the Court reached its intricate conclusion:

> [A] State which has made and maintained a reservation which has been objected to by one or more of the parties to the Convention but not by others, can be regarded as being a party to the Convention if the reservation is compatible with the object and purpose of the Convention; otherwise, that State cannot be regarded as being a party to the Convention, [but] if a party to the Convention objects to a reservation which it considers to be incompatible with the object and purpose of the Convention, it can in fact consider that the reserving State is not a party to the Convention; [and] if, on the other hand, a party accepts the reservation as being compatible with the object and purpose of the Convention, it can in fact consider that the reserving State is a party to the Convention.[79]

Although the compatibility test is a reasonable one, in practice it leaves considerable discretion to the states concerned, except, of course, in the infrequent instance, such as the *Genocide Convention* case itself, when the matter is submitted to international adjudication. In general, as one observer concludes respecting the interpretation of reservations and declarations, "many states continue to regard any

[78] 151 I.C.J. Reports 15, at 21, 24.
[79] Id. at 29-30.

infringement by a non-state entity of their sovereign right to determine the scope of their treaty relations as unacceptable."[80]

In the United States, the Senate plays a special role in making reservations to international agreements. The Restatement (Fourth) provides that the Senate can insist upon reservations and understandings to treaties when it gives its advice and consent and that if "a condition attached by the Senate purports to modify the legal effect of a treaty provision and the President proceeds to ratify the treaty, he or she must include the condition in the instruction of ratification or accession or otherwise manifest to the other treaty parties that U.S. adherence to the treaty is subject to the condition."[81] In 1986, the Senate gave its long-awaited advice and consent to the self-same Genocide Convention, but subject to two "reservations," five "understandings," and one "declaration."[82] It has been suggested that the attachment of so many qualifications to treaties tends to "undermine the credibility of U.S. participation in the international legal process."[83]

"A treaty enters into force in such manner and upon such date as it may provide or as the negotiating states may agree."[84] Usually, a multilateral treaty provides that it will enter into force after its ratification or accession by certain states and/or by a certain number of states. For example, the Non-Proliferation Treaty provides that it is to come into force only after its ratification by the United States, the United Kingdom, the Soviet Union, and 40 other states.[85]

[80] Kohana, Some Notable Developments in the Practice of the UN Secretary-General as Depositary of Multilateral Treaties: Reservations and Declarations, 99 *American Journal of International Law* 433, 450 (2005). See Swaine, Treaty Reservations in *The Oxford Guide to Treaties* 285 (Duncan B. Hollis ed., 2d ed. 2020).

[81] Restatement (Fourth), supra, at 45.

[82] Leich, Contemporary Practice of the United States Relating to International Law, 80 *American Journal of International Law* 612, 612-613 (1986). The reservations required the specific consent of the United States to the submission of any dispute to the International Court of Justice and excluded any Conventional requirement or authorization that might violate the U.S. Constitution. Id. at 615-618. The understandings, *inter alia*, more specifically defined terms in the Convention, id. at 618-619, and the declaration provided "[t]hat the President will not deposit the instrument of ratification until after the implementing legislation referred to in Article V [of the Convention] has been enacted." Id. at 613, 621-622.

[83] Riesenfeld & Abbott, Foreword, *Parliamentary Participation in the Making and Operation of Treaties: A Comparative Study* 1 (Riesenfeld & Abbott eds. 1994).

[84] Vienna Convention, supra, art. 24(1).

[85] Art. IX(3), 21 U.S.T. 483, T.I.A.S. No. 6839, 729 U.N.T.S. 161 (done at Washington, London, and Moscow July 1, 1968; entered into force March 5, 1970).

Since the late nineteenth century, there has been a considerable body of opinion against "secret" treaties and, accordingly, favoring the public registration of all international agreements. A registration requirement was first implemented pursuant to Article 18 of the 1919 Covenant of the League of Nations. Nowadays, treaties are often formally deposited with a state or an international organization such as the United Nations. The depositary is typically asked to register the treaty with the Secretariat of the United Nations, a step presently required by Article 102 of the U.N. Charter and without which the treaty may not be invoked "before any organ of the United Nations,"[86] for example, the International Court of Justice. Other functions of the depositary may include taking custody of the original text, preparing certified copies, receiving signatures and instruments of ratification and accession, informing parties to the treaty of the acts of other states as to the treaty, and informing states "when the number of signatures or of instruments of ratification, acceptance, approval or accession required for the entry into force of the treaty has been received or deposited."[87] Despite the injunction of Article 102 of the U.N. Charter, it seems that many treaties still are not registered. Although in some cases this may be due to a desire for confidentiality, one study concluded that "lack of concern and carelessness perhaps are the major reasons,"[88] while another attributed the failure to register to "the ephemeral, purely administrative, or highly technical nature of the agreements concerned."[89]

2. *The Effect of Treaties*

The basic principle regarding the observance of treaties, *pacta sunt servanda,* finds its place in the Vienna Convention: "Every treaty in force is binding upon the parties to it and must be performed by them in good faith."[90] The notion of good faith in the observance of international agreements is, of course, a fundamental principle of international

[86] UN Charter, supra, art. 102.

[87] Vienna Convention, supra, art. 77(1).

[88] Lillich, The Obligation to Register Treaties and International Agreements with the United Nations, 65 *American Journal of International Law* 771, 772 (1971).

[89] Zemanek, Secret Treaties, 7 *Encyclopedia of Public International Law* 505, 506 (1984).

[90] Vienna Convention, supra, art. 26.

law.[91] As Judge Lauterpacht observed in his separate opinion in the *Norwegian Loans* case in 1957: "Unquestionably, the obligation to act in accordance with good faith, being a general principle of law, is also part of international law."[92]

Generally, "[a] party may not invoke the provisions of its internal law as justification for its failure to perform a treaty."[93] Although occasionally a treaty may be deemed invalid because a "manifest" violation of a "fundamental" internal law of a state invalidated its consent,[94] this is a rare event. The Permanent Court of International Justice held in its 1932 advisory opinion on the *Treatment of Polish Nationals and Other Persons of Polish Origin or Speech in the Danzig Territories* that "a State cannot adduce as against another State its own Constitution with a view to evading obligations incumbent upon it under international law or treaties in force."[95]

Usually, a state will be obliged at international law to faithfully observe its treaty obligations even if the treaty for one reason or another has no legal force in its own municipal legal system, a scenario to which we return in the next section [see below]. A state is often positively obliged to ensure that an international agreement is incorporated into its municipal law. As the Convention on the Settlement of Investment Disputes Between States and Nationals of Other States provides: "Each Contracting State shall take such legislative or other measures as may be necessary for making the provisions of this Convention effective in its territories."[96]

Even though a treaty may not yet have come into force, the Vienna Convention provides that a "State is obliged to refrain from acts which would defeat [its] object and purpose" if "it has signed the treaty or has exchanged instruments constituting the treaty subject to ratification, acceptance or approval, until it shall have made its intention clear not to become a party to the treaty" or if "it has expressed its consent to be bound by the treaty, pending the entry into force of the treaty

[91] See J.F. O'Connor, *Good Faith in International Law* (1991); E. Zoller, *La bonne foi en droit international public* (1977).

[92] 1957 I.C.J. Reports 9, 53.

[93] Vienna Convention, supra, art. 27.

[94] Id., art. 46(1).

[95] 1932 P.C.I.J. Reports, ser. A/B, no. 44, at 24.

[96] Art. 69, 17 U.S.T. 1270, T.I.A.S. No. 6090, 575 U.N.T.S. 159 (done at Washington March 18, 1965; entered into force October 14, 1966).

and provided that such entry into force is not unduly delayed."[97] The wording "defeat the object and purpose of a treaty" was inserted by the Vienna Conference to replace the International Law Commission's suggested language, "tending to frustrate the object of a proposed treaty," which was felt to be too loose a construction.[98]

A treaty or a part of a treaty may be applied provisionally if "the treaty itself so provides . . . or the negotiating states have in some other manner so agreed."[99] Occasionally, a treaty will explicitly provide for means of consultation to satisfy states that a treaty's purposes are not defeated before its coming into force. Such provision, for example, was made in the agreement enlarging the European Common Market from six to nine members.[100]

Treaties may, by their terms, apply retroactively, but the presumptive rule is that treaty provisions are not retroactive.[101] The Vienna Convention provides that "[u]nless a different intention appears from the treaty or is otherwise established, its provisions do not bind a party in relation to any act or fact which took place or any situation which ceased to exist before the date of the entry into force of the treaty with respect to that party."[102] Unless rebutted, the presumption is that a "treaty is binding upon each party in respect of its entire territory."[103]

In assessing the legal effect of treaties and to better interpret their provisions, international law sometimes employs four descriptive concepts: *ratione personae, ratione materiae, ratione loci,* and *ratione temporis.* A good brief description of the four concepts, useful in the analysis of non-treaty norms, like customary international law, as well as treaty norms is:

> The norm *N* establishes a legal relationship between two or more particular international legal subjects (i.e. *N* is applicable *ratione personae*) relative to a particular action or factual state of affairs (i.e. *N* is applicable *ratione materiae*) occurring at a particular geographical location (i.e. *N* is applicable *ratione loci*) at a particular point in time or during a particular time period (i.e. *N* is applicable *ratione temporis*).[104]

[97] Vienna Convention, supra, art. 18.

[98] Sinclair, supra, at 43.

[99] Vienna Convention, supra, art. 25(1).

[100] Sinclair, supra, at 43-44.

[101] Id. at 85.

[102] Vienna Convention, supra, art. 28.

[103] Id., art. 29.

[104] Linderfalk, The Application of International Legal Norms over Time: The Second Branch of Intertemporal Law, 58 *Netherlands International Law Review* 147, 153 (2011).

B. The Law of Treaties

As a political matter, treaty interpretation is made more complex because any given treaty may be interpreted and applied in a variety of settings. Any given treaty, for example, may be interpreted not only by an international court and the parties in their diplomatic relations, but also by two or more municipal courts. It may be useful to have a treaty interpreted similarly in different forums, and, occasionally, a treaty will give to some institution the right of authoritative interpretation. One example is found in the European Union's original Treaty of Rome where it was provided in Article 164 that the European Court of Justice "shall ensure that in the interpretation and application of this Treaty the law is observed."[105] Similar provision is made in the European Convention for the Protection of Human Rights and Fundamental Freedoms for the European Court of Human Rights.[106] These are obviously very helpful provisions, giving the European Court of Justice and the European Court of Human Rights interpretative roles vis-à-vis their treaties somewhat comparable to that of the U.S. Supreme Court vis-à-vis the U.S. Constitution [see Chapters 8 and 9]. Most often, however, no such designation is made.

It is, of course, to be hoped that similar results will be reached by different states, courts, or observers by reference to a more or less settled body of international rules governing the interpretation of treaties. One, however, should not be overly optimistic. Lord McNair reflected that there was "no part of the law of treaties which the text-writer approaches with more trepidation than the question of interpretation."[107] Moreover, the provisions in treaties are always just words, never facts; though often more precise than other sorts of international law rules, treaty rules will always be uncertain to some degree.[108] A newer problem with treaty interpretation is the splintering of general international law into "specialist regimes of trade law, human rights

[105] Treaty Establishing the European Economic Community, U.K.T.S. 15 (1979) (with authoritative English language text), 298 U.N.T.S. 11 (signed at Rome March 25, 1957; entered into force January 1, 1958; not in force for the United States).

[106] Arts. 19, 52, 53, U.K.T.S. 71 (1953), E.T.S. 5, 213 U.N.T.S. 221 (signed at Rome November 4, 1950; entered into force September 3, 1953; not in force for the United States).

[107] A.D. McNair, *The Law of Treaties* 364 (2d ed. 1961) [hereinafter cited as "McNair"].

[108] See Lim & Elias, The Role of Treaties in the Contemporary International Legal Order, 66 *Nordic Journal of International Law* 1, 3-11 (1997).

law, environmental law, the law of the sea," etc., which makes much interpretation inherently "multifaceted."[109]

The Vienna Convention provides in Article 31 that a "treaty shall be interpreted in good faith in accordance with the ordinary meaning to be given to the terms of the treaty in their context and in the light of its object and purpose."[110] According to the Vienna Convention, treaties are to be interpreted primarily by reference to the terms of the treaty's text, giving rather less emphasis than might some municipal laws of contract to the circumstances surrounding the explicit agreement of the parties. The "context" referred to in the Convention means only a treaty's own preamble and annexes, as well as "any agreement relating to the treaty which was made between all the parties in connexion with the conclusion of the treaty" and "any instrument which was made by one or more parties in connexion with the conclusion of the treaty and accepted by the other parties as an instrument related to the treaty."[111] Although not part of a treaty's context, the Vienna Convention also permits the following to be taken into account: subsequent agreements among the parties, subsequent practices of the parties in the application of the treaty, and "any relevant rules of international law applicable in the relations between the parties."[112] The Convention restricts the use of supplementary means of interpretation to those situations where they "confirm the meaning resulting from the application of Article 31" or when the means used in Article 31 yield an ambiguous or obscure meaning or "a result which is manifestly absurd or unreasonable."[113] Thus, the Vienna Convention would have us turn to a treaty's legislative history, its *travaux preparatoires*, only when the more formal documentation fails to provide a clear or sensible meaning.

The question remains: How is one to know when a treaty's terms are unclear or unreasonable? Lord McNair has argued, for example, that the true function of treaty interpretation is to elucidate the real intent of the parties and that, accordingly, the terms of a treaty must be interpreted not only by referring to the text of the treaty, but also by

[109] Fitzmaurice, Book Review, 104 *American Journal of International Law* 329, 329-330 (2010). See Cali, Specialized Rules of Treaty Interpretation: Human Rights, *The Oxford Guide to Treaties* 525 (D. Hollis et al. eds. 2012).

[110] Vienna Convention, supra, art. 31(1).

[111] Id., art. 31(2)(a), (b).

[112] Id., art. 31(3)(c).

[113] Id., art. 32.

taking into account the context in which the treaty was made.[114] A contrary inclination, however, was demonstrated by the Permanent Court of International Justice in the *Lotus* case in 1927, when it refused to consider the *travaux preparatoires* of the Lausanne Convention even though the record of the negotiations seemed to show that France and England had in fact meant to restrict Turkey's extraterritorial jurisdiction with the words "principles of international law." The Permanent Court held that "there is no occasion to have regard to preparatory work if the text of a convention is sufficiently clear in itself."[115] The *Lotus* court preferred to rely instead solely on the meaning in general international law of the term "international law" and decided that ordinary international law had no rule prohibiting Turkey's exercise of extraterritorial jurisdiction.[116]

The Vienna Convention, on its face, falls somewhere between McNair and *Lotus,* since it leaves considerable discretion to the interpreter of the rule to determine whether treaty terms are so unclear or so unreasonable as to require reference to the *travaux preparatoires.* If only in curiosity we refer to the *travaux preparatoires* of Article 32 of the Vienna Convention itself, we find considerable reluctance on the part of many states to permit courts or anyone else to look beyond a treaty's express terms.[117] A Spanish negotiator, for example, felt that what should be stressed was "the will of the parties expressed objectively in the text rather than . . . the intention of the parties reconstructed subjectively from the preparatory work."[118]

In the United States, many courts strive to give treaties the same interpretation they would have before an international court. However, there is sometimes a greater willingness shown in the United States than internationally to interpret a treaty by ascertaining the meaning intended by the parties rather than by strictly reading the text.[119] Furthermore, a U.S. court or agency may well use interpretative materials supplementary to those relied on by an international court, such as Congressional

[114] McNair, supra, at 365.
[115] 1927 P.C.I.J. Reports, ser. A, no. 10, at 16.
[116] Id. at 16-32.
[117] See [1966] 2 *Yearbook of the International Law Commission* 91-101.
[118] U.N. Doc. A/CONF.39/5, vol. I, at 198.
[119] Restatement (Fourth), supra, at 55-70.

Reports and debates and other internal documentation relating to the negotiation or ratification of an international agreement.[120]

"Although courts in the United States have the final authority to interpret a treaty for purposes of applying it as law in the United States, at least since the mid-20th century the Supreme Court has stated that it gives 'great weight' to the executive branch's interpretation of a treaty."[121] For example, in Sumitomo Shoji America, Inc. v. Avagliano, the Supreme Court decided to follow the interpretation of a treaty as it was made by both the U.S. and the Japanese governments and held that "[a]lthough not conclusive, the meaning attributed to treaty provisions by the Government agencies charged with their negotiation and enforcement is entitled to great weight."[122]

Oftentimes treaties are rendered in more than one language. The Seabed Arms Control Treaty, for example, was drafted in English, Russian, French, Spanish, and Chinese texts.[123] Normally, each version is equally authoritative, though, of course, the treaty by its terms may give one text preeminence.[124] If the texts in different languages cannot be reconciled on their face, then the Convention provides that "the meaning which best reconciles the texts, having regard to the object and purpose of the treaty, shall be adopted."[125]

Generally, "[a] treaty does not create either obligations or rights for a third state without its consent."[126] A third state is held to have accepted an obligation set forth in a treaty only upon its express consent, but it may be deemed to have accepted a right implicitly.[127] Of

[120] Id. at 201. See Eastern Airlines v. Floyd, 499 U.S. 530 (1981), where Justice Marshall turned to many sources including French doctrine and an Israeli court judgment. A useful note about researching treaty interpretation, literally addressed to the law clerks of Mr. Justice Scalia, but helpful to any student, clerk, lawyer, or judge, is Vagts, Senate Materials and Treaty Interpretation: Some Research Hints for the Supreme Court, 83 *American Journal of International Law* 546 (1989).

[121] Restatement (Fourth), supra, at 60.

[122] 457 U.S. 176, 184-185 (1982).

[123] Treaty on the Prohibition of the Emplacement of Nuclear Weapons and Other Weapons of Mass Destruction on the Seabed and in the Subsoil Thereof, art. XI, 23 U.S.T. 701, T.I.A.S. No. 7337 (done at Washington, London, and Moscow February 11, 1971; entered into force May 18, 1972).

[124] Vienna Convention, supra, art. 33(1).

[125] Id., art. 33(4).

[126] Id., art. 34.

[127] Id., arts. 35, 36.

course, it is always possible for a rule in a treaty to bind third states if the rule enters into customary international law, a possibility considered by the International Court of Justice in the *North Sea Continental Shelf* case.[128] The Convention contains no provision concerning treaties establishing "objective regimes," such as those delineating territory, which may be held to be good against all the world. The International Law Commission thought this too controversial an issue.[129]

3. *The Amendment, Invalidity, and Termination of Treaties*

The terms of a treaty may be altered; the general rule set forth by the Vienna Convention is that a "treaty may be amended by agreement between the parties."[130] Such amendments are treaties in their own right and are themselves governed by the law of treaties. Treaties often have terms providing for their amendment. For example, the Charter of the Organization of American States provides: "[A]mendments to the present Charter may be adopted only at an Inter-American Conference convened for that purpose."[131]

For its purposes, the Vienna Convention distinguishes between the "amendment" and the "modification" of multilateral treaties. The International Law Commission felt that an amendment formally altered a treaty with respect to all parties, while a modification altered an agreement only with respect to certain parties.[132] The Convention reads that unless a multilateral agreement provides otherwise, all contracting states have a right to participate in a decision to amend a treaty and in the negotiation and conclusion of any amendment, as well as a right to become a party to the amended treaty.[133] An amendment "does not bind any state already a party to the treaty which does not become a party to the amending agreement."[134] Instead, "[w]hen the parties

[128] Id., art. 38; see Chapter 3; 1969 I.C.J. Reports 4.

[129] Sinclair, supra, at 104.

[130] Vienna Convention, supra, art. 39.

[131] Art. 111, 2 U.S.T. 2394, T.I.A.S. No. 2361, 119 U.N.T.S. 3; as amended, 21 U.S.T. 607, T.I.A.S. No. 6847 (signed at Bogota April 30, 1948; entered into force December 13, 1951).

[132] Sinclair, supra, at 106-107.

[133] Vienna Convention, supra, art. 40.

[134] Id., art. 40(4).

to a later treaty do not include all the parties to the earlier one . . . the treaty to which both States are parties governs their mutual rights and obligations."[135] With respect to modification, the Convention provides that several of the parties to a treaty may agree to a modification of the treaty affecting only their relations so long as either such a modification is provided for by the treaty or the modification is not prohibited by the treaty and "does not affect the enjoyment by the other parties of their rights under the treaty or the performance of their obligations; [and] does not relate to a provision, derogation from which is incompatible with the effective execution of the object and purpose of the treaty as a whole."[136] Some sorts of treaty may be more amenable to modification than others.[137]

Outside the bounds of the Vienna Convention, it has been argued that customary international law knows the possibility that a treaty may be amended or modified by the tacit consent of the parties, which is shown by a pattern of consistent and accepted practice by the parties at variance from the treaty's provisions. For example, in the *Soering* case in 1989, the European Court of Human Rights held that in principle, though not in this instance, "[s]ubsequent practice in national penal policy, in the form of a generalized abolition of capital punishment, could be taken as establishing the agreement of the Contracting States to abrogate the exception provided for under Article 2(1)" of the European Human Rights Convention permitting the taking of life by a state following "conviction of a crime for which this penalty is provided by law."[138] The Vienna Conference voted 54 to 15 to delete an article proposed by the International Law Commission permitting the modification of treaties by subsequent practice. It was feared that the erroneous interpretation of a treaty by low-ranking officials might lead to modifications of the treaty actually undesired by the states involved.[139]

Normally, "[a] ground for invalidating, terminating, withdrawing from or suspending the operation of a treaty . . . may be invoked

[135] Id., art. 30(4)(b).

[136] Id., art. 41(1)(b).

[137] Fitzmaurice, Dynamic (Evolutive) Interpretation of Treaties: Part I, 21 *Hague Yearbook of International Law* 101 (2008).

[138] European Court of Human Rights, Judgment of 7 July 1989, ser. A, no. 161, at 103.

[139] Kearney & Dalton, The Treaty on Treaties, 64 *American Journal of International Law* 495, 525 (1970).

only with respect to the whole treaty."[140] It may, however, be possible to object to some treaty clauses and accept the rest either if the treaty so provides or if the objectionable clauses are both "separable from the remainder of the treaty with regard to their application" and "not an essential basis of the consent" of other parties, so long as "continued performance of the remainder of the treaty would not be unjust."[141]

A treaty is not invalid on the grounds that its conclusion violated the municipal law of one of its parties "unless that violation was manifest and concerned a rule of its internal law of fundamental importance."[142] "A violation is manifest if it would be objectively evident to any state conducting itself in the matter in accordance with normal practice and in good faith."[143] The test for invalidity on the grounds of violation of municipal law is rarely satisfied in practice. The active presumption is that a state's executive officers and foreign ministers have proper domestic authority to conclude international agreements.

For example, when France repudiated an agreement with the United States, made July 4, 1831, which provided for the installment payment of more than $5 million to satisfy American maritime claims against France arising from the Napoleonic Wars, it did so on the grounds that pursuant to French constitutional law, the French legislature needed to be consulted in order to appropriate the necessary funds. The United States protested and threatened reprisals. Finally, in 1836, payments began to be made. Lord McNair agreed with the U.S. position that the French repudiation based on constitutional infirmities was illegal at international law.[144] For Great Britain's part, McNair wrote that "our Government cannot plead any defect in our municipal law or its administration as an excuse for our failure to discharge an international obligation."[145]

The Vienna Convention provides that other permissible grounds for objecting to the validity of a treaty include error relating to a fact

[140] Vienna Convention, supra, art. 44(2).

[141] Id., art. 44(1), (3).

[142] Id., art. 46(1).

[143] Id., art. 46(2).

[144] A.D. McNair, *Lord McNair: Selected Papers and Bibliography* 85 (1974) [hereinafter cited as "McNair, Selected Papers"].

[145] Id. at 157. So, too, may an international organization be bound by a treaty illegal in terms of the organization's own internal law. Kingston, External Relations of the European Community—External Capacity Versus Internal Competence, 44 *International & Comparative Law Quarterly* 659, 669 (1995).

or situation forming "an essential basis" of a state's consent to be bound,[146] the "fraudulent conduct" of another negotiating state, and corruption or coercion of a state's representative by another negotiating state.[147] More absolutely, "[a] treaty is void if its conclusion has been procured by the threat or use of force in violation of the principles of international law embodied in the Charter of the United Nations."[148] The Convention also provides that a treaty is void if "it conflicts with a peremptory norm of general international law," that is, *jus cogens*,[149] which, as we discuss in the next chapter, is the notion that there exist some rules of international law so fundamental that they prohibit acts by states even if such conduct is expressly sanctioned by state consent [see Chapter 3.B.3].

It must be remarked that the notion of invalidity based on error, fraud, corruption, coercion, and a peremptory norm is rather controversial in customary international law. Here the conventional rules cannot be said to necessarily codify existing practices. As Sinclair noted with respect to the principle of *jus cogens*: "[I]t is striking that a concept so widely supported in doctrine and in the writings of jurists has found so little application in state practice."[150]

A treaty may be terminated or a party withdraw from it either "in conformity with the provisions of the treaty; or at any time by consent of all the parties after consultation with the other contracting states," a good example being the abrogation, as of 2005, of some 29 obsolete treaties pertaining to the International Labor Organization.[151] Quite frequently, a treaty explicitly provides for its own termination either after a fixed period or by a specified process.[152] For example, Article IV of the Limited Nuclear Test Ban Treaty reads:

> Each Party shall in exercising its national sovereignty have the right to withdraw from the Treaty if it decides that extraordinary events, related to the subject matter of this Treaty, have jeopardized the supreme

[146] Vienna Convention, supra, art. 48.

[147] Id., arts. 49, 50, 51.

[148] Id., art. 52; see Chapter 6.

[149] Vienna Convention, supra, art. 53.

[150] Sinclair, supra, at 18.

[151] Vienna Convention, supra, art. 54; Helfer, Understanding Change in International Organizations: Globalization and Innovation in the ILO, 59 *Vanderbilt Law Review* 649, 713-715 (2006).

[152] Helfer, Exiting Treaties, 91 *Virginia Law Review* 1579, 1582 (2005).

> interests of its country. It shall give notice of such withdrawal to all other Parties to the Treaty three months in advance.[153]

Treaties are commonly terminated by the explicit terms of a new agreement negotiated and concluded by the parties to the original convention. If a treaty has no provision for termination and does not provide for denunciation or withdrawal, then in principle a state may not denounce the treaty or withdraw from it unless the parties intended to permit denunciation or withdrawal or such a right can "be implied by the nature of the treaty."[154] In practice, problems respecting the termination and breach of treaties are second in number only to those respecting the interpretation of treaties in the ordinary course of international law.[155]

"A material breach of a bilateral treaty by one of the parties entitles the other to invoke the breach as a ground for terminating the treaty or suspending its operation in whole or in part."[156] In a multilateral treaty, a material breach entitles the other parties by unanimous agreement to terminate or suspend the treaty either in relations between themselves and the defaulting state or among all parties. A material breach includes "the violation of a provision essential to the accomplishment of the object or purpose of the treaty."[157]

An understanding that treaty obligations must sometimes yield to exceptional circumstances is present in international law as it is in some form in every legal system. The notion appears in a cluster of separate but related doctrines often referred to collectively as "changed circumstances." A legal excuse occasioned by *force majeure*, an unavoidable and insurmountable obstacle to performance, is more or less universally accepted. More controversial are excuses in situations when performance, though not impossible, has become drastically more onerous. In municipal law, this is sometimes called frustration, *imprévision*, or *rebus sic stantibus*, doctrines with a long lineage.[158] Although their early

[153] Treaty Banning Nuclear Weapon Tests in the Atmosphere, in Outer Space and Underwater, 14 U.S.T. 1313, T.I.A.S. No. 5433, 480 U.N.T.S. 43 (done at Moscow August 5, 1963; entered into force October 10, 1963).

[154] Vienna Convention, supra, art. 56.

[155] G. Haraszti, *Some Fundamental Problems of the Law of Treaties* 10-11 (1973).

[156] Vienna Convention, supra, art. 60(1).

[157] Id., art. 60(2), (3)(b).

[158] U. Draetta, R. Lake & V. Nanda, *Breach and Adaptation of International Contracts: An Introduction to* Lex Mercatoria 86 (1992).

recognition as an exception to the obligations of states under international law was perhaps oblique,[159] they are now widely accepted and acknowledged with important limitations in Article 62 of the Vienna Convention on the Law of Treaties:

> 1. A fundamental change of circumstances which has occurred with regard to those existing at the time of the conclusion of a treaty, and which was not foreseen by the parties, may not be invoked as a ground for terminating or withdrawing from the treaty unless:
>
> (a) the existence of those circumstances constituted an essential basis of the consent of the parties to be bound by the treaty; and
>
> (b) the effect of the change is radically to transform the extent of obligations still to be performed under the treaty.[160]

If there has been a "severance of diplomatic or consular relations between parties to a treaty [this] does not affect the legal relations established between them by the treaty except in so far as the existence of diplomatic or consular relations is indispensable for the application of the treaty."[161] In U.S. constitutional law, if the states parties to a treaty refuse to invoke *rebus sic stantibus*, "a private person who finds the continued existence of the treaty inconvenient may not invoke the doctrine on their behalf."[162]

In interstate relations, change of circumstance can be invoked when the burden of performance on the disadvantaged party has increased drastically. Though the International Court of Justice has ruled that the change in circumstances must "imperil the existence or vital development of one of the parties,"[163] in practice the excuse is not reserved for cases sometimes termed *force majeure* where performance has become literally impossible.[164] Various events can trigger assertions of a change of

[159] Bederman, The 1871 London Declaration, *Rebus Sic Stantibus* and a Primitivist View of the Law of Nations, 82 *American Journal of International Law* 1 (1988).

[160] Vienna Convention, supra, art. 62.

[161] Id., art. 63.

[162] Trans World Airlines v. Franklin Mint Corp., 466 U.S. 243, 253 (1984).

[163] Fisheries Jurisdiction Case, United Kingdom v. Iceland, 1973 I.C.J. Reports 3, at ¶38; see Vagts, *Rebus* Revisited: Changed Circumstances in Treaty Law, 43 *Columbia Journal of Transnational Law* 459 (2005).

[164] Rimke, Force Majeure and Hardship: Application in International Trade Practice with Specific Regard to the CISG and the UNIDROIT Principles of International Commercial Contracts (1999-2000), https://web.archive.org/web/20200304065053/http://www.cisg.law.pace.edu/cisg/biblio/rimke.html.

circumstance. For example, tribunals have dealt with claims of change of circumstance based on war, boycotts, changes in law, severe inflation, and changes in exchange rates. The critical inquiry is whether those events have destroyed the assumed bases of the contract, that is, in the terms of the Vienna Convention, those changes that "radically . . . transform the extent of obligations still to be performed under the treaty."[165] The reluctance of the International Court of Justice in 1997 to accept the defense of changed circumstances due to the transformation of the political and economic systems of Hungary and Slovakia in the *Gabcíkovo-Nagymaros Project* case was based on its finding that, as significant as those changes were, they were "not of such a nature either individually or collectively, that their effect would radically transform the extent of their obligations still to be performed in order to accomplish the Project," which had multiple energy, environmental, navigation, and financial goals and implications.[166]

States may also invoke the justification of necessity to avoid their international legal commitments. Much of the recent discussion of necessity springs from the arguments of Argentina repudiating its foreign debt and the ensuing and still-continuing international arbitration.[167] It is important that the doctrine of necessity be applied cautiously. At root, necessity often may be little more than an asserted justification of an illegal act based on a perceived significant state interest, an assertion which may undermine the very foundation of international law.

If there are successive treaties relating to the same subject matter, then if "a treaty specifies that it is subject to, or that it is not to be considered as incompatible with, an earlier or later treaty, the provisions of that other treaty prevail."[168] A later treaty may terminate an earlier treaty if both treaties have all the same parties and if either the later treaty provides "that the matter should be governed by that treaty" or

[165] Vienna Convention, supra, art. 62.

[166] Case Concerning the Gabcíkovo-Nagymaros Project, Hungary/Slovakia, 1997 I.C.J. Reports 3, at ¶104. Despite the ICJ judgment, the case lingers on. See Baranyai & Bartus, Anatomy of a Deadlock: A Systemic Analysis of Why the Gabcikove-Nagymaros Dam Dispute Is Still Unresolved, 18 *Water Policy* 39 (2015).

[167] See CMS Gas Transmission Co. v. Argentina, ICSID Case No. ARB/01/96, Decision on Annulment, Sept. 25, 2007; Sloan, On the Use and Abuse of Necessity in the Law of State Responsibility, 106 *American Journal of International Law* 447 (2012).

[168] Vienna Convention, supra, art. 30(2).

"the provisions of the later treaty are so far incompatible with those of the earlier one that the two treaties are not capable of being applied at the same time."[169] However, if not terminated, the earlier treaty may still be applied "to the extent that its provisions are compatible with those of the later treaty."[170]

A state may terminate or suspend a treaty because of the emergence of a new peremptory norm of general international law.[171] An invalid treaty is void and has no legal force.[172] If a treaty is properly terminated, then the parties are ordinarily released "from any obligation further to perform the treaty."[173] If a treaty is suspended, then usually the parties are released "from the obligation to perform the treaty in their mutual relations during the period of the suspension."[174]

Treaties are not normally terminated upon a change in the government of one of the parties. As Lord McNair pointed out, "[t]here is now an abundance of authority for the view that treaties continue to bind a State whatever changes of Government may have occurred since they were concluded, whether the change of government takes place in a constitutional or in a revolutionary manner."[175] Thomas Jefferson, then U.S. Secretary of State, advised President Washington in 1793 that "[Franco-American treaties are] not the treaties between the United States and Louis Capet, but between the two nations of America and France, and the nations remaining in existence, though both of them have since changed their form of government, the treaties are not annulled by these changes."[176]

In the United States, the power to suspend or terminate a treaty or to decide not to suspend or terminate a treaty is vested in the President.[177] This is a power not found in explicit terms in the Constitution, but rather developed in practice. "[T]he United States has terminated dozens of treaties, and almost all of the terminations have been accomplished by unilateral presidential action," which generally "have not generated

[169] Id., art. 59(1).
[170] Id., art. 30(3).
[171] Id., art. 64; see Chapter 3.
[172] Id., art. 69.
[173] Id., art. 70(1).
[174] Id., art. 72.
[175] McNair, Selected Papers, supra, at 377.
[176] Ibid.
[177] Restatement (Fourth), supra, at 126.

much controversy in Congress."[178] In an exception, the Supreme Court in 1979 dismissed a suit brought by Senator Goldwater and others complaining that President Carter had failed to properly consult Congress in terminating the Mutual Defense Treaty of 1954 with the Taiwanese government. Four members of the Court held that the issue was a "political question" beyond the Court's judicial competence and better "left for resolution by the Executive and Legislative Branches of the Government," and one found for the President on the grounds that the unilateral power to terminate treaties "rests upon the President's well-established authority to recognize, and withdraw recognition from, foreign governments."[179]

[178] Id. at 132.
[179] Goldwater v. Carter, 444 U.S. 996, 1002-1007 (1979).

CHAPTER 3

Custom and Other Sources of International Law

A large number and a wide variety of international legal rules are generated by means other than the explicit consent of states expressed in treaties. Sometimes these other sources of international law are grouped together under descriptive rubrics like "the law of nations," "general international law," or "international common law," but they are usually better known by their more specific appellations: customary international law, the general principles of law, natural law, *jus cogens* or fundamental norms, and equity. In this chapter, these non-treaty sources are explored in turn. Despite their considerable diversity, international rules not based on treaties share certain characteristics. Among other things, they may be more generally applicable to states than are rules emanating from international agreements. However, such non-treaty rules are typically less definite in their formulation and less certain as to their authority, so often more subject to doubt in practice.

A. CUSTOMARY INTERNATIONAL LAW

1. Custom as International Law

The idea of custom as a source of legal rules is ancient. Roman law knew an "[u]nwritten law consist[ing] of rules approved by usage; for long-continued custom approved by the consent of those who use it imitates a statute."[1] Grotius, a founder of modern international law and deeply influenced by the classical tradition, suggested in 1625 that "[t]he proof for the law of nations is similar to that for unwritten municipal law; it is found in unbroken custom and the testimony of those who are skilled in it."[2] Vattel, in the principal international law text of the late eighteenth and early nineteenth centuries, defined the "customary law of nations" as "certain maxims and customs consecrated by long use, and observed by nations in their mutual intercourse with each other as a kind of law."[3] More recently, Brierly explained that customary international law was "a usage felt by those who follow it to be an obligatory one."[4]

For many modern international lawyers, customary international law is, alongside treaty law, one of the two central forms of international law. Indeed, until the twentieth century, custom was often viewed as the principal source of international law. Today, however, the accepted listing of the sources of international law, Article 38 of the Statute of the International Court of Justice, gives "international custom, as evidence of a general practice accepted as law" pride of only second place, ranking it after international agreements.[5] Nonetheless, treaties, despite their considerable proliferation, leave many international topics untouched, and most states are not party to most treaties. So custom remains a very useful second source of international law, supplementing treaty rules and having the potential to reach out more generally to regulate parties in their international relations.

The fundamental idea behind the notion of custom as a source of international law is that states by their international practice may implicitly consent to the creation and application of international legal rules. In this sense, the theory of customary international law is simply an implied side to the contractual theory that explains why treaties are

[1] The Institutes of Justinian, *The Elements of Roman Law* 45 (bk. I, tit. II, §9) (4th ed. Lee 1956).

[2] H. Grotius, *De Jure Belli ac Pacis Libri Tres* 44 (bk. 1, ch. 1, §14) (Kelsey trans. 1925) [hereinafter cited as "Grotius"].

[3] E. de Vattel, *The Law of Nations, or Principles of the Law of Nature, Applied to the Conduct and Affairs of Nations and Sovereigns xv* (1797) [hereinafter cited as "Vattel"].

[4] J. Brierly, *The Law of Nations* 60 (4th ed. 1949).

[5] Statute of the International Court of Justice, art. 38(1)(b), as annexed to the Charter of the United Nations, 59 Stat. 1031, T.S. No. 993, 3 Bevans 1153 (signed at San Francisco June 26, 1945; entered into force October 24, 1945) [hereinafter cited as "ICJ Statute"].

international law. For those international lawyers who insist on some ultimate positive act of state consent to make any international legal norm, treaties and custom constitute the only two definitive sources of international law.[6] Most international lawyers, however, are willing to go beyond treaties and custom to general principles of law, natural law, *jus cogens,* and equity to find international law, though virtually all would still agree that treaties and custom are international law's principal sources.[7]

One of the advantages of customary international law is that it may often be more generally applicable than is the international law drawn from treaties. Indeed, customary international law is sometimes said to be "general international law," a characteristic it may share with other non-consensual sources when it applies to all, not only particular, states. So, for example, a rule of customary international law may be presumed to be, as the U.S. Supreme Court held in 1820, a "universal law of society."[8] Nonetheless, some customary international law may be determined to be merely regional, and some states may be found not to be bound by even general customary international law if they have expressly dissented to the rule's formulation. So, for example, in the *Asylum* case in 1950, the International Court held that even if Colombia could prove a customary American regional rule that a state granting protection in its embassy was legally competent to qualify the refugee as a political offender entitled to asylum, such a custom "could not be invoked against Peru which, far from having by its attitude adhered to it, has, on the contrary, repudiated it by refraining from ratifying the Montevideo Conventions of 1933 and 1939, which were the first to include a rule concerning the qualification of the offence in matters of diplomatic asylum."[9]

The lines that separate state practice that violates customary international law, state practice that dissents from customary international law,

[6] G.I. Tunkin, *Theory of International Law* 89-203 (Butler trans. 1974) [hereinafter cited as "Tunkin"].

[7] A.A. D'Amato, *The Concept of Custom in International Law* 1-10 (1971); Lillich, The Growing Importance of Customary International Human Rights Law, 25 *Georgia Journal of International & Comparative Law* 1, 10-21 (1995/96); *Custom's Future: International Law in a Changing World* C.A. Bradley ed. 2016).

[8] United States v. Smith, 18 U.S. (5 Wheaton) 153, 161 (1820).

[9] 1950 I.C.J. Reports 266, 268-269, 277-278; Green, The Right of Asylum in International Law, 3 *University of Michigan Law Review* 223 (1961).

and state practice that replaces old with new customary international law are oftentimes hard to discern. From the perspective of those who view international law as a study of national and international public policy, claims and counterclaims about customary international law make up the meat of their subject.[10] One example of the claims/counterclaims process is the clash between assertions of territorial waters and high seas freedoms explored in Chapter 7.

One could suppose a customary international law that along with treaties formed a more or less complete body of law, one that addressed the great number of problems that might come to it with applicable and discernible rules. In actual fact, the set of legal rules made up by treaties and customary international law is incomplete. One of the recurrent problems of international law is that there are areas of behavior that could be covered by conventional and customary rules, but where no rules based on either explicit or implicit state consent can be discovered. It is at this stage that international lawyers often turn to non-consensual forms of international law like general principles of law, natural law, and fundamental norms, as well as to equity, to fill the gaps.

2. *The Art of Customary International Law*

The determination of customary international law is more an art than a science. This art is well seen in the judicial reasoning of the best-known U.S. case relying on customary international law, *The Paquete Habana.*[11] In April 1898, at the outset of the Spanish-American War, two Cuban fishing smacks, the *Paquete Habana* and the *Lola,* were on the high seas routinely fishing and completely unaware that hostilities had broken out between the United States and Spain, then the colonial ruler of Cuba. The *Paquete Habana* and the *Lola* were captured by U.S. warships, brought into Key West, Florida, condemned by the local U.S. district court as prizes of war, and sold at auction, the proceeds going into the U.S. Treasury, probably destined as prizes of war for the officers and

[10] See M.S. McDougal & W.M. Reisman, *International Law in Contemporary Perspective* (1981).

[11] 175 U.S. 677 (1900). See Dodge, *The Paquete Habana*: Customary International Law as Part of Our Law, in *International Law Stories* 287 (Noyes, Dickinson, Janis & Vázquez eds. 2d ed.).

crew of the seizing U.S. naval ships. The Cuban masters of the vessels complained that the capture and sale of the two boats by the United States was a violation of customary international law.

The Supreme Court began its analysis of custom with the following proposition:

> By an ancient usage among civilized nations, beginning centuries ago, and gradually ripening into a rule of international law, coast fishing vessels, pursuing their vocation of catching and bringing in fresh fish, have been recognized as exempt, with their cargoes and crews, from capture as prize of war.[12]

The great bulk of the Court's decision was then given over to the demonstration of this thesis.[13] The Court's substantiation of the customary rule began with a chronological survey of state practice from "the earliest accessible sources, through the increasing recognition of [the rule], with occasional setbacks, to what we may now justly consider as its final establishment in our own country and generally throughout the civilized world."[14] The first bits of data examined were orders of King Henry IV of England made in 1403 and 1406 pursuant to a treaty between him and the King of France. These fifteenth-century English acts provided that French fishermen were not to be disturbed when fishing off England or when they proceeded to and from their fishing grounds. It was understood that English fishermen were to be accorded reciprocal privileges by the French king. The Court then cited similar protections detailed in a 1521 treaty between France and the German Emperor and in reciprocal edicts of France and the Netherlands in 1536.[15]

It is doubtful that the Court expected that these early examples of state practice demonstrated that there was an international legal rule as early as the fifteenth or sixteenth century shielding fishermen from wartime seizure. Rather, the evidence tended to demonstrate much the opposite. If it were already accepted customary international law that fishermen were not to be disturbed even in times of war, such special

[12] 175 U.S. 677, 686.
[13] Id. at 686-711.
[14] Id. at 686.
[15] Id. at 687-688.

protection would not have been necessary. The Supreme Court did not, of course, need to determine whether an international legal rule existed in the fifteenth and sixteenth centuries; it sought only to find a rule at the turn of the twentieth. Its own language, quoted above, referred to "an ancient usage . . . ripening into a rule of international law." Presumably the very notion of customary law is that what is at first only practice becomes, in time, law. The question is how to know when and whether the usage has ripened.

One ripening requirement is that the practice must have become more or less uniform. In *The Paquete Habana,* references were made to protective state practices from 1403, 1406, 1521, 1536, 1543, 1584, 1661, 1675, 1681, 1692, 1779, 1780, 1785, 1793, 1796, 1798, 1799, 1806, 1828, 1846, 1854, 1859, 1870, and 1894. Though there were also examples of instances where fishermen were declared to be fair game for wartime capture, the Court found these much fewer in number and less persuasive. Practice, though it should be consistent, need not be unanimous. Nor need it necessarily be ancient. As the International Court of Justice held in the *North Sea Continental Shelf* cases, a "passage of only a short period of time is not necessarily, or of itself, a bar to the formation of a new rule of customary international law," so long as the practice is "both extensive and virtually uniform."[16]

Determining customary international law is not only a matter of documenting reasonably consistent state practice. Even when it is established that the bulk of the evidence of state practice tips in a certain way, the question remains as to how or why such uniform state practice establishes a rule of law. It is at this point of the analysis that international lawyers begin to speak of a psychological, as well as a historical, element to customary international law: what is called *opinio juris vel necessitatis* or, as the *Restatement (Third) of the Foreign Relations Law of the United States* put it in 1987, "a sense of legal obligation."[17]

In terms of its function, *opinio juris* may be thought of as a solvent that transforms the nitty-gritty of a historical rendition of examples of state practice into a more liquid form: a rule of customary international law that may be applied to current problems. Without *opinio juris,* there

[16] 1969 I.C.J. Reports 3, 43.

[17] American Law Institute, *Restatement (Third) of the Foreign Relations Law of the United States* §102(2) (1987). The *Restatement (Fourth)*'s only published volume to date does not cover customary international law. For a consideration of *opinio juris,* see B.D. Lepard, *Customary International Law: A New Theory with Practical Applications* (2010).

may exist only a history lesson more or less devoid of legal significance. As the International Court has held: "The States concerned must therefore feel that they are conforming to what amounts to a legal obligation. The frequency, or even habitual character of the acts is not in itself enough."[18]

How then does one know if this sense of "legal obligation" has done its work? One way is to ask whether states when they acted in a consistent fashion did so only out of convenience or if they acknowledged that they did so because they felt compelled by international law. This may, however, be a difficult question of fact. For example, in *The Paquete Habana* we can find only traces of acknowledged compulsion. In the 1521 treaty between France and Germany mentioned above, it was said that the industry of the fishermen was "bestowed by heaven to allay the hunger of the poor."[19] Might this imply that to some extent the monarchs of France and the Empire were complying with a kind of religious mandate in agreeing to protect fishermen? An order of Louis XVI in 1779 referred, post-Voltaire and in a more rationalistic frame of mind, to "the sentiments of humanity which inspired [the King]."[20] Are such humanitarian sentiments sufficient to make a case for legal compulsion? More helpful was Napoleon's complaint in 1801 that English seizures of French fishing boats were "contrary to all the usages of civilized nations, and to the common law which governs them, even in time of war."[21]

However, such examples of formal state expressions of *opinio juris*, weak as they are, are rare in *The Paquete Habana* and indeed far from prevalent in practice generally. Oftentimes, what one finds is simply state practice unadorned with any explicit acknowledgment of compliance with the rules of international law. This should come as no surprise. States often act in customary ways but usually have no need to pronounce that they do so because they somehow feel legally obliged. Indeed, official state expressions about rules of customary international law are more likely to be generated in situations of conflict and doubt about those rules than when customary rules are well accepted.

Jurists and judges, rather than states, are often the more helpful sources for expressions of opinions that international practice has

[18] North Sea Continental Shelf Cases, 1969 I.C.J. Reports 3, 44.

[19] 175 U.S. 677, 688 (1900).

[20] Id. at 689-690.

[21] Id. at 692.

at some stage become customary international law. Here it might be worthwhile to remember that Article 38(1)(d) of the Statute of the International Court of Justice refers to "judicial decisions and the teachings of the most highly qualified publicists of the various nations, as subsidiary means for the determination of rules of law."[22] As we discuss below, one of the significant ways in which judges and publicists contribute to international law is by cumulating the practice of states and opining when such practice has reached the point where it may truly be considered customary international law. Jurists and judges, rather more frequently than states, are the effective brewers of that magic potion, *opinio juris.* Custom and all of the non-consensual sources are explained and justified by a goodly number of legal theories.[23]

3. The Evidences of International Law

The material evidences used to determine international law are exceedingly various. The U.S. Department of State lists the "sources of international lawmaking" as including "treaties, executive agreements, legislation, Federal regulations, Federal court decisions, testimony and statements before Congressional and international bodies, diplomatic notes, correspondence, speeches, press conference statements, and even internal memoranda."[24] The mere collection of relevant information to be used in weighing and evaluating legal arguments about rules of international law is sometimes a daunting task, much more complicated than a search for evidences of rules of municipal law.[25]

To begin with, there are all the many treaties we have noted above, to be found not only in the international treaty series,[26] but also in the

[22] ICJ Statute, supra.

[23] See *Custom's Future: International Law in a Changing World* (Bradley ed. 2016); Sivakumaran, The Influence of Teachings of Publicists on the Development of International Law, 66 *International and Comparative Law Quarterly* 1 (2017).

[24] *Digest of United States Practice in International Law 1973 v* (Rovine ed. 1974).

[25] Keeping up to date on international law can be an intimidating chore; another very useful annual compendium is provided by the International Law Section of the American Bar Association, e.g., Buys et al., International Legal Developments Year in Review: 2013, 48 *ABA/SIL Year in Review* 1 (2014); Buys et al., International Legal Developments Year in Review: 2014, 49 *ABA/SIL Year in Review* 1 (2015).

[26] For 1648-1919, *The Consolidated Treaty Series* (Parry ed.); for 1920-1946, *The League of Nations Treaty Series*; since 1946, *The United Nations Treaty Series.* L.N.T.S. and U.N.T.S. are also available at http://treaties.un.org (visited Jan. 12, 2024).

many national treaty series, for example, those prepared for or by the United States.[27] Additionally there are a great number of reports of the decisions of international courts[28] and of municipal courts on issues of international law.[29] And, of course, there is a vast amount of scholarly material on international law available in books and periodicals.[30]

[27]Before 1949, U.S. treaties were published in the *Statutes at Large.* Compilations covering the period from 1776 to the middle of the twentieth century are Malloy, *Treaties, Conventions, International Acts, Protocols, and Agreements Between the United States and Other Powers,* and Bevans, *Treaties and Other International Agreements of the United States of America.* Since 1949, treaties are first published in "slip" format as part of the *Treaties and Other International Agreements Series.* The publication in print of treaties in this series lags. The Office of Treaty Affairs at the Department of State has made those texts of treaties in this series from 1981 and 2025 available online at https://www.state.gov/bureaus-offices/treaty-affairs/ (accessed Mar. 18, 2026), pursuant to 1 U.S.C. §112a(d). The text of treaties published as Senate Treaty Documents may be accessed through the Library of Congress's THOMAS website. Through 1984, the "slip" treaties were collected and published in the hard-bound volumes of *United States Treaty Series.* No new volume has been published since then, however, and no mention of this title is made at the Department of State Treaty Affairs website so its status is uncertain. The Department of State does publish the very useful annual *Treaties in Force* in print with the most recent 2025 edition online at https://www.state.gov/treaties-in-force/, which lists bilateral treaties in force for the United States nation by nation and multilateral treaties in force for the United States by subject matter and shows which other states are party to those agreements. The online edition also links to full text when available. Month-to-month treaty practice that was published in the *Department of State Bulletin* (later titled the *Department of State Dispatch*) until 1999 is now found from 1996 to the present online in *Treaty Actions* at https://www.state.gov/1996-TIAS, and https://state.gov/depositary-information/ (accessed Mar. 18, 2026).

[28]These include *The Reports of the Permanent Court of International Justice,* available online at http://www.icj-cij.org/en/pcij (accessed Mar. 18, 2026); *The Reports of the International Court of Justice,* available online at https://icj-cij.org/en/annual-reports (accessed Mar. 18, 2026); the decisions of the European Court of Justice reported in the *Common Market Law Reports,* in the *European Court Reports,* and online at the Court's website https://infocuria.curia.europa.eu/tabs/tout, and the decisions of the European Court of Human Rights reported in *The Publications of the European Court of Human Rights, Series A: Judgments and Decisions* until 1998, and in all instances online in the court's HUDOC, accessible via the Court's website (http://www.echr.coe.int).

[29]Besides the regular national law reports, municipal decisions concerning international law are sometimes published in *The International Law Reports* and in *International Legal Materials.* There are also special national collections devoted to international law such as *American International Law Cases, British International Law Cases,* and *Commonwealth International Law Cases.*

[30]The three principal general periodical legal bibliographies, the *Index to Legal Periodicals,* the *Index to Foreign Legal Periodicals,* and the *Legal Resources Index,* are helpful

Most distinctive of all as collections of evidences of international law are the digests of national practice in international law. The United States has been a pioneer in this field, having long published official encyclopedic digests of its international law practice: by Cadwalader in 1877,[31] by Wharton in 1886,[32] by Moore in 1906,[33] by Hackworth beginning in 1940,[34] and by Whiteman beginning in 1963.[35] Beginning in 1973, supplemental annual digests of international law have been prepared by the Office of Legal Adviser of the Department of State.[36] The value of such collections as a means for determining customary international law has been widely recognized. The Council of Europe, for example, has recommended that its member states "publish digests concerning national practice in the field of public international law" and has suggested guidelines for the organization and content of such digests.[37]

---

starting points for international law research. Other useful bibliographies for doctrine are *Public International Law,* a semiannual publication of Germany's Max-Planck-Institut für ausländisches öffentliches Recht und Völkerrecht, Harvard Law School Library, *Catalog of International Law and Relations* (20 vols. 1965), and the research site of the American Society of International Law (http://www.asil.org).

[31] J.L. Cadwalader, *Digest of the Published Opinions of the Attorney-General, and of the Leading Decisions of the Federal Courts, with Reference to International Law, Treaties and Kindred Subjects* (1877).

[32] F. Wharton, *A Digest of the International Law of the United States* (3 vols. 1886).

[33] J.B. Moore, *A Digest of International Law* (8 vols. 1906).

[34] G.H. Hackworth, *Digest of International Law* (8 vols. 1940-1944).

[35] M.M. Whiteman, *Digest of International Law* (15 vols. 1963-1973).

[36] E.g., *Digest of United States Practice in International Law 1973* (Rovine ed. 1974). Printed *Digests* were published until 1989. In 2000, the Office of the Legal Adviser published one volume for 1989-1990 and another for 1991-1999, and resumed publication of annual volumes. The renewed *Digest* follows a slightly different format than before, https://www.state.gov/office-of-the-legal-adviser/digest-of-united-states-practice-in-international-law#:~:text=Hard%20copies%20of%20the%20annual,105%20of%20the%20Copyright%20Act (accessed January 29, 2026).

[37] Council of Europe, Committee of Ministers, Resolution 64(10) of Oct. 6, 1964, and Resolution 68(17) of June 28, 1968. Nowadays, collections of state practice are to be found, e.g., in the *Australian Yearbook of International Law,* the *British Digest of International Law,* the *Canadian Yearbook of International Law,* the *Annuaire français de droit international, La prassi italiani di dritto internazionale,* the *Japanese Annual of International Law,* the *Netherlands Yearbook of International Law,* the *Revista española de derecho internacional,* and the *Repertoire Suisse de droit international public.*

4. *The Resolutions and Recommendations of International Organizations*

While there is little doubt that state practice constitutes good evidence of customary international law, what else may be counted as admissible data is more controversial. Especially debated is the legal effect of the practice of international organizations. There is no question that international organizations can be delegated rulemaking powers by treaty, thereby diminishing the sovereign prerogatives of member states. Such, for example, is the case with an important number of economic functions delegated to the European Union by its member states [see Chapter 9]. Much less sure is the value of resolutions and recommendations of international organizations when there has been no such explicit delegation of legislative powers.

Much of the controversy surrounds the practice of the General Assembly of the United Nations, which is empowered by the U.N. Charter to "initiate studies and make recommendations for the purpose of promoting international cooperation in the political field and encouraging the progressive development of international law and its codification."[38] Such studies and recommendations are not in and of themselves a form of international legislation. Nonetheless, General Assembly resolutions are not infrequently used as evidence of customary international law. For example, in its advisory opinion on the *Western Sahara*, the International Court relied heavily on General Assembly resolutions to establish basic legal principles concerning the right of peoples to self-determination.[39] The General Assembly itself has recommended that its declarations and resolutions be "taken into consideration by the International Court of Justice" as one way in which "the development of international law may be reflected."[40]

The soundest way to account for the legal effect of the resolutions and recommendations of international organizations is to note that such resolutions and recommendations are a particularly useful evidence of the simultaneous attitudes of a number of states with respect to a specific legal issue or topic. The vote of a state on a matter before an international organization is itself an act of that state, and the balloting of

[38] Art. 13(1), 59 Stat. 1031, T.S. No. 993, 3 Bevans 1153 (signed at San Francisco June 26, 1945; entered into force October 24, 1945).

[39] 1975 I.C.J. Reports 12, 31-37.

[40] Preamble, U.N.G.A. Res. 3232 (XXIX), November 12, 1974.

many states on a specific question may in some circumstances illustrate a consensus (or a lack of one) about a customary rule. So, for example, in an arbitration between Texaco and Libya, the sole arbitrator, Professor Dupuy of France, looking to the votes of states on U.N. resolutions to help determine the customary international law applicable to nationalizations of foreign property, rejected three 1974 U.N. resolutions because of the opposition of Western countries and relied instead on a 1963 U.N. resolution where developed and developing countries were in agreement: "The consensus by a majority of States belonging to the various representative groups indicates without the slightest doubt universal recognition of the rules therein incorporated."[41]

As we explore below, much of the work of discerning and developing customary international law is done by judges in the process of preparing and rendering judicial decisions and by scholars in researching and writing legal doctrine. A rather comparable role has been played by the International Law Commission (ILC). Created by the U.N. General Assembly in 1947, the ILC is composed of 34 jurists from as many countries. Its task is to help develop and codify international law, giving priority to requests of the General Assembly. It may also put on its agenda items suggested by itself, by other international organizations, and by states. The ILC has prepared early drafts of a number of important international conventions [see Chapters 2 and 10].[42]

As with the resolutions and recommendations of international organizations, the probative value of the reports and drafts of the International Law Commission may be sometimes uncertain. Article 15 of the Commission's Statute recognizes that there is a distinction between the "progressive development of international law," that is, "the preparation of draft conventions on subjects which have not yet been regulated by international law or in regard to which the law has not yet been sufficiently developed in the practice of states," and the "codification of international law," that is, "the more precise formulation and systemization of rules of international law in fields where there already has been extensive State practice, precedent and doctrine."[43] The less an ILC report or draft

[41] Texaco Overseas Petroleum Co. v. Libyan Arab Republic, Award on the Merits of January 19, 1977, 17 *International Legal Materials* 1, 30 (1978).

[42] See H.W. Briggs, *The International Law Commission* (1965) [hereinafter cited as "Briggs"]; I. Sinclair, *The International Law Commission* (1987); the annual *Yearbook of the International Law Commission* (1949 et seq.).

[43] Briggs, supra, at 362, 364-365; U.N. Doc. A/CN.4/4/Rev.1 (1962).

represents a "progressive development" and the more it is taken to be a "codification," the better an evidence of customary international law it is. However, such a characterization may not be easy to make. Looking at the long years the ILC spent preparing a draft convention on the law of treaties, Sinclair noted that the distinction between progressive development and codification "proved extremely difficult for the Commission to sustain in practice."[44]

5. *"Soft Law"*

Resolutions of international organizations are sometimes regarded as a sort of "soft law": "rules which are neither strictly binding nor completely void of any legal significance."[45] These may in time "harden" into customary international law.[46] The notion of "softness" has also been applied to treaties with a less-than-obligatory nature,[47] a notion akin to that of "aspirational treaties" [see Chapter 2].

Perhaps the most important use of "soft law" in practice has involved the development of international environmental law [see Chapter 7]. The 1972 Stockholm Conference, the U.N. Environmental Programme, and regional and non-governmental international organizations have all elaborated "soft law" norms that have to some degree molded state behavior, yielding "harder" customary international law.[48]

However new the term "soft law" may be, there have always been times when states have concluded treaties not meant to be legally binding.[49] Moreover, there have always been and always will be debates about which international norms are "legal" and which are "non-legal"

[44] I. Sinclair, *The Vienna Convention on the Law of Treaties* 11 (2d ed. 1984).

[45] Bernardt, Customary International Law, 7 *Encyclopedia of Public International Law* 61, 62 (1984).

[46] Seidl-Hohenveldern, International Economic "Soft Law," 163 *Hague Recueil* 165, 194-213 (1979).

[47] Francioni, International "Soft Law": A Contemporary Assessment, *Fifty Years of the International Court of Justice: Essays in Honour of Sir Robert Jennings* 167 (Lowe & Fitzmaurice eds. 1996).

[48] Dupuy, Soft Law and the International Law of the Environment, 12 *Michigan Journal of International Law* 420, 422-431 (1991).

[49] Hillgenberg, A Fresh Look at "Soft Law," 10 *European Journal of International Law* 499, 499-502 (1999).

and, of course, about what difference "legality" makes in practice.[50] It can even be argued that "soft law" is now used for so many different purposes that the term "has lost its identifiable conceptual concept and become vague and sometimes even meaningless."[51]

6. *The Inelegance of Customary International Law*

Without denigrating the considerable utility of customary international law, it must be admitted that this form of international law is highly controversial.[52] This is so for at least three reasons. First and foremost is the fact that, oftentimes, state practice is so diverse that it may be difficult or even impossible to find enough consistency of practice to warrant drawing a customary international legal rule from it. This was a problem in the *Lotus* case, where the Permanent Court of International Justice held that neither state practice nor the opinion of publicists was so settled as to permit finding an international rule restraining Turkey from asserting jurisdiction to criminally prosecute a Frenchman involved in a high seas collision between French and Turkish boats.[53] The difficulty was highlighted by Justice Harlan

[50] Bothe, Legal and Non-Legal Norms—A Meaningful Distinction in International Relations?, 11 *Netherlands Yearbook of International Law* 65 (1980); Pronto, Understanding the Hard/Soft Distinction in International Law, 48 *Vanderbilt Journal of International* Law 941 (2015).

[51] Blutman, In the Trap of a Legal Metaphor: International Soft Law, 59 *International & Comparative Law Quarterly* 605, 624 (2010).

[52] See Chimini, Customary International Law: A Third World Perspective, 112 *American Journal of International Law* 1, 7-14 (2018); *The Oxford Handbook of the Sources of International Law* (Besson & d'Astremont eds. 2017).

[53] 1927 P.C.I.J. Reports, ser. A, no. 10. See Guilfoyle, *SS Lotus (France v. Turkey, 1927)*, in *Landmark Cases in Public International* Law 89 (Bjorger & Miles eds. 2017). As a matter of maritime law, states strongly disagreed with the *Lotus* decision. In the 1952 Brussels Convention, the flag state was given exclusive jurisdiction over a ship's officers in cases involving a collision on the high seas, a rule followed in Article 11 of the 1958 Geneva Convention on the High Seas. W.W. Bishop, *International Law* 547-548 (3d ed. 1971). A similar rule is to be found in Article 97 of the 1982 United Nations Convention on the Law of the Sea. U.N. Doc. A/CONF.62/122 (done at Montego Bay December 10, 1982; entered in force November 16, 1994; not in force for the United States), reprinted in 21 *International Legal Materials* 1261 (1982) [hereinafter cited as "U.N. Law of the Sea Convention"].

in the *Sabbatino* case, where he noted in dismay that "[t]here are few if any issues in international law today on which opinion seems to be so divided as the limitations on a state's power to expropriate the property of aliens."[54] The same is sometimes true with the customary international law of human rights.[55] If no treaty can be found to authoritatively regulate a matter, it is by no means certain that customary international law will be able to provide a definite rule to fill the gap.

Second, even if one state, judge, or other observer decides that the available evidences establish a norm of customary international law, there is no assurance that another decision-maker will reach the same conclusion. Customary international law is ordinarily found by a more or less subjective weighing of the evidence, and subjective scales tilt differently in different hands. So, for example, the United States is persuaded that certain of its high seas freedoms are protected by customary international law regardless of its failure to ratify the Law of the Sea Treaty, a conclusion resisted by other states [see Chapter 7].

Third, the very process of making customary international law often stimulates, rather than diminishes, conflict. When states have differing views of what international law ought to be and when they cannot agree to make common rules by treaty, then they may well act and react in practice in a fashion consciously designed to make new customary international law or, at least, to block another state's preferred version of the right rule from becoming customary international law or to establish an exception to the rule. So, in the *Fisheries* case, the International Court held that Norway was not obliged to follow the ordinary customary rules about the drawing of maritime baselines because it had long enforced a contrary principle.[56] Nowadays, maritime states and coastal states are often found locked in serious lawmaking or lawbreaking confrontations, for example, protecting high seas freedoms on the one hand and extending national maritime zones on the other, as in the Gulf of Sidra.[57]

[54] Banco Nacional de Cuba v. Sabbatino, 376 U.S. 398, 428 (1964).

[55] Kadens & Young, How Customary Is Customary International Law?, 54 *William & Mary Law Review* 885 (2013).

[56] 1951 I.C.J. Reports 116.

[57] See Blum, The Gulf of Sidra Incident, 80 *American Journal of International Law* 668 (1986).

B. NON-CONSENSUAL SOURCES OF INTERNATIONAL LAW

Gaps or faults in the fabric of international law as woven by treaties and custom may sometimes make it desirable to find other sources of international law. However, whether such sources exist and what they might be are matters of considerable debate. Since many, especially legal positivists, believe that a vital step in the making of any international legal rule is state consent and since other sorts of international legal rules are mostly based on non-consensual foundations, such other rules may be suspect to some. A natural law perspective makes non-consensual rules easier to accept. Whatever the theoretical stumbling blocks, in practice, non-consensual sources play an important role in international law. As Professor Cassese put it, international law is no longer, if it ever was, "a faithful reflection of the existing constellation of power"; rather it now "incorporates a large body of 'oughts.'"[58]

1. *General Principles of Law*

A frequently relied upon non-treaty, non-customary source of international law is what is termed *general principles of law*. A typical formulation of this source appears in Article 38(1)(c) of the Statute of the International Court of Justice, where, in the third place after treaties and custom, the Court is instructed to apply "the general principles of law recognized by civilized nations" in deciding "in accordance with international law such disputes as are submitted to it." Although at one time the term *civilized nations* was meant to restrict the scope of the provision to European states or states recognized as actors in the European system of international politics, such as the United States and, somewhat later, Japan, nowadays it is recognized that a search for general principles of law should include all corners of the globe.[59]

[58] A. Cassese, *International Law in a Divided World* 400 (1988).

[59] G.W. Gong, *The Standard of "Civilization" in International Society* (1984). One might also follow the example of the International Law Commission, which in 2023 used the term "recognized by the community of nations." Jalloh, The Principles of International Law and Other Topics, 118 *American Journal of International Law* 120, 122 (2024).

Although some liberally suggest that the availability of general principles as a source of international law permits international lawyers to apply natural law, while others restrictively contend that general principles of law may be international law only when drawn from customary international practice, the most usual approach to general principles of law as a source of international law relies upon techniques of comparative law.[60] The basic notion is that a general principle of law is some proposition of law so fundamental that it will be found in virtually every legal system. When treaties and customary international law fail to offer a needed international rule, a search may be launched in comparative law to discover if national legal systems use a common principle. If such a common principle is found, then it is presumed that a comparable principle should be attributed to fill the gap in international law.

A search for general principles of law as an exercise in comparative law is a method familiar to lawyers in the common law tradition where courts often survey judicial decisions from other states. Although such foreign cases are not binding as precedent, the rulings from other jurisdictions may have persuasive value. Indeed, if a court has no precedent to guide it, but if most other legal systems tend in one direction, the judge may be inclined to follow the mainstream. Of course, when other legal systems have decided in different ways on a similar point, the judge may feel freer to choose at will from among the conflicting decisions.

Similarly, lawyers and judges in the civil law tradition are familiar with the problem of *lacunae*, gaps in the law, a concept based on the premise that only formal legislative institutions are empowered to make legal rules. When there is no statute available to settle a disputed matter, then there may need to be an explicit authorization permitting courts to fill the legislative vacuum. In this fashion, Article 38(1)(c) of the International Court's Statute can be read as expressly authorizing the Court to draw upon general principles of law to fill gaps left by conventional and customary law.

Whatever the municipal law analogies to Article 38(1)(c), there still remains the question as to what the theoretical foundation or justification is for using general principles of law as a source of international

[60] Friedmann, The Uses of "General Principles" in the Development of International Law, 57 *American Journal of International Law* 279, 282-283 (1963); Waldock, General Course on Public International Law, 106 *Hague Recueil* 1, 54 (1962).

law. It could be argued that the authority to apply general principles of law issues only from the provisions of the Statute of the International Court of Justice, in which case only that court has the power to find rules by reference to general principles of law and it has the power to do so only because states have explicitly so agreed. Although this may be a satisfactory formal explanation for the International Court, it cannot be generally sufficient; there are too many examples of other courts and other bodies drawing upon general principles of law as a source of international law.

One might also contend that there is some sort of implicit consensual agreement among the sovereign states to permit general principles of law to be used as a source of international law,[61] or argue that because various states have a certain norm common to their national legal systems, they do not object to seeing the same norm applicable in their international relations. However, these explanations are more satisfactory in appearance than in substance. Outside the Statute of the International Court of Justice, one does not always find any evidence of explicit or implicit state consent to the use of general principles of law. Perhaps the best that can be said if one wishes to rely on a theory based on state consent is to note that if the states mean not to permit general principles of law to be a source of international law, they could protest, but have not usually done so.

In practice, there has been little problem in accepting general principles of law as a source of international law. This is so partly because of the quasi-consensual explanations given to general principles of law and partly because of the explicit reference in Article 38(1)(c). But it is largely due to the fact that general principles of law have rarely been used to reverse or modify existing rules of international law. Rather, general principles of law are usually used merely to fill gaps or, occasionally, to substantiate determinations of customary international law.

As gap fillers, general principles of law are more a feature of court cases than of other kinds of international legal process. In the *AM & S* case, the European Court of Justice had to decide whether certain company documents sought in an investigation of economic competition were to be protected from inspection by the Commission of the European Economic Community on the grounds that the materials

[61] Tunkin, General Theory of Sources of International Law, 19 *Indian Journal of International Law* 474, 482 (1979).

were privileged communications between lawyers and clients. Neither the Common Market Treaty nor its regulations established such a privilege of confidentiality. However, the European Court of Justice decided to take "into account the principles and concepts common to the laws of those States concerning the observance of confidentiality, in particular, as regards certain communications between lawyer and client." Having been provided with various comparative law surveys, the Court concluded that, despite differences in the rules of the members of the Common Market, there were "common criteria inasmuch as those laws protect, in similar circumstances, the confidentiality of written communications between lawyer and client provided that, on the one hand, such communications are made for the purposes and in the interests of the client's rights of defence and, on the other hand, they emanate from independent lawyers, that is to say, lawyers who are not bound to the client by a relationship of employment."[62] *AM & S* also demonstrates the possibility of regional general principles of law, not dissimilar to regional customary international law. The ECJ may have "recourse to general principles inherent in the community legal order instead of falling back on general international law."[63]

Other courts have used general principles of law as gap fillers in a wide variety of circumstances. The International Court, for example, turned to them in the *Corfu Channel* case to justify its use of circumstantial evidence, arguing that such evidence was "admitted in all systems of law."[64] In the *AMCO* case, in 1984, an international arbitral tribunal used a comparative analysis of Indonesian, Dutch, Belgian, Italian, German, Danish, English, and United States laws to find a general principle of law applicable in international law defining a "contract" as "an agreement based on a meeting of minds and wills and creating obligations."[65] Judge Mosler of the International Court of Justice found that international tribunals have employed a comparative methodology to establish general principles of law for international rules concerning

[62] [1982] 2 *Common Market Law Reports* 264, 297-318, 322-323.

[63] Simma & Pulkowski, Of Planets and the Universe: Self-Contained Regimes in International Law, 17 *European Journal of International Law* 483, 505 (2006); Tridimo, *The General Principles of European Community Law* 4 (2007).

[64] 1949 I.C.J. Reports 4, 18.

[65] AMCO Asia Corp. v. Indonesia, Decision of November 21, 1984, International Centre for the Settlement of Investment Disputes, 24 *International Legal Materials* 1022, 1027-1029 (1985).

liability for damages, unjust enrichment, right of passage over territory, administrative law, and the doctrine of *res judicata*.[66]

General principles of law have also been used, especially in U.S. courts, as a means for substantiating proofs of customary international law. For example, in Filartiga v. Peña-Irala,[67] Judge Kaufman, after reviewing the prohibition of torture by various international conventions, noted a survey that showed that torture had been banned in over 55 national constitutions. This comparative study was then accumulated, along with treaties, state practice, and opinions of judges and publicists, to prove a rule of customary international law prohibiting official torture.[68]

Not infrequently, contracts made between a private party and a foreign state, especially in an investment setting, include a reference to general principles of law as a choice-of-law provision. In these cases, the parties have chosen to rely on general principles of law as a substitute for or a supplement to a specific municipal law. A tribunal's determination of general principles of law in such circumstances will usually be effected by a comparative law analysis more or less identical to that which would be conducted pursuant to a search for general principles to fill a gap in international law or to substantiate a finding of customary international law.[69]

2. *Natural Law*

For many years, natural law was thought to be the principal source of international law. Indeed, many texts of the sixteenth, seventeenth, and eighteenth centuries characterized themselves as studies of the "laws of nature and of nations." In his book so named, Vattel described

> [a] necessary law of nations which consists in the application of the law of nature to nations. It is necessary, because nations are absolutely bound to observe it. This law contains the precepts prescribed by the law of nature to states, on whom that law is not less obligatory than on

[66] Mosler, General Principles of Law, 7 *Encyclopedia of Public International Law* 89, 97-101 (1984).

[67] 630 F.2d 876 (2d Cir. 1980).

[68] Id. at 878-885.

[69] A.D. McNair, *Lord McNair: Selected Papers and Bibliography* 276-294 (1974).

> individuals; since states are composed of men, their resolutions are taken by men, and the law of nature is binding on all men, under whatever relation they act.[70]

An example of such a rule drawn from natural law was the principle of the equality of nations:

> Since men are naturally equal, and a perfect equality prevails in their rights and obligations, as equally proceeding from nature, nations composed of men, and considered as so many free persons living together in the state of nature, are naturally equal, and inherit from nature the same obligations and rights. Power or weakness does not in this respect produce any difference. A dwarf is as much a man as a giant; a small republic is no less a sovereign state than the most powerful kingdom.[71]

Perhaps the best known and still prevalent international legal rule drawn from natural law is the one dating at least from 1748, when Montesquieu in *The Spirit of the Laws* wrote that "the law of nations is naturally founded on the principle that the many nations ought to do to each other, in times of peace the most good, and in times of war the least bad, that is possible without injuring their genuine interests."[72]

A belief in the relevance of natural law to international law may, but need not, stem from religious principles. The early sixteenth- and seventeenth-century Spanish international lawyers Vitoria and Suárez, for example, based the law of nations on Catholic natural law foundations.[73] However, Grotius, a Protestant, later looked to more general biblical sources, as well as to classical authors and to right reason, to ground his theory of natural law.[74] In the eighteenth century's Age of

[70] Vattel, supra, at *lviii.*

[71] Id. at *lxiii.*

[72] "Le droit des gens est naturellement fondé sur ce principe: que les diverses nations doivent se faire, dans la paix, le plus de bien, et, dans la guerre, le moins de mal qu'il est possible, sans nuire à leurs véritables interêts." Montesquieu, L'esprit des lois, *Oeuvres complètes* 527, 531 (Editions du Seuil 1964).

[73] C. Sepulveda, *Derecho Internacional* 13-23 (20th ed. 1998) [hereinafter cited as "Sepulveda"].

[74] Janis, Religion and the Literature of International Law: Some Standard Texts, *The Influence of Religion on the Development of International Law* 61, 61-66 (Janis ed. 1991) [hereinafter cited as "Janis, Religion and International Law"]; Kunz, Natural-Law Thinking in the Modern Science of International Law, 55 *American Journal of International Law* 951, 951-952 (1961).

Reason, Vattel thoroughly repudiated any religious foundations for natural law.[75] In a standard American text of the nineteenth century, Henry Wheaton wrote that there existed "absolute international rights of states," rights to which a state was "entitled as an independent moral being."[76] Wheaton enumerated several such absolute international rights: self-preservation, independence, equality, and property.[77]

In retrospect, much of what passed in the traditional law of nations as natural law looks rather like what we know nowadays as general principles of law. Many of Grotius' laws of nature, for example, were drawn from precedents of Roman law as well as from "the testimony of philosophers, historians, poets; finally also of orators."[78] As with our modern general principles of law, the object of Grotius' exercise of natural law was to find international rules basic or useful, though not clearly consented to, by states.

When nineteenth-century legal positivists began deriding international law as being mere morality and not law at all [see Chapter 8], many international lawyers took affright and tried to sever their ties with natural law altogether. There was a suspicion that intimately linking international law to natural law debased international law. William Manning, the author of one of the earliest English works on international law, wrote in 1839 that "the fundamental principles of the law of nations" did indeed "arise from the law of nature," but that overly discussing the law of nature swamped Englishmen "with a vast quantity of extraneous matter" that "embarrassed and disgusted" them. Better to write, he thought, a book that made little reference to natural law.[79]

The suspicion that international law might be mere morality persists. In a well-known attack, George Kennan wrote that "the most serious fault" of U.S. foreign policy has been a "legalistic-moralistic approach to international problems."[80] Kennan has gone so far as to assert "that there are no internationally accepted standards of morality to which the U.S. government could appeal if it wished to act in the name of moral principles."[81] In the light of such visions, it should be no

[75] Janis, Religion and International Law, supra, at 66-69.

[76] H. Wheaton, *Elements of International Law with a Sketch of the History of the Science* 81 (1st ed. 1836).

[77] Id. at 81, 95, 130, 137.

[78] Grotius, supra, at 23 (prolegomena §40).

[79] W. Manning, *Commentaries on the Law of Nations* 3-4 (1839).

[80] G. Kennan, *American Diplomacy 1900-1950* 95 (1951).

[81] Kennan, Morality and Foreign Policy, 64 *Foreign Affairs* 205, 207 (1985/1986).

surprise that many international lawyers, along with Oppenheim and Lauterpacht, while respecting the contribution that natural law had made to their discipline—"[t]he modern law of nations in particular owes its very existence to the theory of the law of nature"—refused to recognize natural law as a modern source of international law.[82]

Although there are many theories of natural law, the basic idea, as the words themselves imply, is that there is a law so natural that it is to be found in any community, including the community of states. Although most international lawyers accept the idea of an international community, some do not. Soviet theorists like Tunkin saw a fundamental distinction between socialist and capitalist states because they were based on radically dissimilar socioeconomic foundations.[83] Those who hold such presumptions, of course, rarely expect that there will be laws "natural" to different sides of the divide.

3. Jus Cogens

Rather close to natural law is the notion of *jus cogens*, compelling law. *Jus cogens* is a norm thought to be so fundamental that it even invalidates rules drawn from treaty or custom. Usually, a *jus cogens* norm presupposes an international public order sufficiently potent to control states that might otherwise establish contrary rules on a consensual basis. In a seminal article written in the face of the Nazi takeover of Austria, Alfred von Verdross wrote that "it is the quintessence of norms of this character that they prescribe a certain positive or negative behavior unconditionally; norms of this character, therefore, cannot be derogated from by the will of the contracting parties."[84] Needless to say, the very possibility of such a fundamental law is hotly controverted by positivists who rely exclusively on state consent for the making of international law.

[82] L. Oppenheim, 1 *International Law* 92-94, 24-35 (8th ed. Lauterpacht 1955). For reviews of Oppenheim and Brownlie, see Janis, Religion and International Law, supra, at 75-81.

[83] Tunkin, supra, at 233; see Janis, The Soviet Theory of International Law and International Economic Relations, *Soviet Law and Economy* 235 (Ioffe & Janis eds. 1986).

[84] Verdross, Forbidden Treaties in International Law, 31 *American Journal of International Law* 571-572 (1937).

The most notable positive appearance of *jus cogens* is in Article 53 of the Vienna Convention on the Law of Treaties,[85] where the term is rendered in English as "peremptory norm" [see Chapter 2]:

> A treaty is void if, at the time of its conclusion, it conflicts with a peremptory norm of general international law. For the purposes of the present Convention, a peremptory norm of general international law is a norm accepted and recognized by the international community of states as a whole as a norm from which no derogation is permitted and which can be modified only by a subsequent norm of general international law having the same character.[86]

The Convention also provides that a new peremptory norm voids and terminates previously existing treaties with which it comes into conflict.[87]

Albeit explicitly accepted in the Vienna Convention, the notion of *jus cogens* continues to be highly controversial. How are its norms to be determined? Do such norms also trump rules outside of the law of treaties?[88] It is generally accepted that *jus cogens* norms are effective vis-à-vis customary international law.[89] At the very least, if a *jus cogens* norm "occupies the field," contrary practice will be seen only as a violation and not as state practice contributing to the development of a new norm.[90]

Although *jus cogens* is sometimes viewed as a form of customary international law, it is really of a different character. Customary international law is, by its very nature, not an apt instrument for the establishment of non-derogable rules, norms with a potency superior even to treaty rules. As usually conceived, customary international law is weaker than conventional international law. Both are based on state practice, but treaties show the practice explicitly in the form of written

[85] U.N. Doc. A/CONF.39/27 (1969), reprinted in 63 *American Journal of International Law* 875 (1969).

[86] Id., art. 53.

[87] Id., art. 64.

[88] Paulus, *Jus Cogens* in a Time of Hegemony and Fragmentation, 74 *Nordic Journal of International Law* 297 (2005).

[89] Bianchi, Human Rights and the Magic of *Jus Cogens,* 19 *European Journal of International Law* 491 (2008).

[90] Vidmar, Rethinking *Jus Cogens* After *Germany v. Italy:* Back to Article 53, 60 *Netherlands International Law Review* 1, 23 (2013).

rules, while the rules of custom must be drawn awkwardly from the various evidences of state diplomacy or pronouncements. Furthermore, both treaty and custom are grounded on the idea of agreement. Here again, treaties are ordinarily stronger, since consent is shown by a ratification process, while the consensual foundations of custom must be demonstrated more uncertainly by expressions about the law-like character of the rules, e.g., the vague notion of *opinio juris*. That any form of customary international law can be said to be so firmly rooted that it can be employed to prospectively repudiate subsequent treaty rules is a proposition that makes nonsense of the usual theory of customary and conventional international law.

It makes better sense to view *jus cogens* as a modern form of natural law, a viewpoint supported both in history and by function. Essentially, *jus cogens* establishes a set of "core values."[91] Historically, it is significant that the proponents of the idea of peremptory norms invalidating treaty rules were, in no small measure, reacting to the abuses of Nazism during the Second World War.[92] They rejected the positivist proposition that state acts, even the making of treaties, should be always thought capable of making binding law. Verdross explained that the concept of *jus cogens* was quite alien to legal positivists, but "[t]he situation was quite different in the natural law school of international law."[93] Natural lawyers are ready to accept "the idea of a necessary law which all states are obliged to observe . . . , [that is, an] ethics of the world."[94]

When the first drafts of what were to become the Vienna Convention's peremptory norm provisions were introduced in the International Law Commission by Lauterpacht in 1953, he made a clear distinction between the new notion, as yet untermed, and customary international law: "[T]he test was not inconsistency with customary international law pure and simple, but inconsistency with such overriding principles of international law which may be regarded as

[91] Shelton, Sherlock Holmes and the Mystery of *Jus Cogens*, 25 *Netherlands Yearbook of International Law* 23, 48 (2016).

[92] See E. Jiménez de Arechaga, *El derecho internacional contemporáneo* 79 (1980).

[93] Verdross, *Jus Dispositivum* and *Jus Cogens* in International Law, 60 *American Journal of International Law* 55, 56 (1966).

[94] Ibid. Those who insist that *jus cogens* must really be a form of customary international law seem especially frustrated by the employment of the concept in practice. Weisburd, American Judges and International Law, 36 *Vanderbilt Journal of Transnational Law* 1475, 1488-1531 (2003).

constituting principles of international public policy."[95] And as Schwelb noted, though the term *jus cogens* may be new, "the concept of an international *ordre public* has been advocated for a very long time."[96] *Jus cogens* is a legal emanation that grew out of the naturalist school, from those who were uncomfortable with the positivists' elevation of the state as the sole source of international law.

Functionally, a rule of *jus cogens* is, by its nature and utility, a rule so fundamental to the international community of states as a whole that the rule constitutes a basis for the community's legal system. Perforce and per Article 53 of the Vienna Convention, a rule of *jus cogens* is ordinarily non-derogable and invalidates subsequent norms generated by treaty or by custom, that is, by the ordinary consensual forms of international legislation. Thus, it is a sort of international law that, once ensconced, cannot be displaced by states, either in their treaties or in their practice. *Jus cogens* therefore functions like a natural or constitutional law that is so fundamental that states cannot avoid its force.

Partly because of its perceived potency, a peremptory norm is even more difficult to prove and establish than is a usually controversial rule of customary international law. In the *North Sea Continental Shelf* cases, the International Court of Justice explicitly put itself on record as not "attempting to enter into, still less pronounce upon any question of *jus cogens*."[97] It has been argued that there is no example in modern international practice of a treaty's being voided by a peremptory norm.[98]

Nonetheless, there have been frequent assertions by states, judges, and others that certain principles of law are so fundamental as to be considered *jus cogens*. For example, there are the principles of Articles 1 and 2 of the U.N. Charter, which guarantee the sovereignty of states. Some human rights, too, are claimed to be protected by rules of *jus cogens*.[99] In the *Chinn* case, Judge Schucking wrote that the International

[95] Schwelb, Some Aspects of International *Jus Cogens* as Formulated by the International Law Commission, 61 *American Journal of International Law* 946, 949 (1967).

[96] Ibid.

[97] 1969 I.C.J. Reports 3, 42.

[98] Gaja, *Jus Cogens* Beyond the Vienna Convention, 172 *Hague Recueil* 271, 286-289 (1981).

[99] Robledo, Le *jus cogens* international: sa genése, sa nature, ses fonctions, 172 *Hague Recueil* 9, 167-187 (1981).

Court would never "apply a convention the terms of which were contrary to public morality."[100]

In 1992, in the *Siderman* case, the U.S. Ninth Circuit ruled that "the right to be free from official torture is fundamental and universal, a right deserving of the highest status under international law, a norm of *jus cogens*." Judge Fletcher distinguished customary international law and *jus cogens*: "Whereas customary international law derives solely from the consent of states, the fundamental and universal norms constituting *jus cogens* transcend such consent, as exemplified by the theories underlying the judgments of the Nuremberg tribunals following World War II." Given an "extraordinary consensus" of state declarations and doctrinal expositions, the court held that the "crack of the whip, the clamp of the thumb screw, the crush of the iron maiden, and, in these more efficient modern times, the shock of the electric cattle prod are forms of torture that the international order will not tolerate."[101]

In 1987, the Inter-American Commission on Human Rights [see Chapter 8] found the United States in violation of *jus cogens* for permitting the execution of two persons convicted of crimes committed before their eighteenth birthdays.[102] In 2002, in Prosecutor v. Furundžija, the Appeals Chamber of the International Tribunal for the Former Yugoslavia held:

> Clearly, the *jus cogens* nature of the prohibition against torture articulates the notion that the prohibition has now become one of the most fundamental standards of the international community. Furthermore, this prohibition is designed to produce a deterrent effect, in that it signals to all members of the international community and the individuals over whom they wield authority that the prohibition of torture is an absolute value from which nobody must deviate.[103]

In 2019, the International Law Commission's Special Rapporteur for Preemptory Norms of General International Law, Dire Tladi of South

[100] 1934 P.C.I.J. Reports, ser. A/B, no. 63, at 148, 150.

[101] Siderman de Blake v. Republic of Argentina, 965 F.2d 699, 715-717 (9th Cir. 1992).

[102] Fox, Inter-American Commission on Human Rights Finds United States in Violation, 82 *American Journal of International Law* 601 (1988).

[103] Prosecutor v. Furundžija, Case IT-95-17/1 (Appeals Chamber, International Criminal Tribunal for the Former Yugoslavia, 2002), 121 *International Law Reports* 213 (2002).

Africa, released an Annex to a draft report featuring "a non-exhaustive list of norms" that might qualify for *jus cogens* status: prohibitions on aggression, genocide, crimes against humanity, racial discrimination and apartheid, slavery, and torture, as well as basic rules of international humanitarian law and the right of self-determination.[104]

Perhaps no rule better fits the definition of a norm of *jus cogens* than *pacta sunt servanda,* for it is essential to the theory of both conventional and customary international law that contracts between states be legally binding. It is difficult to understand how the obligatory force of agreements can be attributed to either treaty or custom without making a circular argument. If either a treaty or a customary rule is said to impose the rule *pacta sunt servanda,* why should that treaty or customary rule be valid unless it relied upon the very rule of legal obligation that is itself at issue?

It makes much better sense to conceive of *pacta sunt servanda* as a rule of neither conventional nor customary international law; rather, it is a norm fundamental to the legal system from which both treaty and customary rules derive. Indeed, it might do to view *pacta sunt servanda* as just the kind of non-derogable rule that is described as a peremptory norm in the Vienna Convention. In effect, this compelling law, *jus cogens,* is not a form of customary international law, but a form of international constitutional law, a norm that sets the very foundations of the international legal system.

In another sense, *pacta sunt servanda* may be seen to be a form of natural law if we take an organic view of the term *natural.* A rule such as *pacta sunt servanda* is natural to the international community of states because there would be no such community without it. The norm is intrinsic to the very existence of the given community. This does not mean that the rule is one prescribed by nature to every community or every legal system or to any given community's legal system at any given time. Rather, the word *natural* has to do with the organic

[104] Murphy, Peremptory Norms of General International Law (*Jus Cogens*) and Other Topics of the Seventy-First Session of the International Law Commission, 114 *American Journal of International Law* 68, 71 (2020). The ILC later concluded that *jus cogens* norms "are hierarchically superior to other rules of international law." *Report of the International Law Commission, Seventy-Third Session,* U.N. Doc. A/77/10, at 11 (2022).

or constitutional aspect of the rule: that it concerns the fundamental order of the community and its legal system.[105]

C. EQUITY AND INTERNATIONAL LAW

Equity, like a non-consensual source of international law, is sometimes employed to supplement or modify the rules of conventional and customary international law. How much one approves or disapproves of the use of equity in international practice may depend on how one feels generally about the creation of international law by any means other than the explicit or implicit consent of states, and, as might be expected, attitudes often vary between those holding positivist and naturalist positions. Best to say that equity in international law has no settled meaning.[106] It is convenient to divide theories of equity and international law and its practice into two general areas, one mostly procedural and the other substantive, that is, equity as a form of judicial discretion and equity as a form of distributive justice.

1. *Equity as a Form of Judicial Discretion*

Some form of equity has played a role in most every legal system.[107] Equity acting as a form of judicial discretion is an old and a generally accepted role for equity in international law. Grotius in his seminal treatise cited Aristotle for the proposition that all treaties should be interpreted upon the principle of equity: "For since all contingencies can neither be foreseen nor set forth, a degree of freedom is needed in order to make exceptions of cases which the person who has spoken

[105] A debate about the essential nature of *jus cogens* is to be found in the colloquy between the author and Turpel and Sands, 3 *Connecticut Journal of International Law* 359, 364, 370, 371 (1988).

[106] Janis, The Ambiguity of Equity in International Law, 9 *Brooklyn Journal of International Law* 7 (1983); C. Titi, *The Function of Equity in International Law* (2021).

[107] Perhaps the most comprehensive treatment of equity in general is *Equity in the World's Legal Systems* (R. Newman ed. 1973).

would make an exception of, if he were present."[108] This was a fair use of the philosopher. Aristotle indeed defined equity as the "corrective of what is legally just" and wrote that "in a situation in which the law speaks universally, but the case at issue happens to fall outside the universal formula, it is correct to rectify the shortcoming, in other words, the omission and mistake of the lawgiver due to the generality of his statement."[109]

Following the classical model and Grotius' injunction, numerous nineteenth- and twentieth-century arbitration treaties have provided for the application of the "principles of international law and equity." Such a provision has been interpreted as meaning "that something more than the strict law must be used in the grounds of decision of arbitral tribunals in certain cases."[110]

Between the two World Wars, equity was mooted as a possible means for moderating the impact of the Versailles Treaty, provisions of which were seen by some to impose onerous terms on Germany.[111] An international equity tribunal was even contemplated which would "adjust the rights of the parties—by reference not merely to the strict law, but to the rule which is fair in all the circumstances of the particular case."[112] Advocates of an international equity tribunal admitted that such an equity court would have "a quasi-legislative function," but feared that unless such an institution were created to "find an equitable and fair solution" to the problems facing Europe, "war will abolish us."[113]

Based in part on arbitral and judicial practice and in part on aspirations for a greater role for international judges and arbitrators, there is by now a considerable body of international law doctrine about when and in what manner an international judge or arbitrator should

[108] Grotius, supra, at 425 (bk. 2, ch. 16, §26).

[109] Aristotle, *Nicomachean Ethics* 141-142 (bk. 5, ch. 10) (Ostwald trans. 1962) [hereinafter cited as "Aristotle"].

[110] Cayuga Indians Case of January 22, 1926, American and British Claims Arbitration, *Nielsen Reports* 203, 314 (1926).

[111] Kraus, Revision of the Peace Treaties *Ex Aequo et Bono,* 1 *New Commonwealth Quarterly* 33 (1935-1936).

[112] Holdsworth, Preface to W. Friedmann, *The Contribution of English Equity to the Idea of an International Equity Tribunal* x (New Commonwealth Inst. Monograph, ser. B, no. 5, 1935).

[113] Davies, *A Substitute for War* 8-9 (New Commonwealth Soc. Pamph., ser. B, no. 8.B, May 1935).

apply equity instead of strict rules of international law.[114] Most important, the doctrine draws a distinction between "equitable principles" and decisions taken *ex aequo et bono,* that is, by what is fair and good. The distinction arises from the terms of Article 38(2) of the Statute of the International Court of Justice and that of the Permanent Court of International Justice before it: "This provision [Article 38] shall not prejudice the power of the Court to decide a case *ex aequo et bono,* if the parties agree thereto."[115] Parties have never conferred an *ex aequo et bono* power on the International Court.

In order to defeat any possible equivalence between a judge's inherent power to use equity in international law and the *ex aequo et bono* provision of Article 38(2), the application of equity has been seen as being authorized under the "general principles of law" provision of Article 38(1)(c), where no special party consent is required [see Chapter 3.B.1].[116] In his opinion in the 1937 *Meuse* case, Judge Hudson wrote:

> Article 38 of the Statute expressly directs the application of "general principles of law recognized by civilized nations," and in more than one nation principles of equity have an established place in the legal system. The Court's recognition of equity as a part of international law is in no way restricted by the special power conferred upon it "to decide a case *ex aequo et bono,* if the parties agree thereto."[117]

Interpreting Article 38(1)(c) as permitting the Court to look to municipal examples to establish equitable principles in international law, Hudson drew on the equitable traditions of common law and civil law countries to find the rule that "where two parties have assumed an identical or a reciprocal obligation, one party which is engaged in a continuing non-performance of that obligation should not be permitted to take advantage of a similar non-performance of that obligation

[114] See V. Degan, L'équité et le droit international (1970); Berlia, Essai sur la portée de la clause de jugement en équité en droit des gens (1937); Janis, Equity in International Law, 7 *Encyclopedia of Public International Law* 74 (1984); Cheng, Justice and Equity in International Law, 8 *Current Legal Problems* 185 (1955); Strupp, Le droit du juge international de statuer selon l'équité, 33 *Hague Recueil* 351 (1930).

[115] ICJ Statute, supra, art. 38(2).

[116] Id., art. 38(1)(c).

[117] 1937 P.C.I.J. Reports, ser. A/B, no. 70, at 73, 76.

by the other party."[118] Similarly, the international arbitral tribunal in the *Rann of Kutch* case between India and Pakistan decided that although it did not have authority to adjudicate *ex aequo et bono*, "equity forms part of International Law; therefore, the Parties are free to present and develop their cases with reliance on principles of equity."[119]

There are also helpful doctrinal distinctions between equity *intra legem, praeter legem,* and *contra legem.* A judge acts *intra legem,* that is, within the law, when equity is applied to specific cases in such a way as to achieve the law's intent, but without exceeding the law's formal language. Equity *praeter legem,* that is, beyond the law, is a bolder use of equity since the judge is then called on to fill in gaps and supplement the law with equitable rules necessary to decide the case at hand. Most debatable of all is a judge's use of equity *contra legem,* that is, against the law, where the rules of the law are disregarded and the equitable result achieved despite the law's explicit injunction.[120]

These doctrinal notions of equitable principles versus *ex aequo et bono* and of equity *intra, praeter,* and *contra legem* are often employed to justify or attack a judge's or an arbitrator's use of discretion. Characterizing a specific judicial decision as the employment of equitable principles is generally more favorable than characterizing it as an unauthorized use of judicial discretion *ex aequo et bono.* Correspondingly, it is less hostile to portray an application of equity as *intra legem* or *praeter legem* than to insist that an equitable decision was made *contra legem.* In an international system so much based on notions of sovereignty and state consent, it seems wrong to many, especially those of a positivist persuasion, to permit international judges or arbitrators to substitute their own discretion for rules made by the parties. Those more inclined to a naturalist philosophy will usually permit judges and arbitrators to go further in substituting equitable considerations and their own discretion for strict rules of international law.

The potential for and the problems of equity as a form of judicial discretion are well illustrated by the recent maritime delimitation cases,

[118] Id. at 77.

[119] The Indo-Pakistan Western Boundary Case Tribunal, Award of February 19, 1968, citing the decision of February 23, 1966, 17 *Reports of International Arbitral Awards* 1, 11.

[120] Sohn, Arbitration of International Disputes *Ex Aequo et Bono, International Arbitration Liber Amicorum for Martin Domke* 330, 332 (Sanders ed. 1967).

the leading example of which is the ruling of the International Court of Justice in 1969 in the *North Sea Continental Shelf* cases.[121] The disputes came to the Court by special agreements among Denmark, Germany, and the Netherlands asking, "What principles and rules of international law are applicable to the delimitation as between the Parties of the areas of the continental shelf in the North Sea,"[122] areas rich in oil and gas. The three states had been unable to negotiate a delimitation. Because Germany's North Sea coast is concave and the Netherlands' and Denmark's coasts are convex, application of the equidistance rule as sought by the Netherlands and Denmark (drawing a line each point of which is equally distant from each shore) would have folded in the German portion of the shelf. Germany argued that it should be awarded a larger slice of the continental shelf pie and suggested that the actual length of coastlines be used as the measuring factor.

Viewed in terms of the traditional doctrinal characterizations, the *North Sea Continental Shelf* cases can be seen as an example of equity *praeter legem.* The Court first examined and rejected the claims by the parties that any existing rules of conventional or customary international law, including the equidistance rule urged on the Court by the Netherlands and Denmark, were applicable to the delimitation of this continental shelf.[123] Strict positivist views of international law and of the role of international judges dictated that the Court simply declare a gap in the conventional and customary international legal rules binding the three states and, with no explicit *ex aequo et bono* discretion vested in the Court by the parties, pronounce itself unable to further assist in the delimitation of the shelf.[124] However, rather than find itself powerless to decide, the Court held as follows:

> [D]elimitation is to be effected by agreement in accordance with equitable principles, and taking account of all the relevant circumstances, in such a way as to leave as much as possible to each Party all those parts of the continental shelf that constitute a natural prolongation of its land

[121] 1969 I.C.J. Reports 3.

[122] Id. at 7.

[123] Id. at 19-32.

[124] Friedmann, The *North Sea Continental Shelf* Cases—A Critique, 64 *American Journal of International Law* 229 (1970).

territory into and under the sea, without encroachment on the natural prolongation of the land territory of the other.[125]

If the Court had only gone so far as to suggest that equitable principles should be applied by the parties, perhaps its decision would have been not much more than a somewhat obfuscated version of a decision *non liquet,* that is, finding no relevant international law and holding that the Court had no authority itself to make a rule. The International Court, however, was truly assertive in that it also chose to decide what the applicable equitable principles should be:

> Here indeed is a case where, in a theoretical situation of equality within the same order, an inequity is created. What is unacceptable in this instance is that a State should enjoy continental shelf rights considerably different from those of its neighbors merely because in the one case the coastline is roughly convex in form and in the other it is markedly concave, although those coastlines are comparable in length.[126]

Hence the Court urged the parties to "abat[e] the effects of an incidental special feature [Germany's concave coast] from which an unjustifiable difference of treatment could result."[127] Following the Court's decision, the states negotiated an international agreement awarding Germany much of the additional shelf it had sought.[128]

Since 1969, there have been more international adjudications involving the delimitation of maritime areas. These other cases have had the judges and arbitrators, at the parties' requests, actually drawing the lines delimiting maritime space and, in so doing, using considerable discretion. They have generally applied *North Sea Continental Shelf*'s notions of equitable principles.[129]

[125] 1969 I.C.J. Reports 4, 53.

[126] Id. at 50.

[127] Ibid.

[128] Von Schenck, Die verträgliche Abgrenzung des Festlandsockels unter der Nordsee zwischen der Bundesrepublik Deutschland, Dänemark und den Niederlanden nach dem Urteil des Internationalen Gerichtschofes vom 20. Februar 1969, 15 *Jahrbuch für internationales recht* 370 (1970). The trilateral agreement is reproduced in an English translation in 65 *American Journal of International Law* 901 (1971).

[129] Some of the many subsequent delimitation judgments include Maritime Delimitation in the Black Sea (Romania v. Ukraine), ICJ, Feb. 3 2009; Territorial and Maritime Dispute Between Nicaragua and Honduras in the Caribbean Sea, ICJ, Oct. 8,

C. Equity and International Law

The maritime delimitation cases are all excellent illustrations of the traditional doctrinal equity distinctions at work. Although the International Court in *North Sea Continental Shelf* declared that its application of equitable principles was the use of equity "within the rules" of international law,[130] the *intra legem* argument is really a justification that could be better relied upon by the subsequent judicial and arbitral panels. They, after all, had the *North Sea Continental Shelf* decision to guide them as a prior judicial decision and hence, per Article 38(1)(d) of the International Court's Statute, could use the *North Sea Continental Shelf* case as a subsidiary source of international law [see below]. The *North Sea Continental Shelf* case itself was, as mentioned above, really equity *praeter legem* since the Court found no existing rule of international law to decide the case and used equity to go beyond the law. The *North Sea Continental Shelf* Court did argue that past practice among states delimiting shelf called for the use of equitable principles.[131] However, that past practice had not established a rule permitting international judges to use their discretion to delimit shelf when no existing rule of international law did the job and when the states involved had been unable to agree.

The International Court in *North Sea Continental Shelf* characterized its use of equity as being pursuant to "principles" of law, rather than as an instance of its acting "*ex aequo et bono*, such as would only be possible under the conditions prescribed by Article 38, paragraph 2, of the Court's Statute."[132] Like Judge Hudson in *Meuse*, the *North Sea Continental Shelf* judges sought to rebut the presumption that they were constrained in using equity because there they had not been given an *ex aequo et bono* authorization. Unlike Judge Hudson in 1937,

2007; Maritime Delimitation and Territorial Questions Between Qatar and Bahrain, 2001 I.C.J. Reports 40; Maritime Delimitation in the Area Between Greenland and Jan Mayen (Denmark v. Norway), 1993 I.C.J. Reports 38; Continental Shelf case (Libyan Arab Jamahiriya/Malta), 1985 I.C.J. Reports 13; Delimitation of the Maritime Boundary in the Gulf of Maine Area case (Canada v. United States), 1984 I.C.J. Reports 246; Continental Shelf case (Tunisia/Libyan Arab Jamahiriya), 1982 I.C.J. Reports 18; Arbitration Between the United Kingdom of Great Britain and Northern Ireland and the French Republic on the Delimitation of the Continental Shelf, Decisions of the Court of Arbitration, June 30, 1977, March 14, 1978, 18 *International Legal Materials* 397 (1979).

[130] 1969 I.C.J. Reports 3, 48.

[131] Id. at 46-48.

[132] Id. at 48.

however, the judges in 1969 did not rely on municipal practice to demonstrate equitable principles in international law. They may well have chosen to employ the term *equitable principles* simply because the term had already been doctrinally differentiated from *ex aequo et bono* and therefore seemed a less questionable justification than merely referring to equity unadorned.

In any event, because it was first, the *North Sea Continental Shelf* case was a bolder use of judicial discretion than the subsequent maritime delimitation cases. There have been 15 maritime delimitation judgments between 1945 and 2009, decisions characterized as involving "a large element of subjective discretion."[133] Later judges were more ready to acknowledge their discretionary powers. The International Court in the *Tunisia/Libya* case noted that the term *equitable* can refer both to the means to be applied and to the result to be achieved; what was most important was that the result be equitable.[134] In his dissent in the *Gulf of Maine* case, Judge Gros lamented that the Court's equity had become "an equity beyond the law, detached from any established rules, based solely on whatever each group of judges seised of a case declares itself able and free to appreciate in accordance with its political or economic views of the moment."[135]

The judicial assertion of equitable powers has not passed unnoticed. The doctrinal debate about the power of judges or arbitrators to modify or supplement rules of international law with equity has raged in great heat.[136] Much of the controversy has had to do with the question of whether judges and arbitrators should make international law rules, the traditional form of the dispute concerning equity as a

[133] Tanaka, Reflections on Maritime Delimitation in the *Romania/Ukraine* Case before the International Court of Justice, 56 *Netherlands International Law Review* 397, 398, 427 (2009). Since 2009, there have been three more I.C.J. maritime delimitation judgments: Nicaragua v. Colombia, 2012 I.C.J. Reports 624; Peru v. Chile, 2014 I.C.J. Reports 3; and Costa Rica v. Nicaragua, 2018 I.C.J. Reports 15. See *Maritime Boundary Delimitation: The Case Law* (A.G. Oude Elferink, T. Henricksen & S.V. Busch eds. 2018).

[134] 1982 I.C.J. Reports 18, 59-61.

[135] 1984 I.C.J. Reports 246, 388.

[136] C.R. Rossi, *Equity and International Law: A Legal Realist Approach to International Decision Making* (1993); Lapidoth, Equity in International Law, *Proceedings of the 81st Annual Meeting of the American Society of International Law, April 8-11, 1987* 138 (1990); Lowe, The Role of Equity in International Law, 12 *Australian Yearbook of International Law* 54 (1988-89); Reuter, Quelques réflexions sur l'équité en droit international, 15 *Révue belge de droit international* 165 (1980).

form of judicial discretion. An assertion of the equitable powers of the international judge came in the *Al-Jedda* judgment of the European Court of Human Rights: "Our guiding principle is equity which above all involves flexibility and an objective consideration of what is fair and reasonable in all the circumstances of the case."[137]

A few general conclusions about this traditional equity and international law controversy are possible. First, there is no doubt that international judges and arbitrators can be given explicit equitable powers to supplement or modify international law rules in specific cases before them. The difficult issue is whether any equitable powers are to be presumed when there is no explicit authorization. In the maritime delimitation and other cases, judges and arbitrators have sometimes assumed implicit equitable authority and have thereby opened themselves to positivist critiques.

Second, given the absence of any general international legislature to make, modify, or repudiate rules of international law, there is a special temptation for judges and arbitrators to act *praeter legem* when new rules are needed to decide actual cases before them and when the consensual sources of international law yield no certain answers to specific questions. Once found and employed in a given case, any equitable decision then becomes available as a possible source of judge-made law in subsequent cases insofar as one recognizes judicial decisions as a source of international law. A comparable "hardening" of judge-made equity into rules of law, of course, happens in municipal practice as well—witness the course of equity in Anglo-American law.

Third, given the importance of state consent as a foundation of modern international law, it is less permissible, however, for an international judge or arbitrator to impose an equitable variation upon an explicitly dissenting state. In such an instance, it probably makes sense to return to Grotius and Aristotle and say that such equitable corrections are allowed only in those specific cases where the intent of the legislator would be frustrated by a strict application of the formal rule. Much the same conclusion was reached by Blackstone:

> And law, without equity, tho' hard and disagreeable is much more desirable for the public good, than equity without law; which would make every judge a legislator, and introduce most infinite confusion; as there

[137] Al-Jedda v. United Kingdom, European Court of Human Rights, Judgment of 7 July 2011, at para. 114.

> would then be almost as many different rules of action laid down in our courts as there are differences of capacity and sentiment in the human mind.[138]

2. *Equity as a Form of Distributive Justice*

One can think of equity in international law as having both a procedural and a substantive side. In terms of process, equity, as we have seen, is usually viewed as involving an explicit or implicit mandate to an international judge or arbitrator to modify or supplement the rules of international law. In terms of substance, the application of equity often results in some form of distributive justice. Again, Aristotle is helpful. He defined distributive justice by saying that it is "the just share [which] must be given on the basis of what one deserves, though not everyone would name the same criterion of deserving."[139]

If this is all too abstract, it may be easier to understand the procedural and substantive sides of equity in the light of the *North Sea Continental Shelf* cases. The procedural side of equity was the Court's decision that the delimitation of the continental shelf should be accomplished by the application of equitable principles and that the Court itself was competent in international law to decide what those principles were to be. The substantive side of equity was the Court's decision that equity required that the length of Germany's coastline, not the coastline's concavity, be given effect as the decisive measure.

Equity's procedural side gave the Court the power to apply a special rule to the case. Equity's substantive side turned to a specific measure of distributive justice, the length of the coastline, as the standard used to actually decide the case. While it was by no means certain that every international judge or arbitrator would have chosen the coastline as the crucial equitable measure for delimiting the shelf, the grant of equitable discretion to the Court meant in practice that the Court would take a more or less arbitrary step in deciding what equitable measure to use. To paraphrase in this context Aristotle's definition of distributive justice, we might say that though it might be generally agreed that Germany and the Netherlands and Denmark should have that portion of the shelf that they deserve, not everyone would name

[138] W. Blackstone, 1 *Commentaries on the Law of England* 62 (1st ed. 1765).
[139] Aristotle, supra, at 118-119 (bk. 5, ch. 3).

the length of the coastlines as the right equitable criterion for authoritatively delimiting the shelf.

Although the maritime delimitation cases have sometimes been attacked on the grounds that international judges and arbitrators should not be making such equitable determinations,[140] the maritime cases are a not unusual sort of equity in international practice; they are well in keeping both with traditional equity doctrine and with the usages of many courts and arbitral panels. Note, too, that the maritime delimitation decisions have been seemingly approved by those states that have not only abided by the judgments, but also continued to submit maritime delimitation cases to international adjudication and arbitration, knowing full well that judges and arbitrators are inclined to apply equitable principles to maritime delimitation cases even without explicit equitable authority.

Furthermore, equity as a feature of maritime delimitation has been enshrined in uncontroversial parts of the 1982 U.N. Convention on the Law of the Sea.[141] Article 74 concerning delimitation of exclusive economic zones and Article 83 dealing with delimitation of the continental shelf both require that delimitation "shall be effected by agreement on the basis of international law, as referred to in Article 38 of the Statute of the International Court of Justice, in order to achieve an equitable solution."[142]

Much more controversial are the many claims made for equity as part of a new international economic order. These claims have little or nothing to do with equity as a form of judicial discretion. They almost entirely concern equity as a form of distributive justice. The newer equity usages derive from the economics and politics of decolonization. When the newly freed countries of Asia and Africa discovered that the gaps in standard of living between themselves and the West had grown and not diminished in the 1950s and 1960s, they began to argue against the traditional international economic order of trade and development.[143] In 1973, the Organization of Petroleum Exporting Countries demonstrated that at least some developing countries had

[140] Blecher, Equitable Delimitation of Continental Shelf, 73 *American Journal of International Law* 60 (1979).

[141] U.N. Law of the Sea Convention, supra.

[142] Ibid.

[143] Bhagwati, Introduction, *The New International Economic Order: The North-South Debate* 5-6 (Bhagwati ed. 1977).

more bargaining power than had been previously thought.[144] This mix of economic frustration with perceptions of greater bargaining power led to assertions by developing countries that there should be established a new international economic order where global wealth would be spread more equitably among developed and developing countries.

The call for a new international economic order took explicit form in three well-known 1974 U.N. General Assembly resolutions: the Declaration on the Establishment of a New International Economic Order,[145] the Programme of Action on the Establishment of a New International Economic Order,[146] and the Charter of Economic Rights and Duties of States.[147] All three resolutions make numerous references to equity. The Charter of Economic Rights and Duties of States, for example, provides that "relations among States" should be governed, *inter alia*, by the principle of "[m]utual and equitable benefit" and urges states to "cooperate in facilitating more rational and equitable international economic relations."[148]

Some Western observers argued that the many claims for equity in the debate about the new international economic order are devoid of any legal content; that they simply denote the economic, political, and moral aspirations of the developing countries; and that equity in the new international economic order context has no meaning in international law except as a signal made by some countries that they intend to strive for the goal of achieving a better economic equilibrium between developing and developed countries.[149] While such arguments devaluing equity as a legal concept in international economic relations have force, they must be balanced against two countervailing phenomena: first, some international law doctrine does ascribe a legal quality to the role of equity in the new international economic order,

[144] J. Singh, *A New International Order: Toward a Fair Redistribution of the World's Resources* 6 (1977).

[145] U.N.G.A. Res. 3201 (S-VI), 6 (Special) U.N. GAOR Supp. (No. 1) 3, U.N. Doc. A/9556 (May 1, 1974).

[146] U.N.G.A. Res. 3202 (S-VI), 6 (Special) U.N. GAOR Supp. (No. 1) 5, U.N. Doc. A/9556 (May 1, 1974).

[147] U.N.G.A. Res. 3281 (XXIX), 29 U.N. GAOR Supp. (No. 31) 50, U.N. Doc. A/9631 (December 12, 1974).

[148] Id., ch. I(e), ch. II(8).

[149] Brownlie, Legal Status of Natural Resources in International Law (Some Aspects), 162 *Hague Recueil* 245 (1979).

and, second, this legal quality is, to a degree, supported by some of the actual references made to equity in recent international legal practice.

Aristotle's definition of distributive justice has already been noted, and we have seen how in the actual equitable determination of cases like *North Sea Continental Shelf* a form of distributive justice is sometimes used by international judges and arbitrators to settle disputes before them. International lawyers from the developing countries also insist that there are new equitable principles in international law that impose obligations on rich countries to redistribute wealth to poor countries.[150] One of the most prominent proponents of an equitable rule of distributive justice in international law is Mohammed Bedjaoui, an Algerian international lawyer elected in 1982 to the International Court of Justice, and between 1994 and 1997, President of the Court. Before joining the ICJ, Bedjaoui argued that a new international law ought to replace what he called the old "law of coexistence and indifference":

> The new law is gradually putting a certain "interventionism" in the place of the "laisser-faire and unconstraint" of traditional law. This international law of participation, genuinely all embracing and founded on solidarity and co-operation, must give great prominence to the principle of equity (which corrects inequalities) rather than to the principle of equality. In doing so, it must keep the objective in view, which consists of reducing and, if possible, even of eradicating the gap that exists between a minority of rich nations and a majority of poor nations. There is no doubt at all that it is a far-reaching legal revolution to have given international law this task of fostering a policy of development and to have made this "an international legal duty" for the rich States and a "subjective international right" for the developing countries.[151]

Doctrinal assertions such as those made by Bedjaoui are buttressed by the appearance in recent international practice of references to equity that seem to be explicable only as notions of distributive justice based on a measure of relative wealth. For example, The Set of Multilaterally Agreed Equitable Principles and Rules for the Control of Restrictive Business Practices explicitly treats equity as "preferential or

[150] Haq, From Charity to Obligation: A Third World Perspective on Concessional Resource Transfers, 14 *Texas International Law Journal* 389 (1979).

[151] M. Bedjaoui, *Towards a New International Economic Order* 127 (1979).

differential treatment for developing countries."[152] The U.N. Agreement Concerning the Activities of States on the Moon and Other Celestial Bodies provides for an "equitable sharing" in the benefits derived from outer space resources, giving "special consideration" to the "interests and needs of the developing countries."[153] The U.N. Convention on the Law of the Sea has several provisions employing equity as a form of distributive justice, including Article 155(2) requiring the "equitable exploitation" of the seabed "for the benefit of all countries, especially the developing States" and Article 69(1) giving landlocked states "the right to participate, on an equitable basis, in the exploitation of an appropriate part of the surplus of the living resources of the exclusive economic zones of coastal States of the same subregion or region, taking into account the relevant economic and geographical circumstances of all the States concerned."[154]

The debate about equity as a form of distributive justice raises anew many of the same issues about non-consensual rulemaking in international law that we have encountered above [see above]. Plainly, any doubt about the legal force of a non-consensual source or about equity dissipates when states are seen to explicitly or implicitly consent to the disputed rule in question. Insofar as equity as a form of distributive justice comes to be embodied in ratified international agreements, it takes on a hardened and less doubtful form. Otherwise, the assertion of equity as a form of distributive justice is bound to be controversial.

In these circumstances, policy may well be more important than philosophy. This may be true, too, respecting the debate about whether equity should guide the world community respecting international environmental law[155] or in the law of international trade.[156] Albeit the views

[152] U.N. Doc. TD/RBP/CONF.10 (May 2, 1980).

[153] U.N. Doc. A/34/664 (November 12, 1979).

[154] U.N. Law of the Sea Convention, supra.

[155] For policy arguments that equity should guide the world community as it faces environmental challenges, see Brown Weiss, Climate Change, Intergenerational Equity, and International Law, 9 *Vermont Journal of Environmental Law* 615 (2007); Morgera, The Need for an International Legal Concept of Fair and Equitable Benefit Sharing, 27 *European Journal of International Law* 353 (2016); Carlarne & Colavecchio, Balancing Equity and Effectiveness: The Paris Agreement and the Future of International Climate Change Law, 27 *New York University Environmental Law Journal* 107 (2019).

[156] See M. Paparinskis, *International Minimum Standard and Fair and Equitable Treatment* (2013); and A. Gourgouinis, *Equity and Equitable Principles in the World Trade Organization* (2017).

of some may vary depending on their positivist or naturalist persuasions, for most, policy positions will dictate opinions about any asserted equitable rules. The appeal to equity in these controversies[157] squarely raises the longstanding question of what, if any, non-consensual substantive norms or principles do or should regulate relations among states.

D. THE ROLE OF JUDGES AND PUBLICISTS

The decisions of judges (including arbitrators) and the doctrines of scholars have played a surprisingly important part in the development of international law. In what one author calls the "heroic period" of international law—the sixteenth, seventeenth, and eighteenth centuries—Vitoria, Grotius, Vattel, and their contemporaries provided not only the very structure of the discipline, but many of its fundamental principles as well.[158] Nowadays, Article 38(1)(d) of the Statute of the International Court of Justice lists "judicial decisions and the teachings [in French, *la doctrine*] of the most highly qualified publicists of the various nations, as subsidiary means for the determination of rules of law."[159]

Given their classification as "subsidiary means" and because Article 38 lists international conventions, international custom, and the general principles of law ahead of judicial decisions and the opinion of publicists, it is often suggested that the most important modern role for judges and scholars is collecting the data necessary to establish or explicate rules drawn from the other three (and implicitly higher) sources of international law. A classic statement of the cumulative role of judges and scholars is found in the U.S. Supreme Court's decision in *The Paquete Habana*:

> [We turn] to the customs and usages of civilized nations; and, as evidence of these, to the works of jurists and commentators, who by years of labor, research and experience, have made themselves peculiarly well acquainted with the subjects of which they treat. Such works are resorted to by judicial tribunals, not for the speculations of their authors

[157] 1984 I.C.J. Reports 128, 388.
[158] Sepulveda, supra, at 106.
[159] ICJ Statute, supra.

> concerning what the law ought to be, but for trustworthy evidence of what the law really is.[160]

Only somewhat less generally accepted than the judges' and scholars' role as accumulator is their role as evaluator. "The most delicate and elusive phase of the study of international law is that which exacts of the investigator a rigid examination of, and a judicial conclusion with respect to, the actual condition of the law at any given time."[161] There is, of course, an implicit evaluative role in the cumulative function, since one needs to evaluate the possible evidences of international law to decide what to include in and exclude from the collecting process. Beyond this, a judge or a jurist may also measure the practices and rules of international law against some sort of standard, one plain standard being simply that of consistency, that is, that a legitimate rule be regularly followed. More dramatically, some extrinsic standard, such as one drawn from religious or ethical principles, may be employed.

A third role for decisions and doctrine is what one might call aspirational. Here the judge or scholar frames a rule or some principle of international law in the belief that it ought to be adopted. Many of the efforts made to formulate rules to limit or even prohibit war may be understood in this way [see Chapter 6].

Probably the judge's and scholar's most controversial function in international law has to do with rule formation: the role that most impinges upon the power of sovereign states. For those positivists who believe that only states create international legal rules, the very idea that individuals may contribute to the making of an international law may be heresy. There is a fine, though necessary, line between the role of rule formation and the roles of accumulation, evaluation, and aspiration. In the latter cases, the individual may in fact sometimes be part of the rule development process. As accumulator, the individual may help mold rules through the collection of evidence of customary

[160] 175 U.S. 677, 700 (1900). Even this modest role may be suspect. It has been reported that between the years 1965 and 1979 "no scholarly writings on international law were published in the People's Republic of China." Chiu, Chinese Attitudes Toward International Law in the Post-Mao Era, 1978-1987, 21 *International Lawyer* 1127 (1987).

[161] C.C. Hyde, 1 *International Law, Chiefly as Interpreted and Applied by the United States* *viii* (1945).

international law or the general principles of law. As evaluator or idealist, the individual may set the development of international law off on an important new course. In some circumstances, it may be that a judge or scholar contributes to the process by which a norm becomes a definite rule of international law.[162]

The most usual argument about this sort of rulemaking involves judges. In the tradition of the common law, judicial decisions have long been treated as a source of law. The basis for such treatment rests historically on the medieval theory that the king's judges were speaking and acting for the sovereign. By the seventeenth century, Coke and others were advancing the proposition that even the king was subject to the law as interpreted and applied by the courts. Such ideas of judicial supremacy were sanctified in American legal practice where constitutional theory holds that the Constitution, as interpreted and applied by the Supreme Court, empowers and limits the U.S. government.

In the countries of the civil law, there has been much more suspicion of the powers of judges. Based, in part, on the role of judges in the *ancien regime* in France, civil lawyers assign formal rulemaking powers only to the legislature. They look askance at the notion that a judge can make rules of law. The French Civil Code reads: "It is forbidden for judges to decide on the basis of general and regulatory dispositions on the cases which are submitted to them."[163]

The division between common and civil lawyers regarding the authority of judges to make law is reflected in Article 38(1)(d). There, where both judicial decisions and doctrine are listed as "subsidiary" means of determining international law, the duality accommodates the two principal Western legal traditions. However, Article 59 of the Statute provides that "[t]he decision of the Court has no binding force except between the parties and in respect of that particular case,"[164] a clause similar to the prohibition of the French Civil Code. Such a

[162] Sivakumaran, The Influence of Publicists on the Development of International Law, 66 *International & Comparative Law Quarterly* 1 (2017); Roberts, Comparative International Law? The Role of National Courts in Creating and Enforcing International Law, 60 *International and Comparative Law Quarterly* 57 (2011).

[163] "Il est défendu aux juges de prononcer par voie de disposition générale et réglémentaire sur les causes qui leur sont soumises." Art. 5, Code Civil. See M.W.Janis, J.E. Noyes & L.N. Sadat, *International Law Cases and Commentary (Seventh Edition)* 347-352 (2025).

[164] ICJ Statute, supra.

prohibition may not diminish the power of judges to cumulate or even evaluate the law, but it does mean to restrict their power to authoritatively formulate legal rules.

Although it would be too much to claim that judges have a generally acknowledged rulemaking function in international law, there are at least two interstices in which some judicial power lies. First, domestic judges, especially in common law jurisdictions, do sometimes make pronouncements about international law that have a legally binding effect within a municipal legal system. One thinks, for example, of the judicially created rules pertaining to the act of state doctrine in the United States [see Chapter 10]. Of course, it may well be objected that in such circumstances judges act not as individuals, but as functionaries. At least, however, the judges are not usually acting as representatives of the state, and they do not have to adopt the government's position on a matter.

Second, despite Article 59, the International Court of Justice, as well as other international tribunals and municipal courts, does rely heavily on judicial precedent. Although in theory the International Court cannot base its decision on its earlier decisions as might a common law court, in practice the International Court makes constant reference to its own holdings. In this respect, like many civil law courts, the International Court follows a doctrine known in France as a *jurisprudence constante*, rendering decisions that are sequentially consistent. Furthermore, the decisions of courts, especially those of the International Court, are often employed in other forums as evidence of customary international law or of general principles of law [see Chapter 5].

CHAPTER 4

International Law and Municipal Law

International law often plays a role on the national stage. When international legal rules are interpreted and applied by a judge, the setting is usually a case before a domestic, not an international, court or tribunal. So, when lawyers deal with international legal problems, they usually find themselves engaged in a municipal legal proceeding or negotiation. In this chapter, as our attention turns from international legal rules to international legal process, it is fitting to begin with the ways in which international law are employed in national legal systems.

A. DUALISM AND MONISM

The prevalent U.S. doctrinal approach to the relationship between international and municipal law is called "dualist." Dualism views every national and international legal system as a separate and discrete entity, each with its own power to settle the effect any outside rule of law might have within it. Thus, international law is generally thought to make itself effective in a domestic legal order dependent upon the constitutional rules of the municipal system itself, a process called "incorporation."

Conversely, municipal law is thought to be incapable of imposing itself on the international legal system. A state ordinarily may not rely on its own domestic law as a ground for repudiating an international legal obligation. As the Permanent Court of International Justice explained in the *Greco-Bulgarian Communities* case: "It is a generally accepted principle of international law that in the relations between Powers who are contracting Parties to a treaty, the provisions of municipal law cannot prevail over those of the treaty."[1] As we have seen in Chapter 2, a similar rule is found in the Vienna Convention.[2] Thus, it is entirely possible for an obligation to be legally binding in international law and be effective in the international legal system, for example, before an international court or in international relations generally, but have no legal force in one or another municipal legal system, for example, before a domestic court, because of some obstacle posed by municipal law.

Another theoretical approach to the relationship between international and national law is called "monist." Monism views the international legal order and national legal systems as component parts of a single "universal legal order" in which international law may have a certain supremacy.[3] Whatever the logical attractions of monism, it is not usually as reliable a guide to practice as dualism. Most states and most courts, especially those in the United States, usually view national and international legal systems as discrete entities and routinely discuss in a dualist fashion the incorporation of rules from one legal system to the other.[4]

B. TREATIES IN MUNICIPAL LAW

We first turn to the relationship between treaties and national law. Treaties are, by far, the sort of international law most often seen in domestic practice. What is dealt with below is largely constitutional law about the incorporation of international law. Pertinent U.S. rules are introduced, along with a few from other countries.

[1] 1930 P.C.I.J. Reports, ser. B, no. 17, at 32.

[2] Art. 27, U.N. Doc. A/CONF.39/27 (1969), reprinted in 63 *American Journal of International Law* 875 (1969) (signed at Vienna May 23, 1969; entered into force January 27, 1980; not in force for the United States).

[3] See H. Kelsen, *Principles of International Law* 553-588 (2d ed. Tucker 1966).

[4] For a study exploring dualism and monism in practice, see Verdier & Versteeg, International Law in National Legal Systems: An Empirical Investigation, 109 *American Journal of International Law* 514 (2015).

B. Treaties in Municipal Law

1. *Treaties in U.S. Law*

The U.S. Constitution mentions treaties several times and in somewhat different ways. In Article II (2), the President of the United States is granted the "Power, by and with the Advice and Consent of the Senate, to make Treaties, provided two thirds of the Senators present concur." Article III (2) extends the judicial power of the United States "to all Cases, in Law and Equity, arising under this Constitution, the Law of the United States, and Treaties made, or which shall be made, under their Authority." Article VI (2) instructs that the "Constitution, and the Laws of the United States which shall be made in pursuance thereof; and all Treaties made, or which shall be made, under the Authority of the United States, shall be the supreme Law of the Land; and the Judges in every State shall be bound thereby, any Thing in the Constitution or Laws of any State to the Contrary notwithstanding." Finally, the Constitution explicitly restricts the states of the Union in Article I (10): "No State shall enter into any Treaty, Alliance, or Confederation," though U.S. states may make some international compacts. The Constitution's delicate balances between the treaty powers of the legislature and those of the President and between the states and the federal government vis-à-vis treaty implementation were the result of hard-fought compromises at the Constitutional Convention of 1787.[5]

Amplifying these explicit constitutional provisions are more than two centuries of judicial practice. As early as the time of the first President, George Washington, in Ware v. Hylton in 1796, the Supreme Court enforced a treaty, the 1783 Peace Treaty with Great Britain, against a recalcitrant state, Virginia.[6] If the Peace Treaty had not been enforced, war with Britain might have ensued.[7] The Supreme Court "would perhaps never perceive itself to be on firmer ground in enforcing treaties than when enforcing the very treaty whose violation had led to the Constitutional Convention."[8]

[5] See Janis & Wiener, Treaties in U.S. Law from the Founding to the Restatement (Third), in *Supreme Law of the Land?: Debating the Contemporary Effects of Treaties Within the United States Legal System* 15, 15-19 (G.H. Fox, P.R. Dubinsky & B.R. Roth eds. 2017) [hereinafter cited as "*Supreme Law of the Land?*"].

[6] Ware v. Hylton, 3 U.S. (3 Dall.) 199 (1796).

[7] Ramsey, The Power of the States in Foreign Affairs: The Original Understanding of Foreign Policy Federalism, 75 *Notre Dame Law Review* 341, 422 (1999).

[8] Wu, Treaties' Domain, 93 *Virginia Law Review* 571, 606 (2007).

Case law by now provides many more constitutional rules about treaties than does the Constitution itself.[9] Chief among them is the judge-made doctrine of self-executing treaties, itself a significant contribution made by the United States to international law. The doctrine, though not the term itself, emerged in 1829, in the judgment of Chief Justice John Marshall in Foster & Elam v. Neilson. *Foster & Elam* sought to determine the rightful owner of land in territory that had been known as West Florida and then became part of the state of Louisiana east of New Orleans. Between 1800 and 1821, the territory was transferred back and forth between Spain and France and eventually to the United States, but the relevant treaties among the three countries were ambiguous, and there was some doubt as to which sovereign state possessed West Florida at any given moment in that period. What was indisputable was that after the ratification in 1821 of an 1819 treaty of amity between Spain and the United States, West Florida belonged to the latter. The 1819 Spanish-American treaty provided, *inter alia*, that "all the grants of land made before the 24th of January 1818 by [the King of Spain] in the said territories ceded by his majesty to the United States, shall be ratified and confirmed to the persons in possession of the lands, to the same extent that the same grants would be valid if the territories had remained under the dominion of his catholic majesty."[10] Foster and Elam claimed land under a grant made by the Spanish King in 1804. Neilson alleged that the plaintiffs' grant was void because by 1804, the land had already been ceded by Spain to France.[11] Rather than determine who rightfully possessed the territory in 1804, the Supreme Court asked this question: Could plaintiffs in any circumstances rely on the 1819 Spanish-American treaty's confirmation of Spanish grants?

Chief Justice Marshall wrote:

> A treaty is in its nature a contract between two nations, not a legislative act. It does not generally effect, of itself, the object to be accomplished,

[9] See Damrosch, *Medellín* and *Sanchez-Llamos*: Treaties from John Jay to John Roberts, in *International Law in the U.S. Supreme Court: Continuity and Change* 451 (D.C. Sloss, M.D. Ramsey & W.S. Dodge eds. 2011).

[10] Foster & Elam v. Neilson, 27 U.S. (2 Pet.) 253, 310 (1829).

[11] For more on the background of the case, see Vázquez, *Foster v. Neilson* and *United States v. Percheman*: Judicial Enforcement of Treaties, *International Law Stories* 259 (J.E. Noyes, L.A. Dickinson, M.W. Janis & C.M. Vázquez eds.,2d ed. 2025) [hereinafter cited as "Noyes, Dickinson, Janis & Vázquez"]; Mirow, The Supreme Court, Florida Land Claims, and Spanish Colonial Law, 31/32 *Tulane European & Civil Law Forum* 181 (2017).

> especially so far as its operation is infra-territorial; but is carried into execution by the sovereign power of the respective parties to the instrument.
>
> In the United States a different principle is established. Our constitution declares a treaty to be the law of the land [by the supremacy clause of Article VI]. It is, consequently, to be regarded in courts of justice as equivalent to an act of the legislature, whenever it operates of itself without the aid of any legislative provision. But when the terms of the stipulation import a contract, when either of the parties engages to perform a particular act, the treaty addresses itself to the political, not the judicial department; and the legislature must execute the contract before it can become a rule for the Court.[12]

Thus, *Foster & Elam* held that a legal rule drawn from a treaty may be applied in a case by the U.S. courts without any legislative act so long as its provisions are interpreted as being aimed directly at the courts and not at the Congress requiring legislative action. However, in *Foster & Elam* itself, the Supreme Court read the specific provision of the 1819 treaty as aimed at the lawmakers:

> The article under consideration does not declare that all the grants made by his catholic majesty before the 24th of January 1818, shall be valid to the same extent as if the ceded territories had remained under his dominion. It does not say that those grants are hereby confirmed. Had such been its language, it would have acted directly on the subject, and would have repealed those acts of congress which were repugnant to it; but its language is that those grants shall be ratified and confirmed to the persons in possession, etc. By whom shall they be ratified and confirmed? This seems to be the language of contract; and if it is, the ratification and confirmation which are promised must be the act of the legislature.[13]

Interestingly, in *Percheman* a few years later, Marshall, seeing the Spanish-language version of the treaty, held that the self-same article *was* self-executing,[14] as good an example as any of the interpretative discretion of the courts. Since Marshall's decisions in *Foster & Elam* and *Percheman*, U.S. judges have generally recognized the distinction

[12] 27 U.S. (2 Pet.) 253, 314 (1829).

[13] Id. at 314-315.

[14] United States v. Percheman, 32 U.S. (7 Pet.) 51 (1833).

between self-executing and non-self-executing treaties.[15] The actual term "self-executing" itself does not seem to have been employed by the Supreme Court until 1887, in an opinion of Mr. Justice Field in Bartram v. Robertson.[16] The term received rather more publicity the next year in Whitney v. Robertson, another Field holding.[17] A rendering of the distinction between self-executing and non-self-executing treaty provisions in U.S. law is that of Section 310 of the American Law Institute's 2018 *Restatement (Fourth) of the Foreign Relations Law of the United States*: "Courts will evaluate whether the text and context of the provision, along with other treaty materials, are consistent with an understanding of the States."[18] Professor Wuerth underlines that the Restatement (Fourth) puts particular emphasis on the intent of U.S. treaty-makers.[19]

Self-executing treaty provisions are, because of the supremacy clause of Article VI, also binding upon each of the several states of the United States. Whether any part of a treaty is self-executing and thus, in a case of conflict, invalidates state law, must be determined on a case-by-case basis. In Asakura v. Seattle, on the one hand, the U.S. Supreme Court had before it a complaint by a Japanese national residing in the United States that a Seattle city ordinance prohibiting the issuance of pawnbroker licenses to aliens violated a 1911 friendship, commerce, and navigation treaty between the United States and Japan. The relevant treaty language read: "The citizens or subjects of each of the High Contracting Parties shall have liberty to enter, travel and reside in the territories of the other to carry on trade . . . upon the same terms as native citizens or subjects." The Court decided that the 1911 treaty operated "of itself without the aid of any legislation, state or national; and it will be applied and given authoritative effect by the courts." Finding that the business of a pawnbroker was "trade" within

[15] Paust, Self-Executing Treaties, 82 *American Journal of International Law* 760, 771-775 (1988) [hereinafter cited as "Paust"]. For an appraisal of different approaches to the distinction between self-executing and non-self-executing treaties in U.S. law, see Vazquez, The Four Doctrines of Self-Executing Treaties, 89 *American Journal of International Law* 695 (1995).

[16] 122 U.S. 116, 120 (1887).

[17] 124 U.S. 190, 194 (1888). See Paust, supra, at 766.

[18] American Law Institute, *Restatement of the Law Fourth: The Foreign Relations Law of the United States: Selected Topics in Treaties, Jurisdiction, and Sovereign Immunity* 87 (2018) [hereinafter cited as "Restatement (Fourth)"].

[19] Wuerth, Self-Execution, in *Supreme Law of the Land?*, supra, at 148, 176.

the definition of the treaty, the Court ruled that the city ordinance violated the treaty.[20]

On the other hand, in Sei Fujii v. State of California, where plaintiff argued that the U.N. Charter invalidated a state law barring certain aliens from owning land, the California Supreme Court held, first, that the Charter's Preamble and Article 1 were not self-executing: "They state general purposes and objectives of the United Nations Organization and do not purport to impose legal obligations on the individual member nations or to create rights in private persons." The court then held:

> It is equally clear that none of the other provisions relied on by plaintiff is self-executing. Article 55 declares that the United Nations "shall promote . . . universal respect for, and observance of, human rights and fundamental freedoms for all without distinction as to race, sex, language, or religion," and in Article 56, the member nations "pledge themselves to take joint and separate action in cooperation with the Organization for the achievement of the purposes set forth in Article 55." Although the member nations have obligated themselves to cooperate with the international organization in promoting respect for, and observance of, human rights, it is plain that it was contemplated that future legislative action by the several nations would be required to accomplish the declared objectives, and there is nothing to indicate that these provisions were intended to become rules of law for the courts of this country upon the ratification of the charter.[21]

Though not self-executed into U.S. law in *Sei Fujii*,[22] it has been argued that the human rights provisions of the U.N. Charter indirectly contributed to the progressive development of U.S. civil rights law.[23]

[20] 265 U.S. 332, 340-344 (1924). Relations between the United States and Japan worsened in the 1930s when Japan invaded China. In response, the United States terminated the treaty in *Asakura*. On December 7, 1941, Japan launched a surprise attack on Pearl Harbor in Hawaii and the United States was precipitated into World War II. See M.W. Janis, J.E. Noyes & L.N. Sadat, *International Law: Cases and Commentary* 237-238 (2d ed. 2025) [hereinafter cited as "Janis, Noyes & Sadat"].

[21] 242 P.2d 617, 620-622 (1952). For a more recent judgment holding that the Treaty of Non-Proliferation of Nuclear Weapons was not self-executing, see Republic of Marshall Islands v. United States, 865 F.3d 1187 (3d Cir. 2017).

[22] At the time, Professor Wright thought the provisions were indeed self-executing. See Wright, National Courts and Human Rights—The Fujii Case, 45 *American Journal of International Law* 62 (1951).

[23] Lockwood, The United Nations Charter and United States Civil Rights Litigation: 1946-1955, 69 *Iowa Law Review* 901 (1984).

In 1954, the Supreme Court appears to have incorporated the Charter's norm against racial discrimination into the Fourteenth Amendment in Brown v. Board of Education.[24]

The supremacy of legislatively executed or self-executed treaty provisions as against state law has long been upheld by the U.S. courts.[25] In Missouri v. Holland, the Court hinted that it sometimes might even be constitutionally possible for Congress to enact laws pursuant to international agreements which would otherwise infringe upon the residual sovereign power of the states. In the *Missouri* case, federal district courts had struck down earlier federal laws regulating migratory birds because these U.S. statutes were held to be unconstitutional infringements upon the residual rights left to the states by the Tenth Amendment. The President then negotiated a treaty with Canada providing for similar migratory bird regulation. The Canadian-American treaty went to the Senate, which gave its advice and consent, the President ratified the international agreement, and Congress enacted implementing legislation. The Supreme Court upheld the constitutionality of the new federal law. In the words of Justice Holmes:

> We do not mean to imply that there are no qualifications to the treaty-making power; but they must be ascertained in a different way. It is obvious that there may be matters of the sharpest exigency for the national well being that an act of Congress could not deal with but that a treaty followed by such an act could. . . .[26]

Here the treaty and the implementing legislation concerned "a national interest of very nearly the first magnitude," which could "be protected only by national action in concert with that of another power."[27]

[24] 347 U.S. 483 (1954). See Sloss, How International Human Rights Transformed the U.S. Constitution, 38 *Human Rights Quarterly* 426 (2016).

[25] Concluding his review of judicial precedent before and after *Foster*, Professor Van Alstine comments that the Supreme Court has "consistently affirmed that courts have not only the ability, but the 'obligation' to give direct effect to individual rights that a self-executing treaty establishes." Van Alstine, Federal Common Law in an Age of Treaties, 89 *Cornell Law Review* 892, 916 (2004).

[26] 252 U.S. 416, 433 (1920).

[27] Id. at 433. Justice Holmes was three times wounded fighting to preserve the Union in the Civil War. He wrote that though it "was enough for [the founders of the

B. Treaties in Municipal Law

In 2014, in Bond v. United States, the Supreme Court resisted calls that it limit or overturn *Missouri*,[28] holding instead that the Chemical Weapons Convention did not apply to a minor domestic dispute.[29] Even so, some lamented that the *Bond* Court did not go further in affirming to the world community that the United States would remain true to its international commitments.[30]

The Supreme Court has limited state assertions of authority in international law and relations in some cases. In 1968, in *Zschernig*, an Oregon judgment testing the "'democratic quotient' of a foreign regime" was held to be an unconstitutional infringement upon the federal government's authority to regulate the international relations of the United States.[31] Similarly, a Massachusetts statute punishing Burma for violating human rights was found unconstitutional in 2000 in *Crosby*.[32] Reaffirming that "valid executive agreements are fit to preempt state law, just as treaties are," the Supreme Court in 2002, in *Garamendi*, struck down a California Holocaust statute, finding a state/federal conflict: "The basic fact is that California seeks to use an iron fist where the President has consistently chosen kid gloves."[33]

Other times, states have been permitted to be more assertive in foreign affairs. The Supreme Court's judgment in 2008, in Medellín v. Texas, denied the power of the President to order state compliance with a judgment of the International Court of Justice, a questionable

Constitution] to realize or to hope that they had created an organism; it has taken a century and cost their successors much sweat and blood to prove that they had created a nation." Id. at 434. See Janis, *Missouri v. Holland*: Birds, Wars, and Rights, in Noyes, Dickinson, Janis & Vázquez, supra, at 317.

[28] See Rosenkranz, Bond v. United States: Concurring in the Judgment, *2014 Cato Supreme Court Review* 285 (2014).

[29] 564 U.S. 844 (2014). See Liptak, Chemical Weapons Treaty Does Not Apply to Petty Crime, Justices Rule, *N.Y. Times*, June 3, 2014, at A13.

[30] See Glennon & Sloane, The Sad Quiet Death of Missouri v. Holland: How Bond Hobbled the Treaty Power, 41 *Yale Journal of International Law* 51 (2016).

[31] Zschernig v. Miller, 389 U.S. 429, 435 (1988).

[32] Crosby v. National Trade Council, 530 U.S. 363 (2000). For comparable state and local laws attempting to punish Sudan for the repression in Darfur, see Bechky, Darfur, Divestment, and Dialogue, 30 *University of Pennsylvania Journal of International Law* 823 (2009).

[33] American Insurance Ass'n v. Garamendi, 539 U.S. 396, 416, 427 (2003). See Denning, Foreign Affairs Powers of the United States, 97 *American Journal of International Law* 950 (2003).

holding.[34] In Gingery v. City of Glendale in 2016, the Ninth Circuit permitted a municipality to erect a peace memorial remembering the "comfort women" abducted by the Japanese in World War II, even though the U.S. federal government was reluctant to pressure Japan to accept the account of the atrocities. The court held that states and cities may make statements conflicting with U.S. foreign policy so long as they do not enact interfering laws or regulations.[35]

An assertion of state foreign affairs authority recently in dispute is a prohibition of the use of Sharia law or international law in state courts.[36] An Oklahoma provision was passed by a popular referendum amending the state constitution in November 2010.[37] It was struck down by a U.S. district court, largely on the grounds that the Oklahoma amendment was an establishment of religion in violation of the First Amendment of the U.S. Constitution.[38]

Of course, no treaty provision will be applied by a U.S. court if found to be in direct contravention of the U.S. Constitution.[39] As the Supreme Court held in Reid v. Covert, "no agreement with a foreign nation can confer power on the Congress, or on any other branch of Government, which is free from the restraints of the Constitution."[40] Moreover, treaties have no absolute supremacy vis-à-vis federal statutes. Rather, between treaty law and federal statutory law there is thought to be a virtual equivalence. In the *Head Money* cases, the Supreme Court held that "so far as a treaty made by the United States with any foreign nation can become the subject of judicial cognizance in the courts

[34] Medellín v. Texas, 552 U.S. 491 (2008). See Vazquez, Treaties as the Law of the Land: The Supremacy Clause and the Judicial Enforcement of Treaties, 122 *Harvard Law Review* 599 (2008).

[35] 831 F.2d 1222 (9th Cir. 2016).

[36] As of November 2018, there were, according to the National Conference of State Legislatures, some 11 states with anti-Sharia laws, www.ncsl.org/research (Nov. 20, 2018). See The Law of the Land, *ABA Journal* (April 2011), at 14.

[37] Oklahoma Constitutional Amendment Barring Consideration of Sharia and International Law, 105 *American Journal of International Law* 123 (2011).

[38] McKinley, U.S. Judge Blocks a Ban on Islamic Law, *N.Y. Times*, Nov. 30, 2010, at A21.

[39] The Cherokee Tobacco, 78 U.S. (11 Wall.) 616, 620-621 (1870); Geofroy v. Riggs, 133 U.S. 258, 267 (1890). See Section 307 of the Restatement (Fourth), supra, at 70-75.

[40] 354 U.S. 1, 16 (1957).

of this country, it is subject to such acts as Congress may pass for its enforcement, modification, or repeal."[41]

Faced in practice with apparently conflicting treaties and statutes, U.S. courts first attempt to reconcile their clashing provisions. If no such reconciliation is possible, then the rule is that the treaty or federal statutory law later in time controls. Section 309 of the Restatement (Fourth) explains: "When there is a conflict between a self-executing treaty provision and a federal statute, courts in the United States will apply whichever reflects the latest expression of the will of the U.S. political branches."[42] An often-cited statement of this principle was given in the *Whitney* case:

> By the Constitution a treaty is placed on the same footing, and made of like obligation, with an act of legislation. Both are declared by that instrument to be the supreme law of the land, and no superior efficacy is given to either over the other. When the two relate to the same subject, the courts will always endeavor to construe them so as to give effect to both, if that can be done without violating the language of either; but if the two are inconsistent, the one last in date will control the other, provided always the stipulation of the treaty on the subject is self-executing.[43]

As noted above, in international law a nation may not usually interpose its own law as a justification for failing to comply with an otherwise legally binding treaty obligation. Accordingly, in the case of a subsequent and conflicting act of Congress, though a treaty provision might no longer have force in the U.S. courts, it may still be legally binding in the international legal system, a difficulty in the opinion of the *Whitney* court best left to the concern of the executive and legislative branches of government.[44] In any case, there is "a firm and obviously sound canon of construction against finding implicit repeal of a treaty in ambiguous congressional action. . . . Legislative silence is not sufficient to abrogate a treaty."[45] Similarly, where both Congress and the President agree that a treaty is still in force, the courts, "because of the deference [they]

[41] 112 U.S. 580, 599 (1884).
[42] Restatement (Fourth), supra, at 80.
[43] Whitney v. Robertson, 124 U.S. 190, 194 (1888).
[44] Id. at 194-195.
[45] Trans World Airlines v. Franklin Mint Corp., 466 U.S. 243, 252 (1984).

owe to the political branches of the government in treaty matters," will ordinarily not challenge a treaty's validity or enforceability.[46]

The *Head Money* and *Whitney* cases involved treaties modified by later acts of Congress, but, as the statement of principle in *Whitney* makes clear, treaties may also supersede earlier federal laws. In the *Cook* case, for example, the Treaty of May 22, 1924, with Great Britain was held to supersede, "so far as inconsistent with the terms of the Act [of 1922], the authority which had been conferred by section 581 upon officers of the Coast Guard to board, search and seize beyond our territorial waters." Thus, the Court held that the United States could not lawfully seize a ship of British registry beyond the limits set forth in an agreement concluded with the United Kingdom.[47]

Faced with a decision of whether to reconcile conflicting treaty rules and statutes or to accord one or another precedence, courts sometimes opt for reconciliation, but perhaps beyond plausible grounds. In the *Palestine Liberation Organization* (PLO) case, a federal district court heard a suit brought by the U.S. Justice Department, seeking to close the PLO's U.N. observer mission in New York.[48] This seemed to be the intent of the Anti-Terrorism Act of 1987, albeit the closure would probably violate the international obligations of the United States under its treaty as a host country for the United Nations. The federal court, noting that "statutes and treaties are both the supreme law of the land" and that "the Constitution sets forth no order of precedence to differentiate between them," concluded that the text and legislative history of the Anti-Terrorism Act failed "to disclose any clear legislative intent that Congress was directing the Attorney General, the State Department or this Court to act in contravention of the Headquarters Agreement."[49] There seemed to be "unanimous belief" in the Justice Department that the *PLO* decision should have been appealed, but the State Department felt that it would have been "a grave mistake" to close the PLO office.[50]

[46] New York Chinese TV Programs v. U.E. Enterprises, 954 F.2d 847, 852-854 (2d Cir. 1992).

[47] Cook v. United States, 288 U.S. 102, 118-122 (1933).

[48] United States v. Palestine Liberation Organization, 695 F. Supp. 1456 (S.D.N.Y. 1988).

[49] Id. at 1464, 1465.

[50] Pear, U.S. Officials Split on Whether to Appeal Ruling for P.L.O., *N.Y. Times*, Aug. 28, 1988, at A5.

The interagency dispute was settled by President Reagan who, citing "foreign policy considerations," chose not to appeal the district court's judgment.[51] England's Professor Rosalyn Higgins, now a judge on the ICJ, has termed the *PLO* judgment "admirably purpose-oriented but unpersuasive."[52]

Even more doubtful was the opinion of Chief Justice Rehnquist, writing for a 6-3 majority of the Supreme Court, in *Alvarez-Machain,* where reversing the Ninth Circuit, the Court ruled that the kidnapping of a Mexican citizen in Mexico by agents of the U.S. government was not to be construed as an act covered by the terms of the 1978 U.S.-Mexico Extradition Treaty: "The language of the Treaty, in the context of its history, does not support the proposition that the Treaty prohibits abductions outside of its terms."[53] This interpretation was resisted by Justice Stevens, writing for the minority, who cited the language of the Ninth Circuit approvingly: The provisions of the Extradition Treaty "only make sense if they are understood as *requiring* each treaty signatory to comply with those procedures whenever it wishes to obtain jurisdiction over an individual who is located in another treaty nation."[54] Justice Stevens predicted that "most courts throughout the civilized world—will be deeply disturbed by the 'monstrous' decision the Court announces today."[55] Indeed, the Mexican government, among others, expressed its outrage with the judgment and demanded the renegotiation of the Extradition Treaty.[56] Professor Henkin, then President of the American Society of International Law, lamented that the majority of the Supreme Court had failed to take "international law

[51] Pear, U.S. Will Allow P.L.O. to Maintain Its Office at U.N., *N.Y. Times,* Aug. 30, 1988, at A1.

[52] R. Higgins, *Problems and Process: International Law and How We Use It* 215 (1994).

[53] United States v. Alvarez-Machain, 504 U.S. 655, 666 (1992).

[54] Id. at 673-674 (Stevens, J., dissenting).

[55] Id. at 687 (Stevens, J., dissenting).

[56] Golden, After Court Ruling, Mexico Tells U.S. Drug Agents to Stop Activity, *N.Y. Times,* June 16, 1992, at A19. Mexico was disappointed again by U.S. actions vis-à-vis a treaty when in 2002, despite a personal appeal by Mexican President Fox to U.S. President Bush, the United States refused to intervene to discourage Texas from executing a Mexican national who had been convicted despite not being informed of his rights under the International Consular Convention. President Fox then called off meeting with President Bush on other topics. *The Times* (London), Aug. 17, 2002, at 17.

seriously."[57] The lamentation continues; in 2007 legal counsel representing the United States in a British court was mocked when citing *Alvarez-Machain* asserting the U.S. government's right to kidnap foreign citizens abroad.[58]

Treaties that have the benefit of Article VI and the supremacy clause need not necessarily be "treaties" made pursuant to the Constitution's Article II, that is, agreements that have received the two-thirds advice and consent of the Senate. Indeed, most treaties binding the United States are not Article II–type treaties. A study of all the international agreements made by the United States between 1946 and 1972 found that only 6 percent were treaties sent to the Senate for its formal advice and consent; 86.7 percent were so-called statutory agreements or "congressional-executive" agreements where the President acted pursuant to ordinary legislation, that is, statutes passed by a majority of both the House of Representatives and the Senate; and 7.4 percent were "executive agreements," that is, compacts concluded by the President alone without any congressional participation.[59] Another study of the period 1990 to 2012 found that only 6.2 percent of U.S. international agreements were Article II–type treaties.[60] Nowadays, very few treaties are submitted to or consented to by the Senate.[61]

[57] Henkin, Notes from the President: Will the U.S. Supreme Court Fail International Law?, *Newsletter of the American Society of International Law* 1 (August-September 1992). The Supreme Court's mistake in *Alvarez-Machain* was underlined all the more painfully when the federal trial judge ultimately acquitted the Mexican doctor because the evidence presented against him "had been based on 'hunches' and the 'wildest speculation' and had failed to support the charges that he had participated in the torture of the drug agent." Mydans, Jury Clears Mexican in Agent's Killing, *N.Y. Times*, Dec. 15, 1992, at A20.

[58] Leppard, US Says It Has Right to Kidnap British Citizens, *Sunday Times* (U.K.), Dec. 2, 2007 at 1, 2.

[59] L.K. Johnson, *The Making of International Agreements* 13 (1984). A more general survey found that only about 10 percent of about 12,000 international agreements entered into by the United States between 1776 and 1986 had been ratified after an Article II advise and consent by the Senate. Kennedy, Conditional Approval of Treaties by the U.S. Senate, 19 *Loyola International & Comparative Law Journal* 89, 91 (1996).

[60] Bradley & Goldsmith, Presidential Control over International Law, 131 *Harvard Law Review* 1201, 1210 (2018).

[61] John Bellinger, formerly Legal Adviser to the State Department, complained that President Obama secured Senate consent to only nine new treaties in his first term in office. Bellinger, Obama's Weakness on Treaties, *N.Y. Times*, Dec. 19, 2012, at A31.

B. Treaties in Municipal Law

A treaty not of the Article II type was at issue in United States v. Belmont where the supremacy as against state law of an agreement concluded by the President with the Soviet Union was questioned.[62] The United States sought to recover funds deposited with Belmont's bank by a private Russian company later nationalized by the Soviet Union. These funds were included in amounts assigned by the Soviet government to the United States in a U.S.-U.S.S.R. executive agreement to be used to help satisfy outstanding claims of private American parties against the Soviet Union. Faced with the objection that the executive agreement had not been submitted to or voted on by the Senate, the Supreme Court held:

> But an international compact, as this was, is not always a treaty which requires the participation of the Senate. There are many such compacts, of which a protocol, a modus vivendi, a postal convention, and agreements like that now under consideration are illustrations. . . .
>
> Plainly, the external powers of the United States are to be exercised without regard to state laws or policies. . . . And while this rule in respect of treaties is established by the express language of cl. 2, Art. VI, of the Constitution, the same rule would result in the case of all international compacts and agreements from the very fact that complete power over international affairs is in the national government and is not and cannot be subject to any curtailment or interference on the part of the several states.[63]

It may even be that a reference to a "treaty" in an act of Congress will be construed to include treaties not of the Article II type. For example, looking at a statute that provided for direct appeal to the Supreme Court in cases concerning "treaties," the Supreme Court held that a commercial agreement between the United States and France, "[i]f not technically a treaty requiring ratification, nevertheless . . . was a compact authorized by the Congress of the United States, negotiated and proclaimed under the authority of its President" and thus "a treaty under the Circuit Court of Appeals Act."[64]

The power of the President or of the President and Congress to make international agreements outside the boundaries of Article II is a controversial and still-developing area of the law. In United States

[62] 301 U.S. 324 (1937).
[63] Id. at 330-331.
[64] Altman v. United States, 224 U.S. 583, 601 (1912).

v. Curtiss-Wright,[65] the Supreme Court advanced the thesis that the federal government had special powers in international affairs, powers that might even be extra-constitutional:

> [T]he investment of the federal government with the powers of external sovereignty did not depend upon the affirmative grants of the Constitution. The powers to declare and wage war, to conclude peace, to make treaties, to maintain diplomatic relations with other sovereignties, if they had never been mentioned in the Constitution, would have vested in the federal government as necessary concomitants of nationality. . . . [T]he power to make such international agreements as do not constitute treaties in the constitutional sense . . . which is [not] expressly affirmed by the Constitution, nevertheless exist[s] as inherently inseparable from the conception of nationality.[66]

The *Curtiss-Wright* Court found the grant of such a power "not in the provisions of the Constitution, but in the law of nations."[67]

Later courts have not adopted such a broad theoretical view of the extra-constitutional international powers of the President or Congress, but they have been ready to accept extraordinary incursions by the President into municipal law when the President is acting pursuant to international agreements, at least when the President acts with the explicit or implicit consent of Congress. The outstanding modern example of such permissible incursions is Dames & Moore v. Regan.[68] There, the Court unanimously upheld the effectiveness in U.S. law of presidential orders made to fulfill the terms of the U.S.-Iranian agreement settling the Iran hostage crisis. In exchange for the release of the U.S. diplomats held hostage by Iran, the United States ordered the termination of private litigation against Iran in U.S. courts and the release of Iranian assets that had been attached in the proceedings. Terminated litigation could be recommenced before a specially created international arbitral tribunal in The Hague, and $1 billion of the released assets was devoted to a fund set aside to satisfy the awards of the arbitrators. The *Dames & Moore* Court, though careful to narrow its decisions to the facts of the case, held that where "we can conclude that

[65] 299 U.S. 304 (1936).
[66] Id. at 318.
[67] Ibid.
[68] 453 U.S. 654 (1981).

Congress acquiesced in the President's action, we are not prepared to say that the President lacks the power to settle such claims."[69]

It is safe, albeit perhaps confusing, to conclude by recalling that the term "treaty" has at least three meanings in U.S. law. First is the definition of a "treaty" in the Vienna Convention, sometimes but not always followed in the U.S. legal system: "an international agreement concluded between States in written form and governed by international law."[70] Second is the Article II–type "treaty" of the U.S. Constitution made by the President with the advice and consent of two-thirds of the Senators present who concur. Third are other U.S. international agreements entitled to the protection of the Constitution's supremacy clause for "all treaties made, or which shall be made, under the authority of the United States" in Article VI, and as elaborated by case law like *Belmont* and *Dames & Moore.*[71]

2. *Treaties in the Law of Some Other States*

Turning to the constitutional rules of other states concerning incorporation of treaties into their municipal legal systems, we encounter such a considerable variety of specific provisions that Professor Brownlie laments, "The whole subject resists generalization."[72] Nonetheless, some generalization, however superficial, may be useful in highlighting a few of the ways in which the U.S. approach to the incorporation of treaties into municipal law is and is not characteristic of other countries.

Probably the most significant difference between the constitutional rules of the United States and those of other states, especially those in the common law tradition, has to do with self-executing treaties. Quite simply, most other common law countries deny the very possibility of self-execution. They do not permit treaties to take effect in their municipal legal systems without legislative enactment.

Such is the rule, for example, in England, where the Crown is constitutionally authorized to conclude and ratify international

[69] Id. at 688.

[70] Vienna Convention, supra, art. 2(1)(a).

[71] See Spiro, Executive Agreements and the (Non)Treaty Power, 77 *North Carolina Law Review* 134 (1988).

[72] I. Brownlie, *Principles of Public International Law* 48 (6th ed. 2003) [hereinafter cited as "Brownlie"].

agreements without parliamentary participation, but Parliament alone has power to incorporate treaties into English law, an incorporation accomplished by an enabling act of legislation.[73] In *The Parlement Belge*, when the British government argued that a ratified, but unenacted, treaty between the United Kingdom and Belgium shielded a Belgian state-owned mail boat from the jurisdiction of the English courts, Sir Robert Phillimore held that to so find an immunity would be "a use of the treaty-making prerogative of the Crown which I believe to be without precedent, and in principle contrary to the laws of the constitution," and if Belgium should feel wronged because the protection afforded by the treaty was not provided, then that should be settled by "proper measures of compensation and arrangement, between the Governments of Great Britain and Belgium."[74]

The traditional English rule against self-execution of treaties still holds sway. As Jennings and Watts put it: "Where a treaty affects private rights or, generally, requires for the implementation of its obligations a modification of existing law, the necessary changes in the law must be the subject of action by or under the authority of an Act of Parliament before an English court can give effect to the changes in the law called for by the treaty."[75] In 1989, the House of Lords reaffirmed the rule against the self-execution of treaties in English law. Writing in a unanimous decision in *International Tin*, Lord Oliver held:

> [A]s a matter of the constitutional law of the United Kingdom, the Royal Prerogative, whilst it embraces the making of treaties, does not extend to altering the law or conferring rights upon individuals or depriving individuals of rights which they enjoy in domestic law without the intervention of Parliament. Treaties, as it is sometimes expressed, are not self-executing. Quite simply, a treaty is not part of English law unless and until it has been incorporated into the law by legislation.[76]

[73] Sales & Clement, International Law in Domestic Courts: The Developing Context, 124 *Law Quarterly Review* 388 (2008).

[74] [1878-1879] 4 P.D. 129, 154-155.

[75] 1 *Oppenheim's International Law: Ninth Edition* 58-59 (R. Jennings & A. Watts eds. 1992) [hereinafter cited as "Jennings & Watts"].

[76] Australia v. New Zealand Banking Group Ltd. v. Commonwealth of Australia, House of Lords, Judgment of October 26, 1989, 29 *International Legal Materials* 670, 694 (1990).

B. Treaties in Municipal Law

The English rule obtains in most countries that like the United States were once part of the British Empire.[77] In Canada, perhaps the best-known general statement of the principle is to be found in the opinion of Lord Atkin in Attorney-General for Canada v. Attorney-General for Ontario:

> Within the British Empire there is a well-established rule that the making of a treaty is an executive act, while the performance of its obligations, if they entail alteration of the existing domestic law, requires legislative action. . . . Once [treaties] are created, while they bind the state as against the other contracting parties, Parliament may refuse to perform them and so leave the state in default.[78]

India, too, follows the English rule. The Indian courts may not apply the terms of a treaty unless the treaty has been given a legal sanction by an enactment of the Indian Parliament.[79] Although Article 51 of the Indian Constitution provides, *inter alia,* that there is a "directive principle of state policy" to "foster respect for international law and treaty obligations in the dealings of organized peoples with one another," directive principles are not justiciable in Indian law; rather, they are merely meant to guide the Indian government.[80]

In countries where the executive can unilaterally conclude and ratify treaties, the potential national embarrassment of the legislature's refusing to enact a ratified treaty into municipal law is sometimes avoided by the simple expedient of the executive postponing ratification of a treaty until the legislature is ready to act. The United Kingdom and other states in the English tradition, for example, all ordinarily delay ratifying treaties until appropriate laws are enacted.[81]

Although the doctrine of self-executing treaties is rejected by most other common law countries, the notion of self-execution is accepted

[77] Opponents of a broad policy of self-executing treaties sometimes encourage a return to the English approach of a stricter dualism. See Moore, Do U.S. Courts Discriminate Against Treaties?: Equivalence, Duality, and Non-Self-Execution, 111 *Columbia Law Review* 2228, 2249 (2010).

[78] [1937] A.C. 326, 347-348 (Judicial Committee of the Privy Council).

[79] S.D. Mahajan, *Public International Law* 104 (5th ed. 1973).

[80] See M.P. Tandon, *Public International Law* 74 (14th ed. 1973).

[81] See Jennings & Watts, supra, at 60-61; O. Schachter, M. Nawaz & J. Fried, *Toward Wider Acceptance of U.N. Treaties* 95-97 (1971).

in one form or another by many nations with a civil law tradition. In civil law countries, which make up most of all states, the authority for the incorporation of treaty rules into municipal law is usually to be found in explicit constitutional provisions. For example, Article 55 of the French Constitution of 1958 reads that "treaties or international agreements regularly ratified or approved have, from the date of their publication, an authority superior to municipal law on the basis of reciprocity by the other state."[82] In practice, this means that a treaty has effect in French municipal law when it is embodied in a decree signed by the French president and printed in the Official Journal.[83]

The doctrine of self-executing or directly applicable treaties in France is, however, much restricted by explicit constitutional limits. The very terms of Article 55 dictate that a ratified treaty has no force in French municipal law if it has not been duly published.[84] Article 55 also imposes a condition of reciprocity; that is, the French courts will not apply a treaty in French municipal law if it is not in force in the municipal law of the other party.[85] Furthermore, there are constitutional limits on the French executive's power to conclude international agreements. Article 52 of the Constitution reads that "[t]he President of the Republic negotiates and ratifies treaties,"[86] but Article 53 provides that treaties regulating certain subject matters may not be ratified or approved except by statutory enactment.[87] Such parliamentary approval is needed for treaties that modify French municipal law or that affect the financial commitments of the state, as well as for matters of considerable international importance such as treaties of peace, commerce, or concerns relative to international organizations.[88]

It may be that the French president has at least some temporary special treaty-making powers under the emergency provisions of

[82] "[L]es traités ou accords régulièrement ratifiés ou approuvés ont, des leur publication, une autorité supérieure a celle des lois, sous réserve, pour chaque accord ou traité, de son application par l'autre partie."

[83] P. Manin, *Droit international public* 63 (1979).

[84] Conseil d'État, Judgment of 23 December 1981, Commune de Thionville et autres, 1981 *Récueil des décisions du Conseil d'État* 484, 486.

[85] Lachaume, Jurisprudence française rélative au droit international (Année 1981), 28 *Annuaire français de droit international* 972, 976-981 (1982).

[86] "Le Président de la République négocie et ratifie les traités."

[87] "[N]e peuvent être ratifiés ou approuvés qu'en vertu d'une loi."

[88] Lesage, Les procedures de conclusion des accords internationaux de la France sous la Ve République, 8 *Annuaire français de droit international* 873, 879-880 (1962).

Article 16.[89] But another limit on the French executive's freedom to conclude treaties is found in Article 54 of the Constitution, which prohibits the government from ratifying or approving treaties that violate the Constitution unless the Constitution is first amended.[90]

Other civil law states have adopted a wide variety of rules about self-executing treaties, again mostly to be found in explicit constitutional provisions. In Japan, the 1946 Constitution provides that "[t]reaties concluded by Japan and established laws of nations shall be faithfully observed," a provision that most scholars agree makes treaties directly applicable in Japanese municipal law.[91] In practice, however, judges in Japan have been reluctant to find treaties self-executing for fear of over-riding municipal law.[92]

Some civil law countries have more closely followed the U.S. precedent. Mexico, for example, as early as its first constitution in 1824, more or less replicated Article VI (2) of the U.S. Constitution. Mexico's old Article 161 provided that each state was obliged to comply with the Mexican Constitution, general laws of the Union, and treaties made or that would be made by the supreme authority of the Federation with foreign powers.[93] Similar provisions have been included in subsequent constitutions. Article 133 of the present Mexican Constitution makes the Constitution, the laws of Congress, and treaties "the supreme law of all the Union."[94] This article raises many of the same problems as those generated by the comparable supremacy clause of the U.S. Constitution.[95]

[89] Id. at 883-884.

[90] Blumann, L'article 54 de la Constitution et le controle de la constitutionalité des traités en France, 82 *Révue générale de droit international public* 537 (1978). In general, see Janis, Noyes & Sadat, supra, at 350-351.

[91] Iwasawa, The Relationship Between International Law and National Law: The Japanese Experiences, 64 *British Yearbook of International Law 1993* 333, 344-345 (1994).

[92] Id. at 349-366.

[93] "[C]ada uno de los Estados tiene obligación. . . . (II) De cuidar y hacer cuidar la Constitución y leyes generales de la Unión y los Tratados hechos o que en adelante se hicieren por la autoridad suprema de la Federación con alguna potencia extranjera." C. Sepulveda, *Derecho internacional* 76 (14th ed. 1984).

[94] "Esta Constitución, las leyes del Congreso de la Unión que emanan de ella y todos los tratados que estén de acuerdo con la misma, celebrados y que se celebren por el Presidente de la República con aprobación del Senado, serán la Ley suprema de toda la Unión." Id. at 77.

[95] Id. at 77-80.

C. THE LAW OF NATIONS IN U.S. LAW

1. *The Law of Nations as Common Law*

In the United States, international law that originates from sources other than treaties was traditionally considered to be part of common law. The principle dates back to a number of cases decided by the English courts in the eighteenth century.[96] Blackstone, in 1769, stated the proposition thus: "[T]he law of nations (wherever any question arises which is properly the object of its jurisdiction) is here adopted in its full extent by the common law, and is held to be a part of the law of the land."[97]

In the United States, the Constitution itself employs the term "the law of nations." Indeed, it may be difficult to understand how the Constitution separates powers among the Congress, the President, and the courts, and between the federal government and the states without understanding and applying the law of nations.[98] However, unlike the explicit provision in the Constitution about the incorporation of treaties, there is no constitutional provision about the incorporation of the law of nations. Rather, as Professors Bellia and Clark remark, "U.S. courts, lawyers and judges must evaluate such law on its own terms and determine—in every case—how it interacts with the Constitution's precise text and structure."[99]

In 1784, the principle that the law of nations is part of the law of the land took judicial hold in the United States even before the Constitution was drafted or ratified. In Respublica v. De Longchamps, McKean, the Chief Justice of Pennsylvania, held that an assault on the French consul general in Philadelphia was "an infraction of the law of Nations. This law, in its full extent, is part of the law of this State, and is to be collected from the practice of different Nations, and the authority

[96] See Barbuit's Case, T. Talbot 281, 25 Eng. Rep. 777 (1736); Triquet v. Bath, 3 Burr. 1478, 96 Eng. Rep. 273 (1764) [hereinafter cited as "Barbuit's case"].

[97] W. Blackstone, 4 *Commentaries on the Laws of England* 67 (1st ed. 1765-1769) [hereinafter cited as "Blackstone"].

[98] Bellia & Clark, The Law of Nations as Constitutional Law, 98 *Virginia Law Review* 729 (2012).

[99] A.J. Bellia Jr. & B.R. Clark, *The Law of Nations and the United States Constitution* 272 (2017).

of writers."[100] The classic utterance by the Supreme Court on the topic is that of Mr. Justice Gray in *The Paquete Habana*: "International law is part of our law, and must be ascertained and administered by the courts of justice of appropriate jurisdiction, as often as questions of right depending upon it are duly presented for their determination."[101] Albeit, Justice Gray's statement "was not new," as Professor Dodge observes, "it was nonetheless significant in affirming that this was *still* true" in an age of high positivism.[102]

As we saw in *The Paquete Habana* in Chapter 3, U.S. courts do not usually treat customary international law, the general principles of law, judicial decisions, and the opinions of publicists as discrete sources of international law as would the International Court of Justice. Rather, U.S. courts tend to collect evidences from all these diverse sources in hopes of establishing some rule of international common law, a legacy of the law of nations tradition. In United States v. Smith, Justice Story explained that the law of nations "may be ascertained by consulting the works of jurists, writing professedly on public law; or by the general usage and practice of nations; or by judicial decisions recognising and enforcing that law."[103] Thus, the terms "the law of nations" or perhaps "international common law" probably is more descriptive of the sort of international law, beyond treaty law, that is found and applied in the U.S. legal system.

The eclectic and inclusive nature of the U.S. courts' perception of non-treaty international law is reflected in Filartiga v. Peña-Irala. There, Judge Kaufman of the Second Circuit held that "[h]aving examined the sources from which customary international law is derived—the usage of nations, judicial opinions and the works of jurists—we conclude that official torture is now prohibited by the law of nations."[104] The evidence reviewed by the court in specifying the rule included affidavits of international legal scholars, the U.N. Charter, U.S. judicial decisions, the Universal Declaration of Human Rights, other General

[100] 1 U.S. (1 Dallas) 111, 116 (1784).

[101] 175 U.S. 677, 700 (1900).

[102] Dodge, *The Paquete Habana*: Customary International Law as Part of Our Law, *International Law Stories*, Noyes, Dickinson, Janis & Vázquez, supra, at 287, 302.

[103] 18 U.S. (5 Wheat.) 153, 160-161 (1820). See Samuels, The Full Story of United States v. Smith: America's Most Important Piracy Case, 1 *Pennsylvania State Journal of Law & International Affairs* 320 (2012).

[104] 630 F.2d 876, 884 (2d Cir. 1980).

Assembly resolutions, the opinions of publicists in law review articles, the European Human Rights Convention and other regional agreements, constitutional provisions of "over fifty-five" nations, U.S. diplomatic contacts, and a judgment of the European Court of Human Rights. None of these evidences was given any special priority. Such a collective approach is typical whenever it is argued that international law is a part of the common law.

In *Filartiga*, the federal court turned to international law because a federal statute, the Alien Tort Statute of 1789 (ATS), gave it jurisdiction over "any civil action by an alien for a tort only, committed in violation of the law of nations."[105] There are also jurisdictional foundations for applying international law in federal court cases arising under the laws and treaties of the United States, in diversity jurisdiction involving foreign citizens or states, in admiralty cases, and in cases involving foreign diplomats.[106]

Filartiga's expansive view of the 1789 Alien Tort Statute was upheld by the Supreme Court in 2004, in Sosa v. Alvarez-Machain. Though Alvarez-Machain proved no more successful recovering damages for his abduction than he was on resisting its execution, his second case led the Supreme Court to agree that the Alien Tort Statute provided a cause of action without need for a further enabling statute: "[T]here is every reason to suppose that the First Congress did not pass the ATS as a jurisdictional convenience to be placed on the shelf for use by a future Congress."[107] Justice Souter, in a masterful opinion for the Court, went on to hold "that Congress intended the ATS to furnish jurisdiction for a relatively modest set of actions alleging violation of the law of nations," such as crimes against ambassadors, safe conducts, prize captures, and piracy.[108] Importantly, the Court disagreed with a

[105] 28 U.S.C. §1350. See Casto, The Federal Courts' Protective Jurisdiction over Torts Committed in Violation of the Law of Nations, 18 *Connecticut Law Review* 467 (1986).

[106] 28 U.S.C. §§1331-1333, §1251; see American Law Institute, *Restatement (Third) of the Foreign Relations Law of the United States* 42-46 (1987) [hereinafter cited as "Restatement (Third)"]. The latest restatement, the Restatement (Fourth), supra, hesitated in covering the entire field, and goes only to three topics: treaties, jurisdiction, and sovereign immunity. Hence, here respecting customary international law and the law of nations, we can only refer to the Restatement (Third), supra.

[107] Sosa v. Alvarez-Machain, 542 U.S. 692, 697, 719 (2004).

[108] Id. at 720.

dissenting Justice Scalia about the possible creation of new causes of action. Justice Souter wrote: "[I]t would be unreasonable to assume that the First Congress would have expected federal courts to lose all capacity to recognize enforceable international norms simply because the common law might lose some metaphysical cachet on the road to modern realism."[109] As one commentator notes, *Sosa* both giveth and taketh away: "[C]alculated to bring a sharp halt to the expansion of the scope of ATS-enabled claims[, it] nonetheless appears to confirm the main current of ATS jurisprudence that has been allowed to develop without Supreme Court review in the lower courts over the course of twenty-four years."[110]

A further refinement of the Alien Tort Statute came in 2013, when in Kiobel v. Royal Dutch Petroleum, the Supreme Court held that the reach of the ATS was limited by a presumption against extraterritoriality.[111] Professor Steinhardt observes that the large majority of the Court preserved claims that "touch and concern" the United States, such as, for example, in *Filartiga* where the defendant was found in the United States.[112] However, *Kiobel* was welcomed by foreign governments concerned with the extensive extraterritorial reach of the ATS.[113]

However, the reach of the ATS was significantly limited in 2018, when, in Jesner v. Arab Bank, the Supreme Court ruled 5-4 that the statute does not extend to foreign corporations.[114] Justice Kennedy for a plurality held that Congress, not the courts, was the proper place to determine corporate liability. For the majority, Kennedy stressed that diplomatic tensions with Jordan, the bank's corporate domicile,

[109] Id. at 730. Looking, however, at the particular claim of Alvarez-Machain, the Court held that his invocation of "a general prohibition of 'arbitrary' detention . . . expresses an aspiration that exceeds any binding customary rule having the specificity we require." Id. at 731-738.

[110] Roth, Scope of Alien Tort Statute—Arbitrary Arrest and Detentions as Violations of Custom, 98 *American Journal of International Law* 798, 803 (2004).

[111] 569 U.S. 108 (2013). See Swaine, *Kiobel* and Extraterritoriality: Here (Not) There, (Not Even) Everywhere, 69 *Oklahoma Law Review* 23 (2016). Further limiting the ATS for corporations is Nestle USA v. Doe, 593 U.S. 628 (2021).

[112] Steinhardt, Kiobel and the Weakening of Precedent: A Long Walk for a Short Drink, 107 *American Journal of International Law* 841, 844 (2013).

[113] Kohl, Corporate Human Rights Accountability: The Objections of Western Governments to the Alien Tort Statute, 63 *International & Comparative Law Quarterly* 665 (2017).

[114] 584 U.S. 281 (2018).

underscored the wisdom of the Court excluding foreign corporations from the jurisdiction of the ATS. Professor Hamilton laments that the ATS was no longer "a beacon of hope for survivors of human rights atrocities."[115] It has been suggested that state courts in the United States should now come to the rescue of international human rights law.[116]

Forty years after its resurrection in *Filartiga*, we now know at least five things about the Alien Tort Statute. First, it is a jurisdictional statute. Second, the ATS provides for those causes of action found in 1789 in Blackstone's common law. Third, norms of international common law may become new causes of action if definitely defined. Fourth, the ATS is to be read with a presumption against extraterritoriality. And, fifth, it does not ordinarily reach corporations.

In addition, of course, the ATS and indeed any claim based on the law of nations must demonstrate that state practice proves a customary rule. So, in *The Paquete Habana*, the Supreme Court found sufficient practice to prove a rule exempting coastal fishing vessels from seizure.[117] In *Amerada Hess*, the Second Circuit held that there was sufficient evidence for a rule protecting neutral shipping in international waters from attack in the Falkland Islands conflict.[118] However, in *Echeverria-Hernández*, a panel of the Ninth Circuit rejected a claim that "international law requires the United States to provide temporary asylum to all persons fleeing internal armed conflict"; evidences that states actually did provide such refuge were held to be only acts "of understandable humanitarian concern."[119]

As to supremacy in U.S. law, international common law has much the same status vis-à-vis state law as do treaties and other international agreements. Although there is no constitutional supremacy clause for customary international law as there is for treaty law, it makes "no sense that questions of international law should be treated as questions of

[115] Hamilton, *Jesner v. Arab Bank*, 112 *American Journal of International Law* 720, 724 (2018).

[116] Davis & Whytlock, State Remedies of Human Rights, 98 *Boston University Law Review* 397 (2018).

[117] 175 U.S. 677, 686-711 (1900).

[118] Amerada Hess v. Argentine Republic, 830 F.2d 421 (2d Cir. 1987), *rev'd on other grounds*, 485 U.S. 1005 (1989).

[119] Echeverria-Hernandez v. United States Immigration & Naturalization Serv., 923 F.2d 688, 692-693 (9th Cir. 1991), *vacated*, 946 F.2d 1481 (9th Cir. 1991).

state rather than federal law."[120] Customary international law is appropriately viewed as an area of federal common law where the Supreme Court is given the final say in setting the rules for the state and federal courts alike.[121] The Supreme Court in Banco Nacional de Cuba v. Sabbatino held that customary international law, in this case the act of state doctrine, "must be treated exclusively as an aspect of federal law."[122] However, as U.S. federal courts are increasingly limited in their application of international law, state courts have been encouraged to step in.[123]

Compared with other federal law, the law of nations or international common law has no more supremacy than have treaties. So, statutes later in time prevail. Whether international common law has as much potency as international agreements is a matter of some dispute. When, in a tentative draft of the Restatement, the Reporters wrote that new international common law as well as new international agreements superseded preexisting municipal law, there were protests that there were no cases awarding international common law this status, and in a later draft, the Reporters retreated, stating only that new treaty provisions superseded preexisting domestic law.[124] As to state law, Professor Vázquez points out, "[T]he constitutional structure strongly supports denying the States the power to place the nation in breach of its obligations under customary international law."[125]

[120] Henkin, International Law as Law in the United States, 82 *Michigan Law Review* 1555, 1559 (1984).

[121] Friendly, In Praise of Erie and of the New Federal Common Law, 39 *New York University Law Review* 383 (1964); Jessup, The Doctrine of Erie Railroad v. Tompkins Applied to International Law, 33 *American Journal of International Law* 740 (1939). A persuasive rebuttal of arguments that customary international law might be something less or other than federal common law is to be found in Koh, Is International Law Really State Law?, 111 *Harvard Law Review* 1824 (1998).

[122] 376 U.S. 398, 425-426 (1964).

[123] See Colangelo, International Law in U.S. State Courts: Extraterritoriality and "False Conflicts" of Law, 48 *International Lawyer* 1 (2014); Born, Customary International Law in United States Courts, 92 *Washington Law Review* 1641 (2017).

[124] See American Law Institute, *Restatement (Revised) of the Foreign Relations Law of the United States*, Tent. Draft No. 1, §135(1) (1980) and Tent. Draft No. 6, §135 and Reporters' Note 4 (1985). On the Reporters' retreat, see Maier, The Authoritative Sources of Customary International Law in the United States, 10 *Michigan Journal of International Law* 450, 464-473 (1989).

[125] Vázquez, Customary International Law as U.S. Law: A Critique of the Revisionist and Intermediate Positions and a Defense of the Modern Position, 86 *Notre Dame Law Review* 1495, 1552 (2011).

In practice, conflicts between U.S. law and international law do not often arise. Judges are usually able to reconcile possibly conflicting provisions. As Chief Justice Marshall wrote in the much-cited *Charming Betsy*: "[A]n act of Congress ought never to be construed to violate the law of nations if any other possible construction remains."[126] Professor Alford applauds the *Charming Betsy* doctrine, arguing that when properly construed, it is "an indispensable device for pursuing our nation's foreign policy objectives.[127]

2. *Customary International Law in the Law of Some Other States*

Unlike the incorporation of treaties into municipal law, where the United States differs so greatly from other common law countries, U.S. practice with respect to the domestic incorporation of the law of nations or international common law is rather close to that of other common law jurisdictions. Brownlie puts the proposition for England and the Commonwealth as follows: "The dominant principle, normally characterized as the doctrine of incorporation, is that customary rules are to be considered part of the law of the land and enforced as such, with the qualification that they are incorporated only so far as is not inconsistent with Acts of Parliament or prior judicial decisions of final authority."[128]

In England, the incorporation of international law is judge-made, rather than publicist-made, doctrine. There is a continuing "controversy . . . whether, if rules of international law are part of English law, they are, once they have been pronounced upon by English courts, subject to the rules of English law relating to the binding force of judicial precedent"[129] or may be modified against precedent by lower courts following perceived changes in customary international law.[130] Such controversies continue to swirl, for as Lord McNair noted, "We have

[126] Murray v. Schooner Charming Betsy, 6 U.S. (2 Cranch) 64, 118 (1804).

[127] Alford, Foreign Relations as a Matter of Interpretation: The Use and Abuse of *Charming Betsy*, 67 *Ohio State Law Journal* 1339, 1338 (2006).

[128] Brownlie, supra, at 41.

[129] Jennings & Watts, supra, at 58.

[130] Trendtex Trading Corp. v. Central Bank of Nigeria [1977], 1 Q.B. 529 (Court of Appeal).

never attempted to rationalize the relations between international law and English law. . . . [S]uch controversies as that between the monist and the dualist theories, into which the late Professor Oppenheim in vain tried to lead us, have found no abiding-place in our literature."[131] Accordingly, the workings of the doctrine must be picked out in a common law fashion case by case. Of course, England shares *Barbuit's Case*, Triquet v. Bath, and Blackstone with the United States.[132] Another English formulation of the incorporation rule is found in West Rand Central Gold Mining Co. v. The King:

> It is quite true that whatever has received the common consent of civilized nations must have received the assent of our country, and that to which we have assented along with other nations in general may properly be called international law, and as such will be acknowledged and applied by our municipal tribunals when legitimate occasion arises for those tribunals to decide questions to which doctrines of international law may be relevant. But any doctrine so invoked must be one really accepted as binding between nations, and the international law sought to be applied must, like anything else, be proved by satisfactory evidence, which must shew either that the particular proposition put forward has been recognised and acted upon by our own country, or that it is of such a nature, and has been so widely and generally accepted, that it can hardly be supposed that any civilized State would repudiate it.[133]

In Canada, "customary rules of international law are adopted automatically into our law, amid a few caveats about sovereignty and then directly applied unless they conflict with statute or some fundamental constitutional principle in which case legislation is required to enforce them."[134] Although this practice is reasonably consistent in Canada, it is, as in England, largely unsupported by any forthright judicial theory. As Professor Macdonald remarks: "[I]f this absence of theory is remarkable,

[131] A.D. McNair, *Lord McNair: Selected Papers and Bibliography* 147 (1974); see Sales & Clement, International Law in Domestic Courts: The Developing Framework, 124 *Law Quarterly Review* 388 (2008).

[132] Barbuit's Case, supra; Blackstone, supra.

[133] [1905] 2 K.B. 391, 406-407.

[134] Macdonald, The Relationship Between International Law and Domestic Law in Canada, *Canadian Perspectives on International Law and Organization* 88, 111 (Macdonald, Morris & Johnston eds. 1974).

it is also in keeping with what can only be described as the common law tradition of doing first and theorizing about it afterwards."[135]

In India, the courts "treat customary rules of international law as part of the Indian municipal law unless there is such conflict between the two that they cannot be reconciled."[136] This was the rule in India before its independence, and, according to Article 372 of the Indian Constitution, such a pre-independence rule stays in effect unless specifically repealed. Article 13 of the Indian Constitution, however, invalidates any law, including a customary international law, that violates fundamental rights.[137]

Outside the common law legal systems, most civil law countries rely on explicit constitutional provisions incorporating international law other than treaties into municipal law. The French jurist Rousseau divides such constitutional solutions into three groups.[138] First are those constitutional provisions, often found in preambles, where the state indicates its readiness in principle to submit to general international law.[139] For example, the preamble to the present French Constitution, that of October 4, 1958, reads that "the French people solemnly proclaim their commitment to human rights and to the principles of national sovereignty which have been defined by the Declaration of 1789 and confirmed and elaborated by the preamble to the Constitution of 1946."[140] The Constitution of October 27, 1946, so incorporated by reference in the present Constitution, explicitly provided that "the French Republic, faithful to its traditions, adheres to the rules of public international law."[141]

Second, some constitutions expressly incorporate general international law into municipal law and leave to the legislators or the courts the duty of harmonizing any conflicts between international and

[135] Id. at 88.

[136] R.C. Hingorani, *Modern International Law* 30 (1979).

[137] Id. at 30-31.

[138] C. Rousseau, 1 *Droit international public* 47-48 (1970) [hereinafter cited as "Rousseau"].

[139] Id. at 47.

[140] "Le peuple français proclame solennellement son attachément aux Droits de l'homme et aux principes de la soverainété nationale tels qu'ils ont été definis par la Déclaration de 1789, confirmée et complétée par le préambule de la Constitution de 1946."

[141] "La République française, fidèle a ses traditions, se conforme aux règles du droit public international."

municipal rules.[142] So, for example, in the Philippines, Article 2(3) of the Constitution provides that "[t]he Philippines . . . adopts the generally accepted principles of international law as part of the law of the Nation."

Third, some constitutions not only incorporate international common law into national law, but also give it priority over domestic rules in case of conflicts.[143] In the Constitution of the Federal Republic of Germany, Article 25 provides that "the general rules of the law of nations are part of federal law. They take precedence against domestic law and directly create rights and duties for persons in the country."[144] In the Czech Republic's 1992 Constitution, human rights treaties are given both direct effect and supremacy over domestic legislation.[145]

In general, it seems that some sort of incorporation of customary or general international law into municipal legal systems is quite common worldwide. A recent survey of 101 countries concluded that it found "remarkable consistencies across countries: the vast majority of national legal systems now recognize custom as directly applicable, at least in principle."[146]

D. FOREIGN RELATIONS LAW

In the United States, the relationship between international law and municipal law is sometimes treated as one aspect of what is called "foreign relations law."[147] Indeed, the Restatements of the American Law Institute devoted to international law topics are entitled "Foreign

[142] Rousseau, supra, at 47-48.

[143] Id. at 48.

[144] "Die allgemeinen Regeln des Völkerrechtes sind Bestandteil des Bundesrechtes. Sie gehen den Gesetzen vor und erzeugen Rechte und Pflichten unmittelbar für die Bewohner des Bundesgebietes."

[145] Stein, International Law in Internal Law: Toward Internationalization of Central-Eastern European Constitutions, 88 *American Journal of International Law* 427, 441 (1994).

[146] Verdier & Versteeg, International Law in National Legal Systems: An Empirical Investigation, 109 *American Journal of International Law* 514, 515 (2015).

[147] Bradley, What Is Foreign Relations Law?, *The Oxford Handbook of Comparative Foreign Relations Law* (Bradley ed. 2019).

Relations Law of the United States."[148] The Restatement (Third) defines the subject as follows:

> The foreign relations law of the United States, as dealt with in this Restatement, consists of
>
> (a) international law as it applies to the United States; and
>
> (b) domestic law that has substantial significance for the foreign relations of the United States or has other substantial international consequences.[149]

The international part of the Restatement's foreign relations law is the principal theme of this book, but some rules from the domestic part of U.S. foreign relations law figure here, too. Domestic norms have, as we have already seen, a great deal to do with incorporating international law into municipal law and with limiting the international role of the component states of the United States. Furthermore, in many substantive areas of international law, especially in those fields traditionally known as "international business law" and "international conflicts of law," municipal rules play the major part [see Chapters 9 and 10].

Moreover, U.S. domestic law plays a critical part in international politics generally in that it allocates powers among the branches of the federal government for the conduct of foreign relations.[150] The U.S. Constitution explicitly grants Congress the "Power to lay and collect Taxes, Duties, Imposts and Excises, to pay the Debts and provide for the common Defence and General Welfare of the United States."[151] Congress is also empowered to "regulate Commerce with foreign Nations," to "define and punish Piracies and Felonies committed on the high seas, and Offences against the Law of Nations," to "declare War, grant Letters of Marque and Reprisal, and make Rules concerning Captures on Land and Water," to "raise and support Armies," and to "provide and maintain

[148] Confusingly, the first published version was named the Restatement (Second) because the subject was first addressed in the second set of Restatements in general. American Law Institute, *Restatement (Second) of the Foreign Relations Law of the United States* (1965). The second and third versions accordingly have been called the Restatement (Third), supra, and the partial Restatement (Fourth), supra.

[149] Restatement (Third), supra, §1.

[150] See L. Henkin, *Foreign Affairs and the Constitution* (1972); Dames & Moore v. Regan, 453 U.S. 654 (1981); United States v. Curtiss-Wright Export Corp., 299 U.S. 304 (1936).

[151] U.S. Constitution, art. I, §8.

a Navy."[152] The President of the United States is to "be Commander in Chief of the Army and Navy." The President also has power "by and with the Advice and Consent of the Senate, to make Treaties provided two thirds of the Senators present concur," to "appoint Ambassadors [and] other public Ministers and Consuls," and to "receive Ambassadors and other public Ministers."[153] The Supreme Court has vested in it the judicial power of the United States, which includes "all Cases, in Law and Equity, arising under this Constitution, the Laws of the United States, and Treaties made, or which shall be made, under their Authority;—to all Cases affecting Ambassadors, other public Ministers and Consuls;—to all Cases of admiralty and maritime Jurisdiction;—to Controversies . . . between a State, or the Citizens thereof, and foreign States, Citizens or Subjects."[154]

In practice, some of the most controversial issues of domestic politics have to do with the separation of powers among the three branches of government with respect to foreign affairs. For example, we have already looked at questions involving a President's right, with and without Congress, to make binding international agreements for the United States. There are also important questions about the limits on the Supreme Court's power to make judicial determinations affecting international relations; these underlie, for example, the act of state doctrine [see Chapter 10].

Congress, too, may be constitutionally restricted in matters of foreign affairs. In Immigration & Naturalization Service v. Chadha, the Supreme Court declared unconstitutional a so-called legislative veto that Congress had employed to prevent the President from waiving the deportation of an alien.[155] The *Chadha* decision cast in doubt a great many statutes by which Congress has attempted to limit the President's powers in international relations.[156] The case has, for example, serious implications for the 1973 War Powers Resolution wherein Congress, over President Nixon's veto, strove to ensure that a President

[152] Ibid.

[153] Id., art. II, §§2, 3.

[154] Id., art. III, §2.

[155] 462 U.S. 919 (1983).

[156] Franck & Bob, The Return of Humpty-Dumpty: Foreign Relations Law After the *Chadha* Case, 79 *American Journal of International Law* 912 (1985); M.J. Berry, *The Modern Legislative Veto: Macropolitical Conflict and the Legacy of Chadha* (2017).

would have to consult meaningfully with Congress before committing U.S. forces to combat.[157]

When carefully defined, the concept of foreign relations law is a useful addition to the theoretical constructs of international law and its municipal cousins. One leading U.S. casebook, for example, explains that foreign relations law has as its subject "the interaction between the conduct of United States foreign relations and the constitutional distribution of powers, prerogatives and rights within the nation."[158] Sometimes, however, the notion of foreign relations law conflates U.S. law and international law, usually with the result that U.S. foreign policy objectives are held to ordain findings of international law by a U.S. court. So, in *Alvarez-Machain*, Chief Justice Rehnquist seemed compelled to follow an implausible Executive Branch interpretation of the U.S.-Mexican Extradition Treaty in order to conclude that the Treaty permitted governmental kidnapping within the territory of a foreign sovereign. Faced with a real conflict between U.S. foreign policy and a rule of international law, it better serves the values of international law for a court to admit the difference between foreign relations law and international law, whatever the choice of law it prefers to apply.[159] This is especially true at a time when all three branches of the U.S. government—legislative, executive, and judicial—have, in the words of Thomas Franck, the President of the American Society of International Law, "frittered away the great opportunities" of the post–Cold War decade to transform international relations paying greater attention to the development of international law.[160]

Since the United States is faced with so many problems respecting international law compliance posed not only by the kidnapping of Alvarez-Machain, but also by U.S. obedience or not to ICJ judgments [see Chapter 5], to the laws of armed conflict [see Chapter 6], by

[157] Pub. L. No. 93-148, 87 Stat. 555, 50 U.S.C. §§21541-1548. See Glennon, The War Powers Resolution Ten Years Later: More Politics than Law, 78 *American Journal of International Law* 571 (1984).

[158] T.M. Franck & M.J. Glennon, *Foreign Relations and National Security Law v* (2d ed. 1993).

[159] United States v. Alvarez-Machain, 504 U.S. 655 (1992). That there can be a judicial failure to promote either international or constitutional law when judges hesitate in reviewing governmental actions in international affairs is one of the lessons taught in H.H. Koh, *The National Security Constitution: Sharing Power After the Iran-Contra Affair* (1990).

[160] Franck, Notes from the President, *ASIL Newsletter* (May-June 1998), at 1, 8.

U.S. treatment of enemy combatants [see Chapter 6], by obedience or not to international environmental and trade law [see Chapters 7 and 9], and obedience or not to international criminal law [see Chapter 8], it was good to hear then U.S. Secretary of State, Condoleezza Rice, declare to the American Bar Association in November 2005: "For the United States, an essential element of the rule of law has always been, and still remains, law among nations."[161] There have long been arguments about so-called American exceptionalism in international law, a battle perhaps never so heated as today.[162]

E. INTERNATIONAL LAW, THE INTERPRETATION OF U.S. LAW, AND THE REPUTATION OF THE UNITED STATES

There has also long been controversy about whether or not international law and foreign law may be used to interpret U.S. law and the U.S. Constitution. For example, in 1857, Chief Justice Taney, in his much-reviled opinion for the Supreme Court in Dred Scott v. Sanford, held that African Americans were constitutionally incapable of being citizens of the United States and argued that "[n]o one, we presume, supposes that any change in public opinion or feeling, in relation to this unfortunate race, in the civilized nations of Europe or in this country, should induce the court to give to the words of the Constitution a more liberal construction in their favor than they were intended to bear when the instrument was framed and adopted."[163] In his dissent, Justice McLean took the opposite position, submitting that at least as of 1857, there was "no nation in Europe which considers itself bound to return to his master a fugitive slave, under the civil law or the law of nations" and that since "the great principles of international law" were part of the common law, Dred Scott should go free.[164]

[161] Secretary of State Emphasizes the Rule of Law Internationally and Internally, 100 *American Journal of International Law* 215, 216 (2006).

[162] See Sitaraman & Wuerth, The Normalization of Foreign Affairs Law, 128 *Harvard Law Review* 1897 (2015).

[163] 60 U.S. (19 How.) 393, 399, 426 (1857).

[164] 60 U.S. (19 How.) 393, 529, 534, 554-555 (McLean, J. dissenting).

The debate about the propriety of using international law and foreign law in the interpretation of U.S. law is presently most heated about issues such as the death penalty, government regulation of same-sex relationships, and U.S. conduct in international affairs. International law skeptics, like Professor Rubenfeld, complain that international law is used as a vehicle for anti-American resentments: "A case in point is the position taken by the 'international community' with respect to the continuing use of capital punishment in some American jurisdictions."[165] International law enthusiasts, like Dean Koh, lament American "exceptionalism" when it justifies unilateralism, and argues instead for a "norm-based internationalism, in which American power derives not just from hard power, but from perceived fidelity to universal values of democracy, human rights, and the rule of law."[166]

In U.S. case law, the modern debate dates to the 1977 opinion of Justice White in Coker v. Georgia, where he found it "not irrelevant here that out of 60 major nations in the world surveyed in 1965, only 3 retained the death penalty for rape where death did not ensue."[167] In 2005, in Roper v. Simmons, there was spirited disagreement among the members of the Supreme Court about international law and foreign opinion. Dissenting from the Court's judgment that it was unconstitutional to execute a juvenile offender who was younger than 18 when the crime was committed, Justice Scalia wrote, "More fundamentally, however, the basic premise of the Court's argument that American law should conform to the laws of the rest of the world ought to be rejected out of hand."[168] However, in his opinion for the Court, Justice Kennedy, looking both at international law and foreign law, held that "[o]ur determination that the death penalty is disproportionate punishment for offenders under 18 finds confirmation in the stark reality that the United States is the only country in the world that continues to give official sanction to the juvenile death penalty."[169]

[165] Rubenfeld, The Two World Orders, in What Good Is International Law?, *Wilson Quarterly* (Autumn 2003), at 21, 22, 32.

[166] Koh, On American Exceptionalism, 55 *Stanford Law Review* 1479, 1527 (2003).

[167] 433 U.S. 584, 596 n.10 (1977).

[168] 543 U.S. 551, 607, 624 (Scalia, J. dissenting).

[169] Id. at 555, 575. For an interesting story about Justice Kennedy's views on the use of international law and foreign law, see Toobin, Swing Shift: How Anthony Kennedy's Passion for Foreign Law Could Change the Supreme Court, *The New Yorker*, Sept. 12, 2005, at 42.

E. International Law, the Interpretation of U.S. Law

A fundamental question from *Dred Scott* to *Alvarez-Machain* and so on to the present day remains the same: How far is the United States willing to go in disregarding international law and foreign opinion in the conduct of our affairs?[170] Does American "exceptionalism" make us an outlier in the world community and diminish our standing?[171] Sadly, the problem of such non-compliance extends not only to traditional "bad actors" in international law, but to other countries that, like the United States, had been longstanding international law enthusiasts. As *The Economist* complained in September 2020 about the United Kingdom, how can the European Union "do a trade deal with a country that is talking of ripping up a treaty it agreed with them less than a year ago?"[172] It was Grotius who reminds us in *The Laws of War and Peace*, written in 1625: "Law is not founded on expedience alone[;] there is no state so powerful that it may not sometime need the help of others outside itself, either for purposes of trade, or even to ward off the forces of many foreign nations united against it."[173]

[170] Janis, *Dred Scott* and International Law, 43 *Columbia Journal of Transnational Law* 763, 807-810 (2005); Agora: The United States Constitution and International Law, 98 *American Journal of International Law* 42 (2004); U.S. Supreme Court Holds Juvenile Death Penalty Unconstitutional, Citing Treaties and Foreign Practice, 99 *American Journal of International Law* 487 (2005).

[171] See the comparative study in Pollack, Who Supports International Law and Why?: The United States, the European Union, and the International Order, 13 *International Journal of Constitutional Law* 873 (2016); S. Patrick, *The Sovereignty Wars: Reconciling America with the World* (2017); International Law and Disorder: The World's Rules-Based Order is Cracking, *The Economist*, May 11, 2024.

[172] Brexit and International Law: A Shocking Breach: Threatening to Break International Law as a Negotiating Tactic Is Both Foolish and Dangerous, *The Economist*, Sept. 12, 2020, at 12.

[173] H. Grotius, *De Jure Belli ac Pacis Libri Tres* 16 (1648) (Kelsey trans. 1913).

CHAPTER 5

International Courts

Idealists have long looked to international adjudication as a means for authoritatively and peacefully settling international disputes. In the wake of the First World War and based on earlier arbitral precedents, history's first universal court of international law, the Permanent Court of International Justice (PCIJ), was established in 1921 under the aegis of the League of Nations. The PCIJ collapsed with its parent organization in the Second World War, but in 1945, a more or less identical tribunal, the International Court of Justice (ICJ), was constituted as the judicial branch of the new United Nations.

Despite the creation of what is known collectively as the International Court or the World Court, two of international law's most persistent and fundamental riddles have bedeviled the PCIJ and the ICJ: How can states be encouraged or even compelled to submit their international conflicts to judges for settlement? How can international judicial decisions, once rendered, be effectively enforced? Though it was long thought that reform of the International Court was the road to progress in international adjudication, today probably more faith is put on the development of alternative regional and specialized international courts. This in turn poses a third question: How does the ICJ fit into an international legal system increasingly characterized by not one, but a multitude of international courts?

A. PUBLIC INTERNATIONAL ARBITRATION

Before turning to the International Court, it might do to briefly set the historical stage. Though a permanent international court is a relatively new phenomenon, public international arbitration, "the settlement of differences between States by judges of their own choice, and on the basis of respect for law,"[1] dates from the earliest recorded times.[2] There was extensive use of international arbitration by the classical Greek city states more than 2,000 years ago, setting an often-admired practice.[3] Early international arbitration was *ad hoc*, taking place only when sovereigns were willing to submit international disputes to impartial umpires. The relatively recent idea of constituting some sort of permanent and compulsory form of international arbitral tribunal is attributed to a number of early modern authors, including Charles Irénée Castel de Saint-Pierre (1658-1743), a French abbot animated by the eighteenth century's passion for reason and by his own disgust with the incessant wars of Louis XIV.[4]

In the nineteenth century, there began to be great and widely shared expectations that someday the courtroom would come to replace the battlefield as the ordinary place for the resolution of interstate conflicts. Such expectations were especially strong in Great Britain and the United States, countries where the rule of law and authoritative courts of law were already important domestic traditions. It seemed only right and proper that what had been achieved domestically should also be gained internationally. There was also, in both countries, a strong religious heritage of pacifism, which played an important part in the outlook of many persons and which encouraged a quest for peaceful alternatives to war.[5] It is easy with the cynicism and hindsight of the

[1] The Hague Convention for the Pacific Settlement of International Disputes, art. XV (signed at The Hague July 29, 1899), *The Hague Conventions and Declarations of 1899 and 1907* 41, 55 (2d ed. Scott 1915) [hereinafter cited as "Hague Arbitration Convention"]. Public international arbitration stands alongside private international arbitration between or among private parties from different countries and mixed international arbitration between private parties and states. See Chapter 9.C.

[2] See J.H. Ralston, *International Arbitration from Athens to Locarno* 153 (1929).

[3] Grynaviski & Hsieh, Hierarchy and Judicial Institutions: Arbitration and Ideology in the Hellenistic World, 69 *International Organization* 697 (2015).

[4] Saint-Pierre, *Projet pour rendre la paix perpétuelle en Europe* (Goyard-Fabre ed. 1981).

[5] P. Brock, *Pacifism in the United States from the Colonial Era to the First World War* (1968).

twenty-first century to forget how genuine and, in many respects, realistic were nineteenth-century aspirations for international adjudication.

The lodestone for many early nineteenth-century Britons and Americans was the Jay Treaty of 1794, an agreement concluded by the governments of the two nations as a means for resolving the many disputes still remaining after Britain's formal acknowledgment of American independence in 1783. The Jay Treaty, which contained several then-remarkable provisions calling for the arbitration of cases concerning territorial delimitation, the seizure of ships at sea, and other confiscations of private property, generated a surprising number of arbitral awards: some 536 between 1799 and 1804.[6] Public international arbitration in its modern form is said to date from the Jay Treaty.[7]

In the wake of the Jay Treaty, more than 200 public international arbitral tribunals were established between 1795 and 1914.[8] A large proportion of these were constituted by one or another of the United States and the United Kingdom, countries where there was considerable popular support for international arbitration as a matter of principle.[9] The United States, for example, was a party to the establishment of various arbitral commissions along the lines of those introduced in the Jay Treaty with Ecuador, Mexico, Peru, Spain, and Venezuela. The busiest of these, the United States-Mexican Mixed Claims Commission of 1868, alone heard more than 2,000 claims between 1871 and 1876.[10]

The success of the Jay Treaty and its progeny stood in stark contrast to the disastrous course of nineteenth-century wars unmoderated by international arbitration. After the War of 1812 engulfed England and the United States in what many saw as a useless and immoral expenditure of life and treasure, there arose, first in the United States

[6] A. Nussbaum, *A Concise History of the Law of Nations* 128-129 (rev. ed. 1954) [hereinafter cited as "Nussbaum"].

[7] A.D. McNair, *Lord McNair: Selected Papers and Bibliography* 198 (1974); Schlochauer, Arbitration, 1 *Encyclopedia of Public International Law* 13, 14 (1981). A useful collection of reports, documents, and commentary about early international arbitration is to be found in the seven volumes of *International Adjudications: Ancient and Modern*, Ancient Series: 1491-1504, Modern Series (6 vols.): 1798-1817 (Moore ed. 1929-1936).

[8] A.M. Stuyt, *Survey of International Arbitrations: 1794-1989* 1-325 (3d ed. 1990), recording 317 arbitrations from the Jay Treaty to the outbreak of World War I; R.L. Buell, *International Relations* 606-607 (2d ed. 1929).

[9] C.D. Davis, *The United States and the First Hague Peace Conference* 16 (1962) [hereinafter cited as "Davis"].

[10] Nussbaum, supra, at 217-218.

and then in the United Kingdom, increasingly vigorous peace societies that actively promoted international courts and arbitration. Beginning with state peace societies organized in New York and Massachusetts by David Low Dodge and Noah Worcester in 1815, peace societies were constructed on a national basis in the United States by William Ladd in 1828 and internationally by Elihu Burritt in 1846. Throughout the nineteenth century, these peace societies, largely made up of religious enthusiasts, provided much of the popular support and a good many of the principles and projects that would culminate in the permanent international courts of the twentieth century.[11]

In the eyes of many, a turning point was reached in 1872 when an international arbitration settled the *Alabama* claims. An *ad hoc* tribunal composed of five judges named by each of the United States, Great Britain, Italy, Switzerland, and Brazil was empowered by the United Kingdom and the United States to decide whether the United Kingdom had violated the rules of international law when it permitted British companies to build warships for the Confederacy and then to supply them during the American Civil War (1861-1865). The *Alabama* tribunal decided that Britain had violated her international obligations as a neutral state and ordered her to pay the United States some $15,500,000 in damages in compensation for the sinking of U.S. shipping.[12] The full sum was paid in British Treasury Bonds on September 9, 1873; the American receipt was framed and hung in 10 Downing Street.[13] Some years earlier, in 1865, Lord Russell, the British Foreign Secretary, had refused to arbitrate the *Alabama* claims on the ground that the British government were "sole guardians of their own honor."[14] The eventual success of the arbitration became a popular demonstration that it was indeed possible for even powerful states to arbitrate important disputes and thereby avoid war.[15] General Grant, who was President during the *Alabama* arbitration, was so encouraged by the

[11] M.W. Janis, *The American Tradition of International Law: Great Expectations 1789-1914* 95-116 (2004).

[12] W.W. Bishop, *International Law* 1023-1027 (3d ed. 1971). Remarkably, the sum constituted about 5% of the U.K.'s government annual budget. Tom Bingham, The *Alabama* Claims Arbitration, 54 *International and Comparative Law Quarterly* 1 (2005).

[13] J.G. Wetter, 1 *The International Arbitral Process: Public and Private* 170-171 (1979).

[14] C.C. Hyde, 2 *International Law Chiefly as Interpreted and Applied by the United States* 120 (1922) [hereinafter cited as "Hyde"].

[15] Nussbaum, supra, at 218-219.

tribunal's deeds that the old warrior predicted "an epoch when a court recognized by all nations will settle international differences instead of keeping large standing armies."[16]

The *Alabama* arbitration also heartened the many members of the peace societies in Great Britain and the United States, some of whom constituted the Association for the Reform and Codification of the Law of Nations in 1873, in hopes that an international code would promote the development of international arbitration.[17] Among others, the American Peace Society and the Universal Peace Union, publisher of an influential magazine, *The Peacemaker*, began to advocate general arbitration treaties and a permanent international arbitral court, as well as gradual disarmament.[18] It was argued that the cause of international adjudication would be much advanced if a permanent arbitral court were available to which countries could submit their disputes.[19] Approaching the turn of the century, British and U.S. pacifists were exerting increasing influence upon their governments. In 1890, a resolution calling for the negotiation of general arbitral agreements was passed by the U.S. House and Senate, and in 1893, the British House of Commons unanimously resolved to cooperate with the United States in negotiating a general arbitration treaty. However, when the two governments finally drafted and signed such an agreement in 1897, the treaty failed ratification by three votes in the U.S. Senate.[20]

Nonetheless, when the Russian Czar convened an international peace conference at The Hague in 1899, the United States, as well as the United Kingdom, pressed for a permanent and universal court of arbitration. Though Germany at first resisted such notions, in time she

[16] Davis, supra, at 13-14.

[17] The group is now known as the International Law Association and has developed a wider ambit, being interested with everything from international commercial arbitration to human rights to space law. See International Law Association, *Report of the Seventy-Second Conference, Toronto 2006* (2006); Stodter, International Law Association, 9 *Encyclopedia of Public International Law* 182 (1986). The ILA has many national branches, including the American Branch of the International Law Association, which usually holds an annual conference in New York City in the Fall.

[18] Davis, supra, at 8-15.

[19] S. Amos, *Remedies for War* 123 (1880). The founder of the American Peace Society, William Ladd, had proposed a "Court of Nations" as early as 1839. G. Schwarzenberger, *William Ladd: An Examination of an American Proposal for an International Equity Tribunal* (1935).

[20] Davis, supra, at 19-34.

weakened her opposition, and the delegates at The Hague adopted the Convention for the Pacific Settlement of International Disputes.[21] This Hague Arbitration Convention, which was somewhat modified by a second Hague Conference in 1907, called on its parties "to use their best efforts to insure the pacific settlement of international differences."[22] States were first to rely on the good offices or mediations of friendly third states to settle their disagreements, that is, on informal diplomatic procedures, but if good offices and mediation proved unsuccessful, then the Convention provided for the establishment of international commissions of inquiry, which were to "elucidat[e] the facts by means of an impartial and conscientious investigation" and then issue non-binding reports.[23] More dramatically, the Convention established the first permanent panel of international arbitrators, the Permanent Court of Arbitration (PCA), from which states could designate specific arbitrators to sit on *ad hoc* tribunals that could hear cases submitted voluntarily by states and render legally binding awards.[24]

The PCA was hailed by one of its creators as the "greatest achievement" of the first Hague Conference.[25] It was confidently predicted that the "nations will, with greater frequency, carry their differences to The Hague; and the Temple, for the construction of which the generous American citizen, Mr. Carnegie, has provided the means, bids fair to be thronged with suitors appealing to reason and international justice for the protection of their national rights."[26] Some peace advocates, however, were greatly disappointed. Professor Holland of Oxford complained that the "substantive provisions contained in the Arbitration Convention really amount to nothing, since everything in them which savoured of an obligatory character was omitted, in deference to the

[21] Id. at 146-172; Bederman, The Hague Peace Conferences of 1899 and 1907, *International Courts for the Twenty-First Century* 9 (M.W. Janis ed. 1992); *The Hague Peace Conferences of 1899 and 1907 and International Arbitration: Reports and Documents* (Rosenne ed. 2001).

[22] Hague Arbitration Convention, supra, art. 1; Eyffinger, A Highly Critical Moment: Role and Record of the 1907 Hague Peace Conference, 54 *Netherlands International Law Review* 197 (2007).

[23] Hague Arbitration Convention, supra, arts. 2-14.

[24] Id., arts. 15-57.

[25] J.H. Choate, *The Two Hague Conferences* 31-32 (1913).

[26] J.W. Foster, *Arbitration and The Hague Court* 76 (1904). Mr. Carnegie's "Temple" is the Peace Palace, presently the home of the International Court of Justice, as well as of the Permanent Court of Arbitration.

arguments of which the German delegation was the mouthpiece."[27] A little less discouraged, President Low of Columbia opined: "No one supposes that this Convention, even if universally signed, will prevent all war, . . . but it will compel the nations, in a new way to justify war to the public opinion of mankind."[28]

In practice, the record of The Hague Arbitration Convention fell somewhere in between the hopes of the optimists and the fears of the pessimists. The Convention was ultimately ratified or adhered to by some 44 states, including the United States, the United Kingdom, Germany, France, Russia, and most of the other then-independent countries of Europe, the Americas, and Asia.[29] By 1914, more than 120 arbitration agreements had been concluded making reference to the PCA,[30] and between 1902 and 1914, there were some 14 arbitral panels and two commissions of inquiry organized under the Convention's auspices.[31]

Two of the better-known rulings emanating from the new arbitral machinery in The Hague were the *Casablanca* and *Dogger Bank* cases. In *Casablanca,* a PCA tribunal settled a potentially explosive dispute over France's measures preventing Germany from removing German and other deserters from the French Foreign Legion in Morocco.[32] In the *Dogger Bank* case, a PCA commission of inquiry composed of admirals from the British, Russian, United States, French, and Austrian navies reported, 4 to 1, that the Russian fleet's attack on English fishing vessels (wildly mistaking them for Japanese torpedo boats in the North Sea) was not justifiable; Russia agreed to pay about $300,000 in compensatory damages.[33]

Overall, however, the great expectations of the nineteenth century for public international arbitration as an alternative to war came to

[27] Quoted in Davis, supra, at 188.

[28] Id. at 191.

[29] Hague Arbitration Convention, supra, at 81-82.

[30] Hyde, supra, at 122.

[31] *Hague Court Reports i-vi* (J.B. Scott ed. 1916) [hereinafter cited as "Hague Court Reports"].

[32] Id. at 110-120; Nussbaum, supra, at 222.

[33] Hague Court Reports, supra, at 403-412. The submission of the *Dogger Bank* case to the PCA in October 1904 probably averted a retaliatory strike by the Royal Navy against the Russian fleet, then *en route* from the Baltic to the Far East to take part in Russia's war with Japan over Manchuria. Lebow, Accidents and Crises: The Dogger Bank Affair, 31 *Naval War College Review* 1 (Summer 1978).

naught. Most important international disputes were, in practice, never submitted to any form of international arbitration. The United States, for example, steadfastly and despite pleas from U.S. pacifists, refused to agree to Spain's request for arbitration to settle the American grievances (such as the sinking of the battleship *Maine*) precipitating the Spanish-American War of 1898.[34] The United States also refused to participate in the Central American Court of Justice, created in 1907, thereby dooming this earliest permanent regional international court [for subsequent and generally more successful permanent regional international courts, see Chapters 8 and 9]. Most fatal of all, Germany and the other great powers of Europe were eager to employ their armies in 1914. There was no European inclination to submit their disagreements to impartial arbiters as urged by U.S. Secretary of State Bryan.[35] Ignoring the PCA, Europe plunged into a most disastrous war.

Between 1914 and its revival in the 1990s, the PCA decided only two inter-state arbitrations.[36] One of the causes for the decline was the emergence of the other Hague courts, the PCIJ in 1921, and the ICJ in 1945. However, this only tells part of the story. Other forms of arbitration, especially investor-state and international commercial arbitral procedures and institutions, have prospered [see Chapter 9].

By itself turning to investor-state and international commercial arbitration in the 1990s, the PCA found a new and useful role to play.[37] Even some public international arbitration returned to the PCA. There were some 31 public or mixed international arbitral awards rendered by the PCA between 1999 and 2009.[38] Since 2014, there have been 29 PCA

[34] Davis, supra, at 35.

[35] Nussbaum, supra, at 222-224. It is interesting to record the mixed voices of the United States. The Central American Court of Justice was actually the proposal of Elihu Root, then U.S. Secretary of State. Scott, The Closing of the Central American Court of Justice, 12 *American Journal of International Law* 380, 380-382 (1918).

[36] Schlochauer, Permanent Court of Arbitration, 1 *Encyclopedia of Public International Law* 157, 162 (1981); www.pca-cpa.org (accessed Mar. 27, 2026); Van Haersolte-Van Hof, The Revitalization of the Permanent Court of Arbitration, 54 *Netherlands International Law Review* 395, 399 (2007) [hereinafter cited as Van Haersolte]. For reports of public international arbitration, PCA and other, after 1920, see United Nations, *Reports of International Arbitral Awards*, Vol. I (1948)-Vol. XXI (1997).

[37] Butler, The Hague Permanent Court of Arbitration, *International Courts for the Twenty-First Century* 43, 44, 50-52 (M.W. Janis ed. 1992); Van Haersolte, supra, at 401-409.

[38] Permanent Court of Arbitration, *Summaries of Awards 1999-2009* (B. Macmahon & F.C. Smith eds. 2010).

arbitrated cases involving inter-state, investor-state, and international commercial arbitrations.[39] As of November 2025, there are seven inter-state, 90 investor-state, and 93 international commercial arbitration disputes pending with the PCA.[40] In 2009, a PCA arbitration involved a delimitation dispute between a state and a liberation movement.[41]

Probably the most important modern PCA arbitration is the inter-state *South China Sea* case of 2016, where the Philippines challenged China in the PCA pursuant to the Law of the Sea Convention [see Chapter 7] respecting Chinese claims to maritime areas off the coast of the Philippines.[42] The PCA largely rejected Chinese claims to historic rights,[43] and held that China could not legally claim sovereignty over islands in the region and had violated the international legal rights of the Philippines in its own maritime economic zones.[44] China rejected the PCA decision,[45] while the Philippines has wavered about what to do with its arbitral victory.[46]

Modern public international arbitration outside the structure of the PCA also has had its successes.[47] A renowned arbitration of the later twentieth century, the *Rann of Kutch* case in 1968, saw a three-judge tribunal, by a majority vote, divide territory disputed by India

[39] www.pca-cpa.org (accessed Oct. 2, 2020).

[40] https://pca-cpa.org/en/cases/ (accessed Nov. 7, 2025).

[41] Government of Sudan v. Sudan People's Liberation Movement/Army, July 22, 2009, www.pca-cpa.org; see Lathrop, Abyei Arbitration, 104 *American Journal of International Law* 66 (2010).

[42] Philippines v. China, Award, PCA Case No. 2013-19 (Convention on the Law of the Sea Annex VII Arbitral Tribunal, 2016). See Ndi, *Philippines v. China*: Assessing the Implications of the South Sea Arbitration, 8 *Australian Journal of Maritime & Ocean Affairs* 269 (2016).

[43] Gao & Jia, The Nine-Dash Line in the South China Sea: History, Status and Implications, 107 *American Journal of International Law* 98 (2013).

[44] Reed & Wong, Maritime Entitlements in the South China Sea: The Arbitration Between the Philippines and China, 110 *American Journal of International Law* 746 (2016).

[45] Guilfoyle, A New Twist in the South China Sea Arbitration: The Chinese Society of International Law's Critical Study, *European Journal of International Law: Talk!*, May 25, 2018.

[46] Beech & Gutierez, As Xi Visits Philippines, Critics Blast Duterte's Conciliatory Approach, *N.Y. Times*, Nov. 21, 2018.

[47] Sohn, The Function of International Arbitration Today, 108 *Hague Recueil* 1, 11-21 (1963); Keith, 100 Years of International Arbitration and Adjudication, 15 *Melbourne Journal of International Law* 1 (2014).

and Pakistan. The arbitration ended armed hostilities between the two countries, and the arbitrators' award was respected; India and Pakistan jointly erected over 800 new boundary pillars.[48] France and the United Kingdom constituted an arbitral panel in 1975 to delimit their continental shelf claims in the English channel.[49] In 1983, Guinea and Guinea-Bissau, in the first sub-Saharan post-Colonial African public international arbitration, empowered an *ad hoc* arbitral tribunal to delimit their maritime boundary.[50] In 1988, the Taba Tribunal settled a dispute between Egypt and Israel over land in the Sinai, rendering an award in favor of Egypt that was probably justifiable to Israeli public opinion in a way that a negotiated settlement would not have been.[51]

In 1986 and 1990, New Zealand and France twice held arbitral proceedings relating to the sinking in a New Zealand port of the *Rainbow Warrior*, a Greenpeace vessel sometimes employed to disrupt and protest French nuclear testing in the South Pacific. The first arbitration concluded that France should pay New Zealand $7 million and confine two French secret service agents involved in the sinking and imprisoned in New Zealand to a French Pacific island for at least three years. When France released both agents early, the second tribunal ordered France to pay an additional $2 million.[52]

[48] Case Concerning the Indo-Pakistan Western Boundary (*Rann of Kutch*) Between India and Pakistan, Award of February 19, 1968, 17 *United Nations Reports of International Arbitral Awards* 1 (1980). See Wetter, The Rann of Kutch Arbitration, 65 *American Journal of International Law* 346, 355-356 (1971).

[49] Arbitration Between the United Kingdom of Great Britain and Northern Ireland and the French Republic on the Delimitation of the Continental Shelf, Decisions of the Court of Arbitration, June 30, 1977, March 14, 1978, 18 *International Legal Materials* 397 (1979).

[50] Arbitration Tribunal for the Delimitation of the Maritime Boundary Between Guinea and Guinea-Bissau, Award of February 14, 1985, 25 *International Legal Materials* 251 (1986).

[51] Shaw, The International Court of Justice: A Practical Perspective, 46 *International & Comparative Law Quarterly* 831, 832 (1997). Boundary disputes are a favorite subject of international arbitration. Between 1951 and 2021, international tribunals decided 53 boundary disputes—22 involving land boundaries, 19 maritime, and 12 a mix. Compliance was high, 85% followed in full or in part. Shaffer, The Rule of Law Under Challenge, 39 *American Society of International Law Newsletter*, January/March 2023, at 1.

[52] France-New Zealand Arbitration Tribunal, 74 *International Law Reports* 241, 82 *International Law Reports* 500 (1990). See Davidson, The Rainbow Warrior Arbitration Concerning the Treatment of the French Agents Mafart and Prieur, 40 *International & Comparative Law Quarterly* 446 (1991); Samuel, Sinking of the Rainbow Warrior was Personally Sanctioned by Mitterand, *The Telegraph* (London), July 11, 2005, at 12.

A. Public International Arbitration

Arbitral tribunals decided maritime delimitation cases between Canada and France relating to St. Pierre and Miquelon in 1992, and between Eritrea and Yemen in the Red Sea in 1999.[53] There have also been a fair number of international claims tribunals, not unlike those of the nineteenth century, where states have provided special courts to hear complaints about the expropriation of foreign investments, of which the Iran-United States Claims Tribunal in The Hague is only one example [see Chapter 8].[54]

Inter-state arbitration has been on a roller-coaster ride. While there were some 178 recorded inter-state arbitrations between 1900 and 1945, there were only 43 arbitrations between 1945 and 1990, even though there were many more states than before the Second World War.[55] Some non-Western states, like China, had unhappy experiences with imposed international arbitrations in the nineteenth and early twentieth centuries and are nowadays adverse to participation in either international arbitration or adjudication.[56] However, since the 1990s, inter-state arbitration both within and outside the PCA has increased in numbers and importance. Along with the regional and specialized international courts, public international arbitration challenges the role of the International Court of Justice.[57]

The award was paid into a Friendship Fund, which between 1991 and 2019 supported scholarly exchanges between the two countries. *The New Zealand France Friendship Fund: The Fund's Acievements 1991 to 2019* (2020).

[53] Court of Arbitration for the Delimitation of Maritime Areas Between Canada and France: Decision in Case Concerning Delimitation of Maritime Areas (St. Pierre and Miquelon), June 10, 1992, 31 *International Legal Materials* 1145 (1992); Reisman, Eritrea-Yemen Arbitration, Dec. 17, 1999, 94 *American Journal of International Law* 721 (2000).

[54] See *Iran-United States Claims Tribunal Reports*, Vol. 1: 1981-1982 (1983), to Vol. 38: 2004-2009 (2010); W. Mapp, *The Iran-United States Claims Tribunal: The First Ten Years 1981-1991* (1993); Bederman, The United Nations Compensation Commission and the Tradition of International Claims Settlement, 27 *New York University Journal of International Law & Politics* 1 (1994).

[55] Gray and Kingsbury, Inter-State Arbitration Since 1945: Overview and Evaluation, *International Courts for the Twenty-First Century* 55, 56-57 (M.W. Janis ed. 1992).

[56] Ku, China and the Future of International Adjudication, 27 *Maryland Journal of International Law* 154 (2012).

[57] See Akande, The Peace Palace Heats Up Again: But Is Inter-State Arbitration Overtaking the ICJ?, *European Journal of International Law: Talk!*, Feb. 17, 2014.

B. THE FOUNDATIONS OF THE INTERNATIONAL COURT

The death and destruction wrought by the First World War had a significant impact upon attitudes toward world politics. Many more people than before, statesmen and citizens alike, came to believe that new steps in international organization had to be ventured. There was a feeling that sovereign states and traditional balance of power politics had failed enormously. It was not so much that there had been a war (after all, there had been wars for all of recorded time), but that the so-called Great War had been so unnecessarily brutal and so exceptionally pointless. There seemed to be no good end or justification for World War I's terrible slaughter. In the fourteenth of his famous Fourteen Points, Woodrow Wilson proposed a "general association of nations . . . formed under specific covenants for the purpose of affording mutual guarantees of political independence and territorial integrity to great and small states alike."[58] From this proposal issued the League of Nations [see Chapter 7], part and parcel of which was the Permanent Court of International Justice.

As early as 1918, a British government committee on the League of Nations proposed that a court be designed to settle disputes arising out of the forthcoming treaty of peace and that the tribunal also be empowered to hear cases concerning other international disagreements. At Versailles in 1919, the British and the Americans, the two traditional advocates of international courts, vigorously lobbied the other victorious powers for a League Court. As a result, provisions calling for such a court were included in the Peace Treaty.

In 1920, as one of its first priorities, the Executive Council of the newly created League of Nations commissioned an Advisory Committee of Jurists composed of representatives from Belgium, Brazil, France, Great Britain, Italy, Japan, the Netherlands, Norway, Spain, and the United States to prepare a draft statute for what came to be the PCIJ and later the ICJ. The League of Nations readied a Protocol for the Permanent Court of International Justice, which was signed and ratified

[58] T.W. Wilson, 14th Point in Address of January 8, 1918, *The Public Papers of Woodrow Wilson,* 1 *War and Peace* 161 (R.S. Baker & W.E. Dodd eds. 1925).

by many states. Judges were elected to the Court in 1921. The PCIJ was formally inaugurated on February 15, 1922.[59]

The work of the Permanent Court of International Justice is discussed below, integrated with the work of the International Court of Justice into a discussion of the International Court in general. Suffice it to say at this point that between 1921 and 1945 the PCIJ rendered some 83 judgments, substantive orders, and advisory opinions.[60] The high-water mark for the PCIJ, as for the League of Nations, came in the 1920s. Not only was the Court employed relatively frequently with respect to the post-Versailles settlement in Europe, but also there were thousands of cases decided by the Mixed Arbitral Tribunals and claims commissions set up after World War I.[61]

However, the United States, though it kept a judge on the PCIJ, never ratified the Court's Protocol. In 1934, the Roosevelt administration drafted legislation providing for U.S. adherence to the PCIJ, but the Senate, supporting the measure by a vote of 52 to 36, failed to secure the needed two-thirds majority for passage. As war clouds settled over Europe and Asia later in the 1930s, U.S. isolationism only increased. Hopes for the PCIJ in the United States and elsewhere faded.[62]

The PCIJ played little part in forestalling and none in moderating the Second World War. It held its last public sitting on December 4, 1939, and met in October 1945 only to facilitate the transfer of its archives to the new ICJ. All the judges of the PCIJ resigned on January 31, 1946, and the PCIJ was formally dissolved in April of that year.[63]

Despite the failure of the League of Nations (with which the fate of the PCIJ was inextricably tied) during the awful conflagration of

[59] A.S. Bustamente, *The World Court* 79-111 (Read trans. 1925); O. Spierman, "Who Attempts Too Much Does Nothing Well," The 1920 Advisory Committee of Jurists and the Statute of the Permanent Court of International Justice, 73 *British Yearbook of International Law* 187 (2003); Janis, Book Review: Morris ed., *The League of Nations and the Development of International Law: A New Intellectual History of the Advisory Committee of Jurists,* 10 *Jus Gentium* 419 (1925).

[60] *I.C.J. Yearbook 1984-1985*, 189-194.

[61] League of Nations, *Ten Years of World Co-operation* 125-163 (1930); Gross, The International Court of Justice: Considerations of Requirements for Enhancing Its Role in the International Legal Order, 1 *The Future of the International Court of Justice* 22, 28-29 (Gross ed. 1976) [hereinafter cited as "Gross"].

[62] C. Hull, 1 *The Memoirs of Cordell Hull* 387-390 (1948).

[63] Registry of the International Court of Justice, *The International Court of Justice* 17-19 (1976).

the Second World War, there continued to be considerable interest in a new permanent and universal international court. In January 1942, the foreign ministers of the American republics resolved in Rio de Janeiro to charge the Inter-American Juridical Committee to study and make recommendations about post-war international organization. In July of the same year, U.S. Secretary of State Cordell Hull declared his country's intent to promote the reestablishment of the International Court.[64] Even greater enthusiasm for a new international court was to be found in Britain. In 1941, the British government asked its allies to join with it in studying the future of the International Court, an offer at first declined. By 1943, however, the British were able to constitute an Informal Inter-Allied Committee of Experts to investigate and make suggestions about a new post-war court. Composed of delegates from Britain, Belgium, Canada, Czechoslovakia, France, Greece, Luxembourg, the Netherlands, New Zealand, Norway, and Poland, the Committee of Experts reported in February 1944. Partly because the reputation of the PCIJ had been less sullied by the outbreak of war than had that of the League of Nations,[65] the Committee concluded that a new international court should be constituted after the war in much the same form as the prewar International Court.[66]

At the negotiations among the United States, the Soviet Union, and Great Britain at Dumbarton Oaks in August and September of 1944, it was the governments' turn to decide to reestablish the International Court. Following the recommendation of the Committee of Experts, it was agreed that the statute of the new Court should be more or less the same as that of the PCIJ. The powers at Dumbarton Oaks, however, rejected the suggestion of the Committee that the new post-war Court not be so closely linked to any new international organization as the PCIJ had been joined to the League.[67] In March 1945, a Committee of Jurists made up of delegates of 44 states was constituted to prepare a draft statute for a new Court. The Committee submitted its report to the San Francisco Conference, which in June 1945 included the

[64] S. Rosenne, *The Law and Practice of the International Court* 26-27 (1965) [hereinafter cited as "Rosenne"].

[65] O.J. Lissitzyn, *The International Court of Justice: Its Role in the Maintenance of International Peace and Security* 1 (1951) [hereinafter cited as "Lissitzyn"].

[66] Rosenne, supra, at 27-28.

[67] Id. at 28-31.

Statute of the International Court of Justice in the U.N. Charter. The Charter established the International Court of Justice as "the principal judicial organ of the United Nations" and made all members of the United Nations parties to it.[68] The ICJ Statute in most material respects reflected the provisions of that constituting the PCIJ. Thus, despite differences in name and in some organizational detail, the two courts are fundamentally the same and are usually treated as one continuous organization.[69] New members of the International Court were elected on February 6, 1946; a formal re-inauguration was held in The Hague on April 18, 1946. When the *Corfu Channel* case was submitted to it on May 22, 1947, the war-time hiatus had ended.

The ICJ Statute provides for 15 judges, elected by separate absolute majorities of the General Assembly and Security Council, and serving nine-year renewable terms.[70] Since the first election to the Permanent Court of International Justice in 1921, nationals of France and the United States have always sat on the World Court. From 1946 to 2023, there was always a national of the Soviet Union or Russia. From 1921 to 2017, there was also always a British national. However, in 2017, the U.K. candidate, Sir Christopher Greenwood, a sitting International Court judge, was defeated by the Indian candidate, a blow to British prestige and influence, a development of "huge significance—not just to the court, but to the United Kingdom's standing in the world," and, in 2023, as a consequence of Russia's invasion of the Ukraine, the Russian judge was not re-elected.[71] The other judges have reflected the international political patterns of the day. So, for example, in 1921, there were ten European judges, a U.S. judge, two judges from Latin America, and two from Asia.

[68] Charter of the United Nations, arts. 92, 93(1), 59 Stat. 1031, T.S. No. 993, 3 Bevans 1153 (signed at San Francisco June 26, 1945; entered into force October 24, 1945) [hereinafter cited as "U.N. Charter"].

[69] G. Elian, *The International Court of Justice* 42-43 (1971); Lissitzyn, supra, at 1; Rosenne, supra, at 42.

[70] Statute of the International Court of Justice, as annexed to the Charter of the United Nations, arts. 2-15, 59 Stat. 1031, T.S. No. 993, 3 Bevans 1153 (signed at San Francisco, June 26, 1945; entered into force October 24, 1945) [hereinafter cited as "ICJ Statute"].

[71] Lansdale, How the UK Lost International Court of Justice Place to India, *BBC News*, Nov. 21, 2017, https://www.bbc.com/news/uk-politics-42063664 (Oct. 14, 2020); Russia Loses International Court of Justice Seat for the First Time, https://meduza.io/en/news/2023/11/10/russia-loses-international-court-of-justice-seat-for-the-first-time-in-history, Nov. 10, 2023 (accessed on Nov. 8, 2025)

By 2025, the number of European judges had fallen to four (France, Slovakia, Germany, and Romania); there was still a U.S. judge and two from Latin America (Brazil and Mexico), but now there were three from Asia (China, India, and Japan), three from sub-Saharan Africa (Uganda, South Africa, and Kenya), one from an Islamic country (Jordan), and a judge from Australia.[72]

Judges are permitted to take on supplemental employment as arbitrators, e.g., for the PCA, "outside commitments" that may lamentably "hamper the efficient discharge by the Court of its judicial work."[73] Only after 75 years was a woman finally elected to the ICJ, Professor Rosalyn Higgins of the United Kingdom in 1995.[74] Judge Higgins is no longer on the Court, but as of 2025, there are five women—from Australia, China, Uganda, Kenya, and the United States.[75] Traditionally, there has also been a disparity between male and female advocates before the Court.[76] *Ad hoc* judges may be appointed to the Court for particular cases when a state party to a dispute does not have a national on the Court. Although *ad hoc* judges, like other sitting judges who are nationals of one of the parties, are not meant to "represent" their states, *ad hoc* judges in practice have several times been in a minority of one respecting a judgment of the Court against their country.[77]

[72] www.icj-cij.org (accessed on Mar. 27, 2026).

[73] Thirlway, The International Court of Justice 1989-2009: At the Heart of the Dispute Settlement System?, 57 *Netherlands International Law Review* 347, 393 (2010).

[74] I.C.J. Communiqué No. 95/20 (July 13, 1995). A good account of the politics attendant to an election of ICJ judges is to be found in Blokker & Muller, The 1996 Elections to the International Court of Justice: New Tendencies in the Post-Cold War Era?, 47 *International & Comparative Law Quarterly* 211 (1998). States tend to elect legally cautious judges, usually former government officials, and may refuse to re-elect judges who show too much judicial independence. Franck, Common Sense and Presumption at the ICJ, 2003-2004 *American Branch (ILA) Proceedings* 25.

[75] www.icj-cji.org (accessed on 8 Nov. 2025).

[76] Kumar & Rose, A Study of Lawyers Appearing Before the International Court of Justice, 25 *European Journal of International Law* 893 (2014).

[77] ICJ Statute, supra, art. 31; Rosenne, supra, at 204-205; Giorgetti, The Challenge and Recusal of Judges on the International Court of Justice, *Challenges and Recusals of Judges and Arbitrators in International Courts and Tribunals* 3 (C. Giorgetti ed. 2015). For more on the structure and procedure of the ICJ and other international courts, see J.G. Merrills, *International Dispute Settlement* (6th ed. 2017).

C. THE ROLES OF THE INTERNATIONAL COURT

1. The Record of the International Court

There has been a considerable fascination with the International Court, more than the sum of its practice might appear to warrant.[78] Partly the fascination is due to exaggerated hopes and fears about the potential for international adjudication. On the one hand, optimists have long expected that an international court would be a path to world peace. On the other hand, pessimists have equally long dismissed international adjudication as an unrealistic and misleading fantasy.[79] If we look to the actual record, the work of the Court falls in an undramatic way somewhere in between. The true story is that the International Court has been an occasional, but real, actor on the world stage.

The moderate record of the Court is seen in its case load. In 25 years, from 1921 to 1945, the PCIJ issued 31 judgments, roughly one every year. In 80 years, from 1946 to 2025, the ICJ registered some 201 cases, an average between two and three cases annually.[80] Although there have been more and less busy years (the International Court rendered no decision at all in 1921, between 1941 and 1947, and in 1967, 1977, and 1983), over a century there seems to be little change in the level of practice before the Court. After so long, the truth is that the International Court neither grows in prominence (the optimists' dream) nor simply fades away (the pessimists' expectation).

The real but unspectacular utility of the Court seems to be a function of the kinds of cases the Court is able to hear. Article 34 of the Court's Statute dictates that "[o]nly States may be parties in cases

[78] The vast literature relating to the International Court is reflected in the annual bibliography of books and articles relating to the Court published by the Court's Registry. See, for example, *1984 Bibliography of the International Court of Justice* 77 (1985) where, explaining the need to begin renumbering titles, it is mentioned that the numbers in the old series "had run into five figures and reference had accordingly become too complex." This commentary revolves around an average of fewer than four cases a year!

[79] L. Oppenheim, 1 *International Law* 87-88 (8th ed. H. Lauterpacht 1955).

[80] *I.C.J. Yearbook 2017-2018*, www.icj-cij.org (Oct. 17, 2020); International Court of Justice Cases, www.icj-cij. org (Nov. 8, 2025).

before the Court."[81] By closing the door to private parties, the founders of the International Court foreclosed, as it turns out, the most fertile source of international litigation [contrast the records of regional international courts where private litigation is, in some circumstances, permitted; see Chapters 8 and 9]. This leaves it to states to initiate suits and to international organizations to request advisory opinions. Since governmental authorities almost always prefer to settle international disputes themselves in diplomatic and political ways rather than entrust cases to judicial bodies, the presumption in almost any circumstance is that the International Court will not be employed.

When is the presumption against use of the Court actually overcome? In practice, and reflecting the jurisdictional provisions of the ICJ Statute, generally there are three such situations: first, when two or more states agree to engage the Court more or less as an arbiter; second, when a single state, looking to the political capital to be made from using the Court as a public forum, relies on a form of compulsory jurisdiction to make a recalcitrant state a party to a Court proceeding; and, third, when an international organization requests an advisory opinion from the Court. The first category of employment has been by far the most successful in terms of the actual effectiveness of the Court. The second and third have been, as one might expect, far more problematic.

2. *The International Court as Arbiter*

Article 36(1) of the Statute of the International Court confers jurisdiction upon the Court, *inter alia*, in "all cases which the parties refer to it." In cases of specially conferred or *ad hoc* jurisdiction, the International Court functions rather like a public international arbitration, albeit one where the membership of the tribunal is pre-established. In these arbitral-like cases, the Court receives its grant of jurisdiction by way of a special agreement, a *compromis*, concluded between the consenting states. The *compromis* is itself a treaty.

The *compromis* normally not only confers jurisdiction upon the Court, but also exactly defines the legal question set before the judges. It may also indicate the rules of law to be applied by the Court, though, of course, Article 38 of the Statute of the International Court instructs

[81] ICJ Statute, supra.

the Court as to the sources of international law generally available to it.[82] A typical *compromis* is that which generated the *North Sea Continental Shelf* cases [see Chapter 3]. West Germany, Denmark, and the Netherlands specially agreed as follows:

> (1) The International Court of Justice is requested to decide the following question: What principles and rules of international law are applicable to the delimitation as between the Parties of the areas of the continental shelf in the North Sea. . . .
> (2) The governments . . . shall delimit the continental shelf in the North Sea as between their countries by agreement in pursuance of the decision requested from the International Court of Justice.[83]

Most of the Court's truly effective decisions have been made in cases specially submitted to it by such *ad hoc* agreements of states. Perhaps it is all too obvious, but it seems to be the rule that the Court's decision is most often respected when all states concerned have voluntarily come to the Court and have looked to it for an authoritative determination of a legal issue. Such special submissions have, however, not usually been sought in matters highly charged or of great political moment.

As good an example as any of the Court's arbitral-like cases is *Minquiers and Ecrehos*. In a special agreement, dated December 29, 1950, the United Kingdom and France sent the following question to the ICJ: "The Court is requested to determine whether the sovereignty over the islets and rocks (in so far as they are capable of appropriation) of the Minquiers and Ecrehos groups respectively belongs to the United Kingdom or the French Republic."[84] The Minquiers and Ecrehos lie between the British island of Jersey and the French Normandy coast. Perhaps because the islets had so long been of such little value, there had never been a definitive determination of their true sovereign. As the continental shelf and its oil and gas resources began to be delimited among countries, however, it became increasingly important to know who owned the islets. Unable to settle the matter through diplomatic exchange, Britain and France turned to the Court.

[82] Ibid. Article 38 is set out in full in Chapter 2.
[83] 1969 I.C.J. Reports 4, 6-8.
[84] 1953 I.C.J. Reports 47, 49.

Reading through the case, we can see some clues as to why matters like this one are entrusted to international adjudication. First, *Minquiers and Ecrehos* was a dispute where judicial answers to questions of international law could be decisive of the issues at hand. The great bulk of the Court's opinion was given over to an analysis of historical facts concerning displays of sovereignty over the islands.[85] The Court's final decision was based upon a judicial weighing, here with respect to the Ecrehos, of these evidences of sovereignty:

> The Court, being now called upon to appraise the relative strength of the opposing claims to sovereignty over the Ecrehos in the light of the facts considered above, finds that the Ecrehos group in the beginning of the thirteenth century was considered and treated as an integral part of the fief of the Channel Islands which were held by the English King, and that the group continued to be under the dominion of that King, who in the beginning of the fourteenth century exercised jurisdiction in respect thereof. The Court further finds that British authorities during the greater part of the nineteenth century and in the twentieth century have exercised State functions in respect of the group. The French Government, on the other hand, has not produced evidence showing that it has any valid title to the group. In such circumstances it must be concluded that the sovereignty over the Ecrehos belongs to the United Kingdom.[86]

Second, a reading of the case indicates that the resolution of the dispute was not so crucial to Britain or to France that a settlement of it by the Court contrary to either country's wishes would prove to be politically unacceptable. Very few British or French citizens probably knew then or know today where or what the Minquiers and Ecrehos are. Both the British and the French governments probably could

[85] The Court looked at such evidence as medieval grants, domestic legal proceedings, sanitary edicts, regulation of fishing, and criminal inquests. Id. at 53-67. Territorial disputes continue to constitute a good number of the cases actually decided by the ICJ. See http://www.icj-cij.org, e.g., the cases: Land and Maritime Boundary Between Cameroon and Nigeria (Cameroon v. Nigeria; Equatorial Guinea Intervening), Judgment of Oct. 10, 2002; Sovereignty over Pulau Ligitan and Pulau Sipadan (Indonesia/Malaysia), Judgment of Dec. 17, 2002; Frontier Dispute (Benin/Niger), Judgment of July 12, 2005; Territorial and Maritime Dispute (Nicaragua v. Colombia), Judgment of Nov. 19, 2012; and Frontier Dispute (Burkina Faso/Niger), Judgment of Apr. 16, 2013.

[86] 1953 I.C.J. Reports 47, 67.

accept the political repercussions of an adverse decision. In fact, to some degree the losing government might be better off in domestic public opinion having the Court find against it than if it simply gave the islets and rocks away as the result of diplomatic negotiation.[87]

These two factors of decisive legal issues and low political cost characterize many of the ICJ's specially submitted cases. One might, as further examples, note the *Lotus* case between France and Turkey, concerning the legality of Turkish judicial proceedings relating to a collision of ships on the high seas,[88] the *Brazilian Loans* case between France and Brazil about lawful ways to repay certain state borrowings,[89] and the *Sovereignty over Certain Frontier Land* case between Belgium and the Netherlands.[90] In these and other cases, where the Court has served more or less as an arbiter between presently consenting states, the success rate of the Court's decisions has been high.

A manifestation of the occasional inclination of states to use the International Court as an arbiter comes in the recent use of an underutilized provision of the Court's Statute, Article 26, which permits, *inter alia*, the Court "at any time [to] form a chamber for dealing with a particular case[, t]he number of judges to constitute such a chamber [to] be determined by the Court with the approval of the parties."[91] The United States and Canada first had such a chamber constituted in 1982, with five judges to hear the *Gulf of Maine* case decided in 1984.[92] Since then, Burkina Faso and Mali, the United States and Italy, El Salvador and Honduras (twice), and Benin and Niger have constituted five more chambers of five judges; judgments have been rendered by all four.[93] Though it may well be that in theory in some circumstances countries might be more comfortable with a specially

[87] Some Normans still protest British sovereignty over the islets, e.g., temporarily "invading" Ecrehos to raise a Norman flag and hold a mass. See Binney & Hornsby, Jersey Police Outwit Norman Invasion, *The Times* (London), July 11, 1994, at 5. See The British Islands that Disappear Every Day, *BBC Travel*, https://www.bbc.com/travel/article/20220828-the-british-islands-that-disappear-every-day (Aug. 29, 2022).

[88] 1927 P.C.I.J. Reports, ser. A, no. 10.

[89] 1929 P.C.I.J. Reports, ser. A, no. 15.

[90] 1959 I.C.J. Reports 209.

[91] ICJ Statute, supra, art. 26(2).

[92] 1984 I.C.J. Reports 246 (1984), reprinted in 23 *International Legal Materials* 1197 (1984); see Schneider, The Gulf of Maine Case: The Nature of an Equitable Result, 79 *American Journal of International Law* 539 (1985).

[93] www.icj-cij.org (April 4, 2024).

selected chamber of the Court hearing cases than with having the full Court entrusted with the matter,[94] a possibility more thoroughly developed below, in practice, the use of chambers has fallen off, no new chambers having been constituted in more than 20 years.[95]

3. *The Compulsory Jurisdiction of the International Court*

When the International Court hears a case pursuant to a form of compulsory jurisdiction, it acts more or less like any ordinary municipal court where parties are subject to jurisdiction without their immediate consent. However, even in cases of compulsory jurisdiction, states must have originally consented to the Court's jurisdiction. The necessity for consent has been termed a "serious set-back" by Pieter Kooijmans, formerly a Dutch judge on the ICJ.[96] "It prevents the Court from playing a role comparable to that of the European Court of Justice in Luxembourg or the European Court of Human Rights in Strasbourg, whose jurisdiction flows automatically from their basic treaties."[97]

The Court has a general, albeit optional, compulsory jurisdiction provision, Article 36(2), which reads as follows:

> The States parties to the present Statute may at any time declare that they recognize as compulsory *ipso facto* and without special agreement, in relation to any other State accepting the same obligation, the jurisdiction of the Court in all legal disputes concerning:
>
> (a) the interpretation of a treaty;
>
> (b) any question of international law;
>
> (c) the existence of any fact which, if established, would constitute a breach of an international obligation;
>
> (d) the nature or extent of the reparation to be made for the breach of an international obligation.[98]

[94] Ostrihansky, Chambers in the International Court of Justice, 37 *International & Comparative Law Quarterly* 30 (1988).

[95] www.icj-cij.org (Oct. 18, 2020).

[96] Kooijmans, The ICJ in the 21st Century: Judicial Restraint, Judicial Activism, or Proactive Judicial Policy, 56 *International & Comparative Law Quarterly* 741, 743 (2007).

[97] Ibid.

[98] ICJ Statute, supra.

C. The Roles of the International Court

The general compulsory jurisdiction of the International Court is limited to those disputes where both parties have accepted Article 36(2). As of November 2025, some 74 states had accepted the Court's general compulsory jurisdiction.[99] An example of a straightforward acceptance of the Court's Article 36(2) jurisdiction is that made by Sweden by its Permanent Representative to the United Nations on April 6, 1957:

> On behalf of the Royal Swedish Government, I declare that it accepts as compulsory *ipso facto* and without special agreement, in relation to any other State accepting the same obligation, the jurisdiction of the International Court of Justice, in accordance with Article 36, paragraph 2, of the Statute of the said Court, for a period of five years as from 6 April 1957. This obligation shall be renewed by tacit agreement for further periods of the same duration unless notice of abrogation is made at least six months before the expiration of any such period. The above-mentioned obligation is accepted only in respect of disputes which may arise with regard to situations or facts subsequent to 6 April 1947.[100]

The acceptances of many states of the ICJ's general compulsory jurisdiction are saddled with reservations. A well-known example of such a reservation to Article 36(2) was the so-called Connolly Amendment, whereby the United States excepted from the Court's compulsory jurisdiction "disputes with regard to matters which are essentially within the domestic jurisdiction of the United States of America as determined by the United States of America."[101] Since both parties to a dispute must have accepted the Court's general compulsory jurisdiction before the Court can be seized of a case pursuant to Article 36(2) and since a reservation of the complaining state can be invoked by the state against which suit is brought, there is sometimes not much room in which the Court's compulsory jurisdiction can effectively operate. So, for example, in the *Aegean Sea Continental Shelf* case, Greece's reservation excepting "disputes relating to the territorial status of Greece" was held by the Court to leave it without jurisdiction with respect to a maritime claim made by Greece against Turkey.[102] Similarly, in the *Certain Norwegian*

[99] www.icj-cij.org (Nov. 10, 2025).
[100] *2009-2010 Report of the International Court of Justice* 140-141 (2010).
[101] *I.C.J. Yearbook 1984-1985*, 100.
[102] 1978 I.C.J. Reports 3, 22-37.

Loans case, the Court permitted Norway to rely on France's reservation excluding "matters which were essentially within the national jurisdiction as understood by the Government of the French Republic," a reservation modeled on the Connolly Amendment.[103]

Some states, previously submitting to the Article 36(2) compulsory jurisdiction of the Court, have subsequently withdrawn their consent to such general jurisdiction. So, for example, France withdrew from the compulsory jurisdiction of the International Court after the Court accepted jurisdiction in the *Nuclear Tests* cases brought by Australia and New Zealand.[104] The United States, upset with the Court's decision that it had jurisdiction in a suit brought by Nicaragua to complain about the mining of its harbors,[105] also terminated its acceptance of Article 36(2). In the 1985 press conference announcing the decision of the United States to withdraw, President Reagan's office stated that America's "experience with compulsory jurisdiction has been deeply disappointing."[106]

The United States, nonetheless, still accepts in principle the compulsory jurisdiction of the Court when cases are referred to it by treaties and conventions in force.[107] This other form of compulsory jurisdiction is rooted in Article 36(1) of the Court's Statute, which extends the Court's jurisdiction, *inter alia*, to "all matters specially provided for in the Charter of the United Nations or in treaties and conventions in force."[108] Though the U.N. Charter has no such special clause, there are hundreds of bilateral or multilateral treaties that provide that disputes relating to their terms shall be settled by the International Court of Justice.[109] Compulsory jurisdiction based on bilateral or multilateral treaties stands quite apart from general compulsory jurisdiction pursuant to Article 36(2). States that have not accepted or no longer accept Article 36(2) are still often

[103] 1957 I.C.J. Reports 9. See Hudson, The Thirty-Sixth Year of the World Court, 52 *American Journal of International Law* 1-4 (1958).

[104] 1974 I.C.J. Reports 253. Altogether, some 15 states have withdrawn from Article 36(2) jurisdiction between 1951 and 2012, including Bolivia, Brazil, China, El Salvador, France, Guatemala, Iran, Israel, Nauru, South Africa, Thailand, and Turkey. *I.C.J. Yearbook 2015-2016*, 60.

[105] 1984 I.C.J. Reports 169.

[106] *Congressional Record*, Oct. 9, 1985, at E4540.

[107] See Noyes, The Functions of Compromissory Clauses in U.S. Treaties, 34 *Virginia Journal of International Law* 831 (1994).

[108] ICJ Statute, supra.

[109] *I.C.J. Yearbook 2017-2018*, www.icj-cij.org (Nov. 10, 2025).

parties to international conventions vesting Article 36(1) compulsory jurisdiction in the ICJ.[110] Sadly, respecting Article 36(1), here too the United States is "walking away" from the ICJ.[111]

In practice, whether the Court's compulsory jurisdiction is based generally on Article 36(2) or particularly on Article 36(1), the problems of ineffectiveness have been the same. Cases brought pursuant to either form of compulsory jurisdiction usually involve recalcitrant states, unlikely to voluntarily comply with any unfavorable Court decision and unlikely, too, to be compelled by any available means to respect the Court's judgment. In such cases, the Court has sometimes been reluctant to render a decision that it fears will prove ineffectual and instead has sought "refuge in technical niceties in order to escape a politically explosive issue."[112] For example, in the *South West Africa* case, two former members of the League of Nations, Liberia and Ethiopia, asked the Court to rule that South Africa had violated its legal obligations under a League-conferred Mandate for South West Africa. The Court effectively reversed an earlier ruling and decided that South Africa need not answer for its conduct as Mandatory to individual states, even former members of the League, and that Liberia and Ethiopia had no "legal right or interest appertaining to them in the subject-matter,"[113] a decision Professor Gross termed "the nadir in the fortunes of the Court."[114] In the *Nuclear Tests* cases, Australia and New Zealand argued

[110] The U.S. Senate, in voting its advice and consent in 1986 to the 1948 International Convention on the Prevention and Punishment of the Crime of Genocide, a Convention then ratified by 96 states, adopted the following reservation: "[B]efore any dispute to which the United States is a party may be submitted to the jurisdiction of the International Court of Justice under this article, the specific consent of the United States is required in each case." Leich, Contemporary Practice of the United States Relating to International Law, 80 *American Journal of International Law* 612 (1986). This reservation, the first such attached by the Senate to a multilateral agreement, id. at 615, effectively negates the Genocide Convention's article 36(1) compulsory jurisdiction clause, at least in cases where the United States might be a party. The Genocide Convention was ratified by 152 states in 2020. United Nations, The Genocide Convention, www.un.org (Oct. 16, 2020).

[111] Anderson, Walking Away from the World Court, *Lawfare*, Oct. 5, 2018, www.brookings.edu (Oct. 17, 2020).

[112] Dugard, The Nuclear Tests Cases and the South West Africa Cases: Some Realism About the International Judicial Decision, 16 *Virginia Journal of International Law* 463, 465 (1976).

[113] 1966 I.C.J. Reports 6, 10-11, 28-30, 51.

[114] L. Gross, 2 *The Future of the International Court of Justice* 747 (1976).

that the Court should rule that further atmospheric testing of nuclear weapons by France in the South Pacific would be inconsistent with international law. However, taking notice of French statements made out of court that France intended to pursue a policy of underground testing, the Court held that the claims of Australia and New Zealand "no longer [had] any object and that the Court is therefore not called upon to give a decision thereon."[115] Again, the Court was criticized for being afraid to "grapple with real issues."[116]

More forthright than its reliance on "technical niceties" in *South West Africa* and *Nuclear Tests* was the Court's ruling in *Northern Cameroons.* The Federal Republic of Cameroon complained that the United Kingdom had violated its legal obligations as trustee of the Northern Cameroons by organizing a plebiscite that decided that the territory should achieve independence by incorporation into Nigeria. The U.N. General Assembly then endorsed the result of the plebiscite and terminated the trusteeship agreement with the United Kingdom. Deciding it could not revive the trusteeship agreement, the Court refused to decide Cameroon's claim for a declaratory judgment on the grounds that it would "be impossible for the Court to render a judgment capable of effective application."[117] In other compulsory jurisdiction cases, the Court has rejected the application of the claimant state or found itself without jurisdiction.[118] In any event, in many of its compulsory jurisdiction cases, the Court has, for one reason or another, not attempted to compel an unwilling state to do or not do an act.

Such judicial restraint has had its practical causes. When the Court has chosen to order a recalcitrant state to act, its record of effectiveness has been dismal. In the *Corfu Channel* case, for example, Albania has for

[115] 1974 I.C.J. Reports 253, 256, 263-267, 270, 272.

[116] Rubin, The International Legal Effects of Unilateral Declarations, 71 *American Journal of International Law* 1, 28-29 (1977). In 1996, the Court had occasion to consider the legality of the threat or use of nuclear weapons in two advisory opinions; it rejected a request from the World Health Organization that it deemed fell outside the scope of the WHO's activities, 1996 I.C.J. Reports 66, and responded in a *Lotus*-like fashion of ambiguity to a request from the General Assembly, 1996 I.C.J. Reports 226.

[117] 1963 I.C.J. Reports 15, 18-19, 22-24, 32-33.

[118] See, e.g., Barcelona Traction, 1970 I.C.J. Reports 3; Aegean Sea Continental Shelf, 1978 I.C.J. Reports 3; Application of the International Convention on the Elimination of All Forms of Racial Discrimination (Georgia v. Russian Federation), Preliminary Objections (2011), www.icj-cij.org.

more than four decades refused to pay Court-ordered reparations to Great Britain for damage done to British warships by Albanian mines in international straits.[119] In the *Anglo-Iranian Oil Company* case,[120] Iran disregarded the Court's order to refrain from nationalizing a British corporation pending a final judgment of the Court or agreement between the parties.[121] In the *Fisheries Jurisdiction* case, Iceland refused to obey an order not to enforce a 50-mile fishing zone until the Court ruled on suits brought by the United Kingdom and West Germany.[122] After the *Whaling* case brought by Australia and New Zealand, Japan carried on whaling off Antarctica despite an ICJ judgment condemning the practice; Japan argued that its whaling is now merely "scientific."[123]

What, if anything, is the gain in such cases of disregarded ICJ judgments? In the *United States Diplomatic and Consular Staff in Teheran* case,[124] the U.S. Embassy in Teheran had been occupied, and about 50 Americans, mostly diplomats, were taken hostage on November 4, 1979. The United States, alleging that the Government of Iran was giving "direct support and encouragement to the group holding the

[119] 1949 I.C.J. Reports 4.

[120] 1951 I.C.J. Reports 89.

[121] Id. at 93-94. The Court ultimately ruled that it did not have jurisdiction in the case because Iran's submission to the jurisdiction of the Court excluded disputes resulting from treaties entered into by Iran prior to ratification of its declaration. 1952 I.C.J. Reports 93, 104, 110, 115. See Pahuja & Storr, Rethinking Iran and International Law: *The Anglo-Iranian Oil Company* Case Revisited, in *The International Legal Order: Current Needs and Possible Responses, Essays in Honour of Djamchid Momtaz* 53 (J. Crawford, A. Koroma, S. Mahmoudi & A. Pellet eds. 2017).

[122] Fisheries Jurisdiction Case, 1972 I.C.J. Reports 30. The Court later found it had jurisdiction, 1973 I.C.J. Reports 3, 1973 I.C.J. Reports 49, and ultimately ruled that Iceland could not unilaterally exclude British and German fishing boats from the 50-mile zone. 1974 I.C.J. Reports 3, 1974 I.C.J. Reports 175. The issue has been rendered moot by the emerging international consensus permitting 200-mile fishing zones [see Chapter 7]. With respect to the effectiveness of the Court's orders, see Goldsworthy, Interim Measures of Protection in the International Court of Justice, 68 *American Journal of International Law* 258 (1974).

[123] Whaling in the Antarctic (Australia v. Japan: New Zealand Intervening, Judgment of March 31, 2014, 2014 I.C.J. Reports 2260. See Hodgson-Johnson, Murky Waters: Why Is Japan Still Whaling in the Southern Ocean?, *The Conversation,* Jan. 17, 2017, https://theconversation.com/murky-waters-why-is-japan-still-whaling-in-the-southern-ocean-71402 (Oct. 20, 2020).

[124] 1979 I.C.J. Reports 7 [hereinafter cited as "Diplomatic Staff Case Order"]; 1980 I.C.J. Reports 3 [hereinafter cited as "Diplomatic Staff Case Judgment"].

Embassy,"[125] brought Iran to the International Court pursuant to Article 36(1) compulsory jurisdiction provisions in two multilateral agreements, the 1961 and 1963 Vienna Conventions on Diplomatic and Consular Relations, and in a bilateral accord, the 1955 Treaty of Amity, Economic Relations, and Consular Rights Between the United States and Iran.[126]

Iran, however, refused to appear before the International Court. In a telegram directed to the ICJ, the Iranian Minister for Foreign Affairs argued that "the Court cannot and should not take cognizance of the case." Iran objected that the real dispute between Iran and the United States was "not one of the interpretation and the application of the treaties upon which the American Application is based, but results from an overall situation containing much more fundamental and more complex elements." The Iranian communication stressed the "deep-rootedness" of the Iranian revolution and argued that "any examination of the numerous repercussions thereof is a matter essentially and directly within the national sovereignty of Iran."[127]

[125] United States Application and Request for Interim Measures of Protection in Proceeding Against Iran, 18 *International Legal Materials* 1464, 1469 (1979).

[126] Diplomatic Staff Case Judgment, supra, at 24-28. Article I of the Optional Protocols to each of the two Vienna Conventions reads:

> Disputes arising out of the interpretation or application of the Convention shall lie within the compulsory jurisdiction of the International Court of Justice and may accordingly be brought before the Court by an application made by any party to the dispute being a Party to the present Protocol.

23 U.S.T. 3374, T.I.A.S. No. 7502, 500 U.N.T.S. 241 (done at Vienna April 18, 1961; entered into force April 24, 1964; for the United States December 13, 1972); 21 U.S.T. 325, T.I.A.S. No. 6820, 596 U.N.T.S. 487 (done at Vienna April 24, 1963; entered into force March 19, 1967; for the United States December 24, 1969).

Article XXI (2) of the Iranian-United States Treaty of Amity provides:

> Any dispute between the High Contracting Parties as to the interpretation or application of the present Treaty, not satisfactorily adjusted by diplomacy, shall be submitted to the International Court of Justice, unless the High Contracting Parties agree to settlement by some other pacific means.

8 U.S.T. 899, T.I.A.S. No. 3853, 284 U.N.T.S. 93 (signed at Teheran August 15, 1955; entered into force June 16, 1957).

In 1992, Iran brought a claim against the United States for destruction of an Iranian oil platform, basing the jurisdiction of the ICJ upon Article XXI(2) of the 1955 Treaty of Amity. I.C.J. Communiqué No. 92/26 (November 2, 1992).

[127] Diplomatic Staff Case Order, supra, at 10-11.

C. The Roles of the International Court

In December 1979, the International Court rendered a unanimous interim order that granted provisional measures in favor of the United States. The Court rejected Iran's argument that the dispute was a matter exclusively within the sovereign discretion of Iran, responding that a dispute involving diplomatic and consular relations "is one which by its very nature falls within international jurisdiction."[128] The ICJ reminded Iran that by not appearing, it was depriving "itself of the opportunity of developing its own arguments."[129] The Court based its grant of interlocutory relief on the probable violation of well-understood rules of customary international law, stressed the importance of the legal tradition protecting diplomatic and consular officials and premises, and ordered the immediate release of the hostages.[130]

Though Iran failed to comply and refused again to argue, the Court proceeded to its final judgment in May 1980, ruling by 13 votes to 2 "that the Islamic Republic of Iran, by the conduct which the Court has set out in this judgment, has violated in several respects, and is still violating, obligations owed by it to the United States of America under international conventions in force between the two countries, as well as under long-established rules of general international law." By unanimous vote, the Court held "that the Government of the Islamic Republic of Iran must immediately take all steps to redress the situation resulting from the events of 4 November 1979," including the release of the hostages.[131] The Court stressed "the cumulative effect of Iran's breaches of its obligations when taken together" and considered that the Court had a

> duty to draw the attention of the entire international community, of which Iran itself has been a member since time immemorial, to the irreparable

[128] Id. at 15-16.

[129] Id. at 15. The Court has developed a considerable jurisprudence respecting non-appearing defendant states. Since Iceland began the practice in 1972, there have been five states that have refused to appear in compulsory jurisdiction cases even to argue jurisdiction: Iceland in Fisheries Jurisdiction, 1973 I.C.J. Reports 3; India in Trial of Pakistani Prisoners of War, 1973 I.C.J. Reports 328; France in Nuclear Tests, 1974 I.C.J. Reports 253; Turkey in Aegean Sea Continental Shelf, 1978 I.C.J. Reports 3; and Iran in Diplomatic and Consular Staff. See Fitzmaurice, The Problem of the "Non-Appearing" Defendant Government, 51 *British Yearbook of International Law* 89 (1980).

[130] Diplomatic Staff Case Order, supra, at 19-21.

[131] Diplomatic Staff Case Judgment, supra, at 43-45.

harm that may be caused by events of the kind now before the Court. Such events cannot fail to undermine the edifice of law carefully constructed by mankind over a period of centuries, the maintenance of which is vital for the security and well-being of the complex international community of the present day, to which it is more essential than ever that the rules developed to ensure the ordered progress of relations between its members should be constantly and scrupulously respected.[132]

There were at least four ways in which the International Court might have effectively contributed to the resolution of the hostages dispute. First, Iran might have voluntarily complied with the Court's rulings. Iran, as a member of the United Nations, was obliged by Article 94(1) of the Charter of the United Nations "to comply with the decision" of the Court.[133] Although there is some doubt whether a party is legally bound by a mere order of the Court, there is none that a judgment of the Court is legally binding.[134] In this case, Iran treated both the Court's Order and its Judgment with scorn. The Iranian Foreign Minister called the Order "absolutely ridiculous," while Iranian State Radio dismissed the Judgment as ignoring U.S. aggression against Iran.[135] There was no indication that Iran at any time—before, during, or after the Court's consideration of the case—meant to honor its legal commitment under the U.N. Charter to respect the Court's decision.

Second, the Court might have contributed to the settlement of the dispute by providing a basis for Security Council action. The U.N. Charter provides:

> [If a] party to a case fails to perform the obligations incumbent upon it under a judgment rendered by the Court, the other party may have recourse to the Security Council, which may, if it deems necessary, make recommendations or decide upon measures to be taken to give effect to the judgment.[136]

[132] Id. at 42-43.

[133] U.N. Charter, supra.

[134] Rosenne, supra, at 141.

[135] *The Times* (London), Dec. 17, 1979, at 1; *The Times* (London), May 16, 1980, at 4.

[136] U.N. Charter, supra, art. 94(2). It seems that "[i]n its entire history, the Security Council has never employed its Article 94 powers even on occasions of clear non-compliance." Llamzon, Jurisdiction and Compliance in Recent Decisions of the International Court of Justice, 18 *European Journal of International Law* 815, 847 (2007).

So, the United States might have appealed to the Security Council to take measures to enforce the Court's Judgment, though not its Order. However, the Soviet Union in January 1980 had already vetoed a U.S. proposal to the Security Council to impose an economic boycott on Iran.[137] The United States never asked the Council to enforce the Court's Judgment.

Third, despite the apparent failure of the formal enforcement mechanisms in the U.N. Charter, the Court might still have made an effective contribution to the resolution of the hostages crisis insofar as it could help mobilize sentiment of other states in favor of the United States and against Iran. In this fashion, the Court might have been a persuasive force inducing third parties to bring pressure to bear against Iran. Though hard to quantify, such community pressure may often be the most effective means of enforcing international law. Even John Austin, whose positivist doctrine rejected the claims of international law to being really "law" because the international system lacks a sovereign, admitted that international law could be enforced by the "fear on the part of nations . . . of provoking general hostility, and incurring its probable evils."[138]

However, the effectiveness of this sort of public pressure is very difficult to evaluate. In *Diplomatic and Consular Staff*, there is little evidence that the Court did in fact make an appreciable contribution to the community pressure brought to bear on Iran. Largely because Iran's behavior in seizing the diplomatic and consular staff was such an egregious violation of international law, the United States already had considerable community support before the Court ruled. On November 27, 1979, two days before the case was brought to the Court, the United States Ambassador to the United Nations, Donald F. McHenry, stated that he had "not come upon any single delegate . . . who has defended the action which has been taken by the authorities in Iran."[139] The support in the international community for the U.S. position has been

[137] The U.S. draft resolution imposing an economic boycott against Iran, U.N. Doc. S/13735 (January 10, 1980), received ten votes in its favor (France, Jamaica, Niger, Norway, Philippines, Portugal, Tunisia, the United Kingdom, the United States, and Zambia), two against (East Germany and the Soviet Union), two abstentions (Bangladesh and Mexico), and one not voting (China), U.N. Doc. S/PV.2191/Add.1, at 54-55 (January 13, 1980).

[138] J. Austin, *The Province of Jurisprudence Determined* 208 (1st ed. 1832).

[139] 80 *Department of State Bulletin* 49 (January 1980).

characterized as "virtually unanimous."[140] Of course, there can be different levels of support, and it may be true, though it may be difficult to demonstrate, that the Court persuaded some countries to be somewhat firmer with Iran.

Finally, the Court's ruling that Iran was obliged to make a reparation to the United States might have led to some ultimate payment by some Iranian government for the damage inflicted upon the United States. However, in the January 19, 1981, agreement between the two countries finally settling the Iran hostage crisis, the United States agreed to "promptly withdraw all claims now pending against Iran before the International Court of Justice."[141] Given Iran's unwillingness to obey the Court's two orders to release the hostages, it is doubtful that Iran would have been any more willing to pay Court-awarded reparation. Furthermore, the obstacle of the Soviet veto would have probably prevented Security Council enforcement of a reparation award. It is difficult, therefore, to imagine that the concession of claims before the Court weighed heavily in the balance in the treaty negotiations between Iran and the United States. Rather, it appears that the crucial element was the trade of frozen Iranian assets for the U.S. hostages. It may even be, as subsequently pointed out by the Legal Adviser to the State Department at the time, that the Court's judgment "added to the complexity of unraveling the dispute between the two governments."[142]

What, if anything, then, was gained by the United States in bringing the *Diplomatic and Consular Staff* case to the ICJ? In large measure, the true value of the proceedings for the United States or indeed for any complainant state in like circumstances lies in the Court's utility as a public forum. Throughout the Court's proceedings, the United States underscored its goal to use the Court as a means "to maintain support for the American position by the vast majority of nations on Earth."[143] However much such use of the ICJ as a public forum helps applicant states, there must be some question as to whether such applications

[140] Quandt, The Middle East Crises, 58 *Foreign Affairs* 540, 544 (1980).

[141] Rosenbaum, Committee to Settle Claims is Set Up by Pact with Iran, *N.Y. Times*, Jan. 20, 1981, at A74; 20 *International Legal Materials* 223, 227 (1981).

[142] Owens, The Final Negotiation and Release in Algiers, *American Hostages in Iran: The Conduct of a Crisis* 297, 301 (W. Christopher et al. eds. 1985).

[143] President Carter, Address of January 8, 1980, 80 *Department of State Bulletin* 33 (Mar. 1980).

against recalcitrant states do not unduly injure the Court's already battered reputation.[144] In practice, true compulsory jurisdiction cases have, in the words of a long-time member of the ICJ, rarely produced "any meaningful results in the judiciary."[145] It may be that the prospects for the Court would be brighter if states turned to it only in those situations when it seemed likely that the Court's decision, if rendered, could be effectively enforced.[146]

Sadly, the United States itself has played the role of the recalcitrant state in all too many ICJ cases. In 1985, the United States chose not to participate in the merits stage of the *Military and Paramilitary Activities* case brought by Nicaragua after the Court found compulsory jurisdiction against the United States to try it for acts, including the mining of harbors, in Nicaragua. The United States refused to recognize the Court's 1986 adverse judgment, and in 1991, Nicaragua renounced its further rights of action, including any Court-determined reparations.[147]

Most distressing has been the response of the United States to a series of recent ICJ cases brought by Paraguay, then Germany, and finally Mexico, all respecting the 1963 Vienna Convention on Consular Relations.[148] In 1998, Paraguay brought the *Vienna Convention on Consular Relations* case against the United States alleging that the Vienna Convention's rule of prior consular notification would be violated if

[144] Nigeria's Bola Ajibola, a one-time judge on the ICJ, characterized the *Diplomatic and Consular Staff* case's judgment as being "flagrantly flouted, which left a sour taste in the mouth of world jurists and apparently weaken[ing] the effectiveness, importance and very purpose of the Court." Ajibola, Compliance with Judgments of the International Court of Justice, *Compliance with Judgments of International Courts* 9, 20-21 (Bulterman & Kuijer eds. 1996).

[145] Oda, The Compulsory Jurisdiction of the International Court of Justice: A Myth?: A Statistical Analysis of Contentious Cases, 49 *International & Comparative Law Quarterly* 251, 265 (2000). See V. Lamm, *Compulsory Jurisdiction in International Law* (2014).

[146] Janis, The Role of the International Court in the Hostages Crisis, 13 *Connecticut Law Review* 263 (1981).

[147] 1986 I.C.J. Reports 14, see Highet, Between a Rock and a Hard Place—The United States, the International Court, and the *Nicaragua* Case, 21 *International Lawyer* 1083 (1987); Janis, Somber Reflections on the Compulsory Jurisdiction of the International Court, 81 *American Journal of International Law* 144 (1987); Norton, The *Nicaragua* Case: Political Questions Before the International Court of Justice, 27 *Virginia Journal of International Law* 459 (1987); 1991 I.C.J. Reports 47-48.

[148] 596 U.N.T.S. 261, 21 U.S.T. 77.

the state of Virginia executed a Paraguayan national, Angel Francisco Breard, for murder without advising him of his rights to consular assistance. Although the Court unanimously ordered the United States to "take all measures at its disposal" to prevent Breard's execution before the ICJ heard the *Vienna Convention* case, the United States Supreme Court and the governor of Virginia chose not to stay the execution. Astonishingly, the Clinton administration took contradictory positions. The Justice Department in a Supreme Court brief argued that neither the ICJ nor the Vienna Convention could halt Breard's execution, while the State Department "with great reluctance" urged the governor of Virginia to delay the execution for political rather than legal reasons.[149] Finally on November 2, 1998, Paraguay, under U.S. pressure, agreed to ask the ICJ to discontinue the proceedings.[150]

In 1999, in the *LaGrand* case, Arizona acknowledged a violation of the Consular Convention, but still executed two German nationals over Germany's protest and despite an ICJ order to the United States to stay the execution. As Bruno Simma, the German judge on the Court lamented: "*LaGrand* did not show a real effort by U.S. courts to live up to the ICJ's Judgment."[151] In 2003, in *Avena and Other Mexican Nationals*, Mexico, like Paraguay and Germany before it, brought suit under the Consular Convention. Again, the ICJ ordered the United States to delay executions (this time in 54 separate cases) until it fulfilled its obligations to notify defendants about the right to request consular assistance for legal counsel.[152] Consular Convention cases continue to plague U.S. relations with the ICJ and to sully the international reputation of the United States. In a new and disturbing twist, in Medellín v. Texas, the Supreme Court ruled in 2008, that *Avena* was not legally

[149] Richardson, The Execution of Angel Breard by the United States: Violating an Order of the International Court of Justice, 12 *Temple International & Comparative Law Journal* 121, 125, 128-129 (1998).

[150] I.C.J. Communiqué No. 98/13 (April 3, 1998); I.C.J. Communiqué No. 98/7 (April 9, 1998); Breard v. Greene, 523 U.S. 371 (1998); Agora: Breard, *American Journal of International Law* 666 (1998); Stout, Clemency Denied, Paraguayan Is Executed, *N.Y. Times*, Apr. 15, 1998, at A18; *1998-1999 I.C.J. Yearbook* (225).

[151] Simma & Hoppe, The *LaGrand* Case: A Story of Many Miscommunications, *International Law Stories* 371, 390 (J.E. Noyes, L.A. Dickinson & M.W. Janis eds. 2007); The LaGrand Case (Germany v. United States), 1999 I.C.J. Reports 9, 2001 I.C.J. Reports 466.

[152] Avena and Other Mexican Nationals (Mexico v. United States), 2003 I.C.J. Reports; Aceves, Avena and Other Mexican Nationals: Provisional Measures Order, 97 *American Journal of International Law* 923 (2003); Avena (Mexico v. United States),

binding in U.S. law vis-à-vis Texas and that President Bush did not have the authority to order states to comply with the ICJ judgment ordering the United States to delay executions and review murder trials that violated the U.S. obligation to provide consular notification.[153] Meanwhile, the Bush administration repudiated the Vienna Convention's Optional Protocol giving the ICJ jurisdiction over Consular Convention cases, arguing that the ICJ has "interpreted the Vienna Consular Convention in ways that we [the United States] had not anticipated." *Medellín* itself was, in the words of Professor Vázquez "absurd and unconvincing."[154] Professor Bederman was more hopeful, viewing the case as a "*sui generis*" instance of treaty interpretation.[155]

The aftermath of *Medellín* has been pernicious. Medellín himself was executed by Texas in violation of international law on August 5, 2008, an act condemned by the ICJ in January 2009.[156] As late as 2015, Texas continued to disregard the Consular Convention despite pleas not only from Mexico and the Council of Europe, but also from John Bellinger, former State Department Legal Adviser to President George W. Bush: "Observing the treaty is not 'a favor to foreigners' but a 'plainly compelling' national interest in protecting Americans abroad."[157] So far, the U.S. Congress has not acted to reverse *Medellín* with legislation.[158]

2004 I.C.J. Reports 12. In *Sanchez-Llamas*, 548 U.S. 331 (2006), the Supreme Court rejected the claim that the failure of states to follow the Consular Convention necessitated new trials for death row inmates. See Supreme Court Rejects Exclusionary Rule and New Trials as Remedies for Failures of Consular Notifications, 100 *American Journal of International Law* 926 (2006); Sloss, When Do Treaties Create Individually Enforceable Rights?: The Supreme Court Ducks the Issue in *Hamdan* and *Sanchez-Llamas*, 45 *Columbia Journal of Transnational Law* 20 (2006); Daugirdas & Mortenson, Another Mexican National Executed in Texas in Defiance of Avena Decision, 108 *American Journal of International Law* 322 (2014).

[153] 552 U.S. 491 (2008); McGinnis, Medellín v. Texas, 102 *American Journal of International Law* 622 (2008).

[154] Vázquez, Less than Zero, 102 *American Journal of International Law* 563, 572 (2008).

[155] Bederman, *Medellín*'s New Paradigm for Treaty Interpretation, 102 *American Journal of International Law* 529, 539-540 (2008).

[156] ICJ Rejects Mexico's Request to Interpret *Avena* but Finds United States Violated Measures Order, 103 *American Journal of International Law* 362, 362-363 (2009).

[157] Knowlton, Death Row Case Threatens Global Treaty, *International Herald Tribune*, June 16, 2011, at 4.

[158] Ibid. See Kennedy, Fulfilling Our Treaty Obligations and Protecting Americans, June 27, 2011, www.state.gov (May 2015).

The ICJ's efficacy is threatened by such non-compliance. One study found that between 1987 and 2003 there was significant non-compliance in five of the 14 contentious cases decided by the Court. Another study of ICJ cases before 1987 showed a comparable record, concluding that disputes involving recalcitrant defendants were especially prone to inefficacy.[159] It is a sorry state of affairs to have to count the United States as one of the parties most often in non-compliance with ICJ decisions.

4. *The Advisory Jurisdiction of the International Court*

Similar considerations of effectiveness are pertinent to the Court's advisory jurisdiction. The ICJ is competent to "give an advisory opinion on any legal question at the request of whatever body may be authorized by or in accordance with the charter of the United Nations to make such a request."[160] Pursuant to the Charter of the United Nations:

(1) The General Assembly or the Security Council may request the International Court of Justice to give an advisory opinion on any legal question.
(2) Other organs of the United Nations and specialized agencies, which may at any time be so authorized by the General Assembly, may also request advisory opinions of the Court on legal questions arising within the scope of their activities.[161]

The advisory jurisdiction of the ICJ is modeled on that which was granted to the PCIJ: "The Court may also give an advisory opinion upon any dispute or question referred to it by the Council or by the Assembly." This provision of the League Covenant, Article 14, was an innovation in international law. It was meant to be a form of secondary jurisdiction

[159] Paulson, Compliance with Final Judgments of the International Court, 98 *American Journal of International Law* 434 (2004); Charney, Disputes Implicating the Credibility of the Court: Problems of Non-Appearance, Non-Participation and Non-Performance, *The International Court of Justice at a Crossroads* 288 (L. Damrosch ed. 1987).

[160] ICJ Statute, supra, art. 65(1).

[161] U.N. Charter, supra, art. 96.

(less important than the PCIJ's jurisdiction in contentious cases brought by states), and the word *advisory* was included to make it plain that the Court's pronouncements in such cases were always to be non-binding.[162]

The Permanent Court handed down its first advisory opinion in 1922.[163] In its 19 active years, the PCIJ delivered 27 advisory opinions, 11 of which concerned Poland and/or Danzig and six the International Labour Organization.[164] One case pertained to both favorite topics.[165] The PCIJ's advisory function lapsed along with its other operations at the onset of the Second World War.

There was some debate during the War about considerably expanding the International Court's advisory jurisdiction, perhaps even permitting states to request advisory opinions. Ultimately, however, when the new ICJ was established, it was decided to limit the expansion of the advisory function only to additional international organizations.[166] Today not only are the U.N. Security Council and the General Assembly authorized to request advisory opinions from the Court,[167] but so too are several other U.N. bodies and specialized agencies, including the International Labour Organization, the World Health Organization, the International Bank for Reconstruction and Development, the International Monetary Fund, and the International Atomic Energy Agency.[168] As of 2025, some five organs of the United Nations and 16 specialized agencies are empowered to request advisory opinions.[169]

The ICJ rendered its first advisory opinion, *Conditions of Admission of a State to Membership in the United Nations*, in 1948.[170] Altogether, the Court has given some 28 advisory opinions between 1946 and 2024. However, there have been only 19 advisory opinions since 1961, only

[162] M. Pomerance, *The Advisory Function of the International Court in the League and U.N. Eras* 5-10 (1973) [hereinafter cited as "Pomerance"].

[163] Advisory Opinion on the Workers' Delegate for the Netherlands, 1922 P.C.I.J. Reports, ser. B, no. 1.

[164] *1984-1985 I.C.J. Yearbook* 189-194.

[165] Advisory Opinion on the Free City of Danzig and the I.L.O., 1930 P.C.I.J. Reports, ser. B, no. 18.

[166] D. Pratap, *The Advisory Jurisdiction of the International Court* 39-44 (1972) [hereinafter cited as "Pratap"].

[167] U.N. Charter, supra, art. 96(1).

[168] *I.C.J. Handbook 2014-2015* 82, www.icj-cij.org (May 4, 2015).

[169] International Court of Justice, Organs and Agencies Authorized to Request Advisory Opinions, www.icj-cij.org (Nov. 17, 2025).

[170] 1947-1948 I.C.J. Reports 57.

about one every three years in the last six decades.[171] Despite the fact that there are many more international organizations nowadays than in the 1920s and 1930s that can request advisory opinions, they simply do not ask the International Court for its advice. Why not?

In large measure, the reluctance of international organizations to turn to the ICJ for advisory opinions can be attributed to two factors. First, the states participating in international organizations have proved to be unwilling to remove issues from political processes, where they are more in charge of the ultimate outcome, to the courtroom, where they are less in control of any determination (even if the Court's decision be only "advisory").[172] Second, when the advisory jurisdiction of the Court has been employed, the questions sent to the ICJ have been more "political" and less "legal" than those sent to the PCIJ. This, in turn, has discouraged states from more freely permitting international organizations to request opinions.[173]

The "political" nature of recent advisory opinions has generated many of the same sort of effectiveness problems as have afflicted contentious compulsory jurisdiction cases. For example, in the Court's 1975 advisory opinion on the *Western Sahara*, the U.N. General Assembly asked the Court to advise it as to the legal status of the Western Sahara at the time of its colonization by Spain and as to the territory's "legal ties" to Morocco and Mauritania.[174] The larger political question before the United Nations was whether the phosphate-rich Western Sahara should be granted independence as a separate state or, when decolonized by Spain, divided between its two African neighbors, Morocco and Mauritania.[175] Far from attempting to escape a hot political issue, the Court rushed to embrace it. Going beyond the technical legal questions posed by the General Assembly and after a lengthy analysis of the history of the Western Sahara in the context of the United Nations' decolonization debate, the Court pronounced the legal right of the people of the Western Sahara to a referendum to determine their political future. Justifying its own enlargement of its advisory mandate, the Court held that "[b]y lending its assistance in the solution of a problem

[171] *I.C.J. Yearbook 2017-2018* 2, www.icj-cij.org (Oct. 17, 2020).
[172] Pomerance, supra, at 272.
[173] Id. at 171.
[174] 1975 I.C.J. Reports 12.
[175] Marks, Spanish Sahara—Background to Conflict, 1976 *African Affairs* 1-3.

confronting the General Assembly, the Court would discharge its functions as the principal judicial organ of the United Nations."[176] However, shortly thereafter, and thoroughly in disregard of the Court's opinion, Morocco invaded the Western Sahara and declared it annexed without conducting a plebiscite.[177]

Similarly, the 2004 ICJ advisory opinion in *Legal Consequences of the Construction of a Wall in the Occupied Palestinian Territory*, which held that the wall separating Palestinian from Israeli territory was illegal and should be dismantled, has had little impact on the troubled politics of the Middle East.[178] Rather more timidly, in its *Kosovo* advisory opinion, the ICJ merely decided that Kosovo's declaration of independence did not violate international law without expressing an opinion on Kosovo being an independent sovereign state or not.[179]

As a matter of law, it is plain that, unlike its judgments, the advisory opinions of the Court are not legally binding. The history of the founding of the Court, the Court's own holdings, and the united opinion of commentators unanimously concur that an advisory opinion imposes no legal obligation either upon the requesting organization or upon concerned states to heed the Court's advice.[180] As the ICJ commented in the *South West Africa* case, though the Council of the League of Nations could have asked for an advisory opinion of the PCIJ, "that opinion would not have binding force, and the Mandatory [South Africa] could continue to turn a deaf ear to the Council's admonitions."[181]

[176] 1975 I.C.J. Reports 12, 14, 21, 30-31, 40, 68.

[177] Giniger, Moroccans Plan March in Sahara, *N.Y. Times*, Oct. 17, 1975, at A1, A8; Giniger, Moroccans Rally to Join March to Spanish Sahara, *N.Y. Times*, Oct. 18, 1975, at A4. See Charbonneau, Western Sahara Dispute Spills Over in Nuclear Arms Meeting, *Reuters* (Apr. 24, 2015); J.S. Liceras, *International Law and the Western Sahara Conflict* (2014). In December 2020, the Trump Administration reversed U.S. policy and recognized the Moroccan invasion of the Western Sahara to the dismay of James Baker, the former Secretary of State in the first Bush Administration. The dispute remains a hot topic. Algeria, Morocco and Western Sahara: The Disputed Desert, *The Economist*, Nov. 6, 2021, at 43-44.

[178] 2004 I.C.J. Reports 136; see Agora: ICJ Advisory Opinion on Construction of a Wall in the Occupied Palestinian Territory, 99 *American Journal of International Law* 1 (2005); Baker, Israel's Settlement Drive Is Becoming Irreversible, Diplomats Fear, *Reuters*, May 3, 2016, www.reuters.com.

[179] 2010 I.C.J. Reports; see Cogan, The 2010 Judicial Activity of the International Court of Justice, 105 *American Journal of International Law* 477, 484-486 (2011).

[180] Pratap, supra, at 227-230.

[181] 1962 I.C.J. Reports 319, 337.

In 2019, the United Kingdom rejected the ICJ's Advisory Opinion of the Legal Consequences of the Separation of the Chagos Archipelago from Mauritius in 1965, where the Court advised the United Kingdom that continued occupation of the Chagos islands violated the international law of decolonization.[182] The British government also rejected a 116 to 6 resolution of the U.N. General Assembly resolution calling for U.K. withdrawal, noting that neither the advisory opinion nor the General Assembly resolution were legally binding [see Chapter 7].[183] A critic condemned British "intransigence," arguing the U.K. rejection of the ICJ and the General Assembly "seriously weakens its ability to lecture other states about living up to their human rights obligations."[184]

In practice, then, states treat the authority of the Court's advisory opinions in much the same fashion as they accept (or not) the Court's authority to settle contentious cases. This is so because there is as little practical effectiveness to the obligatory provisions of the U.N. Charter with respect to the judgments of the Court as there is to the non-obligatory provisions respecting advisory opinions. Unless states have willingly asked the Court to finally settle a dispute, they usually give the Court's pronouncements (whether made in contentious cases or in advisory opinions) only so much weight as seems politically advantageous. However, it may well be that the ICJ's advisory opinions are just as capable at giving "legal guidance" and being a source of doctrinal authority as are its judgments in contentious cases,[185] a topic to which we now turn.

[182] ICJ Advisory Opinion of Feb. 25, 2019. See Cohen, International Court of Justice—Decolonization—Peoples' Right of Self-Determination, 113 *American Journal of International Law* 784 (2019).

[183] James, UK "An Illegal Colonial Occupier" After Missing UN Deadline to Return Chagos Islands, *The Independent* (U.K.), Nov. 22, 2019, https://www.the-independent.com/news/uk/home-news/uk-chagos-islands-uk-deadline-un-illegal-occupation-indian-ocean-a9213416.html (Oct. 17, 2020).

[184] Allen, The U.K.'s Intransigence Is a Self-Inflicted Wound, *World Political Review*, July 29, 2020, www.worldpoliticalreview.com (Oct.17, 2020).

[185] Falk, The Kosovo Advisory Opinion: Conflict Resolution and Precedent, 105 *American Journal of International Law* 50, 52-53 (2011); Petersen, The International Court of Justice and the Judicial Politics of Identifying Customary International Law, 28 *European Journal of International Law* 357 (2017).

5. *The International Court and the Development of International Law*

It has been suggested that the International Court's greatest utility lies not in its activities as an agency for the pacific settlement of international disputes, but in its capacity for developing international law.[186] Sir Hersch Lauterpacht wrote that though "it would be an exaggeration to assert that the Court has proved to be a significant instrument for maintaining international peace, [it] . . . has made a tangible contribution to the development and clarification of the rules and principles of international law."[187] Lauterpacht referred to this phenomenon as "a heterogeny of aims" where "[i]nstitutions set up for the achievement of definite purposes grow to fulfil tasks not wholly identical with those which were in the minds of their authors at the time of their creation."[188]

Of course, the role of the International Court in the development of international law has been restricted by the limited number of cases that come to it, only a handful each year. However, as we have seen, over time, even this limited case load has built up. Over nearly a hundred years, from 1922 to 2023, the Court has had the opportunity to deliver 439 judgments, advisory opinions, and substantive orders.[189] The grey PCIJ Reports and crimson ICJ Reports fill three or four library shelves. Contained in these volumes is, by now, an impressive collection of judicial opinion about a great many aspects of international law. Of what value is the accumulation?

It must first be remarked that the decisions of the Court are not in and of themselves legally binding precedent in the way that judges' decisions may be in the common law. Article 59 of the Court's Statute reads: "The decision of the Court has no binding force except between the parties and in respect of that particular case."[190] However, Article 38(1)(d) instructs the Court to apply, after treaties, international custom and general principles of law and, "subject to the provisions of

[186] Lissitzyn, supra, at 3.

[187] H. Lauterpacht, *The Development of International Law by the International Court* 4-5 (1958) [hereinafter cited as "Lauterpacht"].

[188] Id. at 5.

[189] 83 by the PCIJ, *1984-1985 I.C.J. Yearbook* 189-194; 356 by the ICJ *2022-2023 I.C.J. Yearbook* 2, www.icj-cij.org (Nov. 17, 2025).

[190] ICJ Statute, supra.

Article 59, judicial decisions and the teachings of the most highly qualified publicists of the various nations, as subsidiary means for the determination of rules of law."[191] Thus, the Statute is of two minds about the International Court's decisions. On the one hand, they are not legally binding precedent. On the other hand, along with other judicial decisions, they constitute a subsidiary means for finding international law.

In practice, the Court refers repeatedly to its own decisions.[192] It cites its own old opinions as justification for its new holdings and goes to great pains to distinguish earlier cases if it must decide inconsistently.[193] The ICJ relies upon PCIJ opinions in much the same fashion that it relies upon its own.[194] In large measure, the Court's style is reminiscent of that of civil law judges developing a *jurisprudence constante*, where the judges consider it necessary to establish a consistent pattern of judicial decision even if they are prohibited from themselves legislating rules of law [see Chapter 3]. As the then-President of the ICJ said in 1962:

> The present Court has since the beginning been conscious of the need to maintain a continuity of tradition, case law and methods of work. . . . Above all, without being bound by *stare decisis* as a principle or rule, it often seeks guidance in the body of decisions of the former Court, and the result is a remarkable unity of precedent, an important factor in the development of international law.[195]

Regardless of the weight one assigns to state consent as the foundation for rules of international law [see Chapters 2 and 3], there is an influential role for the International Court in developing international law. As we have discussed above, neither treaties nor customary international law can be mechanically applied [see Chapter 3]. There will always be uncertainties about even settled rules of international law that call for judicial interpretation.[196] Furthermore, the precedents of the International Court, especially as they have accumulated, now form a body of jurisprudence that greatly contributes to our understanding

[191] Ibid.
[192] Lauterpacht, supra, at 9; M. Shahabuddeen, *Precedent in the World Court* (1996).
[193] Lauterpacht, supra, at 9-11.
[194] Rosenne, supra, at 611.
[195] Winiarski, Address by the President, *1961-1962 I.C.J. Yearbook* 1, 2.
[196] Lissitzyn, supra, at 9.

of customary international law and general principles of law, a development foreseen in some measure by the founders of the Court.[197] The decisions of the Court have taken on considerable importance. This book, like any other about international law, is rightly replete with references to the judgments and opinions of the International Court.

D. THE REFORM OF THE INTERNATIONAL COURT

The International Court is over 100 years old. The ICJ survives very largely in the form of the PCIJ, which was inaugurated in 1922 after the work of the League of Nations Advisory Committee. Today's ICJ is in no small measure a creature of nineteenth century aspirations put into a real twenty-first century world. Could the Court be reformed and refashioned to meet modern challenges? Many reforms have been suggested.[198] Here, only two areas of possible development are explored: (1) vesting the Court with the authority to render preliminary rulings; and (2) refining the Court's new practice of deliberating in chambers.

1. *Preliminary Rulings*

Attacking "the enduring hold of The Hague system" over the Statute of the present Court, Professor Leo Gross singled out Article 34 as the weakest link in the chain constituting the ICJ, stating, "Only states may be parties in cases before the Court."[199] The Court, of course, could be empowered to render decisions in contentious cases involving international organizations.[200] However, of all possible jurisdictional reforms,

[197] Id. at 9-12.

[198] See, e.g., *International Courts for the Twenty-First Century* (Janis ed. 1992); *The Future of the International Court of Justice* (L. Gross ed. 1976); *Judicial Settlement of International Disputes* (Mosler & Bernhardt eds. 1974); Antonio Cassese, *Legalizing Utopia: The Future of International Law* 239-249 (2012).

[199] Gross, supra, at 67.

[200] Id. at 67-71.

the boldest would be to somehow open the Court to suits brought by private parties. The most likely way to effect such a change would be the institution of some sort of ICJ jurisdiction for the rendering of preliminary rulings, that is, opinions delivered to other courts to help them decide issues of international law.[201]

The idea of granting the International Court jurisdiction to give municipal courts "an opinion on difficult or unsettled questions of international law" dates back at least to 1929 and Hersch Lauterpacht.[202] An ordinary modern analogy for the International Court is the power that was vested in the European Court of Justice by EEC Treaty Article 177 "to give [member state municipal courts] preliminary rulings concerning: (a) the interpretation of this Treaty; (b) the validity and interpretation of acts of the institutions of the Community; (c) the interpretation of the statutes of bodies established by an act of the Council, where those statutes so provide."[203]

The power to render preliminary rulings, which is also referred to as interlocutory jurisdiction, has been thought to be advantageous (1) in increasing the workload of the Court; (2) in promoting uniform interpretation of the rules of international law; and (3) in opening "the way for the real parties to the case, in most cases private individuals, to state their views."[204] Professor Gross has argued that granting the Court the power to give advisory opinions in municipal court cases could "outflank" Article 34 of the Statute of the Court, which provides that "only States may be parties in cases before the Court," and that special chambers of the Court could be employed for such advisory

[201] Scheinen, The ICJ and the Individual, 9 *International Community Law Review* 123 (2007); Sohn, Broadening the Advisory Jurisdiction of the International Court of Justice, 77 *American Journal of International Law* 124 (1983).

[202] Lauterpacht, Decisions of Municipal Courts as a Source of International Law, 10 *British Yearbook of International Law* 65, 94 (1929); Schwebel, Preliminary Rulings by the International Court of Justice at the Instance of National Courts, 28 *Virginia Journal of International Law* 495-496 (1988) [hereinafter cited as "Schwebel, Preliminary Rulings"].

[203] Treaty Establishing the European Economic Community, art. 177, U.K.T.S. 15 (1979) (with authoritative English language text), 298 U.N.T.S. 11 (concluded at Rome March 25, 1957; entered into force January 1, 1958; not in force for the United States).

[204] Steinberger, The International Court of Justice, *Judicial Settlement of International Disputes* 193, 262 (Mosler & Bernhardt eds. 1974) [hereinafter cited as "Steinberger"].

opinions.[205] Judge Schwebel wrote that he found the idea of preliminary rulings "fundamentally appealing," because, though municipal judges make important contributions to the development of international law, "knowledge of national courts about international law is variable, and national and parochial perspectives may come into play."[206]

A contrary position was adopted by Ambassador Shabtai Rosenne, arguing that it would "be premature to confer on the International Court any form of reference jurisdiction in any way comparable to that of the Court of Justice of the European Communities."[207] His chief objection is that the juridical world of the ICJ is not the "closely integrated and virtually closed international community of States" of the EEC; the ECJ, unlike the ICJ, is a "supranational" rather than an "international" court.[208]

Fundamentally, the disagreement about widening the jurisdiction of the International Court to permit the Court to hear interlocutory referrals from municipal courts is rooted in differing views about the proper role of the ICJ and about the legal and political importance of state sovereignty. Ambassador Rosenne's objection probably proves too much. Any meaningful reform of the ICJ is, of course, "premature" in the sense that it must go beyond the existing framework of international law and politics. That does not make it wrong. Furthermore, such reforms do not propose that states be compelled to permit their national courts to refer preliminary questions of international law to the ICJ. There seems to be no good reason save an overriding belief in the necessary inviolability of state sovereignty to preclude consenting states from opening the door of the International Court to their own judges. More serious objections might be raised if the jurisdiction of the Court were to be extended to take cases on appeal, either from municipal courts or from other international courts such as the European Court of Justice, the European Court of Human Rights, or the Inter-American Court of Human Rights.[209]

[205] Gross, supra, at 43.

[206] Schwebel, Preliminary Rulings, supra, at 499.

[207] Rosenne, Preliminary Rulings by the International Court of Justice at the Instance of National Courts: A Reply, 29 *Virginia Journal of International Law* 401, 405 (1989).

[208] Ibid.

[209] Steinberger, supra, at 262-263.

2. *Chambers*

One of the more hopeful signs of life in the International Court had been the emergence of special five-judge chambers to settle disputes submitted by *compromis* between states. The origins of the chambers approach go back to proposals made at the 1907 Peace Conference at The Hague and to provisions for chambers in the Statute of the PCIJ. There were, in fact, two chambers of summary procedure constituted by the PCIJ.[210] Provision for the election of chambers was included in the 1945 ICJ Statute, but until the 1980s, use of chambers by the Court "was practically a dead letter."[211]

Development of the modern chambers procedure in the International Court can be dated to 1968 and to a brief note written by James Hyde at the suggestion of Judge Jessup. Looking at the "lengthy and comparatively expensive procedure" of the ICJ, Hyde argued that, compared to *ad hoc* arbitration, the Court might often appear unattractive to states.[212] Accordingly, he suggested that states consider turning to Article 26 of the Court's Statute:[213]

> 1. The Court may from time to time form one or more chambers, composed of three or more judges as the Court may determine for dealing with particular categories of cases; for example, labour cases and cases relating to transit and communications.
>
> 2. The Court may at any time form a chamber for dealing with a particular case. The number of judges to constitute such a chamber shall be determined by the Court with the approval of the parties.
>
> 3. Cases shall be heard and determined by the chambers provided for in this article if the parties so request.[214]

[210] Zimmermann, Ad Hoc Chambers of the International Court of Justice, 8 *Dickinson Journal of International Law* 1, 2-4 (1989) [hereinafter cited as "Zimmermann"]; Treaty of Neuilly, art. 179, Annex par. 4, 1924 P.C.I.J. Reports, ser. A, no. 3; Interpretation of Judgment N. 3, 1925 P.C.I.J. Reports, ser. A, no. 4.

[211] Ostrihansky, Chambers of the International Court of Justice, 37 *International & Comparative Law Quarterly* 30 (1988) [hereinafter cited as "Ostrihansky"].

[212] Hyde, A Special Chamber of the International Court of Justice—An Alternative to Ad Hoc Arbitration, 62 *American Journal of International Law* 439 (1968) [hereinafter cited as "Hyde"].

[213] Id. at 440.

[214] ICJ Statute, supra.

Hyde felt that states had not theretofore employed chambers because "governments parties do not want to 'buy a pig in a poke,' and would rather have the entire bench than a chamber, which is elected by the Court by secret ballot."[215] Hyde thought that since Article 26(2) of the Statute refers to "the approval of the parties," it might be possible for the parties either to request a specific panel or to reject a court-elected panel if it were unsatisfactory.[216]

In 1972 and 1978, the ICJ changed its Rules respecting chambers, the most significant changes coming in Article 17:

> 1. A request for the formation of a Chamber to deal with a particular case . . . may be filed at any time until the closure of the written proceedings. Upon receipt of a request made by one party, the President [or the Court] shall ascertain whether the other party assents.
>
> 2. When the parties have agreed, the President shall ascertain their views regarding the composition of the Chamber, and shall report to the Court accordingly. . . .
>
> 3. When the Court has determined, with the approval of the parties, the number of its Members who are to constitute the Chamber, it shall proceed to their election, in accordance with the provisions of Article 18 . . . of these Rules [providing for elections to Chambers by secret ballot of the Court]. . . .
>
> 4. Members of a Chamber formed under this Article who have been replaced . . . following the expiration of their terms of office, shall continue to sit in all phases of the case, whatever the stage it has then reached.[217]

In practice, the two most important changes made by the new Rules are to provide for consultation with the parties as to the composition of the chamber and to ensure that judges appointed to a chamber can carry on as members despite the fact that they may leave the full Court.[218] The increased role of the parties in decisions about the composition of chambers has also proved to be their most controversial aspect.

[215] Hyde, supra, at 440.

[216] Ibid.

[217] Schwebel, Ad Hoc Chambers of the International Court of Justice, 81 *American Journal of International Law* 831, 838-839 (1987) [hereinafter cited as "Schwebel, Chambers"].

[218] Zimmermann, supra, at 5-6.

Notably, in the first chamber formed under the new Rules, the United States and Canada in the *Gulf of Maine* case chose to have the Court create what some have referred to as a "regional" chamber.[219] There the chamber was composed solely of North Atlantic judges: Ago (Italy), Mosler (Germany), Gros (France), Schwebel (United States), and Cohen (Canada, *ad hoc*).[220] Subsequent ICJ chambers, though still subject to consultation with the parties, have been more broadly based. The *Frontier Dispute* chamber for the case between Burkina Faso and Mali was composed of Lachs (Poland), Ruda (Argentina), Bedjaoui (Algeria), Luchaire (France, *ad hoc*), and Abi-Saab (Egypt, *ad hoc*).[221] *Elettronica Sicula* between the United States and Italy saw Ago (Italy), Schwebel (United States), Jennings (United Kingdom), Oda (Japan), and Singh (India), succeeded by Ruda (Argentina).[222] The chamber for El Salvador and Honduras in *Land, Island and Maritime Frontier Dispute* was constituted with Sette Câmara (Brazil), Oda (Japan), Jennings (United Kingdom), Valticos (Greece, *ad hoc*), and Virally (France, *ad hoc*), succeeded by Torres Bernárdez (Spain, *ad hoc*).[223] In *Frontier Dispute* between Benin and Niger the chamber was made up of Ranjeva (Madagascar), Kooijmans (the Netherlands), Abraham (France), replacing Guillaume (France), Bedjaoui (Algeria), and Bennouna (Morocco).[224]

Nonetheless, as with the *Gulf of Maine* case, the possibility always exists that parties will choose to narrow a chamber to a certain region or ideology. Questions about the formal legality of such narrowing are probably less pressing now after a decade of practice of party choice. However, the debate about the wisdom of party selection is no less interesting today than at the time when the first chamber was being constituted.[225] Certainly, one of the best arguments for party choice is that if states are to be encouraged to use the Court, then their preferences in

[219] Ostrihansky, supra, at 38.

[220] Delimitation of the Maritime Boundary in the Gulf of Maine Area, Constitution of Chamber, Order of 20 January 1982, 1982 I.C.J. Reports 3; Judgment, 1984 I.C.J. Reports 246.

[221] 1986 I.C.J. Reports 554.

[222] 1989 I.C.J. Reports 15.

[223] 1987 I.C.J. Reports 10.

[224] Case Concerning the Frontier Dispute (Benin/Niger), 2005 I.C.J. Reports 90.

[225] See, e.g., Zoller, La première constitution d'une chambre spéciale par la Cour Internationale de Justice, 86 *Revue générale de droit international public* 305 (1982).

terms of the membership of the chamber ought, simply for reasons of utility, to be respected.[226]

In truth, the debate about party choice is only part of a larger issue concerning the universality of the Court and its judgments. Given that the ICJ is uniquely a tribunal with universal aspirations, might not party choice of chambers threaten this promise? Besides the potential problem of regionalization, might not problems of ideology or personality endanger the universality of the ICJ?[227]

At first glance, there seems to be nothing wrong with states' taking the region, ideology, or personality of potential judges into account. After all, so long as states can constitute *ad hoc* arbitral tribunals entirely outside the structure of the Court to settle their disputes, limiting party choice in constituting chambers is not likely to lead to the increased use of the entire Court, but only to the resort to alternative dispute settlement procedures or to the abandoning of judicial mechanisms altogether. Furthermore, in practice, states did spread the work of chambers rather broadly. The choice of judges in the first four chambers shows that 17 judges (including six judges *ad hoc*) were elected to 22 available places in chambers; only five judges, all members of the ICJ (Ago, Schwebel, Ruda, Jennings, and Oda) were selected twice; no judge was chosen three times. Moreover, if in a case or in a succession of cases the parties seem to be unduly undermining the universality of the ICJ with too narrow selections, the Court could simply not accede to the wishes of the parties. After all, although new Rule 17 permits consultation with the parties, only the Court itself may actually elect the members of a chamber.[228]

Given the success of chambers in their first decade, it has been something of a surprise that there have been few disputes submitted to chambers since 1982, and only one chamber's judgment rendered since 1992.[229] Moreover, no case being entrusted to a new standing chamber of seven members created by the Court in 1993 to deal with environmental matters, the Court chose not to elect members for it

[226] Id. at 322-324.

[227] Schwebel, Chambers, supra, at 840-843.

[228] Id. at 852-853.

[229] For an analysis of the most recent chamber's judgment, the 2005 *Frontier Dispute* case between Benin and Niger, see Mathias, The 2005 Judicial Activity of the International Court of Justice, 100 *American Journal of International Law* 629, 634 (2006).

in 2006.[230] Despite these setbacks, it might do to consider a possible expansion of the notion. For example, it has long been suggested that the ICJ consider establishing permanent regional chambers located elsewhere than The Hague to provide a sometimes more convenient forum for dispute settlement, a proposal that might call for amendment of the Court's statute.[231] This would, however, certainly splinter the universality of the Court and could additionally cause real problems for the judges who would have to coordinate schedules between two tribunals on different continents. Another thought has been to employ a chamber to render the kind of preliminary rulings to municipal courts explored above.[232]

E. THE PROLIFERATION OF INTERNATIONAL COURTS

Another reason why the work of the ICJ has not expanded in recent times is the creation of other international courts with a regional or a specialized jurisdiction. When the PCIJ was established in 1921, there were no other permanent international tribunals, save the PCA, which the PCIJ largely supplanted. The ICJ, too, had a virtually exclusive position as *the* international court until late into the 1950s. Since then, new international courts have been added at an ever-quickening pace. We explore many of the principal new international courts elsewhere in the book: the European Court of Human Rights [see Chapter 8], the European Court of Justice and Court of First Instance [see Chapter 9], the Inter-American Court of Human Rights [see Chapter 8], the International Criminal Tribunal for the Former Yugoslavia and that for Rwanda [see Chapter 8], the International Tribunal for the Law of the Sea [see Chapter 7], the Dispute Settlement System of the World Trade Organization [see Chapter 9], the European Free Trade Association Court [see Chapter 9], the Caribbean Court

[230] I.C.J. Communiqué No. 93/20 (July 19, 1993); see Mathias, The 2006 Judicial Activity of the International Court of Justice, 101 *American Journal of International Law* 602, 612 (2007).

[231] Ostrihansky, supra, at 36-38.

[232] Zimmermann, supra, at 31-32.

of Justice [see Chapter 9], and the International Criminal Court [see Chapter 8].

Faced with these new international courts, some like Gilbert Guillaume, formerly President of the ICJ, fear that international law will become fragmented unless the ICJ is recognized as a kind of supreme court for international law.[233] However, it is doubtful that the world community would ever agree to such a hierarchy. Not only would it be politically unlikely that agreement could be reached on such a proposal, but establishing the international judicial supremacy of the ICJ would undermine many of the advantages of the new regional and international courts, such as their more limited state memberships and more expert areas of competence.[234] Thus, it seems inevitable that these new international courts will develop their own areas of the law with a resulting diversity of international legal jurisprudence. Such, for example, is already the case with the European Court of Justice, which has displayed a certain jurisprudential provincialism.[235]

[233] Crook, The 2000 Judicial Activity of the International Court of Justice, 95 *American Journal of International Law* 685, 686 (2001); see Andenas, Reservation and Transformation: From Fragmentation to Convergence in International Law, 46 *Georgetown Journal of International Law* 685 (2015).

[234] Charney, The Impact on the International Legal System of the Growth of International Courts and Tribunals, 31 *New York University Journal of International Law & Politics* 697, 698-699 (1999).

[235] Dupuy, The Danger of Fragmentation or Unification of the International Legal System and the International Court of Justice, 31 *New York University Journal of International Law & Politics* 791, 795-798 (1999).

CHAPTER 6

States and International Law

No international sovereign enforces international law. In great measure, the responsibility for compliance with international legal rules lies with no court, municipal or international, but with the principal subjects of that law, the states themselves. This is especially so with respect to the more or less constitutional rules of international law, for example, those that set out the fundamental character and the rights and duties of states, and the norms respecting war and peace. Our discussion begins with an introduction to the principles of state sovereignty.

A. SOVEREIGNTY AND INTERNATIONAL LAW

Sovereignty and international law are apparently antagonistic. The notion behind sovereignty is that a state ought to be able to govern itself, free from outside interference. Underpinning international law is the idea that external rules ought to be able to limit state behavior. In the real world, neither sovereignty nor international law could reign absolutely without vanquishing the other. The lesson of history seems to be that in practice, neither sovereignty nor international law ever completely wins out. Rather, a balance is struck between the two, an accommodation that is an essential aspect of the constitution of international politics at any point in time.

Both sovereignty and international law can make strong claims to increased importance in today's world order. Sovereignty, on the one hand, can boast of the resurgence of new free and independent states in Central and Eastern Europe—e.g., Poland, the Czech Republic, Slovakia, Hungary, Romania, and Bulgaria—all of which had been Cold War satellites of the Soviet Union. There are also the new sovereign states that emerged from what used to be the Soviet Union itself and from Yugoslavia, for example, Russia, Ukraine, Georgia, Lithuania, Latvia, Estonia, Slovenia, Croatia, and Bosnia-Herzegovina. Thanks to these developments and to the prior decolonization of Africa and Asia, there are nowadays about 200 sovereign states, four times as many as before the Second World War.

International law, on the other hand, can point to the development of international organizations, especially to the United Nations [see Chapter 7], to the European Union striving to step to a new level of European integration [see Chapter 9], and to the World Bank and the International Monetary Fund reaching out to an increasing number of states [see Chapter 7]. Judicially, there is the International Court of Justice [see Chapter 5] and the International Criminal Court [see Chapter 8], as well as the regional international courts, including the Court of Justice of the European Union [see Chapter 9] and the European Court of Human Rights [see Chapter 8], which are remarkably busy and efficacious. The prospering triangle of international courts in The Hague, Luxembourg, and Strasbourg is without precedent in the long history of international arbitration and adjudication.

Given the increasing number of sovereign states, alongside the vibrancy of international organizations and international courts, what new balance has been struck between sovereignty and international law? Although it is far too early to tell for sure, it may be time to look again at the crafting of the original concepts of sovereignty and international law by Thomas Hobbes and Hugo Grotius during the earliest phase of modern international politics. We may be able to better understand some of the emerging realities of the new roles of sovereignty and international law if we remember the basic reasons for the utility and success of the two concepts.

A. Sovereignty and International Law

1. *Hobbes and the Sovereign State*

In 1648, the Peace of Westphalia[1] ushered in a new period of international relations for which new legal and moral principles were needed. These principles Thomas Hobbes' *Leviathan*, a celebration of the sovereign state, helped supply.[2] Hobbes was an Oxford-educated classicist-turned-philosopher and one-time tutor to both the Earl of Devonshire and the young prince who became Charles II—writing in 1651 in exile in Paris, where he was a refugee from the English Civil War.

The medieval era, which the bloody Thirty Years' War shattered, was characterized by criss-crossing political, legal, religious, and moral allegiances. The ties of feudalism, of King and baron, of the Holy Roman Empire, of the Catholic Church, indeed of all the settled order of medieval Europe, bound men and women this way and that. That such ties could pull in contradictory ways was, for example, the lesson in Anouilh's *Becket*, the story of a medieval man tugged one way by his King and another by his Church.[3] The conflicting allegiances of Europe had contributed to the terrible toll of confusion, death, and destruction from 1618 to 1648. In the mid-seventeenth century, many Europeans sought a simpler and, it was hoped, safer set of loyalties.

When in 1618 the Bohemians (today's Czechs) threw the despised agents of a despised Holy Roman Emperor from a window onto a dung heap, the defenestration of Prague signaled not only their scorn for the Emperor, not only the onset of a terrible religious war of Christian Europe, but also an assertion of Bohemian nationalism. The Bohemian claim was that a people of a certain language, society, and tradition had a right to choose their own religion and to govern themselves, free from the competing universalistic claims of Emperor and Pope.

[1] 1 Treaties of Peace Between Sweden and the Holy Roman Empire and Between France and the Holy Roman Empire (Peace of Westphalia, October 14, 1648), 1 C.T.S. 119-356.

[2] T. Hobbes, *Leviathan* (Everyman's Library ed. 1987) [hereinafter cited as "Hobbes"].

[3] *L'Évêque d'York:* "Le Roi est la force et il est la loi!"
Becket: "Il est la loi écrite, mais il est une autre loi, non écrite, qui finit toujours par courber la tête des rois."
J. Anouilh, *Becket ou l'honneur de Dieu,* 3ième acte (1958).

Though hotly disputed for three awful decades (some estimate that half of Germany died as a result of war, siege, starvation, pillage, and disease), similar sovereign assertions were embodied in the two peace treaties of Münster and Osnabrück. The Peace of Westphalia legitimated the right of sovereigns to govern their peoples free of outside interference, whether any such external claim to interfere was based on political, legal, or religious principles. The two 1648 peace treaties elaborated in great detail which sovereign ruled what. The Peace was a great property settlement for Europe, a quieting of title across the continent. It stilled many of the competitions for land and loyalty that had devastated much of what otherwise would have been the prizes of war.

What 1648 most significantly inaugurated, and what Thomas Hobbes significantly conceptualized, was the organizing principle of the state, particularly the sovereign state. Sovereignty as a concept formed the cornerstone of the edifice of international relations that 1648 raised up. Sovereignty was the crucial element in the peace treaties of Westphalia, the international agreements that were intended to end a great war and to promote a coming peace. The treaties of Westphalia enthroned and sanctified sovereigns, gave them powers domestically and independence externally. But what exactly did "sovereignty" mean? How did being a "sovereign" work? Because Hobbes in 1651 provided some answers to these questions raised so critically in 1648, *Leviathan* took on the lasting importance it did.

Hobbes crafted and fit a crucial puzzle piece into an emerging picture of the new Europe. Hobbes' lasting contribution was the envisioning, in his own words, of "that great Leviathan, or rather (to speak more reverently) of that *Mortall God*, to which we owe under the *Immortall God*, our peace and defence." Rather than believing in any number of loyalties, Hobbes believed that all men required "a Common Power, to keep them in awe, and to direct their actions to the Common Benefit."[4] This Common Power, the Leviathan, required a single authoritarian state:

> The only way to erect such a Common Power, as may be able to defend them from the invasion of Forraigners, and the injuries of one another, and thereby to secure them in such sort, as that by their owne industrie, and by the fruites of the Earth, they may nourish themselves and live contentedly; is, to conferre all their power and strength upon one Man, or upon one Assembly of men, that may reduce all their Wills, by plurality

[4] Hobbes, supra, at 89.

> of voices, unto one Will: which is as much as to say, to appoint one Man, or Assembly of men, to beare their Person; and every one to owne, and acknowledge himselfe to be Author of whatsoever he that so beareth their Person, shall Act, or cause to be Acted, in those things which concerne the Common Peace and Safetie; and therein to submit their Wills, everyone to his Will, and their Judgments, to his Judgment.[5]

This "Multitude so united in one Person, is called a Commonwealth in latine Civitas . . . that great Leviathan."[6] The person, be it one man or an assembly, in whom is united the multitude, commonwealth, *civitas*, or leviathan "is called Soveraigne, and said to have *Soveraigne Power*; and everyone besides, his Subject."[7]

Hobbes' celebration of the Leviathan, the sovereign state, provided a crucial bit of the ideological machinery necessary to operate the structure of world politics crafted at Westphalia. Given the long traditions of loyalty to Church as well as to King, to guild as well as to city, to baron as well as to empire, there needed to be some sort of solvent to dissolve these old ties and some sort of glue to fasten a new and simpler allegiance. Hobbes offered both solvent and glue, proffering the notion that the key actor on the world's stage was the sovereign state to which all loyalty was due internally and which was unrestrained externally.

So successful was the political settlement of Westphalia and so useful was Hobbes' concept of Leviathan and the sovereign state that both became deeply imbedded in the public consciousness. It is difficult now even to conceive that a world of sovereign states is fundamentally an intellectual abstraction, a humanly devised creation, albeit one of tremendous force and utility for more than three centuries.

2. *Grotius and the Law of War and Peace*

As Hobbes offered a plausible vision of a sovereign state at the right place at the right time, so Hugo Grotius was timely on the same scene with a workable theory of a law and order for inter-state relations. In 1625, 26 years before *Leviathan*, Grotius' *De Jure Belli ac Pacis* was

[5] Ibid.
[6] Ibid.
[7] Id. at 90.

published in the midst of terrible slaughter. That the excesses of the Thirty Years' War motivated Grotius is plain from the book's Prologue:

> I have had many and weighty reasons for undertaking to write upon this subject. Throughout the Christian world I observed a lack of restraint in relation to war, such as even barbarous races should be ashamed of; I observed that men rush to arms for slight causes, or no cause at all, and that when arms have once been taken up there is no longer any respect for law, divine or human; it is as if, in accordance with a general decree, frenzy had openly been let loose for the committing of all crimes.
>
> Confronted with such utter ruthlessness, many men who are the very furthest from being bad men, have come to the point of forbidding all use of arms to the Christian, whose rule of conduct above everything else comprises the duty of loving all men. To this opinion sometimes John Ferus and my fellow countryman Erasmus seem to incline, men who have the utmost devotion to peace in both Church and State; but their purpose, as I take it, is, when things have gone in one direction, to force them in the opposite direction, as we are accustomed to do, that they may come back to a true middle ground. But the very effort of pressing too hard in the opposite direction is often so far from being helpful that it does harm, because in such arguments the detection of what is extreme is easy, and results in weakening the influence of other statements which are well within the bounds of truth. For both extremes therefore a remedy must be found that men may not believe either that nothing is allowable, or that everything is.[8]

But was there any such remedy? Grotius had not been by any means the first to write or to speculate about what became modern international law.[9] Antecedents of the discipline—treaties, diplomacy, arbitration, laws of war—go back thousands of years.[10] Grotius himself owed an intellectual debt to a number of sixteenth-century Spanish theologians—Vitoria, Suárez, and others—who sought to apply the Catholic Church's medieval theories of natural law to the new realities

[8] H. Grotius, *De Jure Belli ac Pacis Libri Tres* 20 (Kelsey trans. 1913) [hereinafter cited as "Grotius"].

[9] The actual term *international law* was invented in 1789 by the English philosopher Jeremy Bentham in a flurry of new legal definitions. Janis, Jeremy Bentham and the Fashioning of "International Law," 78 *American Journal of International Law* 405 (1984).

[10] A. Nussbaum, *A Concise History of the Law of Nations* 1-16 (rev. ed. 1962).

of international politics as they urged the Spanish Crown to deal justly with the natives that Spain had found and conquered in the Americas.[11]

Some argue that in light of the Spanish tradition, Grotius' truly distinctive contribution was that he "secularized" international law.[12] Indeed, it is true that Grotius, unlike the Spaniards, presumed to write outside a single Christian denomination, seeking to fashion a law of nations that could appeal to and bind Catholics and various denominational Protestants alike.[13] However, it is doubtful, given his times and his character, that Grotius meant to effect a strictly secular refashioning of the medieval Catholic natural law tradition. His approach was very different from a truly secular author like Machiavelli, who felt that princes ought to be fundamentally irreligious and faithfully unscrupulous. Machiavelli believed that Christianity was a less desirable religion for princes than were the pagan faiths of ancient times because Christianity placed "the supreme happiness in humility, lowliness, and a contempt for worldly objects."[14] Machiavelli's belief in the folly of faithfulness for sovereigns is illustrated by his famous parable in *The Prince*:

> A prince being thus obliged to know well how to act as a beast must imitate the fox and the lion, for the lion cannot protect himself from traps, and the fox cannot defend himself from wolves. One must therefore be a fox to recognize traps, and a lion to frighten wolves. Those that wish to be only lions do not understand this. Therefore, a prudent ruler ought not to keep faith when by doing so it would be against his interest, and when the reasons which made him bind himself no longer exist. If men were all good, this precept would not be a good one; but as they are bad, and would not observe their faith with you, so you are not bound to keep faith with them. No legitimate grounds ever failed a prince who wished to show colourable excuse for the non-fulfillment of his promise. Of this one could furnish an infinite number of modern examples, and show how many times peace has been broken, and how many promises

[11] Kunz, Natural Law Thinking in the Modern Science of International Law, 55 *American Journal of International Law* 951 (1961).

[12] Id. at 951-952.

[13] Janis, Religion and International Law: Some Standard Texts, *The Influence of Religion on the Development of International Law* 61, 63 (Janis ed. 1991) [hereinafter cited as "Janis, Religion and International Law"].

[14] N. Machiavelli, *The Prince and the Discourses* 284-285 (Lerner ed. 1950).

> rendered worthless, by the faithlessness of prince, and those that have been best able to imitate the fox have succeeded best.[15]

Grotius' ideas were quite different. His basic notion was that there was an authentic law of nations, which was based on the "mutual consent" of sovereigns acting in the context of a "great society of states."[16] Though meant to be religiously neutral, Grotius' vision of the law of nations was not secular, but rather was a liberal Christian pronouncement.[17] Theologically, Grotius was a Remonstrant, a follower of Arminius, whose pupil he had been at Leiden. Arminius rejected the Calvinist principle of predestination and embraced the concept that Jesus had been sent to the world to redeem all humankind. All could receive God's grace if they believed in God's law. It was this liberal, more or less universalist, doctrine that ultimately led to Grotius' arrest and imprisonment when the Remonstrants were repressed by Prince Maurits and the Calvinist party in the Netherlands.[18] When Grotius wrote *De Jure Belli ac Pacis,* he was in exile in France, as Hobbes would be 26 years later when *Leviathan* was published.

Grotius used religious citations freely in his text.[19] Acknowledging that "I frequently appeal to the authority of the books which men inspired by God have either written or approved," Grotius went on to say that one must distinguish the laws of the Old and New Testaments from the laws of nature.[20] "The New Testament I use in order to explain—and this cannot be learned from any other source—what is permissible to Christians."[21] Grotius considered it "as certain that in that most holy law a greater degree of moral perfection is enjoined upon us than the law of nature, alone and by itself, would require."[22]

Most important, Grotius believed that sovereigns not only made rules, but also were obliged to live with the rules one made, *pacta sunt*

[15] Id. at 64.

[16] Grotius, supra, at 15.

[17] M.W. Janis, *America and the Law of Nations 1776-1939* 49-71 (2010) [hereinafter cited as "Janis, America and the Law of Nations"].

[18] E. Dumbauld, *The Life and Legal Writings of Hugo Grotius* 11-19 (1969); H. Vreeland, *Hugo Grotius: The Father of the Modern Science of International Law* 68-120 (1917).

[19] Janis, Religion and International Law, supra, at 63-65.

[20] Grotius, supra, at 26-27.

[21] Id. at 27.

[22] Ibid.

servanda. The covenants or contracts of sovereigns were legally and morally binding and not just Machiavellian temporary arrangements of mutual convenience. As men and women could bind themselves together in religious communities and to the law of God, so could sovereigns bind themselves to the law of nations. That there was anything transitory to or hypocritical in commitments made in the law of nations was a notion alien to Grotius. God and the law of nature obliged promisors to keep their promises and makers of contracts to honor their commitments.[23] Even more binding was an oath:

> The chief effect of an oath is to put an end to disputes. "In every dispute the oath is final for confirmation," says the inspired writer of *To the Hebrews.* Similar to this is the statement of Philo: "An oath is the witnessing of God in a matter under dispute." Not unlike it is the statement of Dionysius of Halicarnassus: "The strongest pledge of good faith among men, both Greeks and barbarians, which no time will destroy, is that which makes the gods sponsors by means of sworn agreements." Thus among the Egyptians an oath was "the strongest pledge of men to one another."[24]

Compared to private contracts, treaties were a "more excellent kind of agreement" and, though made by the sovereign, binding on the whole of the people.[25] Treaties were to be fulfilled and interpreted in good faith.[26] Even between enemies, good faith, either expressed or implied, was the foundation for all promises.[27]

That Grotius in particular and Protestants in general should put faith in law and covenant as means to moderate the cruelties attending the relations of states should come as no surprise. A respect for law runs deep in the Protestant tradition. As Max Weber wrote about law and Calvinism:

> [A]ll the more emphasis was placed on those parts of the Old Testament which praise formal legality as a sign of conduct pleasing to God. They held the theory that the Mosaic Law had only lost its validity through Christ in so far as it contained ceremonial or purely historical precepts

[23] Id. at 220-361.
[24] Id. at 372.
[25] Id. at 391-408.
[26] Id. at 409.
[27] Id. at 804.

> applying only to the Jewish people, but that otherwise it had always been valid as an expression of the natural law, and must hence be retained. This made it possible, on the one hand, to eliminate elements which could not be reconciled with modern life. But still, through its numerous related features, Old Testament morality was able to give a powerful impetus to that spirit of self-righteous and sober legality which was so characteristic of the worldly asceticism of this form of Protestantism.[28]

Not only were the laws of nations legally and morally binding, but they were also rationally calculated to lead to the long-term advantage of sovereign states. Here, again, Grotius treated the sovereign state as a person and a reasonable person at that:

> [T]he national who in his own country obeys its laws is not foolish, even though, out of regard for that law, he may be obliged to forgo certain things advantageous for himself, so that nation is not foolish which does not press its own advantage to the point of disregarding the laws common to nations. The reason in either case is the same. For just as the national, who violates the law of his country in order to obtain an immediate advantage, breaks down that by which the advantages of himself and his posterity are for all future time assured, so the state which transgresses the laws of nature and of nations cuts away also the bulwarks which safeguard its own future peace.[29]

Grotius' argument was based on natural law in the sense that he believed that sovereign states, like individuals, naturally relied upon communities for their well-being [for natural law, see Chapter 3]. The pacts made within these communities needed to be respected for the benefit of all, even the greatest individual or state. "[L]aw is not founded on expedience alone, there is no state so powerful that it may not some time need the help of others outside itself, either for purposes of trade, or even to ward off the forces of many foreign nations united against it." "[N]o association of men can be maintained without law . . . surely also that association which binds together the human race, or binds many nations together, has need of law."[30]

[28] Max Weber, *The Protestant Ethic and the Spirit of Capitalism* 165 (Parsons trans. 1958).

[29] Grotius, supra, at 16.

[30] Id. at 17.

A. Sovereignty and International Law

Grotius, a diplomat as well as a jurist, was no starry-eyed idealist. His approach to international law and order was quite different from the utopian proposals of the Abbé de Saint-Pierre who, almost a century later, would suggest a peace-keeping league of the principal European powers.[31] Grotius acknowledged that war, as well as law, was a natural feature of human society. His belief was that war and law were inextricably intertwined:

> Least of all should that be admitted which some people imagine, that in war all laws are in abeyance. On the contrary war ought not to be undertaken except for the enforcement of rights; when once undertaken, it should be carried on only within the bounds of law and good faith. Demosthenes well said that war is directed against those who cannot be held in check by judicial processes. For judgements are efficacious against those who feel that they are too weak to resist; against those who are equally strong, or think they are, wars are undertaken. But in order that wars may be justified, they must be carried on with no less scrupulousness than judicial processes are wont to be.[32]

Grotius' ideas, like those of Hobbes, emerged at a critical moment. To settle the Catholic-Protestant disputes underlying the Thirty Years' War, the Treaties of Westphalia of 1648 acknowledged the sovereign authority of Europe's individual princes and nations in matters both religious and political.[33] Not only the authority of the Emperor, but also the temporal jurisdiction of the Church, including its power to regulate and moderate wars, were much restricted in theory and practice. If international conflicts were to be controlled, the Emperor and the Church, through their edicts and regulations, could no longer be counted on as principal instruments of moderation. Rather, sovereign states would have to restrain themselves. Grotius' suggestion that the states could do so with a positive law of nations grounded on moral

[31] Saint-Pierre, *Projet pour rendre la paix perpétuelle en Europe* (Garnier Frères ed. 1981).

[32] Grotius, supra, at 18.

[33] M.W. Janis, The Shadow of Westphalia: Majoritarian Religion and Strasbourg Law, 4 *Oxford Journal of Law and Religion* 75 (2015); B. Straumann, The Peace of Westphalia as a Secular Constitution, 15 *Constellations* 173 (2008).

notions of covenant caught hold in the imagination of those conducting world affairs. Four centuries later, it holds on still.[34]

B. LAW AND WAR

1. *The Development of the Laws of War*

States have long employed law to limit their conflicts. The idea that wars should be subject to legal rules dates back at least to the ancient civilizations of India, China, Israel, Greece, and Rome.[35] Some of the laws of war had and have to do with the rightful manner of war, what international lawyers call the *jus in bello.* Ancient India's *Book of Manu,* which dates from the fourth century B.C., instructed:

> When (the king) fights with his foes in battle, let him not strike with weapons concealed (in wood), nor with (such as are) barbed, poisoned, or the points of which are blazing with fire.
>
> Let him not strike one who (in flight) has climbed on an eminence, nor a eunuch, nor one who joins the palms of his hands (in supplication), nor one who (flees) with flying hair, nor one who sits down, nor one who says "I am thine";
>
> Nor one who sleeps, nor one who has lost his coat of mail, nor one who is naked, nor one who is disarmed.[36]

Other laws of war prescribe when nations could or should go to war, what is termed the *jus ad bellum.* The idea that initiating a war

[34] On the continuing fascination of Grotian thought for international politics, see *Hugo Grotius and International Relations* (H. Bull, B. Kingsbury & A. Roberts eds. 1992); Lesaffer, The Grotian Tradition Revisited: Change and Continuity in the History of International Law, 73 *British Yearbook of International Law* 103 (2003). On dating modern international law to 1648, see American Law Institute, 1 *Restatement (Third) of the Foreign Relations Law of the United States* 17-18 (1987) [hereinafter cited as "Restatement (Third)"].

[35] I. Brownlie, *International Law and the Use of Force by States* 3-4 (1963) [hereinafter cited as "Brownlie"].

[36] 1 *The Law of War: A Documentary History* 3 (Friedman ed. 1972) [hereinafter cited as "Friedman"].

could be either right or wrong goes back at least to the Greeks, while the early Christians believed all wars immoral.[37] In the fifth century, St. Augustine distinguished just from unjust wars:

> Just wars are usually defined as those which avenge injuries, when the nation or city against which warlike action is to be directed has neglected either to punish wrongs committed by its own citizens or to restore what has been unjustly taken by it. Further that kind of war is undoubtedly just which God Himself ordains.[38]

By the Middle Ages, St. Augustine's concept of the just war and the notion that the Church had a role to play in regulating international conflict were generally accepted throughout Europe. A typical device employed by the Church to moderate the military cruelties of the day was the Peace, such as the one imposed by the Archbishop of Arles in 1035, for parts of southern France:

> This is the peace or truce of God which we have received from heaven through the inspiration of God, and we beseech you to accept it and observe it even as we have done; namely, that all Christians, friends and enemies, neighbors and strangers, should keep true and lasting peace one with another from vespers on Wednesday to sunrise on Monday, so that during these four days and five nights, all persons may have peace, and, trusting in this peace, may go about their business without fear of their enemies.[39]

In the sixteenth century, Spanish jurists—Vitoria, Ayala, and Suárez—collected and explicated biblical, classical, and historical sources to fashion theories of just wars to justify and to moderate the

[37] Brownlie, supra, at 3-5.

[38] Id. at 5.

[39] *A Documentary History of Arms Control and Disarmament* 6 (Dupuy & Hammerman eds. 1973) [hereinafter cited as "Dupuy & Hammerman"]. Analogously, Pope John Paul II called for a day-long global truce in all wars for October 27, 1986, a call joined by 155 religious leaders representing, *inter alia*, Buddhists, Hindus, Jews, Moslems, and Shintoists. Suro, 12 Faiths Join Pope to Pray for Peace, *N.Y. Times*, Oct. 28, 1986, at A3. In 2002, in the aftermath of 9/11, Pope John Paul II led a day of prayer in a ceremony at Assisi attended by almost 200 clerics including Christians, Muslims, Jews, Buddhists, and Sikhs praying that religion ought not to motivate international conflict. BBC News, Pope Leads World Prayer Days (Jan. 24, 2002), www.bbc.co.uk (Jan. 31, 2019).

Spanish conquests in the Americas. As we have seen, these works in turn served as an inspiration and foundation for the writings of Hugo Grotius. In part thanks to Grotius and the development of a modern law of nations, at the conclusion of the Thirty Years' War and for almost three centuries thereafter Europe entered a period of what may be termed "the golden age of the *jus in bello*, of formal, positive constraints on the conduct of war."[40] International conflicts in Europe were generally set piece battles waged by professional armies fighting for fixed and limited political objectives. Civilian populations (often perceived as prizes) were usually left more or less unharmed by military forces.

In the nineteenth century, the law of nations continued to develop and, to an extent, to progress. Going well beyond the customary international rules of the seventeenth and eighteenth centuries, the nations turned increasingly to international conventions. Especially notable were treaties concluded to limit war or to remove its causes. For example, in 1815, the principal European powers agreed to the perpetual neutrality of Switzerland, a pact respected to this day.[41] In 1817, the United States and the United Kingdom agreed to limit their naval forces on the Great Lakes, a settlement eventually leading to the demilitarization of the U.S.-Canadian border.[42]

The effort to codify and develop the laws of war and to control the use of arms became even more earnest as the nineteenth century unfolded. There were profound hopes that war might eventually be abolished since civilization had become so advanced. Such hopes were closely linked to the idea that international arbitration and adjudication could come to replace war as a means of international dispute settlement [see Chapter 5]. In 1856, Great Britain, Austria, France, Prussia, Russia, Sardinia, and Turkey signed the Declaration of Paris, hoping to settle outstanding differences concerning the rights of neutral shipping in times of war.[43] In 1864, Switzerland, Baden, Belgium, Denmark, Spain, France, Hesse, Italy, the Netherlands, Portugal, Prussia, and Würtemberg signed the Geneva Red Cross Convention, protecting hospital and ambulance crews.[44] In 1868, 17 countries,

[40] Howard, *Temperamenta Belli:* Can War Be Controlled?, *Restraints on War: Studies in the Limitation of Armed Conflict* 1, 5 (Howard ed. 1979) [hereinafter cited as "Howard"].

[41] See Dupuy & Hammerman, supra, at 38-39.

[42] Id. at 39-41.

[43] Friedman, supra, at 156-157.

[44] Id. at 187-191.

including Great Britain, Austria-Hungary, France, Italy, Prussia, Russia, and Turkey, signed the Declaration of St. Petersburg, renouncing the use of certain explosive projectiles.[45]

Between 1899 and 1907, in a high tide of idealism, there issued the many various and detailed Hague Conventions. The conventions were the product of two Hague Peace Conferences, the first called in 1898 by Tsar Nicholas II of Russia, who declared "'that the present moment would be very favorable for seeking, by means of international discussion, the most effectual means of insuring to all peoples the benefits of a real and durable peace, and, above all, of putting an end to the progressive development of the present armaments.'"[46] The very listing of the Hague Conventions illuminates the aspirations of the time: on the Pacific Settlement of International Disputes (1899); on the Laws and Customs of War on Land (1899); on the Adaption to Maritime Warfare of the Principles of the Geneva Convention of 1864 (1899); on Prohibiting Launching of Projectiles and Explosives from Balloons (1899); on Prohibiting Use of Expanding Bullets (1899); on Prohibiting Use of Gases (1899); on the Exemption of Hospital Ships from Taxation in Time of War (1904); on the Pacific Settlement of International Disputes (1907); on the Limitation of Employment of Force for Recovery of Contract Debts (1907); on the Opening of Hostilities (1907); on the Laws and Customs of War on Land (1907); on the Rights and Duties of Neutral Powers and Persons in War on Land (1907); on the Status of Enemy Merchant Ships at the Outbreak of Hostilities (1907); on the Conversion of Merchant Ships into War Ships (1907); on the Laying of Automatic Submarine Contact Mines (1907); on Bombardment by Naval Forces in Time of War (1907); on the Adaption to Maritime Warfare of Principles of the Geneva Convention (1907); on Restrictions with Regard to Right of Capture in Naval War (1907); on the Establishment of an International Prize Court (1907); on the Rights and Duties of Neutral Powers in Naval War (1907); and on Prohibiting Discharge of Projectiles and Explosives from Balloons (1907).[47]

[45] Id. at 192-193.

[46] Quoted in J.H. Choate, *The Two Hague Conferences* 5 (1913) [hereinafter cited as "Choate"].

[47] Friedman, supra, at 204-256, 270-397; A. Eyffinger, *The 1907 Hague Peace Conference: "The Conscience of the Civilized World"* (2007).

However, the great hopes behind the many Hague and like conventions came to naught. Joseph Choate, the First Delegate of the United States to the Second Hague Peace Conference, wrote in 1913 that there were preparations for a Third Hague Conference in 1915 and plans set "to celebrate the completion of a century of unbroken peace between ourselves and all the other great nations of the earth."[48] No Third Conference was held. The century of unbroken peace was missed by a year.

2. *Great Wars and Futile Laws*

Beginning in 1914, Europe fought what was called the "Great War" with great and novel savagery. Millions were killed. Aerial bombardment and poison gas were employed. Civilization had apparently not progressed all that far. The warring nations issued learned volumes in the midst of the conflict accusing their enemies of destroying the fabric of international law.[49] The truth was that international law had neither kept the peace nor much mitigated the slaughter. What was to be done? Could international law reform help ensure a more pacific future?

Post-war reactions to the failure of international law were curious. On the one hand, many forsook international law as a path to world peace. Some academics, for example, left the discipline of international law to fashion new subjects called "international relations" and "international politics" in the belief that only by integrating politics, economics, sociology, history, and other scholarly perspectives could they adequately identify the causes of interstate conflicts and help prevent future wars.[50] Others turned all the more fervently to international law, thinking that the cause of the Great War was that the laws of war had been theretofore too loosely drafted. Indeed, though the traditional laws of war had attempted to moderate and reduce the chances of conflict, war itself, of course, remained legal and appropriate when undertaken to defend international legal rights.[51]

[48] Choate, supra, at 92.

[49] French Foreign Ministry, *Germany's Violations of the Laws of War* (Bland trans. 1915).

[50] See R.L. Buell, *International Relations vii* (2d ed. 1929).

[51] See L. Oppenheim, 2 *International Law* 177-178 (7th ed. E. Lauterpacht 1952).

B. Law and War

In the spirit of enacting new and more prohibitive laws of war diplomats representing Germany, the United States, Belgium, France, Great Britain, Italy, Japan, Poland, and Czechoslovakia gathered and concluded the Kellogg-Briand Pact of August 27, 1928.[52] The parties condemned "recourse to war for the solution of international controversies, and renounce[d] it as an instrument of national policy in their relations with one another."[53] They agreed "that the settlement or solution of all disputes or conflicts of whatever nature or of whatever origin they may be, which may arise among them, shall never be sought except by pacific means."[54]

The Kellogg-Briand Pact was, however, an exercise in futility. The scholars, in this case, were more prescient than the statesmen. Germany and Japan utterly disregarded their pledge not to use force. A second World War even more dreadful than the first soon ensued. Grotius himself would well have been shocked by the barbarities visited on Europe and across the globe. Between 1939 and 1945, the gap between the theory of the laws of war and the realities of international practice was wider than ever before. The laws of war stood discredited and in disarray.

The discredit and disarray came at a time when the desire to limit war with law was all the greater because of the development of nuclear weapons and other advanced means of destruction. From the end of the Second World War in 1945, and alongside agreement in the United Nations Charter Article 2(4)'s prohibition on the use of force, to the end of the Cold War in 1989, there were countless pleas for arms control and disarmament.[55] Yet the record over eight decades has been dismal. From 1945 to 1980, there were more than 100 wars and more than 25 million war-related fatalities.[56] Writing in 1985, Louis

[52] Treaty Providing for the Renunciation of War as an Instrument of National Policy, 46 Stat. 2343, T.S. No. 796, 2 Bevans 732, 94 L.N.T.S. 57 (signed at Paris August 27, 1928; entered into force July 24, 1929).

[53] Id., art. I.

[54] Id., art. II.

[55] See United Nations Charter, article 2(4) which reads "All Members shall refrain in their international relations from the threat or use of force against the territorial integrity or political independence of any state." June 26, 1945, 59 Stat. 1031; Disarmament Resolutions Adopted by the General Assembly, U.N. Doc. A/AC187/29/Add.1 (1978).

[56] B.H. Weston, R.A. Falk & A.A. D'Amato, *International Law and World Order* 259 (1st ed. 1980).

Sohn lamented that though for "forty years the nations of the world have been obsessed with nuclear weapons and the need to abolish them . . . [t]he results are pitiful."[57] Nuclear weapons and their proliferation, for example, to India and Pakistan, Israel and North Korea, still bedevil us. Moreover, wars never cease; at one estimate there were 28 armed conflicts ongoing in 2016; probably worst of all has been the Russian armed invasion of Ukraine.[58] In his 2009 Nobel Peace Prize Address, President Obama, though commending international law and non-violence, recognized that "[e]vil does exist in the world. A non-violent movement could not have halted Hitler's armies."[59] War is still very much with us.

The causes of the modern deterioration of the edifice of the laws of war as constructed between 1625 and 1914 are, according to the noted military historian Michael Howard, two. First, the golden "Grotian period" of the laws of war was itself attributable to a very useful consensus among the then-ruling aristocracies of Europe that there was more to be lost than could possibly be won by permitting unlimited conflicts. Beginning with the First World War, prevailing opinion welcomed at least some wars as more or less unlimited engagements, it being sometimes popularly justifiable, for example, to aim to totally destroy or to totally transform another society.[60] Second, recent decades witnessed an explosion of the means for mass destruction. Warfare is totally destructive in ways unimagined by earlier generations.[61] Professor Nafziger laments how discouraging it is "to realize how little progress the global community has made in [limiting war with law] since the time of Hugo Grotius nearly four centuries ago."[62]

[57] Sohn, How to Obtain Peace, Security and Justice, 19 *International Lawyer* 599 (1985); Russia Invades Ukraine, 116 *American Journal of International Law* 595 (2022).

[58] Ploughshares, *Armed Conflict Report 2016 Summary*, www.ploughshares.ca (Jan. 31, 2019);

[59] Obama Nobel Lecture Addresses Use of Force in Global Affairs, 104 *American Journal of International Law* 127, 128 (2010)

[60] Howard, supra, at 5-7.

[61] Id. at 8-9.

[62] Nafziger, Going to War and Going Ahead with the Law, 50 *Willamette Law Review* 321, 346-347 (2014); see Cry Havoc and Ignore the Laws of War, *The Economist*, Aug. 9, 2025, at 49.

3. *Arms Control and Disarmament*

Have we now reached a pass comparable to that when Grotius wrote? Are the horrors of war again so vivid that there will be incentive enough to fashion new legal limits to control the use of force by states? The end of the Cold War did not herald a new day for world peace. Like the aspirations for international courts and international organizations [see Chapters 5 and 7], international accords providing for arms control and disarmament seem to offer only limited encouragement. What is the record?

The Congressional Research Service listed more than 40 arms control treaties and agreements in force as of September 2025.[63] The earliest of the agreements that limit nuclear weapons is the 1963 Nuclear Test Ban Treaty, which prohibits "any nuclear weapon test explosion . . . in the atmosphere; . . . outer space; or underwater."[64] The Test Ban Treaty was the result of long and troubled negotiations among the great powers beginning in May 1955. The obvious need addressed by the Treaty was to limit radioactive fallout, which had become a serious health hazard by the 1950s. The Treaty has been ratified or acceded to by 125 states, including the United States, the Soviet Union (now Russia), India, Pakistan, and the United Kingdom, but other nuclear powers, like China and France, have refused to sign or ratify.[65] A new Comprehensive Nuclear Test Ban Treaty was negotiated in 1994 and opened for signature in 1996, but as of the end of 2018 had not yet come into force.[66] Underground nuclear testing is still permitted, although it is limited by 1974 and 1976 treaties between the United States and the Soviet Union.[67]

[63] Congressional Research Service, *Arms Control and Nonproliferation: A Catalog of Treaties and Agreements* (September 25, 2025) [hereinafter cited as "CRS"].

[64] Treaty Banning Nuclear Weapon Tests in the Atmosphere, in Outer Space and Under Water, art. I(1), 14 U.S.T. 1313, T.I.A.S. No. 5433, 480 U.N.T.S. 43 (done at Moscow August 5, 1963; entered into force October 10, 1963).

[65] U.N. Office of Disarmament Affairs, *Treaty Banning Nuclear Weapons Tests in the Atmosphere, in Outer Space and Under Water*, http://disarmament.un.org/treaties (Jan. 31, 2019).

[66] United Nations, *U.N. Treaty Collection*, Comprehensive Nuclear-Test-Ban Treaty, https://treaties.un.org (Jan. 31, 2019). All 44 members of the Conference on Disarmament must ratify the convention before it comes into force; eight members have not ratified. The U.S. Senate rejected ratification in 1999. Ibid.

[67] The two agreements have been substantially modified to provide for better means of verification. Leich, Contemporary Practice of the United States Relating to

Arguably the most important nuclear weapons treaty in practice has been the Non-Proliferation Treaty of 1968 (NPT), as of 2025, ratified by 191 states,[68] which prohibits states that already have nuclear weapons from transferring such weapons to other states and imposes a duty upon states not already possessing nuclear weapons to refrain from acquiring them:

> Each non-nuclear-weapon State Party to the Treaty undertakes not to receive the transfer from any transferor whatsoever of nuclear weapons or other nuclear explosive devices or of control over such weapons or explosive devices directly, or indirectly; not to manufacture or otherwise acquire nuclear weapons or other nuclear explosive devices; and not to seek or receive any assistance in the manufacture of nuclear weapons or other nuclear explosive devices.[69]

The NPT also provides for the conclusion of agreements between non-nuclear-weapons states and the International Atomic Energy Agency (IAEA) to verify compliance.[70] Such safeguards agreements have entered into force for about 140 states.[71] Though not compelled to do so by the Treaty's language, the United States has also entered into a safeguards agreement with the IAEA,[72] an agreement paralleled by treaties between the IAEA and the United Kingdom and France.[73]

International Law: Protocols to Test Ban and Nuclear Explosions Treaties, 84 *American Journal of International Law* 907-908 (1990).

[68] Treaty on the Non-Proliferation of Nuclear Weapons, 21 U.S.T. 483, T.I.A.S. No. 6839, 729 U.N.T.S. 161 (done at Washington, London, and Moscow July 1, 1968; entered into force March 5, 1970). CRS, supra. T. Cotton, 1 *The Law of Arms Control and the International Non-Proliferation Regime: Preventing the Spread of Nuclear Weapons* (2017).

[69] Id., art. II.

[70] Id., art. III.

[71] See International Atomic Energy Agency, *IAEA Safeguards Overview*, www.iaia.org (Oct. 31, 2019); U.N. Office for Disarmament Affairs, *Treaty on the Non-Proliferation of Nuclear Weapons*, http://disarmament.un.org (Feb. 18, 2015). Notable was the agreement of Libya, which ratified the Treaty in 2004, after extensive negotiations with the United States and the United Kingdom. U.S./U.K. Negotiations with Libya Regarding Nonproliferation, 98 *American Journal of International Law* 194, 197 (2004).

[72] Agreement Between the United States of America and the International Atomic Energy Agency for the Application of Safeguards in the United States, Arms Control and Disarmament Agency, *Arms Control and Disarmament Agreements: Texts and Histories of Negotiations* 206 (1996).

[73] Id. at 86. See S. Courteix, *Exportations nucléaires et non-prolifération* (1978).

However, the efficacy of IAEA safeguards was thrown into doubt by the discovery, during and after the 1991 Persian Gulf War, that Iraq had made significant progress, despite the IAEA, in developing a clandestine nuclear weapons program.[74] Moreover, other nations with significant nuclear programs, such as India, Israel, and Pakistan, have refused to join the Non-Proliferation Treaty system altogether.[75] In 2005, the U.S. Department of State spoke of what it called "a crisis of noncompliance" with the NPT.[76] By 2020, whatever power the NPT regime had exerted had waned. Of special significance is Iran's nuclear program.[77] Since 2006, the Security Council has imposed sanctions on Iran, but is still struggling to control Iranian nuclear development, which endangers the sensitive political environment of the Middle East.[78] In the words of one commentator, "the impression of nuclear disorder and bi-power complacency is generating a tangible sense of urgency."[79]

Other treaties limiting nuclear weapons include the ABM Treaty of 1972 and the agreements issuing from the Strategic Arms Limitation Talks (SALT) between the United States and the Soviet Union.[80] Although treaties that control and limit nuclear weapons, like the SALT agreements, are always highly susceptible to the changing tides of domestic and international politics, such as the Russian invasion of Ukraine,[81] there is little question that on balance they have helped, however marginally, in preventing nuclear war.[82]

[74] Carnahan, Protecting Nuclear Facilities from Military Attack: Prospects After the Gulf War, 86 *American Journal of International Law* 524 (1992).

[75] *The Arms Control Reporter*, at 602aNPT05p13 (Jan. 2005).

[76] U.S. Concerns About Declining Effectiveness of Nonproliferation Regime, 99 *American Journal of International Law* 917 (2005).

[77] CRS, supra.

[78] United States and Six Other States Reach Interim Agreement on Iranian Nuclear Program, 108 *American Journal of International Law* 109 (2014).

[79] Joshi, Going Critical: As the Nuclear Non-Proliferation Treaty Reaches Its Half-Century, It Is Creaking at the Joints, *The Economist: The World in 2020* 72 (2020).

[80] Treaty Between the United States of America and the Union of Soviet Socialist Republics on the Limitation of Anti-Ballistic Missile Systems, 23 U.S.T. 3435, T.I.A.S. No. 7503 (signed at Moscow May 26, 1972; entered into force October 3, 1972). Arms Control and Disarmament Agency, supra, at 113-127, 189-217.

[81] The Congressional Research Service terms present U.S. arms control relations with Russia as "uncertain", CRS, supra. In general, see D. Caldwell, *The Dynamics of Domestic Politics and Arms Control: The SALT II Treaty Ratification Debate* (1991).

[82] J. Dahlitz, *Nuclear Arms Control* (1983).

Albeit the proliferation of nuclear weapons remained a serious and deteriorating situation, the nuclear arms race between the superpowers underwent for a time a remarkable turn for the better. On July 31, 1991, the United States and the Soviet Union signed the Treaty on the Reduction and Limitation of Strategic Offensive Arms. This so-called START Treaty was the first to actually reduce strategic nuclear weapons.[83] In 1992 Protocols, the START Treaty was broadened to include the new, post-USSR states of Russia, Belarus, Kazakhstan, and Ukraine.[84] The U.S. Senate voted its consent to the START Treaty on October 1, 1992; the Russian Duma voiced its assent on November 4, 1992.[85] A new treaty, the Strategic Offensive Reduction Treaty (SORT), dramatically reducing the number of nuclear warheads to be deployed by the United States and Russia, was signed by Presidents Bush and Putin on May 22, 2002, approved by the U.S. Senate and the Russian Duma, and entered into force on June 1, 2003.[86] President Obama signed a new START agreement with Russia on April 8, 2010, which was ratified by the U.S. Senate on December 22, 2010, and by the Russian Duma on January 26, 2011, and which, *inter alia*, limited each party to 1,550 strategic nuclear warheads.[87] Both the United States and Russia satisfied the threshold prior to a February 2018 deadline.[88]

However, in 2019, the Trump administration gave formal notification to Russia that the United States was withdrawing from the Intermediate-Range Nuclear Forces Treaty, a move deplored by Germany's Chancellor Angela Merkel as "really bad news." A new START Treaty was signed in

[83] Leich, Contemporary Practice of the United States Relating to International Law: Arms Control and Disarmament: United States-Soviet Union: START Treaty (1991), 86 *American Journal of International Law* 354 (1992).

[84] Leich, Contemporary Practice of the United States Relating to International Law: Arms Control and Disarmament: U.S.-C.I.S. Protocol to START Treaty, 86 *American Journal of International Law* 799 (1992). See Crossette, 4 Ex-Soviet States and U.S. in Accord on 1991 Arms Accord, *N.Y. Times,* May 24, 1992, at A1.

[85] Cushman, Senate Endorses Pact to Reduce Strategic Arms, *N.Y. Times,* Oct. 2, 1992, at A6; *Washington Post,* Nov. 5, 1992, at A3.

[86] Arms Control Association, *U.S.-Russian Nuclear Arms Control Agreements at a Glance,* www.armscontrol.org (Jan. 31, 2019).

[87] Ibid. Crook, Senate Gives Advice and Consent to START Treaty; Resolution of Advice and Consent Sets Numerous Requirements and Conditions, 105 *American Journal of International Law* 358 (2011).

[88] CRS, supra.

2023.[89] Professor Tannenwald laments that "the dream of disarmament now seems more distant than ever," a tragedy she attributes in large measure to the worsened relations between Russia and the United States, which between them possess more than 90 percent of all nuclear weapons. Sadly, some national leaders, notably Russia's Putin, America's Trump, and North Korea's Kim Jong Un "glorify the world's most destructive weapons."[90]

Given the destructiveness of nuclear weapons, arguments are made that their possession and use are outlawed by international law.[91] If this is so, the law regulating nuclear weapons must be an especially ineffective form of international law, since so many nuclear weapons are actually deployed. It may be sounder to conclude that international law permits, though sometimes limits, the possession of nuclear weapons and prohibits the use of nuclear weapons except in certain extraordinary circumstances,[92] propositions more or less in keeping with postwar practice,[93] and consonant with the 1996 advisory opinion of the International Court of Justice on the *Legality of the Threat or Use of Nuclear Weapons* as requested by the General Assembly. In the *Nuclear Weapons* advisory opinion, the ICJ held that there was neither customary nor conventional international law either authorizing or comprehensively prohibiting the threat or use of nuclear weapons, but that any threat or use of force by means of nuclear weapons had to meet the requirements of Articles 2(4) and 51 of the U.N. Charter and of the international law of armed conflict and of international humanitarian law.[94]

Treaties limiting non-nuclear weapons of mass destruction include the Biological Weapons Convention of 1972 (BWC), which prohibits the development, production, and acquisition of "[m]icrobial or other

[89] state.gov/new-start-treaty.

[90] Tannenwald, The Vanishing Nuclear Taboo? How Disarmament Fell Apart, 97 *Foreign Affairs*, No. 6, at 16, 17 (2018).

[91] L. Meyrourtz, R. Falk & J. Sanderson, *Nuclear Weapons and International Law* (1981); Grief, The Legality of Nuclear Weapons, *Nuclear Weapons and International Law* (I. Pogany ed. 1987).

[92] Shaw, Nuclear Weapons and International Law, *Nuclear Weapons and International Law* (I. Pogany ed. 1987) [hereinafter cited as "Shaw"]; *Nuclear Weapons Under International Law* (G. Nystuen, S. Casey-Maslen & A. Bersagel eds. 2014).

[93] See G. Schwarzenberger, *The Legality of Nuclear War* (1958); *Nuclear Weapons, the Peace Movement and the Law* (Dewar, Pailwala, Picciotto & Ruete eds. 1986).

[94] 1996 I.C.J. Reports 226.

biological agents, or toxins whatever their origin or method of production, of types and in quantities that have no justification for prophylactic, protective, or other peaceful purposes."[95] The BWC came into force in 1975 and addressed what many perceive to be a "peculiarly perverse nature of the whole undertaking," that is, to use modern science aimed at relieving humankind of disease instead to inflict disease upon them.[96] Although the first years of the conventional regime were hopeful, the 1980s were characterized by mistrust and setbacks.[97] Despite the prohibitions of the BWC, by 2007, "deadlier and more sophisticated biological weapons than were imaginable in 1992 can now be and have been produced," calling perhaps for a "harder" BWC regime.[98] In the view of one expert, the BWC "is at last moving in the right direction, after years of being pulled this way and that by dissentient forces."[99]

The BWC has been joined by the Chemical Weapons Convention (CWC), which after more than two decades of negotiation, finally emerged in Geneva in 1992, entered into force in 1997, and is now ratified by 193 states including the United States and Russia.[100] Moreover, by now it is accepted that the use of chemical weapons in both international and non-international warfare is prohibited by customary international law.[101] It may be that only six states maintain a chemical weapons program—China, Iran, Israel, Egypt, North Korea, and Syria.[102] In 2013, following

[95] Convention on the Prohibition of the Development, Production and Stockpiling of Bacteriological (Biological) and Toxin Weapons and on Their Destruction, art. I, 26 U.S.T. 583, T.I.A.S. No. 8062, 1015 U.N.T.S. 163 (done at Washington, London, and Moscow April 10, 1972; entered into force March 26, 1975).

[96] N.A. Sims, *The Diplomacy of Biological Disarmament: Vicissitudes of a Treaty in Force, 1975-1985* 5-6 (1988).

[97] Id. at 5, 51-90, 199-252.

[98] Beard, The Shortcomings of Indeterminacy in Arms Control Regimes: The Case of the Biological Weapons Convention, 101 *American Journal of International Law* 271, 271-276, 316-321 (2007).

[99] Nicholas A. Sims, *The Future of Biological Disarmament: Strengthening the Treaty Ban on Weapons* 1 (2009).

[100] U.N. Office for Disarmament Affairs, *Convention on the Prohibition of the Development, Production, Stockpiling and Use of Chemical Weapons and on Their Destruction*, http://disarmament.un.org/treaties (Jan. 31, 2019).

[101] Zimmerman & Sener, Chemical Weapons and the International Criminal Court, 108 *American Journal of International Law* 436 (2014).

[102] Nigel D. White, *Advanced Introduction to International Conflict and Security Law* 20 (2014) [hereinafter cited as "White"].

Syrian nerve gas attacks on civilians, the Security Council implemented a joint U.S.-Russian "Framework for Elimination of Syrian Chemical Weapons."[103] It was announced in September 2014 that, led by the Organization for the Prohibition of Chemical Weapons and the United Nations, 96 percent of Syria's declared chemical warfare stockpile had been destroyed, with work underway to demolish 12 remaining Syrian production facilities.[104] That progress may have been lost. Between 2015 and 2019, there were once again documented Syrian chemical weapons attacks.[105]

As to arms control agreements relating to conventional weapons, the Conventional Armed Forces in Europe (CFE) Treaty was signed in Paris on November 19, 1990. The CFE Treaty limited and reduced armaments in Europe in five categories: battle tanks, armored combat vehicles, artillery, combat aircraft, and attack helicopters.[106] Signatories included most of the states from both the NATO and the Warsaw Pact agreements. In 1992, the United States, Russia, and 27 other states agreed to reduce the number of troops they would station in continental Europe.[107] However, in an important arms control setback, Russia denounced the CFE Treaty in 2007, claiming "extraordinary circumstances."[108] Other conventional weapons arms control treaties include the Convention on the Prohibition of the Use, Stockpiling, Production and Transfer of Anti-Personnel Mines and their Destruction, which was opened for signature in 1997 and came into force on March 1, 1999,[109] and the 2008 Convention on Cluster Munitions in force since August including 104 countries, though not China, Russia, or the

[103] Progress Is Made Implementing U.S.-Russian Framework for Eliminating Syrian Chemical Weapons, 108 *American Journal of International Law* 95 (2014).

[104] news.un.org/en/story/2026/01/1166724.

[105] See Timeline of Syrian Chemical Weapons Activity 2012-2019, www.armscont rol.org; and Jakes, U.S. Says Syria Used Chemical Weapons, *N.Y. Times*, Sept. 27, 2019, at A13.

[106] Leich, Contemporary Practice of the United States Relating to International Law: Arms Control and Disarmament: Conventional Armed Forces in Europe (CFE) Treaty, 85 *American Journal of International Law* 539, 548 (1991).

[107] *Washington Post*, July 7, 1992, at A14.

[108] Y. Zarakhovich, Why Putin Pulled Out of a Key Treaty, *Time*, https://time.com /archive/6940962/why-putin-pulled-out-of-a-key-treaty/ (July 14, 2007).

[109] As of 2019, there were 164 ratifications, https://treaties.un.org (Jan. 31, 2019).

United States.[110] Despite such progress, Nigel White laments that the "UN remains largely ineffectual in the area of disarmament in the post–Cold War era of a world awash with conventional arms fuelled by a market-driven arms industry."[111]

Some arms control treaties protect regions, such as the 1959 Antarctic Treaty, which provides that "Antarctica shall be used for peaceful purposes only" and prohibits the establishment of military bases there, albeit there are fears that the regime is now "falling apart."[112] There are parallel provisions in the 1967 Outer Space Treaty:

> States Parties to the Treaty undertake not to place in orbit around the Earth any objects carrying nuclear weapons or any other kinds of weapons of mass destruction, install such weapons on celestial bodies, or station such weapons in outer space in any other manner.
>
> The moon and other celestial bodies shall be used by all States Parties to the Treaty exclusively for peaceful purposes. The establishment of military bases, installations and fortifications, the testing of any type of weapons and the conduct of military maneuvers on celestial bodies shall be forbidden.[113]

And in the 1971 Seabed Arms Control Treaty:

> The States Parties to this Treaty undertake not to emplant or emplace on the seabed and the ocean floor and in the subsoil thereof beyond the

[110] U.N. Treaty Collection, *Convention on Cluster Munitions,* https://treaties.un.org (Jan. 31, 2019). See Hulme, The 2008 Cluster Munitions Convention: Stepping Outside the CCW Framework (Again), 58 *International & Comparative Law Quarterly* 219 (2009).

[111] White, supra, at 21.

[112] Antarctic Treaty, art. I, 12 U.S.T. 794, T.I.A.S. No. 4780, 402 U.N.T.S. 71 (signed at Washington December 1, 1959; entered into force June 23, 1961). See The Antarctic: Diplomacy on Ice, *The Economist,* Nov. 2, 2024, at 53.

[113] Treaty on Principles Governing the Activities of States in the Exploration and Use of Outer Space, Including the Moon and Other Celestial Bodies, art. IV, 18 U.S.T. 2410, T.I.A.S. No. 6347, 610 U.N.T.S. 205 (done at Washington, London, and Moscow January 27, 1967; entered into force October 10, 1967). See Tronchetti, Legal Aspects of the Military Uses of Outer Space, 1 *Handbook of Space Law* 331 (F. von der Dunk ed. 2015).

> outer limit of a seabed zone . . . any nuclear weapons or any other types of weapons of mass destruction.[114]

There is also a 1967 Treaty for the Prohibition of Nuclear Weapons in Latin America.[115] Treaties prohibit the acquisition of nuclear weapons by Austria, Bulgaria, Finland, Hungary, Italy, and Romania.[116] State-sponsored cyber-attacks are increasingly common and may call for some form of international regulation similar to the traditional arms control agreements.[117]

Better communications to avert the risk of accidental wars are the aim of such treaties as the "Hot Line" Agreements[118] and the "Accident Measures" Agreement.[119] The latter provides that the United States and the Soviet Union will "undertake to notify each other immediately in the event of an accidental, unauthorized or any other unexplained incident involving a possible detonation of a nuclear weapon which could create a risk of outbreak of nuclear war."[120] Russia, the United States, and 22 other countries also agreed in 1992 to permit surveillance flights over North America, Europe, and the Asian part of Russia to help enforce arms control agreements in what is being called the Open Skies Treaty.[121]

[114] Treaty on the Prohibition of the Emplacement of Nuclear Weapons and Other Weapons of Mass Destruction on the Seabed and the Ocean Floor and in the Subsoil Thereof, art. I(1), 23 U.S.T. 701, T.I.A.S. No. 7337, 955 U.N.T.S. 115 (done at Washington, London, and Moscow February 11, 1971; entered into force May 18, 1972).

[115] 634 U.N.T.S. 281 (signed at Mexico City February 1967; entered into force April 22, 1968).

[116] Shaw, supra.

[117] See D. Caldwell & R.E. Williams, Insecurity in Cyberspace, *Seeking Security in an Insecure World* 157 (2016).

[118] See Arms Control and Disarmament Agency, supra, at 19-23, 91-94.

[119] Agreement on Measures to Reduce the Risk of Outbreak of Nuclear War Between the United States of America and the Union of Soviet Socialist Republics, 22 U.S.T. 1590, T.I.A.S. No. 7186, 807 U.N.T.S. 57 (signed at Washington September 30, 1971; entered into force September 30, 1971).

[120] Id., art. 2.

[121] *Washington Post,* Mar. 21, 1992, at A18. As of January 2019, 34 states were party to the agreement. *Final Document of the Second Review Conference on the Implementation of the Treaty on Open Skies,* OSCE Doc. OSCC.RC/39/10 (Jan. 31, 2019).

4. *International Humanitarian Law*

In the long tradition of the *jus in bello,* modern-day international humanitarian law strives to mitigate unnecessary human suffering once war has already begun.[122] The central principle of international humanitarian law is that destruction is lawful only for the sake of military necessity. As the 1868 Declaration of St. Petersburg put it: "[T]he only legitimate object which states should endeavor to accomplish during war is to weaken the military force of the enemy."[123] By 2019, there were 77 international agreements providing for the humanitarian conduct of war in force.[124]

The realm of international humanitarian law is often associated with the activities of the Red Cross. The International Committee of the Red Cross (ICRC) was founded by Henry Dunant, a Swiss citizen shocked by the horrors of the Italian battlefield of Solferino in 1859.[125] An international non-governmental organization, the ICRC has responsibility for promoting and ensuring respect for the four 1949 Geneva Conventions for the Protection of War Victims: the Convention for the Amelioration of the Condition of the Wounded and Sick in Armed Forces in the Field; the Convention for the Amelioration of the Condition of the Wounded, Sick, and Shipwrecked Members of Armed Forces at Sea; the Convention Relative to the Treatment of Prisoners of War; and the Convention Relative to the Protection of Civilian Persons in Time of War.[126] Drafted under the auspices of the Red Cross, the four Geneva Conventions replaced three earlier humanitarian conventions of 1906

[122] *The Handbook of International Humanitarian Law* (D. Fleck 3d ed. 2014).

[123] Friedman, supra, at 192.

[124] ICRC, Treaties and States Parties to Such Treaties, https://ihl-databases.icrc.org/ihl (Jan. 31, 2019).

[125] H. Dunant, *A Memory of Solferino* (English ed. reprinted by the ICRC 1986).

[126] 6 U.S.T. 3114, T.I.A.S. No. 3362, 75 U.N.T.S. 31 (dated at Geneva August 12, 1949; entered into force October 21, 1950; for the United States February 2, 1956); 6 U.S.T. 3217, T.I.A.S. No. 3363, 75 U.N.T.S. 85 (dated at Geneva August 12, 1949; entered into force October 21, 1950; for the United States February 2, 1956); 6 U.S.T. 3316, T.I.A.S. No. 3364, 75 U.N.T.S. 135 (dated at Geneva August 12, 1949; entered into force October 21, 1950; for the United States February 2, 1956); 6 U.S.T. 3516, T.I.A.S. No. 3365, 75 U.N.T.S. 287 (dated at Geneva August 12, 1949; entered into force October 21, 1950; for the United States February 2, 1956). For the work of the ICRC, see their publications, e.g., International Committee of the Red Cross, *1991 Annual Report* (1992).

and 1929.[127] Violations of these earlier conventions constituted some of the grounds for the judgments of the Nuremberg, Tokyo, and other war crimes tribunals [see Chapter 8]. Although the Geneva Conventions have been ratified by most states, there is considerable debate about the extent to which they apply in civil wars or with respect to non-state-sponsored combatants;[128] even two 1977 Protocols failed to settle the uncertainties.[129] The work of the International Committee of the Red Cross carries on. It was, for example, instrumental in the negotiation of the 1997 Convention on the Prohibition of Anti-Personnel Landmines.[130]

There is a close relationship between international humanitarian law and international human rights law [see Chapter 8]. Although for a time some of the doctrine rejected this linkage, due in part to the relative antiquity and hence respectability of international humanitarian law, by now it seems appropriate to recognize international humanitarian law as that part of international human rights law that deals with "the rights of particular categories of human beings—principally, the sick, the wounded, prisoners of war—in particular circumstances, i.e., during periods of armed conflict."[131] Fundamentally, humanitarianism, like human rights law, is grounded on "principles of charity and justice."[132]

Sadly, the United States now stands accused of repeated violations of international humanitarian law. As Anthony Lewis put it, introducing more than 1,200 pages of documentation of

> legal memoranda that sought to argue away the rules against torture. They are an extraordinary paper trail to mortal and political disaster: to

[127] H.S. Levie, 1 *Protection of War Victims* xiii (1979).

[128] See M. Hess, *Die Anwendbarkeit des humanitären Völkerrechts inbesondere in gemischten Konflikten* (1985); M. Venthey, *Guérilla et droit humanitaire* (1976).

[129] Draper, The Implementation and Enforcement of the Geneva Conventions of 1949 and of the Two Additional Protocols of 1977, 164 *Hague Recueil* 1, 25-28 (1979). The United States has ratified neither of the two 1977 Protocols. See Aldrich, Prospects for United States Ratification of Additional Protocol I to the 1949 Geneva Conventions, 85 *American Journal of International Law* 1 (1991).

[130] *The Banning of Anti-Personnel Landmines: The Legal Contribution of the International Committee of the Red Cross* (L. Maresca & S. Maslen eds. 2000).

[131] Robertson, Humanitarian Law and Human Rights, *Studies and Essays on International Humanitarian Law and Red Cross Principles in Honour of Jean Pictet* 793, 797 (Swinarski ed. 1984); Meron, The Humanization of Humanitarian Law, 94 *American Journal of International Law* 239 (2000).

[132] Walzer, On Humanitarianism: Is Helping Others Charity, or Duty, or Both?, 90 *Foreign Affairs* 69, 80 (2011).

> an episode that will soil the image of the United States in the eyes of the world for years to come. They also provide a painful insight into how the skills of the lawyer—skills that have done so much to protect Americans in this most legalized of countries—can be misused in the cause of evil.[133]

Much publicized U.S. violations of international humanitarian law were those at the by-now infamous Iraqi prison, Abu Ghraib, where photographs were taken and then broadly circulated of prisoner abuses by U.S. forces. These abuses were characterized by an official U.S. Army investigation "as egregious acts and grave breaches of international law" and prompted an apology by President Bush, who said he "was sorry for the humiliation suffered by the Iraqi prisoners and the humiliation suffered by their families."[134] The Bush administration's methods of detention and interrogation in general and at Guantánamo in particular have provoked significant challenges at U.S. and international law. In an important group of cases in 2004—*Hamdi, Rasul,* and *Padilla*—the Supreme Court set some judicial limits on Executive Branch assertions of extraordinary authority.[135] In 2008, in *Boumediene v. Bush,* the U.S. Supreme Court ruled that "[e]ven when the United States acts outside its borders, its powers are not 'absolute and unlimited' but are subject to such restrictions as are expressed in the Constitution," and held that prisoners held at Guantánamo were entitled to a constitutional privilege of habeas corpus.[136] New challenges to U.S. practices are posed by unmanned drone strikes on suspected terrorist targets.[137]

[133] Lewis, Introduction, *The Torture Papers: The Road to Abu Ghraib xiii* (K.J. Greenberg & J.L. Dratel eds. 2005).

[134] U.S. Abuse of Iraqi Detainees at Abu Ghraib Prison, 98 *American Journal of International Law* 591, 595, 596 (2004); Dickinson, Abu Ghraib: The Battle over Institutional Culture and Respect for International Law Within the U.S. Military, *International Law Stories* 405 (J.E. Noyes, L.A. Dickinson & M.W. Janis eds. 2007).

[135] Hamdi v. Rumsfeld, 542 U.S. 507 (2004); Rasul v. Bush, 542 U.S. 466 (2004); Rumsfeld v. Padilla, 542 U.S. 426 (2004). See Hathaway, *Hamdan v. Rumsfeld*: Domestic Enforcement of International Law, *International Law Stories* 337 (J.E. Noyes, L.A. Dickinson, M.W. Janis & C.M. Vazquez eds., 2d ed, 2025); see Agora: Military Commissions Act of 2006, 101 *American Journal of International Law* 35-98, 322-381 (2025).

[136] 558 U.S. 723, 765, 798 (2008).

[137] Bowett, Drone Strikes May Violate International Law Says the UN, *Guardian*, Oct. 18, 2013; United States Legal Justification for Drone Strikes on Anwar Al-Awlaki Released, 108 *American Journal of International Law* 550 (2014).

Whatever remedies U.S. domestic law might provide, solving the problems of international humanitarian law posed by modern conflicts such as those in the Middle East and Ukraine is essentially a matter for international law in general.[138] Even the Geneva Conventions are themselves in doubt.[139] As Professor Hathaway puts it, "[i]f the law of war is to survive today's existential challenges, the United States and its allies need to treat it not as an optional constraint to be adjusted or shrugged off as needed but as an unmoving pillar of the global legal order."[140]

C. THE STATE AND INTERNATIONAL RELATIONS

1. States as Subjects of International Law

Like any legal system, international law has its subjects: those entities or legal persons entitled to rely upon legal rights, obliged to respect legal duties, and privileged to utilize legal processes. More than any other legal system, however, international law is concerned with the reciprocal rights and duties of states. Thus, an important part of international law is devoted to the definition and attributes of states, as well as to the determination of the degree to which non-state actors, such as international organizations, private parties, and non-governmental organizations, are entitled to international legal personality [see also Chapters 7 and 8].

Within the ambit of international law, a state is understood to be composed of four essential elements: a defined territory, a permanent population, a government, and a capacity to conduct international

[138] Taub, New Questions About Mideast Events and the Laws of War, *New York Times*, Oct. 20, 2023, at A10. The International Court of Justice has advised that there have been violations of international humanitarian law in Gaza, the West Bank, and elsewhere. See Legal Consequences Arising from the Policies and Practice of Israel in the Occupied Palestinian Territory, Including East Jerusalem, Advisory Opinion, July 19, 2024,

[139] Laws of War for a Wicked World, *The Economist*, Aug. 9, 2025, at 51.

[140] Hathaway, War Unbound: Gaza, Ukraine and the Breakdown of International Law, 103 *Foreign Affairs*, no. 3, at 84-96 (2024).

relations.[141] These elements impart a certain mutual respect among states that we know as sovereignty, one of international law's most important principles. A sovereign state is one that is free to independently govern its own population in its own territory and set its own foreign policy. In his classic eighteenth-century text, Vattel defined nations or states as "political bodies, societies of men who have united together and combine their forces, in order to procure their mutual welfare and society. . . . Every nation which governs itself, under whatever form, and which does not depend on any other nation, is a *sovereign state.*"[142]

States that are subjects of international law are different from constituent states as they may be defined in many municipal laws. In Australia, Mexico, and the United States, for example, what are termed *states* in domestic law lack some of the sovereign attributes, at least an independent capacity to conduct foreign relations, which would be required to qualify them as states for many purposes of international law. Similarly, the provinces of Canada, the Länder of Germany, the regions of Nigeria, and the cantons of Switzerland are all considered to be simply component parts of sovereign states and not themselves sovereign states in international law.[143]

Of course, component states in sovereign unions may be deemed by municipal law to have particular rights and duties in international relations. This can pose difficulties in the practice of international law, for example, in the negotiation, interpretation, application, and observance of treaties.[144] In the United States, complications arise from

[141] See the Convention on Rights and Duties of States, art. 1, 49 Stat. 3097, T.S. No. 881, 3 Bevans 145, 165 L.N.T.S. 19 (done at Montevideo December 26, 1933; entered into force December 26, 1934) [hereinafter cited as "Montevideo Convention"]. Older definitions did not necessarily mention territory: "A sovereign state is generally defined to be any nation of people, whatever may be the form of its internal construction, which governs itself independently of foreign powers." H. Wheaton, *Elements of International Law with a Sketch of the History of the Science* 51 (1st ed. 1836) [hereinafter cited as "Wheaton"]. By 1905, Oppenheim listed four "conditions which must obtain for the existence of a State": a people, a country, a government, and a sovereign government. A Hobbesian high positivist, Oppenheim opined: "Sovereignty is supreme authority, an authority which is independent of any other earthly authority." L. Oppenheim, *International Law* 100-101 (1st ed. 1905).

[142] E. de Vattel, *The Law of Nations* 3-4, 11 (1758 ed. Fenwick trans. 1919).

[143] J.H.W. Verzijl, 1 *International Law in Historical Perspective* 266-269 (1968).

[144] Opeskin, Federal States in the International Legal Order, 43 *Netherlands International Law Review* 353 (1996).

the considerable sovereign powers historically the province of what was originally 13 and is now 50 states. Virginia, for example, found its criminal justice system criticized twice recently in prominent international court cases: by the European Court of Human Rights in the 1989 *Soering* case[145] and by the International Court of Justice in the 1998 *Breard* case.[146] Massachusetts' venture on its own foreign policy vis-à-vis Burma was struck down by the U.S. Supreme Court in *Crosby* in 2000.[147] In 2003, California was prevented from implementing its statute providing for Holocaust Victim Insurance Relief because of constitutionally impermissible interference with the President's authority to conduct foreign policy.[148] A Florida law punishing companies with "business operations in Cuba" was struck down in 2013.[149]

States as subjects of international law usually retain their sovereign personality even when they delegate some of their sovereign powers to other states or to international organizations. Whether a state that has delegated some of its powers remains a sovereign subject of international law is in each case a matter of fact. For example, because Liechtenstein had delegated so many of its sovereign functions to Switzerland, the League of Nations decided that Liechtenstein could no longer be expected to discharge its international obligations adequately to be qualified to be a member of that organization.[150]

[145] Judgment of July 7, 1989, ser. A, no. 161. The European Court of Human Rights held that the conditions and duration of Virginia's death row constituted inhuman treatment under the European Human Rights Convention and ordered the United Kingdom not to extradite a German national to Virginia so long as the death penalty could be imposed.

[146] 1998 I.C.J. Reports 248. Virginia failed both to advise Breard, a Paraguayan national accused of murder, of his treaty right to consular assistance and to respect an ICJ request that his execution be stayed. A similar failure to advise of a treaty right to consular assistance figured for Arizona in the *LaGrand* case brought by Germany to the ICJ. 1999 I.C.J. Reports 9 and for Texas respecting Mexico in *Avena*, 2004 I.C.J., and *Medellín*, 552 U.S. 491 (2008). See Chapter 5.

[147] Massachusetts prohibited companies from doing business with Burma, prompting protests from Japan and the European Union, A State's Foreign Policy: The Mass that Roared, *The Economist*, Feb. 8, 1997, at 60. The Massachusetts statute was held to be unconstitutional. Crosby v. National Trade Council, 530 U.S. 363 (2000).

[148] American Insurance Ass'n v. Garamendi, 539 U.S. 396 (2003).

[149] Odebrecht Constr., Inc. v. Secretary, Florida Dep't of Transp., 715 F.2d 1268 (11th Cir. 2013).

[150] G.H. Hackworth, 1 *Digest of International Law* 48-49 (1940) [hereinafter cited as "Hackworth"]. This is not to say that Liechtenstein, now a member of the United

Contrarily, France, Germany, and the other members of the European Union plainly remain sovereign states and subjects of international law even though they have delegated certain important powers, especially economic, to the European Union [see Chapter 9]. It is highly doubtful that entities constructed on platforms in the sea, usually for purposes of tax avoidance, can be deemed states for the purposes of international law.[151]

2. *The Rights and Duties of States*

By virtue of their sovereign status, states are entitled to an important number of international legal rights and are concomitantly obliged by international legal duties. Central among these is the right of any sovereign state to a status of international legal equality vis-à-vis other states.[152] The United Nations, for example, is explicitly "based on the principle of the sovereign equality of all its Members."[153] Sovereign states are "equal" in the sense that each has an equal right to be free from the threat or use of force against its territorial integrity. Moreover, any state may be entitled to an equal voice or vote in some international organizations, for example, in the General Assembly of the United Nations, and to an equal right to take part generally in international relations, for example, in becoming a party to a treaty or in establishing diplomatic relations with other states. The right of equality of states in international law does not, however, mean that states are legally entitled to equalities of territory or population or of political, economic, cultural, or military influence. States indeed vary widely on all these

Nations and a sometime litigant in the ICJ in the *Nottebohm* case, 1955 I.C.J. Reports 4, is not at present a sovereign state; see Kohn, The Sovereignty of Liechtenstein, 61 *American Journal of International Law* 547, 557 (1967): "[D]espite her smallness, Liechtenstein is legally and politically a sovereign state and deserves the courtesy of being treated as such."

[151] See the German judgment refusing to recognize state status for the "Duchy of Seeland," Case No. 9 K 2565/77 (Federal Republic of Germany, Administrative Court of Cologne, 1978), 80 *International Law Reports* 683; and, more recently, Dean, Abandon Land for a Less-Taxing Life, *The Times* (London), June 16, 2020, at 3.

[152] Lachs, The Development and General Trends of International Law in Our Time, 169 *Hague Recueil* 9, 77-84 (1980).

[153] Charter of the United Nations, art. 2(1), 59 Stat. 1031, T.S. No. 993, 3 Bevans 1153 (signed at San Francisco June 26, 1945; entered into force October 24, 1945).

counts. There are arguments that a new international economic order imposes legal duties on rich countries to redistribute wealth to poor countries [see Chapter 3].

Other rights and duties incidental to state sovereignty are replete in international law. Sovereign states are entitled, *inter alia*, to make international law in conventional and customary forms [see Chapters 2 and 3] and to establish international organizations and tribunals [see Chapters 5, 7, 8, and 9]. They may decide when international law will be incorporated into municipal law [see Chapter 4] and may sometimes escape the jurisdictional reach of foreign courts and laws [see Chapter 10]. As we see below, sovereign states are permitted to defend themselves and to recognize other states. They may participate in international regimes [see Chapter 7] and determine nationality and citizenship. They are also bound to carry out their international legal duties, whether these obligations be to states [see Chapters 2 and 3] or to private parties [see Chapter 8].

It is an increasingly important aspect of international law that states may not, in particular, violate international human rights law no matter whether the duty be owed to aliens or nationals [see Chapter 8]. Rather more controversial is the degree to which states are bound to respect claims of peoples to the right of self-determination.[154] One group's assertion of the right to self-determination is often a threat to another group's state sovereignty, even to a state's territorial integrity and its very existence. Some of the most recent bloody and genocidal atrocities—in the former Yugoslavia, Rwanda, and Chechnya—are examples of the failure of states to tolerantly balance competing claims of state sovereignty and self-determination.[155]

3. State Responsibility

Since ancient times, it has been assumed that states are responsible for giving just satisfaction for injuries that they have illegally or unjustly

[154] In 1960, the U.N. General Assembly resolved that "[a]ll peoples have *those from the Third World* the right to self-determination." Declaration on the Granting of Independence to Colonial Countries and Peoples, G.A. Res. 1514(xv), Dec. 14, 1960.

[155] Kooijmans, Tolerance, Sovereignty and Self-Determination, 43 *Netherlands International Law Review* 211 (1996).

inflicted. Grotius, for example, wrote about damages caused by war: "He who has done injury to another ought first to offer satisfaction to him whom he has injured, through the arbitrament of a fair-minded man; if such an offer of satisfaction is rejected, then his taking up of arms will be without reproach."[156] Nowadays, the law "concerned with the incidence and consequences of illegal acts, and particularly the payment of compensation for loss caused" is ordinarily called the law of state responsibility and includes injuries done by states to individuals [see Chapter 8]. Although the field might also be denominated the law of "international tort," it may be that the term *tort* misleadingly signals too many similarities to the domestic analogue.[157] Among other things, the substance of the law of state responsibility is much less settled than any nation's ordinary law of tort.[158]

The modern employment of the doctrine of state responsibility may be said to have begun with the Jay Treaty arbitration and subsequent nineteenth-century arbitrations led by the United States.[159] The Permanent Court of International Justice adopted the doctrine as early as 1924 in the *Mavrommatis* case.[160] Since 1949, the International Law Commission has struggled to codify the field.[161] The struggles were sharpened by conflicts between Western international lawyers and those from the Third World over claims for reparations for centuries of colonial exploitation, including genocide and slavery.[162] In 2001, the ILC adopted Draft Articles on the Responsibility of States

[156] Grotius, supra, at 185.

[157] I. Brownlie, *Principles of Public International Law* 421 (6th ed. 2003).

[158] Noyes & Smith, State Responsibility and the Principle of Joint and Several Liability, 13 *Yale Journal of International Law* 225 (1988); Sturma, State Succession in Respect of International Responsibility, 48 *George Washington International Law Review* 653 (2016).

[159] I. Brownlie, *State Responsibility (Part I)*, 2-6 (1983).

[160] 1924 P.C.I.J. Ser. A, No. 2.

[161] See Nolte, From Dionisio Anzilotti to Roberto Ago, The Classical International Law of State Responsibility and the Traditional Primacy of a Bilateral Conception of Inter-State Relations, 13 *European Journal of International Law* 1083 (2002).

[162] See Buser, Colonial Injustices and the Law of State Responsibility: The CARICOM Claim for Reparations, 20 *Heidelberg Journal of International Law* 2 (2017); Brunk & Hakimi, Transforming the World with Reparations?, 119 *American Journal of* International Law 380 (2025).

for Internationally Wrongful Acts.[163] However, the doctrine of state responsibility, notwithstanding the efforts of the Draft Article, remains greatly unsettled.[164] [See Chapters 2 and 8.] A noteworthy and remarkable acceptance by a state for responsibility was seen in 2019 in The Netherlands v. Mothers of Srebenica Association, where the Dutch government accepted partial responsibility for a massacre in the former Yugoslavia when the Netherlands withdrew its protecting forces from a strife-torn region.[165]

4. *Self-Defense, Intervention, and Preemptive War*

A sovereign state is entitled to defend itself, including the right to protect its territorial integrity. In his classic nineteenth-century American international law text, Wheaton saw the "right to self-preservation" as an absolute right, lying at the foundation of all of the other rights of states.[166] Subject to often unexercised powers of the Security Council, a state's right of self-defense is nowadays explicitly recognized in Article 51 of the U.N. Charter: "Nothing in the present Charter shall impair the inherent right of individual or collective self-defense if an armed attack occurs against a Member of the United Nations." The right of self-defense is limited by a duty to take only proportional countermeasures, albeit proportionality in any given instance may be difficult to definitively determine.[167] In diplomatic notes surrounding *The Caroline* case of 1837, the United States

[163] *Report of the International Commission on the Work of Its Fifty-Third Session*, UNGAOR, 56th Sess., Supp. No. 10, at 43, U.N. Doc. A/56/10 (2001).

[164] See Sloane, The Use and Abuse of Necessity in the Law of State Responsibility, 106 *American Journal of International Law* 447 (2012); Paparinskis, The Once and Future Law of State Responsibility, 114 *American Journal of International Law* 618 (2020).

[165] No. 17/04567 (Supreme Court of The Hague, 19 July 2019). See Spijkers, Question of Legal Responsibility for Srebencica Before the Dutch Courts, 14 *International Criminal Justice* 819 (2016), and Karasz, Netherlands Was 10 Per Cent Liable in Srebencia Deaths, Dutch Court Finds, *N.Y. Times*, July 19, 2019, https://www.nytimes.com/2019/07/19/world/europe/srebrenica-massacre-netherlands.html.

[166] Wheaton, supra, at 81.

[167] Franck, On Proportionality of Countermeasures in International Law, 102 *American Journal of International Law* 715, 719-734 (2008).

and the United Kingdom agreed that violent counter-measures required a plausible showing of necessity.[168]

Concomitant with Article 51's right to self-defense is Article 2(4)'s prohibition against *"the threat or use of force against the territorial integrity or political independence of any state."* Similarly, the 1933 Montevideo Convention on the Rights and Duties of States provides that "[n]o state has the right to intervene in the internal or external affairs of another."[169] The General Assembly of the United Nations has with only one abstaining and no dissenting vote condemned "armed intervention and all other forms of interference or attempted threats against the personality of the State or against its political, economic and cultural elements."[170] In 1990-1991, in a rare period of relaxed Great Power relations, the Security Council was able to unite to condemn state aggression. However, when one of the Permanent Members of the Security Council is guilty of intervention, little can be done, for example, respecting Russia's intervention in Ukraine.[171]

Although the prohibition against intervention plainly represents an overwhelming consensus of states, there have been constructed so many excuses and exceptions to Article 2(4) that the basic principle against intervention is sometimes greatly whittled down in practice. There is, for example, a generally accepted notion that it is not illegal intervention to send armed forces into a foreign state in order to support a foreign government already in power when the foreign government requests outside assistance. The Soviet Union in this fashion justified its so-called Brezhnev Doctrine, which asserted its right to intervene militarily to prevent a socialist state from leaving the Soviet Union's political orbit.[172] Similarly, the legal justification of collective

[168] 29 *British and Foreign State Papers* 1129, and 30 *British and Foreign State Papers* 195; see Noyes, *The Caroline*: International Law and Resort to Force, in *International Law Stories* 367 (J.E. Noyes, L.A. Dickinson, M.W. Janis & C.M. Vazquez eds., 2d ed. 2025).

[169] Montevideo Convention, supra, art. 8.

[170] U.N.G.A. Res. 2131 (XX), art. 21, December 21, 1965; 10 U.N.G.A.O.R. Supp. (No. 15), at 107, U.N. Doc. A/5815.

[171] Daugirdas & Mortensen, United States Condemns Russia's Use of Force in Ukraine and Attempted Annexation of Crimea, 108 *American Journal of International Law* 784 (2014); Le Goff, Le Droit International en Apesanteur, *Ouest France*, July 25, 2025, at 1.

[172] Cutler, The Right to Intervene, 64 *Foreign Affairs* 96, 108 (1985) [hereinafter cited as "Cutler"].

self-defense at the invitation of the government of South Vietnam figured importantly in official statements supporting the intervention of the United States in the Vietnam War.[173]

The United States, the Soviet Union, and other countries also proclaimed the right to intervene on behalf of insurgents if the rebels were deemed to be "democratic" and fighting against a "repressive regime."[174] The door is thus opened to intervention by foreign states to fight on opposing sides in the same country: one nation justifying its conduct on the grounds of supporting a legitimate regime, another arguing that it is legally permitted to bolster the cause of freedom-fighting revolutionaries.

As for the doctrine, most international lawyers agree that intervention should normally be illegal, and there can ordinarily be a good case made against any state's military intervention in any other state.[175] The International Court of Justice held in the *Corfu Channel* case that "[t]he Court can only regard the alleged right of intervention as the manifestation of a policy of force, such as has, in the past, given rise to most serious abuses and such as cannot, whatever be the present defects in international organization, find a place in international law."[176] However, there has emerged the doctrine of the responsibility to protect, enunciated by the United Nations in the Secretary General's Report of 2009.[177] The Report provides, *inter alia*, that "[i]f a State is manifestly failing to protect its population, the international community must be prepared to take collective action." Fierce debates still divide advocates for and against intervention in specific circumstances,

[173] See Meeker, Viet-Nam and the International Law of Self-Defense, 56 *Department of State Bulletin* 54 (1967); and the general discussion in *The Vietnam War and International Law* (Falk ed. [4 vols.] 1968, 1969, 1972, 1976).

[174] Cutler, supra, at 106-112.

[175] Schachter, The Legality of Pro-Democratic Invasion, 78 *American Journal of International Law* 645 (1984).

[176] 1949 I.C.J. Reports 4, 35. This position was reaffirmed in Military and Paramilitary Activities in and Against Nicaragua (Nicaragua v. United States of America), Merits, Judgment, 1986 I.C.J. Reports 14, 106, reprinted in 25 *International Legal Materials* 1023, 1069 (1986). See Maier, ed., Appraisals of the ICJ's Decision: Nicaragua v. United States (Merits), 81 *American Journal of International Law* 77 (1987).

[177] *Implementing the Responsibility to Protect,* 4/2/677, Jan. 12, 2009.

for example, in Kosovo, Somalia, Rwanda, Libya, Iraq, Afghanistan, Syria, and Ukraine.[178]

Also divisive was the so-called Bush Doctrine, first enunciated in 2002, that the United States has the right to take preemptive military action. As restated in 2006, the Bush administration declared:

> If necessary, however, under long-standing principles of self-defense, we do not rule out the use of force before attacks occur, even if uncertainty remains as to the time and place of the enemy's attacks. When the consequences of an attack with [weapons of mass destruction] are potentially so devastating, we cannot afford to stand idly by as grave dangers materialize. This is the principle and logic of preemption.[179]

The original 2002 declaration raised questions at the United Nations and elsewhere about the legality of the doctrine of preemptive war in the light of Articles 2(4) and 51 of the U.N. Charter [see Chapter 7]. Despite its rhetorical reaffirmation in 2006, the Bush Doctrine may already be dated in U.S. practice. Along with the troubles at Abu Ghraib and Guantánamo, the Bush Doctrine has been perceived as contributing to a decline in U.S. influence overseas, driving away allies and isolating American foreign policy.[180] Moreover, coupled with the 2002 declaration, the unilateral U.S. invasion and occupation

[178] For debate about humanitarian intervention and the responsibility to protect, see B. Lepard, *Rethinking Humanitarian Intervention* (2002); and Editorial Comments: NATO's Kosovo Stahn, Responsibility to Protect: Political Rhetoric or Emerging Legal Norm, 101 *American Journal of International Law* 99 (2007); Chesterman, Leading from Behind: The Responsibility to Protect After the Obama Doctrine and Humanitarian Intervention After Libya, 25 *Ethics & International Affairs* 279 (2011). For the debate about the legality of interventions pursuant to American international political leadership, see Vagts, Hegemonic International Law, 95 *American Journal of International Law* 843 (2001); Mallaby, The Reluctant Imperialist: Terrorism, Failed States, and the Case for American Empire, 81 *Foreign Affairs* (March/April) 2 (2002); and Sloss, Forcible Arms Control: Preemptive Attacks on Nuclear Facilities, 4 *Chicago Journal of International Law* 39 (2003).

[179] The National Security Strategy of the United States of America, March 2006, at https://georgewbush-whitehouse.archives.gov/nsc/nss/2006/. See United States Issues New National Security Document, Reaffirms Possible Preemptive Use of Force, 100 *American Journal of International Law* 690 (2006).

[180] Daniel, Dombrowski & Payne, The Bush Doctrine Is Dead; Long Live the Bush Doctrine?, 49 *Orbis* 199 (2005); Gordon, The End of the Bush Revolution, 85 *Foreign Affairs* 75 (2006).

of Iraq in 2003 threw into question the legitimacy of the U.N. collective security system.[181] The isolating of U.S. foreign policy did not abate during the Obama administration,[182] and became a defining feature of the Trump administration.[183]

5. *The Territory of States*

The rights of a sovereign state extend not only to its land territory. A state is also entitled to claim national maritime zones contiguous to its shores, such as territorial seas, and certain sovereign rights over the resources of their continental shelf and in exclusive economic zones [see Chapter 7]. Furthermore, states may and do claim certain sovereign rights over superadjacent airspace [see Chapter 7].

Over all their territory as well as over their ships on the high seas, states may and do exercise all those rights to which they are normally entitled as subjects of international law, limited, of course, by the obligations imposed by that law. Among a state's territorial rights are the rights to make, adjudicate, and enforce its municipal law, although other states may also have concurrent jurisdiction based on one or another extraterritorial jurisdictional principle [see Chapter 10].

Territory has frequently changed hands as a result of war, revolution, or simple sale; treaties often have been employed to effect the transfer of territory or to settle disputes about territory's delimitation. The 1783 Treaty of Peace between Great Britain and its former 13 colonies, for example, carefully drew lines between the new United States and what is now Canada:

> From the North West angle of Nova Scotia viz, that angle which is formed by a Line drawn due North from the Source of St. Croix River to the Highlands, along the said Highlands which divide those Rivers that empty themselves into the River St. Lawrence, from those which fall into the Atlantic Ocean, to the North-Western-most Head of the Connecticut River; Thence down along the Middle of that River to the Forty Fifth Degree of

[181] Gray, A Crisis of Legitimacy for the UN Collective Security System?, 56 *International & Comparative Law Quarterly* 157 (2007).

[182] Krieg, Externalizing the Burden of War: The Obama Doctrine and U.S. Foreign Policy in the Middle East, 92 *International Affairs* 97 (2016).

[183] Kupchan, *Isolationism* Is Not a Dirty Word, *The Atlantic: Ideas*, Sept. 27, 2020, www.theatlantic.com.

> North Latitude; from thence by a Line due West on said Latitude until it strikes the River Iroquois or Cataraquy; Thence along the middle of said River into Lake Ontario; through the middle of said Lake until it strikes the communication by water between that Lake and Lake Erie.[184]

Sometimes territorial disputes between states have been submitted as cases to international courts or arbitral tribunals. In practice, a fairly large number of international adjudications and arbitrations have involved issues of territorial delimitation. These usually have been resolved by the weighing of collective evidences of state sovereignty to determine either effective occupation or the peaceful and continuous display of state authority or, occasionally, by the application of equitable principles [see Chapter 3].[185] Problems of territorial delimitation persist, especially in Africa, where many of the boundaries established by colonial regimes are particularly artificial.[186] There are longstanding territorial issues between Israel and the Palestinians that have proved impossible of solution.[187]

Some territory is not allocated to any state. International law knows the possibility of a *res nullius*, an unattributed territory; such was the presumptive legal status of much of the territory accumulated by Europe's colonial empires in the fifteenth to the nineteenth centuries. Territory may also be *res communis*, common or international territory, such as the high seas, Antarctica, and the moon and outer space [see Chapter 7]. A condominium prevails when territory is administered by two or several

[184] Treaty of Peace Between the United States and the United Kingdom, art. 2, 12 Bevans 8 (signed at Paris September 3, 1783; entered into force May 12, 1784) [hereinafter cited as "Treaty of Paris"].

[185] See the Minquiers and Ecrehos case, 1953 I.C.J. Reports 47; the North Sea Continental Shelf cases, 1969 I.C.J. Reports 4; Charney, Progress in International Maritime Boundary Delimitation Law, 88 *American Journal of International Law* 227 (1994); Jiménez de Aréchaga, General Course in Public International Law, 159 *Hague Recueil* 1, 183-188 (1978).

[186] See I. Brownlie, *African Boundaries: A Legal and Diplomatic Encyclopedia* (1979).

[187] See Unsettling: America's Decision to Recognize Israeli Settlements Makes Peace Less Likely, *The Economist*, Nov. 23, 2019, at 16-18; Halbfinger & Kershner, Netanyahu Asserts Golan Move "Proves" Exception to International Law, *N.Y. Times International*, Mar. 27, 2019, at A6. Following the illegal invasion of Ukraine, Finland has worried that Russia may attempt to seize the Aaland Islands. See Protecting Aaland: Temptation Islands, *The Economist*, Sept. 21, 2024, at 48.

states as was, for example, the New Hebrides (now Vanuatu) by Britain and France,[188] or, as the ICJ decided in the 1992 *Land, Island and Maritime Frontier Dispute*, over the Gulf of Fonseca by El Salvador, Honduras, and Nicaragua.[189]

6. *The Recognition and Succession of States and Governments*

States, as well as governments of states, may be recognized by other states and governments. In international law the recognition of a state is the act by which one state acknowledges that another state possesses the essential elements of sovereign statehood. Although in practice the determination of whether an entity possesses these elements may be difficult, the criteria are well accepted: a territory, a people, a government, and an independent capacity to conduct foreign relations.[190]

The constitutive theory of recognition maintains that a state does not exist as a subject of international law until it has been recognized by the other states participating in international relations. The declaratory theory of recognition holds that states, when they recognize another state, simply declare what is already both a political fact and a legal reality: that the other state has real existence and that the recognized state is already a subject of international law. The constitutive theory, based on a positivist insistence on state consent, has lost much of its force. It is the declaratory theory, grounded on a naturalist emphasis on objective legality, that is now probably the predominant view.[191]

Although occasionally there are still disputes about the recognition of states, for example, that of Taiwan by China, of Israel by some of

[188] See A. Coret, *Le condominium* 175-186 (1960).

[189] 1992 I.C.J. Reports 351, 601-605; Samuels, Condominium Arrangements in International Practice: Reviving an Abandoned Concept of Boundary Dispute Resolution, 29 *Michigan Journal of International Law* 727 (2008).

[190] Blix, Contemporary Aspects of Recognition, 130 *Hague Recueil* 587, 632-637 (1970).

[191] See Talmon, The Constitutive versus the Declaratory Theory of Recognition, 75 *British Yearbook of International Law* 101 (2005). As Professor Crawford writes, "the creation of states is a matter in principle governed by international law and not left to the discretion of individual states." J. Crawford, *The Creation of States in International Law* v (2d ed. 2006).

the Arab states, or of Kosovo by Serbia and some other European governments,[192] there is nowadays much more controversy about the recognition of governments. Such controversy is, in turn, closely related to questions about the establishment or maintenance of diplomatic relations with foreign governments. States for political reasons sometimes refuse to recognize foreign governments. In the United States, states or governments that are not recognized may be denied both access to the courts and rights to property otherwise belonging to that foreign state in the United States.[193] In Kadic v. Karadzic, Judge Newman for the Second Circuit, held that Radovan Karadzic, the President of Srpska, could be held responsible for state acts of genocide, war crimes, and crimes against humanity even though Srpska was not recognized by the United States: "It would be anomalous indeed if non-recognition by the United States, which typically reflects disfavor with a foreign regime—sometimes due to human rights abuses—had the perverse effect of shielding officials of the unrecognized regime from liability for those violations of international law norms that apply only to state actors."[194]

The theory of recognition of governments knows various distinctions, not only that between constitutive and declaratory approaches as above, but also between *de jure* and *de facto* recognition, that is, between governments recognized to be constitutionally and rightfully in power and those simply in control of a state in practice.[195] Such theoretical distinctions have caused some commentators to lament the condition of the field. Professor Brownlie, for example, complained that the theory

[192] Kosovo Is Recognized but Rebuked by Others, *N.Y. Times*, www.nytimes.com (Feb. 22, 2008); U.S. Department of State, U.S. Relations with Kosovo, www.state.gov (Jan. 29, 2015); Casperson, The Pursuit of International Recognition After Kosovo, 21 *Global Governance* 393 (2015).

[193] Restatement (Third), supra, at 91. On the rights of unrecognized governments and states in U.S. courts, compare National Petrochemical Co. v. M/T Stolt Sheaf, 860 F.2d 551 (2d Cir. 1988), and Autocephalous Church v. Goldberg & Feldman Arts, 917 F.2d 278 (7th Cir. 1990).

[194] 70 F.3d 232, 245 (2d Cir. 1995).

[195] See, e.g., the opinion of William Howard Taft as the sole arbitrator between Great Britain and Costa Rica in the *Tinoco Arbitration*, Award of October 18, 1923, 18 *American Journal of International Law* 147 (1924). In Boumediene v. Bush, the U.S. Supreme Court held that Guantánamo Bay is subject to the *de jure* sovereignty of Cuba and the *de facto* jurisdiction of the United States. 553 U.S. 723, 755 (2008).

of recognition is "like a bank of fog on a still day."[196] Truth be told, the rules about recognition of governments and, for that matter, states are largely matters belonging to different legal systems, municipal and international. The variations in approaches to the theory of recognition can often be explained as simply due to the variety of legal systems that need to deal with such questions in practice.[197]

States, not their governments, are subjects of international law. So long as the state remains the same, a succession of governments does not affect the state's international legal rights and duties.[198] Although it may be that a new state in international law can avoid some of the international legal obligations of a predecessor state, new governments of the same state inherit the legal commitments of their predecessors.[199]

Whether there has been a succession of government or of the state can usually be simply told. So long, for example, as a state's territory and population remain more or less the same, a new political party in power or a new constitution in place merely indicates a succession of governments. After the Revolution of 1918, the Soviet government of Russia argued that it was so different in kind from the Tsarist regime that the Soviet Union should be treated as a new state. However, the Soviet leadership moderated this argument over time as it found it advantageous to retain some of the international rights and privileges that the Tsars had secured for Russia.[200]

At times the basic principles pertaining to the succession of governments have been applied to questions of state succession, for example, when territory is transferred from one state to another.[201] The United States, for example, argued in 1818 that Chile, then newly independent, was bound by the international agreements made by Spain, its former colonial master.[202] More usually, the succession of governments is

[196] Brownlie, Recognition in Theory and Practice, 53 *British Yearbook of International Law* 197 (1982).

[197] For an analysis of different variants of recognition in legal practice, see S. Talmon, *Recognition of Governments in International Law: With Particular Reference to Governments in Exile* 21-111 (1998).

[198] Hackworth, supra, at 127.

[199] D.P. O'Connell, 2 *State Succession in Municipal Law and International Law* 124 (1967).

[200] K. Gryzybowski, *Soviet Public International Law* 92-95 (1970).

[201] D.P. O'Connell, 1 *State Succession in Municipal Law and International Law* 3-8 (1967).

[202] F. Wharton, 1 *Digest of the International Law of the United States* 19 (2d ed. 1887).

distinguished from the succession of states, the former implying a continuity of the state, the latter a discontinuity in the state's existence.[203]

Such discontinuities are omnipresent in the history of international relations. States may simply disappear as Poland did when it was divided among Austria, Prussia, and Russia between 1772 and 1793. States may meld into unions as, over centuries, one after another alpine canton joined Switzerland, or suddenly as East Germany and West Germany united in 1990. New states may spring from the territory of old as did the United States, either, depending upon one's point of view, when the colonies issued the Declaration of Independence on July 4, 1776, or on September 3, 1783, when in the Treaty of Paris George III acknowledged that Britain's 13 American colonies had become "free Sovereign & independent States."[204] And multiple states may emerge from a single sovereign state as did Russia, Ukraine, Azerbaijan, and the other states to emerge from the breakup of the Soviet Union at Alma-Ata in 1991 and Slovenia, Bosnia-Herzegovina, and Croatia from Yugoslavia in the same year.[205]

Generally, except for territorial agreements, successor states, as distinguished from successor governments, are not bound by the international agreements of their predecessors.[206] Successor states may, however, choose to keep some treaties in force rather than begin with an absolutely clean slate.[207] Though successor states normally are entitled to the foreign property of their predecessor states, they are also usually responsible for many of their predecessors' obligations to private parties.[208]

[203] Restatement (Third), supra, at 100.

[204] Treaty of Paris, supra, art. 1; on the negotiation of the Treaty of Paris, see Andrew C. McLaughlin, *The Confederation and the Constitution 1783-1789* 17-35 (1962 ed.).

[205] Blum, UN Membership of the "New" Yugoslavia: Continuity or Break?, 86 *American Journal of International Law* 830 (1992); Stahn, The Agreement on Succession Issues of the Former Republic of Yugoslavia, 96 *American Journal of International Law* 379 (2002).

[206] Restatement (Third), supra, at 108; Hafner & Novak, State Succession in Respect of Treaties, *The Oxford Guide to Treaties* 383 (D.B. Hollis ed., 2d ed. 2020).

[207] Y. Makonnen, *International Law and the New States of Africa* (1983).

[208] Restatement (Third), supra, at 102, 108.

7. *Non-State Actors*

Traditionally, international law viewed states as the sole subjects of international law, the only entities entitled to international legal rights and duties, and capable of making international legal rules and employing international legal process. Today, it is generally accepted that non-state actors may be, to varying degrees, also subjects of international law.

Non-state actors can be roughly divided into three kinds. First are intergovernmental international organizations [see Chapter 7]. Second are private persons, both individuals and private corporations [see Chapter 8]. Third are international non-governmental organizations (NGOs).[209] NGOs like Amnesty International and Greenpeace play an increasingly influential role at treaty-making international conferences and in international litigation, for example, filing *amicus* briefs in domestic courts and the European Court of Justice.[210] NGOs also play important roles in assisting international development and providing humanitarian relief. However, like states, NGOs can be criticized when they fall short, for example, in failing Haiti after its tragic earthquake in 2010.[211]

Besides being subjects of international law, non-state actors may also be crucial in the formation of international norms. For example, judges and jurists have long been crucial in making customary international law [see Chapter 3]. In the nineteenth century, individuals and private associations played leading roles in the creation of the first international institutions, such as the World Court, a sort of "bottom-up" international law-making by non-state actors that is just as important today.[212]

[209] *NGOs in International Law: Efficiency in Flexibility?* (Dupuy & Vierucci eds. 2008).

[210] Spiro, Accounting for NGOs, 3 *Chicago Journal of International Law* 161 (2002).

[211] Doucet, NGOs Have Failed Haiti, *The Nation* (Jan. 10, 2011).

[212] Janis, America and the Law of Nations, supra, at 72-91, 144-175; Charnovitz, Two Centuries of Participation: NGOs and International Governance, 18 *Michigan Journal of International Law* 183 (1997).

CHAPTER 7

International Organizations and Regimes

Though some have dreamed of a new Roman Empire, a universal global government, there is such diversity among the globe's peoples that to join them in a single polity is probably not only unrealistic but also unwise. Better perhaps that we devise ways for separate sovereign states to dwell together peacefully and to cooperate productively. The law of international organizations and regimes is well short of any kind of legal regime for a world state, but still plays a vital part in helping order international relations.

A. INTERNATIONAL ORGANIZATIONS

1. *International Organizations as Subjects of International Law*

Public international organizations are creatures of international agreement constituted by sovereign states to accomplish common goals. Modern international organizations date back at least to the second half of the nineteenth century. Since 1865 and the establishment of the International Telegraphic (now Telecommunications) Union and

1874's founding of the Universal Postal Union,[1] international organizations have proliferated. "It is only a modest exaggeration to say that there is an international organization for practically every field of human endeavour . . . international peacekeeping and peacemaking, human rights, labor relations, food production and distribution, education, promotion of science and of cultural activities, health, economic development, monetary affairs, international trade, civil aviation, postal services, telecommunications, meteorology, maritime commerce, protection of intellectual property, and nuclear energy."[2] There are about 300 public international organizations.[3] Most international organizations display a tripartite form: a permanent secretariat responsible for preparing meetings and for gathering information, an occasional conference of all member-states acting as a general policy-making body, and a council of selected states exercising day-to-day governmental functions.[4] Though international secretariats have little formal power, they are crucial to the success of their organizations by facilitating and mediating decision making.[5]

Because international organizations are created by the express consent of states, international legal theory has little difficulty explaining why international organizations are vested with international legal personality, albeit within the bounds fashioned by their constituent states. In its 1949 Advisory Opinion on *Reparation for Injuries Suffered in the Service of the United Nations*, the International Court of Justice held that it was "indispensable" to attribute international personality to the United Nations because the Charter of the United Nations assigned the organization specific tasks such as international peacekeeping and the promotion of international economic, social, cultural, and humanitarian cooperation.[6] The Court concluded that

[1] G.A. Codding & M.A. Rutkowski, *The International Telecommunications Union in a Changing World* (1982); G.A. Codding, *The Universal Postal Union* (1964).

[2] F.L. Kirgis, *International Organizations in Their Legal Setting* v (2d ed. 1993) [hereinafter cited as "Kirgis"].

[3] A. Bennett, *International Organizations* 4 (7th ed. 2002) [hereinafter cited as "Bennett"]; www.usaid.gov (Feb. 26, 2023).

[4] I.L. Claude, *Swords into Plowshares: The Problems and Progress of International Organization* 36 (4th ed. 1971) [hereinafter cited as "Claude"].

[5] Kishore, A Comparative Analysis of Secretariats Created Under Select Treaty Regimes, 45 *International Lawyer* 1051, 1082 (2011).

[6] 1949 I.C.J. Reports 174, 178-179.

> [the] Organization is an international person. That is not the same thing as saying that it is a State, which it certainly is not, or that its legal personality and rights and duties are the same as those of a State. Still less is it the same thing as saying that it is a super-State, whatever that expression may mean. It does not even imply that all its rights and duties must be upon the international plane, any more than all the rights and duties of a State must be upon that plane. What it does mean is that it is a subject of international law and capable of possessing international rights and duties, and that it has capacity to maintain its rights by bringing international claims.[7]

The status of any international organization as a person in international law is dependent upon the treaty constituting the organization. The usual theory accounting for the international legal personality of international organizations explains that states delegate some of their sovereign powers, thus some of their international personality, to international organizations so those organizations can fulfill designated functions in international relations.[8] Although it is theoretically conceivable that such delegation could be tacitly made in customary international law, in fact, every international organization is the result of an explicit international agreement. It is to the treaty, effectively the constitution, of each international organization that one must first turn to define the organization's functions and powers. Of course, a treaty's provisions may be amplified, as necessary, by custom, general principles, and the other sources of international law [see Chapter 3].

In addition to its status in international law, an international organization's legal personality may be separately defined by municipal law for domestic purposes. So, for example, in the United States, presidential executive orders, pursuant to the International Organizations Immunities Act, designate various international organizations as legal persons for the purposes of U.S. law. Like a foreign state, an international organization may be entitled to extend diplomatic immunities to its personnel [see Chapter 10].

Unlike states, however, which by definition have their own territories, populations, governments, and capacities to conduct international

[7] Id. at 179; see Bederman, *The Reparations for Injuries Case*: The Law of Nations is Transformed into International Law, in *International Law Stories* 423 (J.E. Noyes, L.A. Dickinson, M.W. Janis & C.M. Vázquez eds, 2d ed. 2025).

[8] See D. Sarooshi, *International Organizations and Their Exercises of Sovereign Powers* (2005).

affairs, the attributes of international organizations are usually quite limited. Their competence is restricted to certain designated functions. So, for example, few international organizations have many executive capabilities; these usually remain with the member states. International organizations often serve merely as gatherers of information, organizers of conferences, and makers of recommendations. A few regional international organizations like the European Union and the Council of Europe have been delegated some real legislative powers and, in the cases of the European Courts of Justice and of Human Rights, some effective judicial authority [see Chapters 8 and 9]. Moreover, international organizations exercise an ever-increasing role in international lawmaking.[9]

Although the restrictions on the international legal personality of specific international organizations are many and various, two important general limitations stand out. First, international organizations, unlike states, are not permitted to bring claims to the International Court of Justice.[10] They are, however, empowered in some circumstances to request advisory opinions from the Court[11] [see Chapter 5], and occasionally to be litigants before regional international courts; e.g., the Council and Commission of the European Union have standing to appear before the European Court of Justice[12] [see Chapter 9]. Second, the agreements made by international organizations are not considered to be "treaties" for the purposes of the Vienna Convention on the Law of Treaties.[13] The International Law Commission prepared, and a U.N. Conference revised and adopted, a separate Vienna

[9] For a study of the promise and peril of international lawmaking by international organizations, see J. Álvarez, *International Organizations as Law-Makers* (2005).

[10] Statute of the International Court of Justice, as annexed to the Charter of the United Nations, art. 34(1), 59 Stat. 1055, T.S. No. 993, 3 Bevans 1153 (signed at San Francisco June 26, 1945; entered into force October 24, 1945).

[11] Charter of the United Nations, art. 96, 59 Stat. 1031, T.S. 993, 3 Bevans 1153 (signed at San Francisco June 26, 1945; entered into force October 24, 1945) [hereinafter cited as "U.N. Charter"].

[12] Consolidated Version of the Treaty Establishing the European Community, arts. 230 (ex 173), 232 (ex 175) (signed at Rome March 25, 1957; entered into force January 1, 1958; not in force for the United States).

[13] Arts. 1, 2(1)(a), U.N. Doc. A/CONF.39/27 (1969), reprinted in 63 *American Journal of International Law* 875 (1969) (signed at Vienna May 23, 1969; entered into force January 27, 1980; not in force for the United States).

Convention on Treaties Concluded Between States and International Organizations or Between International Organizations.[14]

Public international organizations are differentiated in theory and practice from international non-governmental organizations (NGOs). NGOs such as the International Red Cross, Amnesty International, and the International Chamber of Commerce are non-profit private associations incorporated under the laws of one or another state. Another term for an NGO is a private international organization. However designated, what chiefly differentiates a public from a private international organization is that the former is constituted by an international agreement rather than by a municipal legal system.[15] Because NGOs are not created by treaty, they do not partake of any international legal personality by way of the express delegation by states. Like other private entities, however, NGOs, which may number more than 40,000, sometimes play considerable roles in international law and relations.[16]

A variety of public international organizations are introduced elsewhere: the Council of Europe [see Chapter 8]; the Organization of American States [see Chapter 8]; the World Trade Organization [see Chapter 9]; and the European Union [see Chapter 9]. At this point, we explore the most general and ambitious form of international organization, the United Nations and its predecessor organization, the League of Nations.

2. *The League of Nations*

Although the first universal international organization, the League of Nations, was not founded until the twentieth century, the League's intellectual and moral foundations were laid long ago. Ideas about the fundamental unity of all peoples and about a peaceful form of

[14] U.N. Doc. A/CONF.129/15 (Mar. 20, 1986), reprinted in 25 *International Legal Materials* 543 (1986).

[15] H.G. Schermers, 1 *International Institutional Law* 6-10 (1972).

[16] Charnovitz, Two Centuries of Participation: NGOs and International Governance, 18 *Michigan Journal of International Law* 183 (1997); P.R. Baehr, *Non-Governmental Human Rights Organizations in International Relations* (2009); Ben-Ari, The International Legal Status of International Non-Governmental Organizations, 23 *Cardozo Journal of International & Comparative Law* 1 (2014).

international organization circulated at least as early as classical Greece. Zeno (335-263 B.C.), the founder of Stoic philosophy, prophesied in his *Republic* about "a world which should no longer be separate states, but one great city under one divine law, where all were citizens and members one of another, bound together not by human laws but by their own willing consent, or by love."[17]

The Roman emperor Marcus Aurelius (A.D. 121-180) followed the path of Stoicism to formulate ideals of universal law and a world community:

> If the intellectual capacity is common to us all, common too is the reason, which makes us rational creatures. If so, that reason also is common which tells us to do or not to do. If so, law also is common. If so, we are citizens. If so, the Universe is as it were a state—for of what other single polity can the whole race of mankind be said to be fellow-members?—and from it, this common state, we get the intellectual, the rational, and the legal instinct, or whence do we get them?[18]

In early modern European political philosophy, Desiderius Erasmus (1466-1536), Thomas More (1477-1535), the Duc de Sully (1560-1641), Hugo Grotius (1583-1645), William Penn (1644-1718), Jean-Jacques Rousseau (1712-1778), and Immanuel Kant (1724-1804) all fashioned utopian schemes involving international law and organization.[19] In 1713, the Abbé de Saint-Pierre (1658-1743) published the first parts of *A Plan for a Perpetual Peace in Europe.* Often revised and expanded, Saint-Pierre's Plan proposed a perpetual Grand Alliance among the European sovereigns, a prohibition against foreign and civil wars, a reduction in armaments, the mediation of international disputes by a general assembly, and the establishment of a court of arbitration whose

[17] *Essential Works of Stoicism xi* (M. Hadas ed. 1961).

[18] Marcus Aurelius, Communings (ch. iv, §4), *Marcus Aurelius* 71-73 (Haines trans. 1916); for more on universal law and organization in ancient Greece and Rome and in early Judaism and Christianity, see G. Zampaglione, *The Idea of Peace in Antiquity* (Dunn trans. 1973).

[19] Purves, Prolegomena to Utopian International Projects, 1 *Studies in the History of the Law of Nations* 100-108 (Grotian Society Papers 1968, Alexandrowicz ed. 1970); E. Wynner & G. Lloyd, *Searchlight on Peace Plans* (1949 ed.); *Sully's Grand Design of Henry IV* (Grotian Society ed. 1921); I. Kant, *Eternal Peace and Other International Essays* (Hastie trans. 1914).

judgments could be enforced by a communal force of arms.[20] Similarly, sometime between 1786 and 1789, Jeremy Bentham (1748-1832) wrote *A Plan for an Universal and Perpetual Peace*, in which he proposed the giving up of all colonies, the breaking of all alliances, the establishment of free trade, the reduction of armies and navies, and the creation of a congress that would serve as "a common court of judicature" to settle international disputes.[21]

In the nineteenth century, alongside the movement for an international court [see Chapter 5], there emerged a popular enthusiasm for an international government. One of the most important publications promoting the idea was the *Essay on a Congress of Nations*, written in 1840 by the president of the American Peace Society, William Ladd (1778-1841). Ladd admitted that he had borrowed heavily from other idealists, but he claimed originality for his "thought of separating the subject into two distinct parts":

> 1st. A congress of ambassadors from all those Christian and civilized nations who should choose to send them, for the purpose of settling the principles of international law by compact and agreement, of the nature of a mutual treaty, and also by devising and promoting plans for the preservation of peace, and meliorating the condition of man. 2d. A court of nations, composed of the most able civilians in the world, to arbitrate or judge such cases as should be brought before it, by the mutual consent of two or more contending nations: thus dividing entirely the diplomatic from the judicial functions, which require such different, not to say opposite, characters in the exercise of their functions. I consider the Congress as the legislature, and the Court as the judiciary, in the government of nations, leaving the functions of the executive with public opinion, "the queen of the world." This division I have never seen in any essay or plan for a congress or diet of independent nations, either

[20] Abbé de Saint-Pierre, *Projet pour rendre la paix perpétuelle en Europe* (Garnier Frères edition 1981).

[21] Bentham proposed a system of graduated sanctions to enforce the decisions of the international congress: first, reporting merely its opinion; second, circulating the opinion in each state in order to excite public opinion; third, "putting the refractory state under the ban of Europe"; and fourth, "as a last resource," sending armies furnished by the member states. A Plan for an Universal and Perpetual Peace, 2 *The Works of Jeremy Bentham* 546, 552, 554 (J. Bowring ed. 1843); Janis, Jeremy Bentham and the Fashioning of "International Law," 78 *American Journal of International Law* 405, 412-415 (1984).

> ancient or modern; and I believe it will obviate all the objections which have been heretofore made to such a plan.[22]

Reviewing Ladd's *Essay*, Georg Schwarzenberger in 1935 opined that there was "a direct line" in the history of ideas about international organization "from Ladd to the achievements of Geneva, and even further, on the foundations of his Equity Tribunal, to a real League of Nations."[23]

American enthusiasm for international government, at least in theory, ran high in the early years of the twentieth century.[24] The onset of the Great War in 1914 only quickened the pace.[25] Notables at a meeting of the First Annual National Assemblage of the League to Enforce Peace in Washington, D.C., in 1916 included the former President of the United States, William Howard Taft; the president of Harvard, A. Lawrence Lowell; the director of the Chamber of Commerce of the United States, Edward Filene; the president of the American Federation of Labor, Samuel Gompers; the senator from Massachusetts, Henry Cabot Lodge; the president of the Federal Council of Churches of Christ in America, Shailer Matthews; and the former president of Princeton and the then-President of the United States, Woodrow Wilson.[26] It was Wilson who put the longstanding aspirations for international government into concrete form, proposing in the last of his Fourteen Points on January 8, 1918, that "[a] general association of nations must be formed under specific covenants for the purpose of affording mutual guarantees of political independence and territorial integrity to great and small States alike."[27] Wilson and others believed that an international organization devoted to collective security could better guarantee the peace than could traditional balance-of-power politics, which not only had failed to prevent the outbreak of

[22] W. Ladd, *An Essay on a Congress of Nations for the Adjustment of International Disputes Without a Resort to Arms xlix-l* (Lawbook Exchange ed. 2007, Carnegie ed. 1916, 1st ed. 1840); M.W. Janis, *America and the Law of Nations 1776-1939* 79-85 (2010).

[23] G. Schwarzenberger, *William Ladd: An Examination of an American Proposal for an International Equity Tribunal* 7, 37 (1935).

[24] See, e.g., N.M. Butler, *The International Mind* (1913).

[25] R. Goldsmith, *A League to Enforce Peace* (1917).

[26] League to Enforce Peace, *Enforced Peace: Proceedings of the First Annual National Assemblage of the League to Enforce Peace, Washington, May 26-27, 1916* (1917).

[27] T. Woodrow Wilson, Address of January 8, 1918, *The Public Papers of Woodrow Wilson: 1 War and Peace* 161 (R.S. Baker & W. Dodds eds. 1926).

war in 1914, but also, because of its triggering system of alliances, had contributed to the expansion of the conflict.[28] The Versailles Treaty establishing the League "had been constructed on the assumption that the United States would be not merely a contracting but an actively executant party."[29] Unfortunately, or as put politely by a Frenchman, "by a strange paradox,"[30] the U.S. Senate refused to consent to the ratification of the Treaty, and the United States stayed out of its own plan to keep the peace.

For a decade, from 1920 to 1930, the League, based in Geneva, even without the United States and also without the new Soviet Union, made real contributions to international law, world health, the protection of minorities, and the settlement of international disputes (for example, the pacific settlement of the dispute between Greece and Bulgaria in 1925).[31] Unfortunately, the next decade was disastrous for the League. The turning point was the Japanese invasion of Manchuria on September 18, 1931, which the League proved powerless to stop.[32] The League finally condemned the Japanese occupation of Manchuria on February 24, 1933, but Japan simply left the League the next month.[33] Dedicated to the prevention of aggression, the League watched helplessly as Italy invaded Ethiopia in 1934, and Germany marched into the Rhineland, Austria, and Czechoslovakia between 1936 and 1938.[34] Finally, when Germany and Russia attacked Poland in 1939, Britain and France took action, but it was too late. Poland was lost, then France itself, and the nations descended into the twentieth century's second world war.

By the time of the invasion of Poland in 1939, the League was, in large measure, already a forgotten institution. Poland, France, and Great Britain made no attempt to involve the League in the new world war.[35] For a year, the functionaries of the League carried on in Geneva,

[28] H.W. Harris, *What the League of Nations Is* 9-20 (1925). Wilson, a long-time international sceptic, belatedly came to be an international law enthusiast. See Janis, How "Wilsonian" was Woodrow Wilson?, 5 *Dartmouth Law Journal* 1 (2007).

[29] H. Nicholson, *Peacemaking 1919* 207 (1965 ed.).

[30] C.A. Colliard, *Institutions internationales* 50 (3d ed. 1966).

[31] E. Drummond, *League of Nations: Ten Years of World Co-operation* (1930); see the biography of Drummond: J. Barros, *Office Without Power: Secretary-General Sir Eric Drummond, 1919-1933* (1979).

[32] F.P. Walters, *A History of the League of Nations* 465-499 (1960 ed.).

[33] Id. at 494.

[34] Id. at 623-783.

[35] Id. at 802.

a situation described by the Deputy Secretary-General of the League as a "situation of abnormal normality."[36] In the summer and autumn of 1940, the League's officials departed Geneva, where they feared a German or Italian invasion, for safer locations. A large part of the Secretariat was based at Princeton University,[37] a fitting, if ironic, twist on the origins of the League with Woodrow Wilson. Almost a year after the foundation of the United Nations in June 1945, diplomats reconvened at Geneva, where on April 8, 1946, Lord Robert Cecil closed his speech to the League Assembly as follows: "The League is dead, Long live the United Nations."[38] Ten days later, the Assembly unanimously voted to dissolve the League and to transfer its powers, functions, buildings, library, and archives to the United Nations.[39]

3. The United Nations

The collapse of the League of Nations in the 1930s and the horrors of the Second World War persuaded many governments to try to create a better form of collective security for the new post-war world. Negotiations leading to the foundation of the United Nations began in 1943 among the United States, the Soviet Union, Great Britain, and China. On August 21, 1944, the four allies met at Dumbarton Oaks to set the basic configuration of a new international organization. Finally, 50 states met in San Francisco to agree on the definite terms of the United Nations,[40] its Charter being signed there on June 26, 1945.[41]

Successor though it might be, the United Nations was meant for obvious reasons to be an improvement on the League. It was expected that the United Nations would be more forceful than had been the League and that it would include countries, especially the United States, that had never been League members. Furthermore, the United Nations was to address a much wider range of international economic and social issues. Its officials were to be given more independent power.

[36] Id. at 804.

[37] Id. at 809-810.

[38] Id. at 815.

[39] Ibid. See White, The Legacy of the League of Nations: Continuity or Change, 71 *Revista Espana de Derecho Internacional* 277 (2019).

[40] Claude, supra, at 57-60.

[41] U.N. Charter, supra.

Though the League of Nations had failed to avert World War II, it was hoped that the United Nations could prevent World War III.[42]

The United Nations was organized into six "principal organs"—the General Assembly, Security Council, Economic and Social Council, Trusteeship Council, International Court of Justice, and Secretariat—and "[s]uch subsidiary organs as may be found necessary."[43] Alongside the International Court [see Chapter 5], the most notable are the General Assembly, the Security Council, and the Secretariat.[44]

The General Assembly is composed of every member of the United Nations[45]—as of December 2025, 193 member states.[46] The General Assembly has the authority to "discuss any questions or any matters within the scope of the present Charter," though it is limited in making recommendations with respect to matters about which the Security Council "is exercising" its "functions." Operationally, perhaps the greatest power of the General Assembly is its right to "consider and approve the budget of the Organization."[47] In terms of the development of international law, probably the most important contribution of the General Assembly has been its power to "initiate studies and make recommendations for the purpose of . . . encouraging the progressive development of international law and its codification."[48] We have already discussed the legal status of General Assembly resolutions and the work of the International Law Commission [see Chapter 3].

Each state has one vote in the General Assembly, where majority voting is employed except for "important questions," when a two-thirds vote of the members present and voting is required.[49] The one-state, one-vote rule makes a mockery of any claim that the General Assembly might be a sort of international parliament. Countries with more than 300 million persons, like China, India, and the United States, are counted the same as states such as Dominica and Vanuatu,

[42] See E. Luard, 1 *A History of the United Nations* 3-16 (1982).

[43] *The Charter of the United Nations: A Commentary* 1-12 (B. Simma 2d ed. 2002) [hereinafter cited as "Simma"].

[44] L.M. Goodrich, E. Hambro & A.P. Simons, *Charter of the United Nations: Commentary and Documents* 102 (3d ed. 1969) [hereinafter cited as "Goodrich"].

[45] U.N. Charter, supra, art. 9(1).

[46] www.un.org (Dec. 3, 2025).

[47] U.N. Charter, supra, arts. 10, 12, 17; see Goodrich, supra, at 148-167; Simma, supra, at 332-352.

[48] U.N. Charter, supra, art. 13(1)(a); Simma, supra, at 298-317.

[49] U.N. Charter, supra, art. 18.

which have much fewer than a million.[50] There have long been proposals to strengthen the General Assembly by basing voting on schemes of proportional representation,[51] but to no avail. Evan Luard, a sympathetic observer of the United Nations system, compared the General Assembly "at most" to "a parliament of several centuries ago, composed of representatives of pocket and rotten boroughs, often varying grotesquely in populations, making occasional pleas to the powers that be, but exerting a decision-making authority which is at best extremely marginal."[52]

The Security Council is the most ambitious U.N. organ, having "primary responsibility for the maintenance of international peace and security,"[53] a topic to which we return shortly. The Council consists of 15 members, including the five permanent members—China, France, Russia, the United Kingdom, and the United States—and ten others elected for two-year terms.[54] Each member of the Security Council has one vote; nine votes are required to pass a measure, but in the case of non-procedural matters, any of the permanent members may veto a resolution, a provision that, while it reflects the realities of international politics, has often stymied Security Council action.[55] Nonetheless, the Security Council has become, in the words of two U.S. diplomatic experts, "an indispensable pillar of world order."[56] Indeed, it has been proposed that the Security Council be enlarged, albeit a suggestion less popular today than before.[57]

Alongside the International Court, the General Assembly, and the Security Council, there is a plethora of other U.N. organs and committees; their listing alone takes some 14 closely printed pages.[58] A small sampling taken from just one page includes the Special Committee

[50] See E. Osmanzyk, *Encyclopedia of the United Nations and International Organizations* (2d ed. 1990).

[51] G. Clark & L.B. Sohn, *World Peace Through World Law* 20-65 (2d rev. ed. 1960).

[52] E. Luard, *The United Nations: How It Works and What It Does* 34 (1979) [hereinafter cited as "Luard"].

[53] U.N. Charter, supra, art. 24(1).

[54] Id., art. 23.

[55] Id., art. 27; Simma, supra, at 476-523.

[56] K.C. McDonald & S.M. Patrick, *UN Security Council Enlargement and U.S. Interests* 30 (2010).

[57] Id. at 5-10; Patrick, Why Is No One Talking About UNSC Reform Anymore, *World Politics Review* (June 3, 2019), www.worldpoliticsreview.com/insights.

[58] United Nations, *Yearbook of the United Nations 1999* 1444-1457 (2001).

on Peacekeeping Operations, the Special Committee on the Charter of the United Nations and on the Strengthening of the Role of the Organization, the Special Committee on the Situation with Regard to the Implementation of the Declaration on the Granting of Independence to Colonial Countries and Peoples, the Special Committee to Investigate Israeli Practices Affecting the Human Rights of the Palestinian People and Other Arabs of the Occupied Territories, the Special Committee to Select the Winners of the United Nations Human Rights Prize, the United Nations Administrative Tribunal, the United Nations Capital Development Fund, the United Nations Commission on International Trade Law, the United Nations Conciliation Commission for Palestine, and the United Nations Conference on Trade and Development.[59] Furthermore, there are 17 intergovernmental organizations related to the United Nations, including the International Atomic Energy Commission; the International Labour Organization; the United Nations Educational, Scientific and Cultural Organization (UNESCO); the World Bank; and the International Monetary Fund.[60] There is a considerable body of international law pertinent to this large and complex United Nations system.[61]

To support this myriad of agencies, organs, committees, and commissions, there has emerged an international bureaucracy of some magnitude. As of February, 2023, there were about 44,000 persons working for the United Nations.[62] The Secretariat is administered by the Secretary-General, who is appointed by the General Assembly upon the recommendation of the Security Council.[63] Besides being the "chief administrative officer" of the United Nations, the Secretary-General may "perform such other functions as are entrusted to him" by the United Nation's various organs; he may also "bring to the attention of the Security Council any matter which in his opinion may threaten the maintenance of international peace and security."[64] Following in the footsteps of the two Secretary-Generals of the League of Nations,

[59] Id. at 1447.

[60] Id. at 1385-1424. For an account of one such international organization, see Helfer, Understanding Change in International Organizations: Globalization and Innovation in the ILO, 59 *Vanderbilt Law Review* 649 (2006).

[61] See *Bowett's Law of International Institutions* (P.Sands & P. Klein eds., 6th ed. 2009); L.B. Sohn, *Cases on United Nations Law* (2d ed. 1967).

[62] https://careers.un.org (Feb. 26, 2023).

[63] U.N. Charter, supra, art. 97.

[64] Id., arts. 97, 98, 99.

who established the first large-scale international civil service,[65] nine have served as Secretary-General of the United Nations, most notably Dag Hammarskjöld (1953-1961) and U Thant (1961-1971).[66] In 2025, the U.N. Secretary-General was Antonio Guterres. In practice, the Secretary-Generals of the United Nations have played more active roles than did their predecessors in the League of Nations, an intention of the United Nations' founders.[67]

The aspirations of the United Nations are set forth in the Charter's Preamble:

> We the Peoples of the United Nations determined to save succeeding generations from the scourge of war, which twice in our life time has brought untold sorrow to mankind, and
>
> to reaffirm faith in fundamental human rights, in the dignity and worth of the human person, in the equal rights of men and women and of nations large and small, and
>
> to establish conditions under which justice and respect for the obligations arising from treaties and other sources of international law can be maintained, and
>
> to promote social progress and better standards of life in larger freedom,
>
> and for these ends,
>
> to practice tolerance and live together in peace with one another as good neighbors, and
>
> to unite our strength to maintain international peace and security, and
>
> to ensure, by the acceptance of principles and the institution of methods, that armed force shall not be used, save in the common interest, and
>
> to employ international machinery for the promotion of the economic and social advancement of all peoples,
>
> have resolved to combine our efforts to accomplish these aims.[68]

Probably the most important of the Charter's provisions is Article 2(4): "All Members shall refrain in their international relations from the threat or use of force against the territorial integrity or political

[65] Luard, supra, at 92-93.

[66] See *Dag Hammarskjöld Revisited: The UN Secretary-General as a Force in World Politics* (Jordan ed. 1983); Thant Myint-U, *Peacemaker: U Thant and the Forgotten Quest for a Just World* (2025).

[67] Luard, supra, at 96-101.

[68] U.N. Charter, supra.

independence of any state, or in any other manner inconsistent with the Purposes of the United Nations."[69] After more than 80 years, how has this prohibition on the threat or use of force worked in practice?

As we have seen, the record of wars since 1945 is all too dismal. In many cases Article 2(4) of the U.N. Charter is no more of a restraint on the use of force than was the ill-fated Kellogg-Briand Pact [see Chapter 6]. Yet, it may be that Article 2(4) is sometimes effective. Abram Chayes, Legal Adviser to the U.S. Department of State during the Kennedy administration, argued, for example, that Article 2(4) was a significant factor when the United States decided against an air strike or invasion and for the lesser measure of a quarantine at the time of the 1963 Cuban Missile Crisis. Chayes wrote that, though the restraint was as much moral as it was legal, it was vital to this application of Article 2(4) or, indeed, to any application of international law that the "lawyers" were called in to participate in the decision-making process.[70] One cannot, of course, always count on such participation.

In terms of legal justification, it is important to note that Article 2(4) does not stand alone in the U.N. Charter. There is, for example, Article 51, which recognizes that states have an "inherent right of individual or collective self-defense" against an armed attack [see Chapter 6]. Although the right of self-defense is limited in time "until the Security Council has taken measures necessary to maintain international peace and security," in practice, the Security Council is often prevented from acting by discord among its members or by the veto of a permanent member. Article 51 has served as the legal justification for many wars since 1945, of which the Vietnam War is only one example.[71] Whether Article 51 was meant to limit or to preserve states' traditional rights of self-defense, for example, a right of anticipatory self-defense, is hotly disputed.[72] The so-called Bush Doctrine of 2002, advocating preemptive action to protect the United States and friendly states from the threat of weapons of mass destruction [see Chapter 6], triggered a hostile response from a U.N. High Level Panel, which contended that

[69] Ibid; Simma, supra, at 112-136.

[70] A. Chayes, *The Cuban Missile Crisis* 39-40 (1974).

[71] U.S. Department of State, The Legality of United States Participation in the Defense of Viet-Nam, 54 *Department of State Bulletin* 474 (Mar. 28, 1966).

[72] Wright, The Cuban Quarantine, 57 *American Journal of International Law* 546 (1963); McDougal, The Soviet-Cuban Quarantine and Self-Defense, 57 *American Journal of International Law* 597 (1963).

working within the U.N. Charter and Article 51 would have been a more appropriate legal response.[73]

The Charter also permits the use of force when authorized by the United Nations. Article 2(5) obliges U.N. members to "give the United Nations every assistance in any action it takes in accordance with the present Charter." However, for most of its life, the United Nations was frustrated in its international security role. The precondition for effective Security Council action in this regard—the unanimity of China, France, the Soviet Union, the United Kingdom, and the United States—was, because of the Great Power veto, a precondition virtually never satisfied in practice during the Cold War.[74] Between 1945 and 1990, the only extensive use of force undertaken by the United Nations was that in Korea in 1950-1953, before the People's Republic of China was admitted to the organization and beginning while the Soviet Union was boycotting the Security Council.[75] In 1988, Sir Michael Howard could write: "In short, because of the dissensions among its leading members, the UN has failed, or rather the nations composing it have failed, to create a framework of international security."[76]

The relaxation of East-West tensions after 1989 and the successful prosecution of the Persian Gulf War in 1990-1991 raised the hope that the United Nations might then be poised to assume more responsibility for maintaining and restoring "international peace and security." During the Persian Gulf War, the Five Great Powers acted more or less in concert. Accordingly, and remarkably, the Security Council was able to vote to condemn Iraq's invasion of Kuwait under Article 39, to impose non-forcible sanctions against Iraq under Article 42, and finally to provide for forcible measures under Article 51 for collective self-defense.[77] Altogether this provided a U.N. framework sufficient ultimately for military forces sent by the United States and many other nations to repel Iraqi troops from Kuwaiti territory. It is important to

[73] White House, *The National Security Strategy of the United States of America* (Sept. 17, 2002), at https://georgewbush-whitehouse.archives.gov/nsc/nssall.html; *A More Secure World: Report of the High-Level Panel on Threats, Challenges, and Change,* U.N. Doc. A/59/565 (Dec. 2004).

[74] Bennett, supra, at 154; Patil, *The UN Veto in World Affairs 1946-1990* (1992).

[75] H.G. Nicholas, *The United Nations as a Political Institution* 50-55 (4th ed. 1971).

[76] Howard, The United Nations and International Security, *United Nations, Divided World: The UN's Roles in International Relations* 31, 44 (Roberts & Kingsbury eds. 1988).

[77] Schachter, United Nations Law in the Gulf Conflict, 85 *American Journal of International Law* 452, 452-461 (1991).

note, however, that the U.N. legal framework in the Persian Gulf War fell short of constituting a true U.N. international security action as envisioned by the organization's founders, a reality both praised and criticized.[78]

It is fair to say that in terms of avoiding global battle, the United Nations is already more than twice as successful as was the League of Nations. Eighty years have passed without such a conflagration. Of course, just as the League was only partly to blame for a second world war, so the United Nations is only partly responsible for the avoidance of a third. During the Cold War, from 1945 to 1990, the United Nations played a much more limited role in peacekeeping than had been hoped, though it must be said that the United Nations was more active than the League ever was, not only having played a part in forcible action in Korea, but also having sent peacekeeping forces to act as buffers in the Arab-Israeli conflict, in that between India and Pakistan, and in those in Lebanon, Yemen, the Dominican Republic, the Congo, Cyprus, West New Guinea, and Syria.[79] After the Cold War, U.N. peacekeeping boomed, for example, in Cambodia, Somalia, and the former Yugoslavia. By 2018, there were over 100,000 U.N. personnel involved in 14 peacekeeping operations in Lebanon, the Democratic Republic of the Congo, the Sudan, Haiti, and elsewhere at an annual cost of almost $4 billion.[80] U.N. peacekeepers, while surely making an important contribution to world peace, have only what one observer calls "a spotty track record," too often "watching helplessly while war rages."[81]

While well short of constituting a world government, the United Nations at least provides an institutional structure that facilitates diplomacy and the moderation of international conflict. Though there are American voices calling for U.S. withdrawal from international

[78] Id. at 470-473. Cf. Rostow, Until What? Enforcement Action or Collective Self-Defense?, 85 *American Journal of International Law* 506 (1991); Weston, Security Council Resolution 678 and Persian Gulf Decision Making: Precarious Legitimacy, 85 *American Journal of International Law* 516 (1991).

[79] R. Thakur, *International Peacekeeping in Lebanon* (1987); United Nations, *The Blue Helmets: A Review of United Nations Peace-keeping* (1985); L.L. Fabian, *Soldiers Without Enemies* (1971).

[80] U.N. Department of Public Information, *United Nations Peacekeeping Operations: Fact Sheet* (31 August 2018), U.N. Doc. DPI/1634/Rev. 208 (2018).

[81] Autesserre, The Crisis of Peacekeeping: Why the UN Can't End Wars, 98 *Foreign Affairs*, January-February 2019, at 101.

institutions,[82] it is doubtful that such isolationist sentiment will dominate U.S. political opinion as it did in the 1920s and 1930s. There is simply too much at stake for the United States to go it alone in world politics.[83] One recent example is the danger of a unilateral response to global health crises.[84] It is important that the United States and other liberal democracies stand up for multilateralism and the United Nations.[85]

B. INTERNATIONAL REGIMES

Short of international organizations, but more structured than naked rules of international law, are international regimes, broadly, "all sets of norms of behaviour and of rules and policies which cover any international issue, and facilitate substantive or procedural arrangements among the States they address."[86] Traditionally, international regimes regulated territories known as *res communis*, international jurisdictions set by custom or by treaty that vest many or all states with similar rights and duties. Chief among these international regimes have been the oceans, the skies, and Antarctica, territories governed by many or all states or, if you will, the international community. Nowadays, it is recognized that there may be need for international regimes not only over these common spaces, but also over national territory when

[82] Mead, The Jacksonian Revolt: American Populism and the Liberal Order, 96 *Foreign Affairs*, March/April 2017, at 2; The New World Disorder: If America Pulls Back from Global Institutions, Other Countries Must Step Forward, *The Economist*, June 20, 2020, at 8.

[83] Tharoor, Why America Still Needs the United Nations, 82 *Foreign Affairs*, September/October 2003, at 67; Nye, The Decline of America's Soft Power: Why Washington Should Worry, 83 *Foreign Affairs*, May/June 2004, at 16.

[84] J. Youde, *Globalization and Health* (2019); United Nations, *United Nations Comprehensive Response to Covid-19*, www.un.org (2019).

[85] Franklin, The New World Disorder, *The Economist*, June 20, 2020, at 3; Raustiala & Jeronimo, Why the UN Still Matters, *Foreign Affairs*, June 23, 2023.

[86] Klein, International Regimes, 9 *Encyclopedia of Public International Law* 202 (1986).

activities there have global effect, most notably upon the international environment.[87]

1. *The Law of the Sea*

Long the most important international regime and long, too, one of the most elaborate parts of international law is the law of the sea. The traditional law of the sea was based in part on ancient maritime codes, such as the Rhodian Sea Law, the Rules of Oleron, and the Consolato del Mare, and was otherwise drawn from the customary practice of maritime states from all over the world.[88] In 1608, in *Mare Liberum*, Grotius advanced what became a widely accepted fundamental principle: that the high seas—the oceans apart from narrow coastal zones—should be open to the ships of all states, an argument he based on the "most specific and unimpeachable axiom of the Law of Nations, called a primary rule or first principle, the spirit of which is self-evident and immutable, to wit: every nation is free to travel to every other nation, and to trade with it."[89] As with other fields of international law [see Chapters 5 and 6], the nineteenth century was a relatively successful era for the law of the sea. It was widely recognized then in theory and in practice that states could usually claim just a three-mile territorial sea, beyond which vessels were on high seas and subject to regulation only by legal rules set by their flag states and by the law of nations. This traditional law of the sea regime was as remarkable a body of customary international law as any in history.[90]

The story of the law of the sea since the later twentieth century is one that can only be told by underscoring the challenge made to traditional high seas freedoms by individual nation-states seeking to enlarge their own maritime jurisdictions. In large measure, the challenge arose from economic causes. The resources of the oceans were once thought to be more or less inexhaustible: Fish, for example, would so replenish themselves that one nation's fishing would not endanger another

[87] C. Archer, *International Organizations* 124-126 (2d ed. 1992); Bennett, supra, at 321-347.

[88] R.P. Anand, *Origin and Development of the Law of the Sea* (1983).

[89] H. Grotius, *The Freedom of the Seas* 7 (Magoffin trans. 1916).

[90] A classic text of the traditional regime is C. Colombos, *The International Law of the Sea* (6th ed. 1967).

nation's catch. When, because of technological developments, the bounty of the sea—not only fish, but more lately oil, gas, and hard minerals—became depletable resources, states began to carve up the international maritime regime. The race to divide the oceans to control economic resources began in earnest in 1945, when the United States in the Truman Proclamation asserted its sovereign jurisdiction over the oil and gas beneath the country's offshore continental shelf, an underwater plateau extending in many places hundreds of miles out to sea.[91] Since the United States also had significant distant water maritime interests in naval passage, ocean shipping, and tuna fishing, the Truman Proclamation was careful to stipulate that national claims to the mineral resources of the continental shelf in no way affected or provided a precedent for limiting other high seas freedoms.[92] However, Chile soon claimed a 200-mile territorial sea, arguing that since it had no appreciable offshore oil and gas reserves, it was entitled to appropriate fishing resources instead.[93] Though the United States was quick to protest the Chilean claim because it failed, "with respect to fishing, to accord appropriate and adequate recognition to the rights and interests of the United States in the high seas,"[94] other Latin American states endorsed the concept of a 200-mile territorial sea. By 1970, Argentina, Brazil, Chile, Ecuador, El Salvador, Nicaragua, Panama, and Peru had joined in the Montevideo Declaration, claiming their "right to establish the limits of their maritime sovereignty and jurisdiction in accordance with their geographical and geological characteristics and with the factors governing the existence of marine resources and the need for their rational utilization."[95] Between 1945 and 1982, there ensued one conflict after another between states claiming expanded national maritime zones and states wishing to exercise high seas freedoms of fishing or navigation in the same waters, for example, the Tuna War between

[91] Proclamation 2667: Policy of the United States with Respect to the Natural Resources of the Subsoil and the Sea Bed of the Continental Shelf, 10 Fed. Reg. 12,303 (Oct. 2, 1945).

[92] Ibid.

[93] Declaration of President of Chile Claiming Jurisdiction over Seas to a Distance of 200 Miles, *Public Policy for the Seas* 85 (N.J. Padelford ed. 1970).

[94] United States Note of Protest to Chile Regarding the Extent of Territorial Waters Claimed Along the Coasts of Chile, Ecuador and Peru. Id. at 87.

[95] Montevideo Declaration on the Law of the Sea, May 8, 1970, U.N. Doc. A/A.C.138/34 (1971).

Peru and the United States,[96] and the Cod War between Iceland on the one hand and Great Britain and West Germany on the other.[97]

As the customary practice underlying the law of the sea began to diversify, there came to be increasing interest in negotiating law of the sea treaties. In 1949, the United Nations asked the International Law Commission to prepare draft law of the sea conventions, work that led to the 1958 Geneva Law of the Sea Conference and to four international agreements: the Convention on the Territorial Sea and the Contiguous Zone, the Convention on the High Seas, the Convention on Fishing and Conservation of the Living Resources of the High Seas, and the Convention on the Continental Shelf.[98] However, the 1958 Geneva Conference was unable to answer the crucial question of what would be the maximum permissible extent of the territorial sea. The Soviet Union and its allies were in favor of a 12-mile territorial sea, a position supported by Arab states interested in restricting Israel's passage into the Gulf of Aqaba. Latin American states pressed for a 200-mile limit.[99] The United States and other maritime states, such as Great Britain, Japan, and the Netherlands, fought to retain the traditional three-mile limit. Finally, no position prevailed; in a 45 to 33 vote, a U.S. compromise resolution providing for a six-mile territorial sea with an adjacent six-mile fishing zone failed to secure the necessary two-thirds vote.[100] A Second United Nations Conference on the Law of the Sea was convened in Geneva in 1960, especially to grapple with the territorial sea problem, but the new Conference rejected by a single vote a joint U.S. and Canadian proposal for a six-mile territorial sea coupled with an additional six-mile contiguous zone to protect fishing.[101]

[96] Loring, The Fisheries Dispute, *U.S. Foreign Policy and Peru* 83 (Sharp ed. 1972).

[97] Bilder, The Anglo-Icelandic Fisheries Dispute, 1973 *Wisconsin Law Review* 37. The Cod War generated the *Fisheries Jurisdiction* case, where Iceland refused to obey the order of the International Court of Justice to refrain from enforcing its 50-mile fishing zone until the Court ruled on the complaints of Britain and Germany, a zone the Court finally found not opposable to the two countries. 1972 I.C.J. Reports 12, 30; 1974 I.C.J. Reports 3, 175. See A. Welch, *The Royal Navy in the Cod Wars: Britain and Iceland in Conflict* (2006).

[98] Dean, The Geneva Conference on the Law of the Sea: What Was Accomplished, 52 *American Journal of International Law* 607 (1958) [hereinafter cited as "Dean"].

[99] Hollick, The Origins of 200-Mile Offshore Zones, 71 *American Journal of International Law* 994 (1997).

[100] Dean, supra, at 608-616.

[101] Dean, The Second Geneva Conference on the Law of the Sea: The Fight for Freedom of the Seas, 54 *American Journal of International Law* 751, 772-776 (1960).

By the late 1960s, national claims beyond three-mile territorial seas had proliferated. Twelve-mile claims, especially, were legion.[102] As more states made more unilateral maritime claims, the two large naval powers, the United States and the Soviet Union, began to consider calling yet another law of the sea conference to protect high seas freedom.[103] The naval interest in a new conference soon had to share the limelight with another maritime concern. Vast and possibly lucrative resources of manganese nodules had been discovered on the ocean floor. In 1967, Arvid Pardo, the Ambassador of Malta to the United Nations, delivered a speech to the First Committee of the General Assembly, calling for an international regime to govern the deep seabed, mine the manganese nodules, and distribute the profits from their sale to the neediest countries.[104] Pardo's speech triggered the establishment of a United Nations Ad Hoc Seabed Committee in 1968, followed by a Permanent Seabed Committee, which met between 1969 and 1973.[105] The Seabed Committees laid the groundwork for the Third United Nations Conference on the Law of the Sea, a truly gargantuan international conference. Thousands of diplomats met some 193 times (not counting even more committee meetings) between 1974 and 1982 in Caracas, New York, Geneva, and Jamaica. Their deliberations inspired a vast amount of international law research and writing,[106] and generated voluminous official records and proceedings.[107]

[102] W. Friedmann, *The Future of the Oceans* 30-31 (1971) [hereinafter cited as "Friedmann"].

[103] A.L. Hollick, *U.S. Foreign Policy on the Law of the Sea* 174 (1981) [hereinafter cited as "Hollick"]; M.W. Janis, *Sea Power and the Law of the Sea* (1976).

[104] Friedmann, supra, at 62-120.

[105] S. Oda, *The Law of the Sea in Our Time*: Vol. II, *The United Nations Seabed Committee: 1968-1973* (1977).

[106] The quantity of the literature can be appreciated by reviewing seven "select" bibliographies on the Law of the Sea prepared by the United Nations: ST/LIB/SER.B/14 (1974), ST/LIB/SER.B/15 (1974), ST/LIB/SER.B/16 (1975), ST/LIB/SER.B/21 (1976), ST/LIB/SER.B/25 (1978), ST/LIB/SER.B/29 (1980), and LOS/LIB/1 (1985). Highly readable accounts of the many years of the Third Law of the Sea Conference may be found in C. Sanger, *Ordering the Oceans: The Making of the Law of the Sea* (1987), and Wertenbaker, A Reporter at Large: The Law of the Sea, *The New Yorker*, Aug. 1, 1983, at 38-65, and Aug. 8, 1983, at 56-83.

[107] The official records are set out in 17 volumes: *Third United Nations Conference on the Law of the Sea: Official Records* (1975-1984).

B. International Regimes

The end result of the Conference was the United Nations Convention on the Law of the Sea of October 7, 1982.[108] Altogether, some 155 states, though not the United States, signed the agreement. The Convention needed 60 ratifications before it could come into force a year later,[109] but it took more than a decade, November 1993, for the sixtieth state to ratify, and none of these, save Iceland, was an industrialized country.[110] The chief stumbling block was the treatment of deep-sea mining, which was viewed as unfair by many states, but in 1994, the General Assembly adopted a state-negotiated agreement that significantly changed the Convention's deep-sea mining regime.[111] After modification of the deep-sea mining provisions, ratifications flowed much more freely. As of February 2023, there were 168 parties to the Law of the Sea Convention, now including most industrialized countries, except the United States: Australia, Canada, Denmark, Germany, Italy, France, Japan, Ireland, the Netherlands, Norway, Russia, Sweden, and the United Kingdom.[112] It is recognized that on the whole the Convention codifies modern customary international law. Much more so than ever before, the law of the sea is now embodied, or at least reflected, in written form. The starting place for most any maritime topic nowadays is to be found somewhere in the 320 articles and nine annexes of the 1982 Law of the Sea Convention.[113] We can only review some of the more important aspects of this increasingly complex subject.

Like ripples from a stone thrown in a pond, national maritime jurisdictions encircle a state's land territory. These zones are measured from baselines; the "normal" baseline is "the low-water line along the coast as marked on large-scale charts officially recognized by the coastal States," although there are special baselines permitted for, for example, deeply indented coasts and across river mouths and bays.[114] Landward

[108] United Nations Convention on the Law of the Sea, Dec. 10, 1982, 1833 *United Nations Treaty Series* 3 [hereinafter cited as "U.N. Law of the Sea Convention"].

[109] Id., art. 308.

[110] U.N. Office of Legal Affairs, 32 *Law of the Sea Bulletin* 1-3 (1996).

[111] Agreement Relating to the Implementation of Part XI of the United Nations Convention on the Law of the Sea of 10 December 1982, July 28, 1994, 1836 *United Nations Treaty Series* 3 [hereinafter cited as "1994 Implementation Agreement"].

[112] www.un.org/depts/los/index.htm (Feb. 26, 2023).

[113] The Convention is reviewed and analyzed in *The Oxford Handbook of the Law of the Sea* (D.R. Rothwell et al. eds. 2015); and L.B. Sohn, J.E. Noyes, E. Franckx & K.G. Juras, *Cases and Materials on the Law of the Sea* (2d ed. 2014).

[114] U.N. Law of the Sea Convention, supra, arts. 5-16. See Aurrecoechea & Pethick, The Coastline: Its Physical and Legal Definition, 1 *International Journal of Estuarine &*

of the baselines are "internal waters," such as landlocked lakes and rivers, which are fully within the ordinary sovereignty of the coastal state. Measured seaward from the baselines is, first, the territorial sea, which may be as wide as 12 nautical miles and is subject, within some limits set by international law, to the sovereign jurisdiction of the coastal state.[115] Second, and beyond the territorial sea, is the contiguous zone, which may not extend beyond 24 nautical miles from the baselines and within which the coastal state may enforce "customs, fiscal, immigration or sanitary laws."[116] A coastal state may, third, establish an "exclusive economic zone," also beyond the territorial sea, in which it has "sovereign rights for the purpose of exploring and exploiting, conserving and managing the natural resources" up to 200 nautical miles from its coast.[117] Fourth, and finally, a coastal state has rights to exploit its "continental shelf," that is, "the seabed and subsoil of the submarine areas that extend beyond its territorial sea throughout the natural prolongation of its land territory to the outer edge of the continental margin, or to a distance of 200 nautical miles from the baselines from which the breadth of the territorial sea is measured where the outer edge of the continental margin does not extend up to that distance."[118] These four zones of national maritime jurisdiction, along with special regions permitted for archipelagic states,[119] greatly expand state sovereignty and jurisdiction in the oceans at the considerable expense of the traditional international regime.

High seas freedoms are, however, still protected, albeit contributing to economic and conservation problems, for example, overfishing[120] in

---

Coastal Law 29 (1986); Strauss, The Future of Baselines as the Sea Level Rises, 6 *Journal of Territorial & Maritime Studies* 27 (2019).

[115] U.N. Law of the Sea Convention, supra, arts. 2-8.

[116] Id., art. 33. See Lowe, The Development of the Concept of the Contiguous Zone, 52 *British Yearbook of International Law* 109 (1981).

[117] U.N. Law of the Sea Convention, supra, arts. 55-75. See Juda, The Exclusive Economic Zone: Compatibility of National Claims and the UN Convention on the Law of the Sea, 16 *Ocean Development & International Law* 1 (1986).

[118] U.N. Law of the Sea Convention, supra, arts. 76-85. See Jewett, The Evolution of the Legal Regime of the Continental Shelf, 22 *Canadian Yearbook of International Law* 153 (1984).

[119] U.N. Law of the Sea Convention, supra, arts. 46-54.

[120] Ellis, Fisheries Conservation in an Anarchical System, 3 *Journal of International Law & International Relations* 1 (2007); Posner & Sykes, Economic Foundations of the Law of the Sea, 104 *American Journal of International Law* 569, 592-594 (2010).

the greatly diminished area still outside national control,[121] but also in the form of special rights preserved within the newly expanded coastal state jurisdictions. Principal among these are the right of "innocent passage" in territorial seas and the right of "transit passage" through straits used for international navigation.[122] Innocent passage is defined as passage "not prejudicial to the peace, good order or security of the coastal State."[123] Transit passage is passage "solely for the purpose of continuous and expeditious transit of the strait between one part of the high seas or an exclusive economic zone and another part of the high seas or an exclusive economic zone," and the Convention provides that it "shall not be impeded" by the coastal State.[124] Both innocent passage and transit passage are more particularly defined and delimited in the Convention, but their major thrust is to ensure rights of peaceful passage for foreign vessels through the newly acquired maritime zones of the coastal states, rights especially important to the United States.[125] In the new exclusive economic zones, for example, foreign vessels are entitled to traditional high seas rights of navigation and overflight.[126] Moreover, the traditional international law of piracy providing for universal jurisdiction for all states [see Chapter 10] carries on under the Law of the Sea Convention, even in some cases in the exclusive economic zone.[127]

In some respects, the new Law of the Sea Convention does not much depart from the traditional law of the sea. For example, the Convention confirms the right of each state to independently decide which ships shall have its nationality,[128] even while requiring that there be some "genuine link" between the vessel and the conferring flag state.[129] As in the traditional regime, the Convention provides that

[121] U.N. Law of the Sea Convention, supra, arts. 86-120.

[122] Id., arts. 17-32, 37-44.

[123] Id., art. 19(1). See Butler, Innocent Passage and the 1982 Convention: The Influence of Soviet Law and Policy, 81 *American Journal of International Law* 331 (1987).

[124] U.N. Law of the Sea Convention, supra, art. 38(1, 2).

[125] S. Kraska & R. Pedrozo, *The Free Sea: The American Fight for Freedom of Navigation* (2018).

[126] Id., art. 58. See Richardson, Law of the Sea: Navigation and Other Traditional National Security Considerations, 19 *San Diego Law Review* 553 (1982).

[127] Roach, Countering Piracy off Somalia: International Law and International Institutions, 104 *American Journal of International Law* 397 (2010).

[128] U.N. Law of the Sea Convention, supra, art. 90.

[129] Id., art. 91(1).

a state has exclusive jurisdiction over ships on the high seas bearing its nationality, though such exclusive jurisdiction may, in exceptional cases, be modified by international treaties or by the Convention.[130]

The most controversial parts of the 1982 Law of the Sea Convention have concerned the seabed and ocean floor and subsoil thereof beyond the limits of national jurisdiction, territory referred to in the Convention as the "Area."[131] Much of the Convention, several of its annexes, and the 1999 Implementation Agreement are devoted to regulating mineral resources in the Area and to the International Sea-Bed Authority (the "Authority").[132] The Area and its resources are declared "the common heritage of mankind."[133] States are prohibited from appropriating any of the Area's mineral resources, except in accordance with the Convention and with Authority regulation.[134]

A principal known deep seabed resource at issue are manganese nodules that lie in great quantities at depths of 12,000 to 20,000 feet.[135] The nodules vary greatly in size and composition, but many of them contain rich amounts of minerals like manganese, nickel, copper, and cobalt. In the 1960s, technology was developed that made mining possible, although the economics of deep seabed mining are not yet such that it is commercially feasible.[136] The Authority, which is empowered to organize and control seabed mining in the Area as set out in the Convention,[137] has for its members all states parties to the Convention, sits in Jamaica,[138] and is composed of an Assembly, a Council, a Secretariat,[139] and an Enterprise, the last being charged to explore and exploit the seabed as well as to transport, process, and market seabed minerals.[140] There may also be mining done by sovereign states or

[130] Id., art. 92(1).

[131] Id., art. 1(1).

[132] Id., arts. 133-191, Annexes III, IV; 1994 Implementation Agreement, supra. Information about the Authority can be found at www.isa.org.jm (Mar. 4, 2023).

[133] U.N. Law of the Sea Convention, supra, art. 136.

[134] Id., art. 137.

[135] Macdonald & Welsh, Next Frontier: Mining the Ocean Floor, *Wall Street Journal*, June 4, 2014.

[136] Id. at 13-14.

[137] U.N. Law of the Sea Convention, supra, art. 157; 1994 Implementation Agreement, supra, art. 1-2.

[138] U.N. Law of the Sea Convention, supra, art. 156 (2, 4).

[139] Id., art. 158(1).

[140] Id., arts. 158(2), 153, 170.

private parties in conjunction with the Authority.[141] Profits and other benefits from seabed mining are to be shared equitably, "taking into particular consideration the interests and needs of developing States and peoples who have not attained full independence or other self-governing status"[142] [see Chapter 3]. The Area, the Authority, and the Enterprise constitute bold ventures in international cooperation.

Until 1981, the United States had generally supported the concept of a new and comprehensive law of the sea treaty. Prevailing U.S. governmental policy, the result of elaborate intragovernmental negotiations, held that such an agreement could best protect U.S. naval and maritime passage rights by securing such protections in exchange for concessions respecting ocean mining and extended national resource zones.[143] Outside the government, however, critics rejected the prospect of a new law of the sea treaty and urged that the United States instead rely on customary international law to protect navigation rights and, especially, that the United States refuse to establish an international seabed organization with any real powers.[144] Unsuccessful during the 1970s, U.S. opponents of a law of the sea treaty gained a prominent position in the new Reagan administration in 1981, and in 1982, the United States decided not to sign, much less ratify, the Convention of which it was so much the author.[145]

The United States at the concluding session of the Law of the Sea Conference stated that it could accept part, but not all, of the new agreement:

> The United States recognizes that certain aspects of the Convention represent positive accomplishments. Indeed, those parts of the Convention dealing with navigation and overflight and most other provisions of the Convention serve the interests of the international community. These texts reflect prevailing international practice. They also demonstrate that the Conference believed that it was articulating rules in most areas that reflect the existing state of affairs—a state of affairs

[141] Id., art. 153(2)(b).

[142] Id., arts. 140(2), 160(2)(F)(i).

[143] See Hollick, supra; E. Wenk, *The Politics of the Ocean* (1972).

[144] *The Law of the Sea: U.S. Interests and Alternatives* (R.C. Amacher & R.J. Sweeney eds. 1976).

[145] Becker, International Law of the Sea, 41 *International Lawyer* 671 (2007); Noyes, The United States, the Law of the Sea Convention, and Freedom of Navigation, 29 *Suffolk Transnational Law Review* 1 (2005).

> that we wished to preserve by enshrining these beneficial and desirable principles in treaty language.
>
> Unfortunately, despite these accomplishments, the deep sea-bed mining regime that would be established by the Convention is unacceptable and would not serve the interests of the international community.[146]

The official position of the United States was that those parts of the Convention protecting high seas freedoms were customary international law upon which the United States was entitled to rely, but that by refusing to sign or ratify the Convention, the United States was not bound by those parts of it relating to the seabed regime and that, therefore, the United States could lawfully authorize deep seabed mining pursuant to its own domestic legislation. Many other countries, however, rejected the idea that the United States could opt for just those provisions of the Law of the Sea Treaty that it wanted and reject the rest. Their position was that the customary limits on national maritime zones had eroded over time and that the 12-mile limit to the territorial sea and the various transit rights guaranteed in the Convention were negotiated trade-offs for the Convention's deep seabed mining provisions.[147]

As of December 2025, the United States is still not a party to the Convention. Nations that do not ratify the Law of the Sea Convention may continue to assert the high seas freedoms, hoping to keep those rights alive as customary international law. Other states will likewise make counter-assertions for extended national zones [see Chapter 3]. For example, between December 1982 and March 1986, the United States issued more than 40 protest notes to foreign governments asserting expanded maritime jurisdictional regimes:

> [T]o illustrate clearly our national resolve, we have not been bashful about exercising the rights we claim. In this regard, the Department of State and the Navy have established an exercise-of-rights program. Subject to definite guidelines and review, the program challenges illicit coastal state maritime claims which exceed what is permitted by international law. A well-known example of such a challenge is the Navy's role in Libya. At issue is not only

[146] Statement of U.S. Delegate Clingan, December 9, 1982, United Nations, 17 *Third United Nations Conference on the Law of the Sea: Official Records* 116-117 (1984).

[147] *The Lawfulness of Deep Seabed Mining* (T.G. Kronmiller & G.W. Smith eds. 3 vols., 1980-1981); Caminos & Molitor, Progressive Development of International Law and the Package Deal, 79 *American Journal of International Law* 871 (1985).

a prior permission requirement to exercise the right of innocent passage in the territorial sea but also a claim by Libya that the Gulf of Sidra constitutes a historic bay the waters of which are internal within a 300-mile straight line closing the gulf.[148]

Whatever the fate of the freedoms of the high seas as customary international law, it is plain that coastal states may now permissibly extend their economic jurisdictions far into the oceans. The United States already has legislation respecting the continental shelf and a 200-mile fishery zone.[149] After claiming a 200-mile exclusive economic zone in 1983, there is now debate about a more extensive regulation of U.S. maritime zones, which at some 3.9 billion acres, are nearly twice as great as the land acreage (2.3 billion acres) of the United States and its territories.[150] The positive effect of U.S. and other national maritime zones on fishing has been remarkable. National fishery management regimes have greatly diminished overfishing and most of the oceans' fishing stocks are now viewed as sustainable over the long term.[151]

Less happy is on-going discord over deep-sea mining. In 1980, the United States enacted the Deep Seabed Hard Mineral Resources Act,[152] which put the nation at loggerheads with the Convention, a development that has generated an international issue of considerable heat and volume, which carries on, as recently as 2025, unabated.[153]

[148] Address by Ambassador Negroponte, Current Developments in U.S. Oceans Policy, March 14, 1986, U.S. Department of State, Current Policy No. 819 (1986).

[149] Outer Continental Shelf Lands Act of 1953, Pub. L. No. 83-212, 43 U.S.C. §§1331-1343; Fishery Conservation and Management Act of 1976, Pub. L. No. 94-265, 16 U.S.C. §§1801 et seq.

[150] Proclamation No. 5030, 48 Fed. Reg. 10605 (Mar. 15, 1983); National Advisory Committee on Oceans and Atmosphere, *The Exclusive Economic Zone of the United States: Some Immediate Policy Issues* 1 (May 1984).

[151] Hilborn, Let Us Eat Fish, *N.Y. Times*, Apr. 15, 2011, at A21.

[152] Pub. L. No. 96-283, 30 U.S.C. §1401, 19 *International Legal Materials* 1003 (1980).

[153] See *Law of the Sea: U.S. Policy Dilemma* (B. Oxman, D. Caron & C. Buderi eds. 1983). The Oceans Act of 2000, Pub. L. No. 106-256, 114 Stat. 644 (2000) established a public commission to report on recommendations for U.S. oceans policy. For some of the recent controversies involving sea-bed mining, see Lipton, Mining Company is Seeking Shortcut Access to Sea Metals, *New York Times*, Mar. 29, 2025, at 21; Mining the Ocean Bed, The Last Frontier: A Trump Shock May Speed Up the Start of Deep-Sea Mining, *The Economist*, May 3, 2025, at 46.

Before the International Seabed Authority was constituted, for more than a decade a Preparatory Commission met in Jamaica and New York to ready the transition to the new international organization. The work of the Preparatory Commission was remarkably slow, albeit the lack of progress makes sense if one realizes that some key maritime states, such as Germany and the United Kingdom, had not yet signed the 1982 Convention and only sent observers to the Preparatory Commission and that the most important maritime actor, the United States, had neither signed the Convention nor sent observers. Over time, it seemed that the divide between North and South about deep seabed mining widened, with most of the newly non-Communist countries of Eastern Europe joining the ranks of the other industrialized countries.[154] The Convention has been in force since 1994, and the Authority itself has begun to function. The Assembly held its first session in November 1994, and in 1996 elected the Authority's first secretary-general, the Fijian Satya Nandan; in the same year the Authority's operations were begun in Kingston, Jamaica.[155]

The negotiations leading to the Convention also resulted in the constitution of a new international court, the International Tribunal for the Law of the Sea, its statute appearing as Annex VI of the Convention.[156] The Tribunal, composed of 21 judges, is based in Hamburg, Germany, and has considered, as of 2023, only 29 cases, not all decided, from its establishment in July 1996.[157] The Convention obliges states parties to submit unresolved disputes concerning the interpretation or application of the Convention to compulsory dispute settlement procedures, which may be chosen to be not only the Tribunal, but also the

[154] Riddell-Dixon, The Preparatory Commission on the International Sea-bed Authority: "New Realism"?, 7 *International Journal of Estuarine & Coastal Law* 195-197, 199-204 (1992).

[155] 3 *Annual Review of United Nations Affairs 1996*, at 3305-3306 (1997).

[156] Rosenne, Establishing the International Tribunal for the Law of the Sea, 89 *American Journal of International Law* 806 (1995); Noyes, The International Tribunal for the Law of the Sea, 28 *Cornell International Law Journal* 109 (1998).

[157] www.itlos.org (Mar. 4, 2023). See Statement by Rüdiger Wolfrum, President of the International Tribunal for the Law of the Sea on the Report of the Tribunal at the Sixteenth Meeting of the States Parties to the Law of the Sea Convention, 19 June 2006 (Sept. 24, 2002). For a discussion of one of the Tribunal's cases, the M/V "Saiga" (No. 2), Saint Vincent and the Grenadines v. Guinea, July 1, 1999, 38 *International Legal Materials* 1323 (1999), see M.W. Janis, J.E. Noyes & L.N. Sadat, *International Law Cases & Commentary* 960-963 (7th ed. 2025).

International Court of Justice or one of two forms of arbitration, a provision which has caused a certain amount of adjudicative competition and confusion.[158] In practice, though the Tribunal has seemed to result in little fragmentation of the substantive law of the sea, has contributed to a "procedural fragmentation caused by a plethora of conflicting and overlapping jurisdictions."[159]

Regardless of the outcome of the debate about the exploitation of the deep seabed, it is plain that international customary practice as well as the Law of the Sea Convention has destroyed much of the traditional international oceans regime. The greatly extended national maritime zones effectively carve up a large part of the old international commons. At the end of the day, nationalist unilateralism on the oceans "often born of narrow agendas, impatience, frustration, or political and bureaucratic ambitions," results in "systemic costs that may ultimately imperil the existing and future foundation for strong international measures necessary to protect the global marine environment and provide a rational global order for the oceans."[160]

Moreover, expansive national maritime claims have led to serious new international strife. Especially troubling are the conflicting national claims of China, Vietnam, the Philippines, and other states to the islands and waters of the South China Sea.[161] In 2016, under the terms of the Law of the Sea Convention, the Philippines brought China to the Permanent Court of Arbitration [see Chapter 5], complaining about China's claim to sovereignty of rocks and islets in the South China Sea. The PCA ruled for the Philippines, holding that

[158] U.N. Law of the Sea Convention, supra, arts. 286, 287; Boyle, Dispute Settlement and the Law of the Sea Convention: Problems of Fragmentation and Jurisdiction, 46 *International & Comparative Law Quarterly* 37 (1997). For more on the proliferation of international courts, see Chapter 5.

[159] Rayfuse, The Future of Compulsory Dispute Settlement Under the Law of the Sea Convention, 36 *Victoria University Wellington Law Review* 683, 688-700, 710 (2005). Also problematic has been the Tribunal's failure to be adequately concerned with the protection of living marine resources. Id. at 692-693.

[160] Oxman, The Territorial Temptation: A Siren Song at Sea, 100 *American Journal of International Law* 830, 851 (2006); *The Future of Ocean Regime-Building: Essays in Tribute to Douglas M. Johnson* (A. Chircop, T.L. McDorman & S.J. Rolston eds. 2009).

[161] See Damrosch & Oxman eds., Agora: The South China Sea, 107 *American Journal of International Law* 95 (2013).

China did not have good legal title to the disputed territories.[162] China has refused to accept the PCA's judgment.[163]

Maritime conflicts still strongly involve and implicate the use of naval power, including that of the United States.[164] For example, the United States navigates warships in waters claimed by China, evoking heated Chinese protests.[165] Despite the codification accomplishments of the 1982 Law of the Sea Convention, much of the law of the sea remains contentious. Four hundred years after Grotius, that illustrious international lawyer would find himself quite at home on the tumultuous waters of the twenty-first century.

2. *Air Law, Space Law, Antarctica, and the Arctic*

Besides the law of the sea, there are several other traditional fields of international jurisdiction. One of these, the skies, is now, thanks to war and economic competition, so subject to the territorial regulation of the individual states that it must be wondered whether it is any longer truly an international regime or merely a field of extensive inter-state cooperation.[166] Air law, a mix of international and domestic rules, has been defined as "a body of rules governing the use of airspace and its benefits for aviation, the general public and the nations of the world."[167] Most of the rules of air law concern the aviation industry, and many of these are to be found in international agreements, for example, the Warsaw Convention, which limits the liability of international air

[162] Philippines v. China, Award, PCA Case No. 2013-19 (Convention on the Law of the Sea Annex VII Arbitral Tribunal, 2016), www.pca-cpa.org.

[163] Chinese Foreign Ministry, The South China Sea Arbitration Awards: A Critical Study, 17 *Chinese Journal of International Law* 207 (2018); Noyes, International Decision: *In re Arbitration Between the Philippines and China,* 110 *American Journal of International Law* 102 (2016).

[164] J. Kraska, *Maritime Power and the Law of the Sea* (2011); Etzioni, Freedom of Navigation Assertions: The United States as the World's Policeman, 42 *Armed Forces & Society* 501 (2015).

[165] See Daugirdas & Mortenson, United States Conducts Naval Operations Within Twelve Nautical Miles of the Spratley Islands in the South China Sea, Prompting Protests from China, 110 *American Journal of International Law* 120 (2016).

[166] P.C. Jessup & H.J. Taubenfeld, *Controls for Outer Space and the Antarctic Analogy* 201 (1959) [hereinafter cited as "Jessup & Taubenfeld"].

[167] I.H.P. Diederiks-Verschoor, *An Introduction to Air Law* 1 (1985).

carriers,[168] and the Chicago Convention, which establishes the rights of states over territorial airspace and civil aircraft.[169] Alongside the basic multilateral treaty framework of air law, there now exists a wide number of supplemental accords and protocols that are regularly modified by periodic international negotiation.[170] Such regular modification is ever more necessary and frequent.[171] Moreover, the basic multilateral accords are increasingly supplemented by a complex network of bilateral agreements.[172]

Outer space was, not so long ago, not even a topic of legal theory,[173] but no sooner was the first satellite, Sputnik, put in orbit by the Soviet Union, on October 4, 1957, than the fundamental question was raised whether outer space should be "subjected to an international rather than to a national solution or, one might better say, to a series of national solutions?"[174] The answer is still uncertain. National rivalries in space are intense, and the fate of what little international regime there is for the area remains very much in doubt. Central to the international law of outer space is the Outer Space Treaty,[175] concluded in 1967 after heated debate in the United Nations.[176] The former president of the International Court of Justice, Manfred Lachs, termed the Treaty "a

[168] Convention for the Unification of Certain Rules Relating to International Transportation by Air, 49 Stat. 3000, T.S. No. 876, 2 Bevans 983, 137 L.N.T.S. 11 (concluded at Warsaw October 12, 1929; entered into force February 13, 1933; for the United States October 29, 1934). There is considerable domestic case law on the Warsaw Convention. See, e.g., Eastern Airlines, Inc. v. Floyd, 499 U.S. 530 (1991); El Al Israel Airlines, Ltd. v. Tseng, 525 U.S. 155 (1999).

[169] International Air Services Transit Agreement, 59 Stat. 1693, 3 Bevans 916, 84 U.N.T.S. 389 (signed at Chicago December 7, 1944; entered into force January 30, 1945; for the United States February 8, 1945).

[170] J. Naveau, *Droit du transport aérien international* (1980); *Shawcross and Beaumont: Air Law* (J.D. McLean et al. eds., looseleaf 2020).

[171] Guldimann, A Future System of Liability in Air Carriage, 16 *Annals of Air and Space Law* 93 (1991).

[172] Mifsund, Schildhaus, Schmidt & Chen, Aviation and Aerospace Law, 34 *International Lawyer* 625, 630-631 (2000).

[173] C.W. Jenks, *Space Law* 97-101 (1965).

[174] Jessup & Taubenfeld, supra, at 251.

[175] Treaty on Principles Governing the Activities of States in the Exploration and Use of Outer Space, Including the Moon and Other Celestial Bodies, 18 U.S.T. 2410, T.I.A.S. No. 6347, 610 U.N.T.S. 205 (done at Washington, London, and Moscow January 27, 1967; entered into force October 10, 1967) [hereinafter cited as "Outer Space Treaty"].

[176] See C.Q. Christol, *The Modern International Law of Outer Space* 13-20 (1982).

rock on which all further principles and rules are built."[177] Specifically, the principles of the Treaty provide that the "exploration and use of outer space, including the moon and other celestial bodies . . . shall be the province of all mankind" and that "[o]uter space, including the moon and other celestial bodies, is not subject to national appropriation."[178] The Treaty protects the moon and other celestial bodies from any but "peaceful purposes" and prohibits states parties from placing nuclear weapons or other weapons of mass destruction in space, certainly volatile modern political issues.[179] It may be that the Outer Space Treaty ought to be strengthened to better limit an arms race and conflicts in space,[180] or that customary international law play a greater role.[181]

The Outer Space Treaty has been supplemented by four additional U.N. outer space agreements respecting astronauts[182] and the registration of objects launched into space.[183] There is the Moon Treaty, as of December 2025 ratified by 18 states, but not yet in force for the United States, Russia, or China.[184] There is also the Convention on the International Liability for Damage Caused by Space Objects.[185]

[177] Lachs, The Treaty on Principles of the Law of Outer Space, 1961-1992, 39 *Netherlands International Law Review* 291, 300 (1992).

[178] Outer Space Treaty, supra, arts. I, II.

[179] Id., art. IV.

[180] See Maogoto & Freeland, The Final Frontier: The Laws of Armed Conflict and Space Warfare, 23 *Connecticut Journal of International Law* 165, 195 (2007).

[181] See Koplow, ASAT-isfication: Customary International Law and the Regulation of Auti-Satellite Weapons, 30 *Michigan Journal of International Law* 1187 (2009).

[182] Agreement on the Rescue of Astronauts, the Return of Astronauts and the Return of Objects Launched into Outer Space, 19 U.S.T. 7570, T.I.A.S. No. 6599, 672 U.N.T.S. 119 (done at Washington, London, and Moscow April 22, 1968; entered into force December 3, 1968).

[183] Convention on Registration of Objects Launched into Outer Space, 28 U.S.T. 695; T.I.A.S. No. 8480; 1023 U.N.T.S. 15 (done at New York January 14, 1975; entered into force September 15, 1976).

[184] Agreement Governing the Activities of States on the Moon and Other Celestial Bodies, U.N. Doc. A/RES/34,68 (December 5, 1979), reprinted in 18 *International Legal Materials* 1434 (1979) (entered into force July 11, 1984; not in force for the United States); www. treaties.un.org (Dec. 4, 2025). See Christol, The Moon Treaty Enters into Force, 79 *American Journal of International Law* 163 (1985); Larsen, Application of the Precautionary Principle to the Moon, 71 *Journal of Air Law & Commerce* 295 (2006).

[185] Convention on the International Liability for Damage Caused by Space Objects, 24 U.S.T. 2389, T.I.A.S. No. 7762 (done at Washington, London, and Moscow March 29,

The only invocation of the Liability Convention was the Cosmos 954 incident when on January 24, 1978, a Soviet nuclear-powered satellite crashed in the Northwest Territories of Canada.[186]

Generally, the treaties making up the law of space provide for the free exploration and use of outer space, prohibit the appropriation of outer space and celestial bodies by any nation, attempt to restrict military activities in space, and establish that outer space is to be part of the common heritage of all mankind.[187] The United States has challenged the exclusion of military activities in outer space, a challenge by and large resisted by other countries.[188] An international space authority along the lines of the International Seabed Authority discussed above has been envisioned, though not created; there is, however, the United Nations Office for Outer Space Affairs in Vienna that coordinates activities surrounding the five U.N. outer space treaties.[189] There is a pressing need for better regulation of space. As of 2015, some 53 countries were responsible for more than 1,300 public and private satellites.[190]

Like outer space, Antarctica became of legal interest only when technology developed, mostly in the twentieth century, making its territory accessible and potentially useful. By the late 1950s, seven countries—Argentina, Australia, Chile, France, New Zealand, Norway, and the United Kingdom—had all made claim to part of Antarctica, and both

1972; entered into force September 1, 1972; for the United States October 9, 1973). See B.A. Hurwitz, *State Liability for Outer Space Activities* (1992); Larsen, Solving the Space Debris Crisis, 83 *Journal of Air Law & Space Commerce* 475 (2018).

[186] The crash scattered radioactive material. In 1980, the U.S.S.R. agreed to pay Canada $3 million without acknowledging liability. Bourbonniere, National-Security Law in Outer Space, 70 *Journal of Air Law & Commerce* 3, 24 (2005). A related problem concerns the possibility of collision with debris in space. Though there is no relevant treaty, a voluntary code of conduct might begin to address the problem. See Mirmina, Reducing the Proliferation of Orbital Debris: Alternatives to a Legally Binding Instrument, 99 *American Journal of International Law* 649 (2005).

[187] See *Space Activities and Emerging International Law* 249-352 (Matte ed. 1984).

[188] Tannenwald, Law Versus Power on the High Frontier: The Case for a Rule-Based Regime for Outer Space, 29 *Yale Journal of International Law* 363 (2004); Freeland, The Laws of War in Outer Space, *Handbook of Space Security: Policies, Applications and Programs* 81 (S. Freeland & E Gruttner eds. 2020).

[189] J.E.S. Fawcett, *Outer Space: New Challenges to Law and Policy* 8-9 (1984). For the work of the United Nations Office for Outer Space Affairs, see www.unoosa.org/oosa/index.html (Mar. 4, 2023).

[190] Baiocchi & Welser, The Democratization of Space: New Actors Need New Rules, 94 *Foreign Affairs*, No. 3, at 98, 103 (2015).

the United States and the Soviet Union had expressed territorial interest.[191] The potential for conflict among these claims led to the negotiation of the Antarctic Treaty, which still provides the basic legal structure for activities in the region and provides that "Antarctica shall be used for peaceful purposes only" and that there shall be "[f]reedom of scientific investigation."[192] Most important, the Treaty "freezes" national claims to Antarctica:

> No acts or activities taking place while the present Treaty is in force shall constitute a basis for asserting, supporting or denying a claim to territorial sovereignty in Antarctica or create any rights of sovereignty in Antarctica. No new Claim, or enlargement of an existing claim, to territorial sovereignty in Antarctica shall be asserted while the present Treaty is in force.[193]

The Antarctic Treaty regime counts as a successful international jurisdiction, albeit one with "a very low level of formal organization and articulation."[194] How well the system copes with increasing pressures to develop Antarctica's resources and to protect Antarctica's environment is, of course, still open to question.[195] A surge in Antarctic tourism has posed new problems not only for the environment but also about jurisdiction over new facilities. Tourist numbers in Antarctica have grown from about 5,000 in 1990-1991, to about 45,000 in 2016-2017, but fell to 23,023 in 2021-2022.[196] It is also unsettled whether or not Antarctica's

[191] Guyer, The Antarctic System, 139 *Hague Recueil* 149, 159-163 (1973).

[192] 12 U.S.T. 794, T.I.A.S. No. 4780, 402 U.N.T.S. 71 (signed at Washington December 1, 1959; entered into force June 23, 1961).

[193] Id., art. IV(2).

[194] J. Vogler, *The Global Commons: Environmental and Technological Governance* 91 (2d ed. 2000).

[195] Id. at 205-297; see E.J. Sahurie, *The International Law of Antarctica* (1992); Bederman & Keskav, Antarctic Environmental Liability: The Stockholm Annex and Beyond, 19 *Emory International Law Review* 1383 (2005); Liggett, An Erosion of Confidence?: The Antarctica Treaty in the Twenty-First Century, *Diplomacy on Ice: Energy and the Environment in the Arctic and Antarctica* 61 (R. Pincus & S. Ali eds. 2015).

[196] Bastmeijer & Roura, Regulating Antarctic Tourism and the Precautionary Principle, 98 *American Journal of International Law* 763, 780-781 (2004); International Association of Antarctic Tour Operators, *2016-2017 Tourism Statistics*, http://iaato.org (Feb. 12, 2019); www.iaato.org (Mar. 4, 2023).

resources should be considered, like the deep seabed above, part of the "common heritage of mankind."[197]

Respecting the other pole, the United States opposes negotiation of a treaty comparable to the Antarctic Treaty for the Arctic. Instead, President Bush's administration reaffirmed the hope that the Law of the Sea Convention would be ratified since that would be the "most effective way to achieve international recognition and legal certainty for our extended continental shelf."[198] Meantime, however, Russia had claimed the Arctic, using a submarine to place a metal Russian flag on the sea floor beneath the North Pole.[199] Canada, Denmark, and the United States all rejected Russia's Arctic claim.[200] There is a commission on the limits of the Continental Shelf and the Arctic, established pursuant to the Law of the Sea Convention, but its progress is slow, and it is likely that there will be no quick resolution of competing national claims to the Arctic.[201]

3. *International Environmental Law*

Protection of the environment faces many of the same legal and political obstacles that threaten other international common spaces like the seas, the skies, outer space, Antarctica, and the Arctic. Although in practice damages to the environment are often transboundary, most legal and political responses to environmental problems are national. The struggle to create viable forms of substantive and procedural international environmental law has taken on much of the urgency that has heretofore characterized what might be thought of as the missionary

[197] Keyuan, The Common Heritage of Mankind and the Antarctic Treaty System, 38 *Netherlands International Law Review* 173 (1991).

[198] Comprehensive New Statement of U.S. Arctic Policy, 103 *American Journal of International Law* 103 (2009).

[199] Warner, One Small Step for a Submersible, One Giant Land Grab for Russiankind: An Evaluation of Russia's Claim to the North Pole Under International Law, 57 *Naval Law Review* 49, 50-51 (2009).

[200] Id. at 51-52.

[201] Jares, The Continental Shelf Beyond 200 Nautical Miles: The Work of the Commission on the Limits of the Continental Shelf and the Arctic, 42 *Vanderbilt Journal of Transnational Law* 1265, 1304-1305 (2009); *Emerging Legal Orders: The Role of Non-Arctic Actors* (A. Shibata et al. eds. 2019).

causes of international law, most notably war prevention and the protection of human rights.

International environmental law is a relatively recent phenomenon, especially when compared to such classical international legal pursuits as the law of war, the law of the sea, the protection of diplomats, and international mercantile law, all of which date in recognizable modern guise back at least to the sixteenth century. Not until the twentieth century did technology develop to such an extent as to pose threats serious enough for any need for international environmental law to emerge.[202] An early noteworthy evidence of international environmental legal practice was the 1941 decision of the United States-Canada *Trail Smelter* arbitration,[203] where a kind of international tort was found in a case involving transboundary air pollution:

> [U]nder the principles of international law, as well as of the law of the United States, no State has the right to use or permit the use of its territory in such a manner as to cause injury by fumes in or to the territory of another or the properties of persons therein, when the case is of serious consequence and the injury is established by clear and convincing evidence.[204]

Trail Smelter is an example of case-by-case protection of the international environment, but it is doubtful that such piecemeal litigation can effectively address the huge problems posed by global environmental degradation. However, the case is held out as an example of the "internationalization of externalities,"[205] and is, of course, also representative of the doctrine of state responsibility [see Chapter 6].

[202] Nanda, Trends in International Environmental Law, 20 *California Western International Law Journal* 187, 188 (1990). For international environmental law even earlier than *Trail Smelter*, see Hall et al., The Boundary Waters Treaty, the International Joint Commission, and the Evolution of Transboundary Environmental Law and Governance, *The First Century of the International Joint Commission* 457 (D. MacFarlane & M. Clemens eds. 2020).

[203] French, *Trail Smelter* (United States of America v. Canada) (1938 & 1941), *Landmark Cases in Public International Law* 159 (E. Bjorge & C. Miles eds. 2017).

[204] *Trail Smelter* Case (United States v. Canada), Decision of March 11, 1941, 3 *U.N. Reports of International Arbitral Awards* 1938, 1965 (1949), 35 *American Journal of International Law* 684, 716 (1941). *Trail Smelter* was perhaps a happy exception, since it has proven difficult to recover damages for breaches of international environmental law, see A. Kiss & D. Shelton, *International Environmental Law* 347-375 (1991).

[205] Norman & Trachtman, The Customary International Law Game, 90 *American Journal of International Law* 541, 563-564 (2005).

B. International Regimes

Modern international environmental law may be said to have truly begun only in 1972, when the United Nations Conference on the Human Environment met in Stockholm and issued a Declaration on the Human Environment, a good example of "soft law" stimulating important legal rules and practice.[206] One of the Stockholm Conference's most concrete results was the United Nations Environment Programme (UNEP), which has, since then, spawned more than two dozen treaties.[207] These include the Convention on International Trade in Endangered Species of Wild Fauna and Flora (CITES)[208] and the Barcelona Convention for the Protection of the Mediterranean Sea Against Pollution.[209] UNEP has also generated "soft law" of its own, as well as providing international assistance to promote national environmental legislation and administration in developing countries.[210] Besides its Secretariat, UNEP has a Governing Council of 58 states that meets in alternate years at UNEP's headquarters in Nairobi, Kenya.[211]

Since 1972, international environmental problems have sadly multiplied. Some authors have identified the troubles of the international environment as equivalent to those of world peace and international economic justice in that they all constitute fundamental challenges to the traditional international political system based on legal and political doctrines of national sovereignty.[212] Others have signaled the need

[206] Gündling, Environment, International Protection, 9 *Encyclopedia of Public International Law* 119, 121-122 (1986); Handl, Environmental Security and Global Change: The Challenge to International Law, 1 *Yearbook of International Environmental Law 1990* 3, 8 (1991) [hereinafter cited as "Handl"].

[207] 11 *International Legal Materials* 1416 (1972). See Petsonk, The Role of the United Nations Environment Programme (UNEP) in the Development of International Environmental Law, 5 *American University Journal of International Law & Policy* 351, 352 (1990).

[208] 27 U.S.T. 1087, T.I.A.S. No. 8249, 993 U.N.T.S. 243, reprinted in 12 *International Legal Materials* 1085 (1973) (signed in Washington March 3, 1973; entered into force July 1, 1975).

[209] 15 *International Legal Materials* 290 (1976).

[210] Sands, Environmental Law in the United Nations Environment Programme, *The Future of the International Law of the Environment* 51, 52-63 (Hague Academy of International Law 1985) [hereinafter cited as "Sands"].

[211] Annual reviews of UNEP's activities are to be found in the *Yearbook of International Environmental Law*, e.g., 11 *Yearbook International Environmental Law 2004* 641-658 (2005).

[212] Dupuy, Introduction of the Subject, *The Future of the International Law of the Environment* 15, 20-21 (Hague Academy of International Law 1985) [hereinafter cited as "Dupuy"].

to conserve "our planet for generations to come" and to recognize a form of "intergenerational equity."[213] However, despite assertions that the problems of the international environment are "incriminating the notion of sovereignty,"[214] the regulatory world of the international environment displays a variegated complexion, an interwoven texture of old-fashioned, as well as new-fangled, national and international law and process. "International environmental law" has been defined as including "not only public international law, but also relevant aspects of private international law, and in some instances has borrowed heavily from national law."[215]

There are by now quite a number of multilateral treaties protecting the environment. Although at first glance such international agreements are simply ordinary, if important, ways of setting international rules to govern national conduct, there is an argument to be made that, in fact, many of these treaties establish new kinds of international regimes, where, by providing for regular meetings of their members and by "internalizing the making and application of international law within their respective issue-areas, international environmental regimes [have developed] into comparatively autonomous sectoral legal systems."[216] Besides the already mentioned 1976 Barcelona Convention for the Protection of the Mediterranean Sea Against Pollution and its Protocols, other such regime-creating environmental treaties might be said to include the 1974 Helsinki Convention on the Protection of the Marine Environment of the Baltic Sea Area, the 1974 Paris Convention for the Prevention of Marine Pollution from Land-Based Sources, the 1979 Geneva Convention on Long-Range Transboundary Air Pollution, the 1985 Vienna Convention for the Protection of the Ozone Layer and its 1987 Montreal Protocol, and the 1989 Basel Convention on the Control of Transboundary Movements of Hazardous Wastes and Their Disposal.[217]

[213] Brown Weiss, International Law, Common Patrimony and Intergenerational Equity: Research in Progress, *The Future of the International Law of the Environment* 445, 449 (Hague Academy of International Law 1985).

[214] Dupuy, supra, at 20.

[215] P. Birnie & A. Boyle, *International Law and the Environment* 1 (2d ed. 2002).

[216] Gehring, International Environmental Regimes: Dynamic Sectoral Legal Systems, 1 *Yearbook of International Environmental Law 1990* 35, 37 (1991) [hereinafter cited as "Gehring"].

[217] Id. at 35.

B. International Regimes

In 1992, 20 years after the Stockholm Conference, the so-called Rio Summit met to frame and stimulate the debate and development of international environmental law for the next several decades. The United Nations Conference on Environment and Development, which met at Rio de Janeiro, included more than 170 countries and a plethora of non-governmental organizations. At the Rio Summit new Conventions on Biological Diversity and Climate Change were opened for signature.[218] At the Johannesburg World Summit on Sustainable Development in 2002, there were no new treaties or institutions created, only "a recognition that governments had failed to make progress in fulfilling the promises they made a decade earlier at the Rio Earth Summit and that there was a need to focus on implementation."[219]

One of the most important contributions of these environmental conferences was the "precautionary principle." The Rio Declaration on Environment and Development proclaimed, *inter alia*:

> In order to protect the environment, the precautionary approach shall be widely applied by states according to their capabilities. Where there are threats of serious or irreversible damage, lack of scientific certainty shall not be used as a reason for postponing cost-effective measures to prevent environmental degradation.[220]

Other international environmental principles are less clear. Even the crucial concept of "sustainable development," endorsed by ICJ Judge Weeramantry in the *Gabcíkovo-Nagymaros Project* case,[221] is frustratingly vague. One expert writes that sustainable development is too often an "all-encompassing concept, if not a *mantra*, which includes everything

[218] Convention on Biological Diversity (done at Rio de Janeiro, June 5, 1992), 31 *International Legal Materials* 818 (1992); Vierros, The Convention on Biological Diversity: Moving from Policy to Implementation, 7 *Sustainable Development Law & Policy* 17 (2006-2007); Framework Convention on Climate Change (done at New York, May 9, 1992), 31 *International Legal Materials* 849 (1992).

[219] Scherr & Gregg, Johannesburg and Beyond: The 2002 World Summit on Sustainable Development and the Rise of Partnerships, *ALI-ABA Course of Study, April 12-13, 2007*, at 681-682.

[220] Rio Declaration on Environment and Development, Principle 15 (adopted at Rio de Janeiro, June 14, 1992), U.N. Doc. A/CONF. 151/26 (August 12, 1992).

[221] 1997 I.C.J. 3, 88, 110.

which is regarded as good for Mother Earth, for humans themselves, and for future generations."[222]

The issue-specific, treaty-based international environmental regimes that are the progeny of Stockholm and Rio have been characterized as providing "permanent mechanism[s] for changing . . . normative prescriptions."[223] Accordingly, they fall somewhere on a spectrum between international rule and international process, between international agreement and international organization. Because of the need to continually refashion rules to changing environmental circumstances, "[d]iplomatic '*ad hocracy*' is being abandoned for institutionalized, periodic and informal review of international regulatory regimes with simplified amendment procedures."[224] At least two phenomena characterize this international environmental state of affairs, both shared with the field of international human rights law.[225]

The first is that Third World governments pose special problems for generalized international standards. There is a call to apply "differential norms" in international environmental law so that developing countries will not be subjected to standards as strict as those for developed nations.[226] Such special claims for Third World states, based in part on national rights to economic development, were enunciated at least as early as the 1972 Stockholm Conference. There, the Brazilian delegate argued:

> It is economic growth that has allowed developed countries to make great advances in the eradication of mass poverty, ignorance, disease and as such to give a high priority to environmental consideration. Mankind has legitimate needs that are material, aesthetic and spiritual. A country that has not yet reached minimum satisfactory levels in the supply of essentials is not in a position to divert considerable resources to environmental protection.[227]

[222] N. Schrijver, *The Evolution of Sustainable Development in International Law, Meaning and Status* 24 (2008).

[223] Gehring, supra, at 55.

[224] Handl, supra, at 5.

[225] Magraw, International Pollution, Economic Development, and Human Rights, *International Law and Pollution* 30 (D. Magraw ed. 1991) [hereinafter cited as "Magraw"].

[226] Id. at 38-40.

[227] Ntambirweki, The Developing Countries in the Evolution of an International Environmental Law, 14 *Hastings International & Comparative Law Review* 905, 906 (1991).

B. International Regimes

Promoting their developmental needs against international environmental concerns, Third World governments have won preferential treatment in international environmental agreements. In the 1987 Montreal Protocol on Substances That Deplete the Ozone Layer, for example, a developing country is permitted to postpone its compliance with the generalized rules for ten years so long as the country's per capita use of chlorofluorocarbons is less than 0.03 kilograms.[228]

A second important modern phenomenon affecting both international environmental law and international human rights law is the remarkable emergence of private advocacy groups both at the national level and as non-governmental international organizations.[229] The ability of the environmental movement to mobilize public sentiment has been a key factor in encouraging national governments to actually respond to international standards in international environmental law.[230] NGOs such as Greenpeace International, Friends of the Earth, and the World Wide Fund for Nature "have come to be the primary source of expression for the international desire to protect the environment, and number among its most effective guardians"; some suggest that non-governmental international organizations be given legal standing to prosecute national governments in cases brought before international tribunals for violations of international environmental law.[231] In part, NGOs are encouraged to play this role because international decision making is increasingly perceived as undemocratic. Improving the responsiveness of international institutions to popular concerns is nowadays discussed as a problem of their legitimacy.[232] Professor Knox argues that "climate change already interferes with the human rights of vulnerable communities and is an enormous threat to human rights everywhere."[233]

Indeed, in the eyes of some, climate change has become the most important international challenge of our times. Faced with "rising

[228] Id. at 910.

[229] Sands, supra, at 64.

[230] Magraw, supra, at 53-54.

[231] Sands, The Environment, Community and International Law, 30 *Harvard International Law Journal* 393, 394, 412-417 (1989).

[232] Bodansky, The Legitimacy of International Governance: A Coming Challenge for International Environmental Law, 93 *American Journal of International Law* 596 (1999).

[233] Knox, Climate Change and Human Rights Law, 50 *Virginia Journal of International Law* 163, 218 (2009).

seas, dying farmlands, and ever more powerful storms and floods," the international community must face up to the need for "world-historical levels of [international] cooperation."[234] In 1992, the United Nations generated the Framework Convention on Climate Change, ratified as of March 2020, by 197 nations, including the United States.[235] The Kyoto Protocol of 1997 added a complicated scheme of emissions permit trading and binding commitments, but has not been accepted by the United States.[236] It has proved difficult to achieve a climate change regime effective to the degree of the regime regulating the ozone layer.[237] Most recently, the Paris Agreement of 2015, embraced by the Obama administration and denounced by the Trump administration, aims to keep average global temperatures down.[238] On January 20, 2021, his first day in office, President Biden issued an executive order committing the United States to rejoining the Paris Climate Treaty, but in his first day back in office for his second term, President Trump ordered the withdrawal of the United States from the Agreement.[239]

So, in the space of only five decades, international environmental law has developed into one of international law's most challenging fields. As Professor Nanda noted, there is a great irony that, though since 1972 and the Stockholm Conference, international environmental legislation and institutions have rapidly developed, "the planet continue[s] to suffer further environmental degradation."[240] After an exciting period of treaty-making and institution-building, international environmental lawyers have now turned to the much more difficult task of building compliance with good laws already made and

[234] Busby, Warming World: Why Climate Change Matters More than Anything Else, 97 *Foreign Affairs,* July/August 2018, at 49.

[235] 1771 U.N.T.S. 107 (May 9, 1992).

[236] 2203 U.N.T.S. 163 (Dec. 10, 1997).

[237] Peloso, Crafting a Climate Change Protocol: Applying the Lessons Learned from the Success of the Ozone Depletion Program, 25 *Journal of Land Use* 305 (2010); Niranjan, Hole in Ozone Layer Over the Antarctic Smallest Since 2019, *The Guardian,* Dec. 2, 2025, at 4.

[238] 55 *International Legal Materials* 740 (2016); Leal-Arcas & Morelli, The Resilience of the Paris Agreement: Negotiating and Implementing the Climate Regime, 31 *Georgetown Environmental Law Review* 1 (2018); Galbraith, Contemporary Practice of the United States Relating to International Law, 114 *American Journal of International Law* 124, 132-136 (2020).

[239] Davenport & Friedman, Rejoining Paris Accord Tops Moves on Climate, *N.Y. Times,* Jan. 21, 2021, at A21, www.whitehouse.gov (Jan. 20, 2025).

[240] V. Nanda, *International Environmental Law & Policy* 299 (1995).

good institutions already in place,[241] a challenge long familiar to international lawyers concerned with armed conflict [see Chapter 6] and human rights [see Chapter 8].

Coming full circle in international environmental law is the surprising re-emergence of *Trail-Smelter*-like domestic adjudication as an enforcement mechanism. Remarkably, there was litigation in Ecuador against the oil company Chevron for pollution damaging the jungle and its native peoples, and in 2011, an Ecuadorean court found Chevron liable for $9 billion in damages.[242] However, Chevron effectively reversed the Ecuadorean judgment before a Permanent Court of Arbitration tribunal [see Chapter 5],[243] also prevailing in U.S. litigation.[244] More hopefully, law students from the University of the South Pacific initiated a successful pursuit of a 2025 advisory opinion from the International Court of Justice [see Chapter 5] on climate change described as "the largest legal proceeding in human history."[245]

[241] See *The Implementation and Effectiveness of International Environmental Commitments: Theory and Practice* (D.G. Victor, K. Raustiala & E.B. Skolnikoff eds. 1998).

[242] Romero & Krauss, Chevron Is Ordered to Pay $9 Billion by Ecuador Judge, *N.Y. Times*, Feb. 15, 2011, at A4.

[243] Nagarkatti & McWilliams, International Tribunal Rules in Favor of Chevron in Ecuador Case, *Reuters*, Sept. 7, 2018.

[244] Chevron Corp. v. Donziger, 833 F.3d 74 (2d Cir. 2016).

[245] Jarvis, The Weight of Small Worlds, *New York Times Magazine*, Sep. 21, 2025, at 53.

CHAPTER 8

Individuals and International Law

There is little doubt that international law may sometimes apply to and its processes be available to individuals, that is to say, private persons, in corporate as well as in human form. Indeed, a large part of the substance and procedure of the international economic law and international conflict of laws that we explore in Chapters 9 and 10 is private in character, hence their occasional designation as "private international law." At this stage, we introduce the relationship between individuals and what is more usually termed "public international law," as well as review the emergence of international human rights law, probably the most remarkable development in international law in the twentieth century.

A. INDIVIDUALS AS OBJECTS AND SUBJECTS OF INTERNATIONAL LAW

1. The Positivist Transformation of the Law of Nations

It is sometimes forgotten that the law of nations, as it was traditionally conceived and formulated in the seventeenth and eighteenth centuries, was a law that was distinguished from municipal law because of its more or less universal sources and general applicability to individuals as well as to states. As Blackstone wrote in 1765:

> The law of nations is a system of rules, deducible by natural reason, and established by universal consent among the civilized inhabitants of the world; in order to decide all disputes, to regulate all ceremonies and civilities, and to ensure the observance of justice and good faith, in that intercourse which must frequently occur between two or more independent states, and the individuals belonging to each.[1]

The traditional law of nations drew no bright line dividing what later came to be understood as public and private international law. In its broad scope, and rather like some aspects of modern international economic law, the law of nations encompassed "mercantile questions, such as bills of exchange and the like," "all marine causes," and "disputes relating to prizes, to shipwrecks, to hostages, and ransom bills, as well as rules relating to passports, rights of ambassadors and piracy."[2] Moreover, the rules of the traditional law of nations were directly applicable in the municipal courts of England. As Blackstone wrote, the law of nations was "adopted in [its] full extent by the common law, and is held to be a part of the law of the land,"[3] a notion long familiar to American lawyers [see Chapter 4].

The very term "international law" was invented in 1789 by the English philosopher Jeremy Bentham in his influential *Introduction to the Principles of Morals and Legislation*,[4] where, in a brief prefatory reference, "international law" was set out simply as one of several topics to be addressed in an ambitious (and, in the case of international law, largely unfulfilled) scheme of publication.[5] Bentham's elaboration of his new concept of international law came in the final chapter of his *Principles*, where the author was interested, *inter alia*, in defining the science of jurisprudence.[6] Bentham distinguished books on jurisprudence that "ascertain what the law is" (what he called "expository

[1] W. Blackstone, 4 *Commentaries on the Laws of England* 66 (1st ed. 1765-1769) [hereinafter cited as "Blackstone"].

[2] Id. at 67-73.

[3] Id. at 67.

[4] J. Bentham, *An Introduction to the Principles of Morals and Legislation* (Burns & Hart eds. 1970) [hereinafter cited as "Bentham"].

[5] "Principles of legislation in matters betwixt nation and nation, or, to use a new though not inexpressive appellation, in matters of *international* law." Id. at 6.

[6] Id. at 293-300.

jurisprudence") from those that "ascertain what it ought to be" ("censorial jurisprudence").[7] He differentiated works on expository jurisprudence between those composed by the legislator himself (thus "authoritative") and those by "any other person at large" ("unauthoritative").[8] Bentham grouped laws into five "assemblages" based, respectively, on extent, political quality, time, expression, and punishment, these five being the "circumstances that have given rise to the principal branches of jurisprudence."[9] It was in this flurry of categorization that the term "international law" emerged. The new term had its place in the description of the "political quality" of laws and was set in counterpoise to "internal" law:

> . . . with regard to the *political quality* of the persons whose conduct is the object of the law. These may, on any given occasion, be considered either as members of the same state, or as members of different states: in the first case, the law may be referred to the head of *internal*, in the second case, to that of *international* jurisprudence.[10]

Bentham footnoted *international* as follows:

> The word *international*, it must be acknowledged, is a new one; though, it is hoped, sufficiently analogous and intelligible. It is calculated to express, in a more significant way, the branch of the law which goes commonly under the name of the *law of nations*: an appellation so uncharacteristic, that, were it not for the force of custom, it would seem rather to refer to internal jurisprudence. The chancellor D'Aguesseau has already made, I find, a similar remark: he says, that what is commonly called *droit* des *gens*, ought rather to be termed *droit* entre *les gens*.[11]

[7] Id. at 293-294.
[8] Id. at 294.
[9] Ibid.
[10] Id. at 296.
[11] Ibid. There are at least two places where D'Aguesseau (1668-1751) expressed the preferences attributed to him by Bentham. Interestingly, D'Aguesseau, like Bentham as we see below, limited his discussion to relations between states:

> [O]n pourroit appeler le droit qui doit s'observer entre les nations, ou *jus inter gentes*; par une expression plus propre et plus exacte que le terme général de droit des nations, ou de *jus gentium*, terme qui, comme on l'a déjà vu, et comme on le verra encore dans la suite, peut avoir un autre sens.

14 H.F. D'Aguesseau, *Oeuvres complètes* 602 (Pardessus ed. 1819).

It seems that in creating the term *international law*, Bentham simply meant to replace one term, the *law of nations*, with another term, *international law*, which he thought better characterized the relevant branch of the law. One might differ here with H.L.A. Hart, who wrote that "Bentham, the inventor of the expression 'international law,' defended it simply by saying that it was 'sufficiently analogous' to municipal law."[12] The difference with Hart is twofold. First, there does not seem to be anything defensive in Bentham's invention or use of the term. Second, it is doubtful that Bentham meant the analogy to be to municipal law. Rather, it is clearer to understand him to say that international law was analogous to the law of nations. This is really the substance of Bentham's explanatory footnote.

Though Bentham asserted that he was just renaming the law of nations, he really went much further. Consider the following paragraph of Bentham's text:

> Now as to any transactions which may take place between individuals who are subjects of different states, these are regulated by the internal laws, and decided upon by the internal tribunals, of the one or the other of these states: the case is the same where the sovereign of the one has any immediate transactions with a private member of the other: the sovereign reducing himself, *pro re natâ*, to the condition of a private person, as often as he submits his cause to either tribunal; whether by claiming a benefit, or defending himself against a burthen. There remain then the mutual transactions between sovereigns as such, for the subject of that branch of jurisprudence which may be properly and exclusively termed *international*.[13]

Note that Bentham made two important assumptions about international law. First, he assumed that international law was exclusively about the rights and obligations of states *inter se* and never about the

---

Sur le *Droit des Gens* proprement dit, c'est-à-dire, celui qui a lieu de nation à nation, et qui auroit dû être appelé *jus inter gentes*, plutôt que *jus gentium*.

15 Id. at 268.

It may be that reading D'Aguesseau sparked Bentham's creation of the term *international*. In any case, Bentham's term moved into French as well as into English. The French, of course, now refer to *droit international*, as well as to *droit des gens*.

[12] H.L.A. Hart, *The Concept of Law* 231 (1961).

[13] Bentham, supra, at 296.

rights and obligations of individuals. Second, he assumed that cases involving foreign transactions adjudicated by municipal courts were always decided by internal, not international, rules. Both of these assumptions about international law flew in the face of Bentham's assertion that he was merely substituting the term *international law* for what had previously gone under the appellation the *law of nations*. Blackstone explicitly referred to the law of nations as involving "that intercourse which must frequently occur between two or more independent states, *and the individuals belonging to each*" and stated that the law of nations was "*adopted in* [*its*] *full extent by the common law*" (emphasis added).[14] Bentham's definition of international law denied both of these fundamental propositions. How closely Bentham read or knew Blackstone or the traditional law of nations is open to question.[15] In any event, Blackstone, not Bentham, reflected the reality of eighteenth-century practice.[16] As Dickinson explained:

> [T]he Law of Nations in the eighteenth century embraced a good deal more than the body of practice and agreement which came later to be called public international law. In the *De Jure Belli ac Pacis* of Hugo Grotius and in the treatises of his successors, it had been expounded as a universal law binding upon all mankind. In countries of the common law, at least, arbitrary distinctions between private and public right or duty were still far in the future. The universal law was law for individuals no less than for states. As such, it was concerned somewhat indiscriminately with matters between individuals, between individuals and states, and between states.[17]

Bentham nowhere appears to admit he knew what he had done to the scope of that discipline he said could be called either the "law of nations" or "international law." Neither in the *Principles* nor in his other work did Bentham explicitly acknowledge that the traditional law of

[14] See Blackstone, supra.

[15] John Stuart Mill wrote unflatteringly about the founder of utilitarianism: "Bentham failed in deriving light from other minds. His writings contain few traces of the accurate knowledge of any schools of thinking but his own." J.S. Mill, Bentham, *Utilitarianism* 78, 93-94 (M. Warnock ed. 1962).

[16] For an early English case involving individual rights before a municipal court, see Lord Mansfield's opinion in Triquet v. Bath, 3 *Burr. 1478* (1764).

[17] Dickinson, The Law of Nations as Part of the National Law of the United States, 101 *University of Pennsylvania Law Review* 26, 26-27 (1952).

nations meant something quite different from what he defined as international law. Bentham excluded from the domain of his new subject all of those rules in the traditional law of nations that concerned private rights and obligations. This is not to say that Bentham's conception of international law was illogical, only that we should recognize that it was quite different from traditional ideas about the law of nations. More or less inadvertently, Bentham changed the boundaries of the field he sought to define.[18]

Even in his lifetime, Bentham saw the success of his new term. In a note added in 1823, 34 years after the first publication of *Principles*, Bentham wrote: "As to the word *international*, from this work, or the first of the works edited in French by Mr. Dumont, it has taken root in the language. Witness Reviews and Newspapers."[19] Not only in English, but in other languages (e.g., *droit international, internationales Recht, derecho internacional, mezhdunarodnoe pravo*), Bentham's concept caught hold. The older term, the *law of nations* (*droit des gens, Völkerrecht, derecho de gentes*), where it is still used, is commonly thought to be fungible with *international law.*[20]

Though this was Bentham's own view of the matter, in some ways the equivalence of the two terms is a troublesome legacy. To illustrate in a simple and certainly non-exhaustive way, consider three definitions of international law. Differentiate them by their purposes. First, take a Benthamite definition of international law, characterizing laws in terms of their subjects. This definition serves a useful function in grouping all those rules that concern sovereign states *inter se*. It is closest, of course, to Bentham's original intent in crafting the term *international.*

Second is a definition modeled on the older notion, the law of nations. Here laws, *à la* Blackstone, are characterized in terms of their sources. It serves a useful purpose in grouping together all those rules that are drawn from multistate agreement or practice or other non-municipal sources. It is more inclusive than Bentham's definition and

[18] See Janis, Jeremy Bentham and the Fashioning of "International Law," 78 *American Journal of International Law* 405 (1984).

[19] Bentham, supra, at 297.

[20] There are probably thousands of examples where judges and publicists have used the *law of nations* and *international law* interchangeably. Let one example suffice: "The Law of Nations, or International Law, may be defined as the body of rules and principles of action which are binding upon civilized states in their relations with one another." J.L. Brierly, *The Law of Nations* 1 (4th ed. 1949).

better encompasses much of what was traditionally thought of as within the realm of the law of nations.

Third comes a definition framed in terms of international transactions. Looking to rules that have to do with matters involving more than one nation, Philip Jessup explained that his new term *transnational law* included "all law which regulates actions or events that transcend national frontiers."[21] Such a definition groups rules concerning any subject and coming from any source so long as they touch on multinational transactions.

Note how the field of what we call *international law* varies depending on the definition adopted. A rule of law sometimes fits within the boundaries of the discipline under all three definitions. For example, a rule that has to do with the limits of the territorial sea (1) concerns states, (2) may be drawn from sources of international customary and conventional law, and (3) has to do with transnational matters. Other times, though, a rule might be international law by one definition, but not another. A source-based definition of international law, for example, might admit a rule relating to a government's mistreatment of its own citizens into the ambit of the discipline, but a subject-based or transaction-based definition might deny such coverage.[22] It is too much to say that one or another of these three definitions is true and the others false. Much might be gained if we simply realize that each definition is limited in its reach and utility. While it was useful for Bentham to categorize certain rules as concerning only relations among states, he went too far in insisting on the necessary equivalence between *international law* so defined and the older *law of nations*. There may be a useful role for more than one concept in the field.

Regardless of its failings, Bentham's definition of international law as a law for states alone has had a potent effect. The states-only view of international law was generally adopted by nineteenth-century

[21] P. Jessup, *Transnational Law* 2 (1956). Jessup thought there was a need for a new term because "the term 'international' is misleading since it suggests that one is concerned only with the relations of one nation (or state) to other nations (or states)." Id. at 1. Whether or not Jessup actually invented the term is open to discussion, but, as one commentator notes, it was Jessup who "famously conceptualized" it. Zumbansen, Transnational Law, *Encyclopedia of Comparative Law* 738 (J. Smits ed. 2006).

[22] See the contrasting points of view in Filartiga v. Peña-Irala, 630 F.2d 876, 884-885 (2d Cir. 1980), and Dreyfus v. Von Finck, 534 F.2d 24, 30-31 (2d Cir. 1976), *cert. denied,* 429 U.S. 835 (1976).

legal positivists who went further than Bentham in elaborating the ramifications of the definition. In 1834, U.S. Supreme Court justice and scholar Joseph Story, in a landmark book, felt compelled to craft a new discipline of "conflict of laws" or "private" international law.[23] In Story's opinion, while there was a public international law that went to international matters affecting states, there should also be a private international law that concerned the international transactions of individuals. John Austin, the leading nineteenth-century English legal positivist, hammered the nail in the theoretical coffin when he wrote that because international law claimed to regulate matters between sovereign states and because sovereigns by his definition could not be regulated by any outside authority, international law was only a form of "positive morality" and not really "law" at all.[24]

Positivist legal theory had taken the law of nations of the seventeenth and eighteenth centuries, a law common to individuals as well as to states, and transformed it into two international legal disciplines, one "public," the other "private." The former was deemed to apply to states, the latter to individuals. Positivists could scorn both sides of the subject: Public international law was "international," but not really "law"; private international law was "law," but not really "international." For most of the nineteenth and early twentieth centuries, the positivist definition of public international law as a law for states alone dominated the theory of international law.[25]

The conceptual obstruction posed by the positivist insistence that international law is a law only for sovereign states remained more of a practical hurdle in the continental tradition.[26] In France, for example, an important domestic doctrinal distinction between a civil law for

[23] J. Story, *Commentaries on the Conflict of Laws, Foreign and Domestic* (1st ed. 1834).

[24] J. Austin, *The Province of Jurisprudence Determined* 126-196, 207-208 (1st ed. 1832). There is some evidence that, later in life, Austin was "ceasing to be Austinian" and was contemplating revising *The Province of Jurisprudence* "to recognize that the three sciences [of positive morality, ethics, and positive law] were 'inseparably connected parts of a vast organized whole.'" L. Hamburger & J. Hamburger, *Troubled Lives: John and Sarah Austin* 189, 180 (1985).

[25] See, e.g., J.L. Brierly, *The Law of Nations* 1 (4th ed. 1949); C.C. Hyde, 1 *International Law Chiefly as Interpreted and Applied by the United States* 1 (2d ed. 1947); T.E. Holland, *Lectures on International Law* 53 (1933); L. Oppenheim, 1 *International Law* 3 (1st ed. 1905); *Kent's Commentary on International Law* 7 (J.T. Abdy ed. 1866).

[26] For the persistence of positivism in French international law theory, see Rogoff, Review Essay: French Studies in International Law, 105 *American Journal of International Law* 819 (2011).

citizens and a public law for the state was thoroughly transposed into the international arena. French jurists long insisted on a fundamental divide between private international law (what Americans, following Joseph Story, call *conflict of laws*), which was part of the domain of the civil law and which regulated international relations of individuals and private companies, and public international law, part of public law, concerning the international relations of sovereign states.[27] However, the French academic tradition increasingly accepts that the public and private sides of international law are often merged in practice.[28] Indeed, since the public/private international law distinction failed to satisfactorily categorize what Americans call international business law, some in France took more of a common law approach to the law of international commercial transactions.[29]

A further practical difficulty posed by the positivist state/individual, public/private distinctions can be seen in the doctrine of the international law of national development, an influential notion in the 1970s that owed much to French theoretical contributions. The doctrine was conceived to be a part of public international law and promoted an international "right" to development on behalf of states in the Third World.[30] However, this doctrine, alongside its political associate, the new international economic order [see Chapter 3], largely failed to address the economic and political rights of individuals in Third World states where governments all too frequently contribute to internal maldistributions of economic resources and political power. Therefore, it made little moral or practical sense to many in the West to impose a legal obligation on their own governments to contribute to the economic advancement of the elites either of the Third World or of what were then the Communist states of the Second World.

[27] See H. Battifol & P. Lagarde, *Droit international public* (7th ed., Vol. I, 1989; Vol. II, 1983); C. Rousseau, *Droit international public* (Vol. I, 1970; Vol. II, 1974; Vol. III, 1977; Vol. IV, 1980; Vol. V, 1983).

[28] Arroyo & Mbengue, Public and Private International Law in International Courts and Tribunals: Evidence of an Inescapable Interaction, 56 *Columbia Journal of Transnational Law* 797 (2018).

[29] See B. Oppetit, *Droit du commerce international* (1977). For a French analysis that eschews the public/private international law distinction in favor of more of a common law approach, see D. Carreau, P. Juillard & T. Flory, *Droit international économique* 7-8 (1978).

[30] See M. Flory, *Droit international du développement* 25-26 (1977).

2. *State Protection of and Responsibility for Individuals*

Despite the positivists' philosophical rejection of individuals as subjects of public international law, legal practice, especially in the common law legal systems, never entirely abandoned the more inclusive doctrine of the traditional law of nations. Even in the high tide of positivism in the late nineteenth and early twentieth centuries, municipal courts sometimes permitted individuals to sue and be sued for violations of public as well as private international law. For example, as we have already seen, in 1900 in *The Paquete Habana*,[31] the U.S. Supreme Court allowed foreign individuals to sue and recover from the U.S. government for its violations of the customary international law of the sea. [See Chapter 3.] To reconcile such practice with their legal theory, positivist theorists opined that international law could be "transformed" into municipal legal rules and thus become applicable to individuals.[32]

Nonetheless, in other respects the positivists' states-only doctrine of international law took hold and denied individuals the status of subjects of international law. Most prominently, the Statute of the International Court, following that of its predecessor the Permanent Court of International Justice, was drafted to provide that "[o]nly states may be parties in cases before the Court."[33] [See Chapter 5.] Similarly, many municipal courts refused to permit individuals to litigate international law issues unless the constitutional law of the state had by one or another means incorporated the relevant international legal rules into municipal law. [See Chapter 4.]

As something akin to giving individuals access to international legal rules and process, positivist international legal theory elaborated doctrine and procedure to provide for states protecting individuals on the international plane.[34] As the Permanent Court of International Justice held in *Mavrommatis Palestine Concessions*:

[31] 175 U.S. 677 (1900). See Dodge, *The Paquete Habana*: Customary International Law as Part of our Law, *International Law Stories* 287 (J.E. Noyes, L.A. Dickinson, M.W. Janis & C.M. Vázquez eds., 2d ed. 2025).

[32] H. Triepel, *Völkerrecht und Landesrecht* (1889).

[33] Art. 34(1), 59 Stat. 1031, T.S. No. 993, 3 Bevans 1153 (signed at San Francisco June 26, 1945; entered into force October 24, 1945).

[34] C.F. Amerasinghe, *Diplomatic Protection* (2008).

> It is an elementary principle of international law that a State is entitled to protect its subjects, when injured by acts contrary to international law committed by another State, from whom they have been unable to obtain satisfaction through the ordinary channels. By taking up the case of one of its subjects and by resorting to diplomatic action or international judicial proceedings on his behalf, a State is in reality asserting its own rights—its right to ensure, in the person of its subjects, respect for the rules of international law.
>
> The question, therefore, whether the present dispute originates in an injury to a private interest, which in point of fact is the case in many international disputes, is irrelevant from this standpoint. Once a State has taken up a case on behalf of one of its subjects before an international tribunal, in the eyes of the latter the State is sole claimant.[35]

The right to state protection is limited, however. For example, the International Court has sometimes insisted that a private party be protected only by a state with which it has a "genuine link." So in *Nottebohm*, the Court concluded that there was an "absence of any bond of attachment" between Nottebohm and Liechtenstein, the protecting state, and refused to permit that state to sue on the individual's behalf.[36] In *Barcelona Traction*, the ICJ held that a company incorporated in Canada could not be protected in a Court action by Belgium, the home of its principal stockholders, because "the general rule of international law authorizes the national State of the company alone to make a claim."[37] *Barcelona Traction*'s concept of "corporate separateness" from corporate

[35] Mavrommatis Palestine Concessions, 1924 P.C.I.J. Reports, ser. A, no. 2, at 12.

[36] 1955 I.C.J. Reports 4, 26. For an argument that *Nottebohm*'s "genuine link" is out of date, see Sloane, Breaking the Genuine Link: The Contemporary International Legal Regulation of Nationality, 50 *Harvard International Law Journal* 1 (2009). For a new "relaxed attitude to layered loyalty," i.e., nationality, even multiple nationalities, chosen by, and not imposed on, individuals, see Franck, Clan and Superclan: Loyalty, Identity and Community in Law and Practice, 90 *American Journal of International Law* 359, 382 (1996); P.J. Spiro, *At Home in Two Countries: The Past and Future of Dual Citizenship* (2016).

[37] 1970 I.C.J. Reports 4, 46. The question of what nationality to assign a multinational corporation for the purposes of state protection may well not be an easy one to answer. See P.I. Blumberg, *The Law of Corporate Groups: Procedural Law* 407-416 (1983); Staker, Diplomatic Protection of Private Business Companies: Determining Corporate Personality for International Law Purposes, 61 *British Yearbook of International Law* 155 (1991).

shareholders may well have outlived its utility.[38] The very doctrine of nationality in international law is often muddled and vague.[39]

Alongside the doctrine of state protection of its own nationals is to be found the principle of state responsibility for injury to foreign nationals. In traditional positivist international law theory, the responsibility of a state is owed the foreign state rather than the foreign national. Professor Brownlie put the proposition thus: "If nationals are subjected to injury or loss by an agency for which another state is responsible in law, then, whether the harm occurs in the territory of a state, or *res communis*, i.e., the high seas or outer space, or in *terra nullius*, the state of the persons harmed may present a claim on the international plane."[40]

In traditional practice, the law of state responsibility has mostly concerned the responsibility of states for the expropriation of or damage to property of aliens. The Restatement (Third), for example, provides as follows:

> A state is responsible under international law for injury resulting from:
>
> (1) a taking by the state of the property of a national of another state that
>
> (a) is not for a public purpose, or
> (b) is discriminatory, or
> (c) is not accompanied by provision for just compensation;
>
> For compensation to be just under this Subsection, it must, in the absence of exceptional circumstances, be in an amount equivalent to the value of the property taken and be paid at the time of taking, or within a reasonable time thereafter with interest from the date of taking, and in a form economically usable by the foreign national.[41]

States may, of course, assume explicit conventional responsibility for the protection of foreign nationals. A typical example is found in

[38] Côté, Piercing the Corporate Veil in International Law: Problems with the Denial of Benefits Clause, *Corporate Citizen: New Perspectives on the Globalized Rule of Law* 247 (O.E. Fitzgerald ed. 2020).

[39] See Special Issue: Nationality and International Law, 65 *Netherlands International Law Review* 267 (2018).

[40] I. Brownlie, *Principles of Public International Law* 519 (4th ed. 1990).

[41] American Law Institute, 1 *Restatement (Third) of the Foreign Relations Law of the United States* 196-197 (1987).

the Friendship, Commerce and Navigation Treaty between the United States and Liberia:

> The nationals of each High Contracting Party shall receive within the territories of the other, upon submitting to conditions imposed upon its nationals, the most constant protection and security for their persons and property, and shall enjoy in this respect that degree of protection that is required by international law. Their property shall not be taken without due process of law and without payment of just compensation.[42]

In the nineteenth century, there also emerged a body of state practice establishing customary rules of state responsibility providing for compensation for nationalizations and expropriations of alien-owned property.[43] The status of such customary norms of international law providing international minimum standards that all states must meet regardless of treaty obligations has at times been highly controversial, the positions of the Western states being much at odds with those of Third World nations.[44] The controversy was crystallized in the debate surrounding the legal force of the 1973 and 1974 resolutions of the U.N. General Assembly concerning the New International Economic Order [see Chapter 3]. On the one hand, the Charter of Economic Rights and Duties of States, for example, provides:

> Each State has the right . . . [t]o nationalize, expropriate or transfer ownership of foreign property, in which case appropriate compensation should be paid by the State adopting such measures, taking into account its relevant laws and regulations and all circumstances that the State considers pertinent. In any case where the question of compensation gives rise to a controversy, it shall be settled under the domestic law of the nationalizing State and by its tribunals, unless it is freely and mutually agreed by all States concerned that other peaceful means be sought on the basis of the sovereign equality of States and in accordance with the principle of free choice of means.[45]

[42] Art. I, 54 Stat. 1739, T.S. No. 956, 9 Bevans 595, 201 L.N.T.S. 163 (signed at Monrovia August 8, 1938; entered into force November 21, 1939).

[43] I. Brownlie, *System of the Law of Nations: State Responsibility (Part I)* 2-6 (1983). Lillich, The Current Status of the Law of State Responsibility for Injuries to Aliens, *International Law of State Responsibility for Injuries to Aliens* 1 (R. Lillich ed. 1983).

[44] See H.J. Steiner, D.F. Vagts & H.H. Koh, *Transnational Legal Problems* 446-513 (4th ed. 1994); C.F. Amersinghe, *State Responsibility for Injuries to Nationals* (1967).

[45] U.N.G.A. Res. 3281 (XXIX), art. 2(2)(c), December 12, 1974.

On the other hand, in his 1977 arbitral award in the *Texaco* case, Professor Dupuy held that this provision of the Charter was "a political rather than . . . a legal declaration" and instead chose to rely upon the 1962 United Nations resolution on Permanent Sovereignty over National Resources, which subjected state nationalizations and expropriations of foreign property to the rules of international, as well as national, law.[46] "Recent international tribunals have consistently affirmed a requirement under international law that full compensation be paid for expropriations of foreign property."[47] In 2001, the International Law Commission [see Chapter 2] adopted Draft Articles on the Responsibility for Internationally Wrongful Acts, a document itself now surrounded by controversy.[48]

Procedurally, problems of expropriation of alien property have sometimes been addressed by *ad hoc* claims tribunals, some of which are merely national commissions, proceeding under local law and distributing shares of lump sum settlements negotiated from foreign governments. For example, between 1819 and 1961, the United States established such national claims commissions to hear claims against Spain, Great Britain, Denmark, France, the Two Sicilies, Peru, Mexico, Brazil, China, Turkey, Yugoslavia, Panama, Bulgaria, Hungary, Romania, Italy, the U.S.S.R., and Czechoslovakia, among others.[49] Other claims tribunals have been, as we have already explored [see Chapter 5], international bodies established by treaty, with judges of mixed nationality applying international law. There has been an explosion of bilateral investment treaties that provide for direct claims by investors against

[46] U.N.G.A. Res. 1803 (XVII), art. 4, December 14, 1962; Texaco Overseas Petroleum Company/California Asiatic Oil Company v. Libyan Arab Republic, Award of January 19, 1977, 17 *International Legal Materials* 1, 27-31 (1978).

[47] Norton, A Law of the Future or a Law of the Past? Modern Tribunals and the International Law of Expropriation, 85 *American Journal of International Law* 474, 503 (1991).

[48] *Report of the International Law Commission on the Work of Its Fifty-Third Session,* UNGAOR, 56th Sess., Supp. No. 10, at 43, U.N. Doc. A/56/10 (2001); see Symposium: The ILC's State Responsibility Articles, 96 *American Journal of International Law* 773-890 (2002).

[49] R.B. Lillich, *International Claims: Their Adjudication by National Commissions* 5-15 (1962). See the, at first, semi-annual, but from 1967 annual, *Report of the Foreign Claims Settlement Commission of the United States.*

governments from 385 in 1989, to at least 2,600 in 2010.[50] Proceedings often take the form of international commercial arbitration, a topic more fully explored below. [See Chapter 9.]

One of the most important of the recent claims tribunals has been the United States-Iran Claims Tribunal. Set up in 1981 at The Hague, it consists of nine members, three chosen by the United States, three by Iran, and three by agreement among the nationally chosen arbitrators. Hearing claims of nationals of both countries and applying "such choice of law rules and principles of commercial and international law as the Tribunal determines to be applicable, taking into account relevant usages of the trade, contract provisions and changed circumstances," the Tribunal has generated a considerable body of case law.[51]

Comparable to such state-sponsored claims tribunals is the Claims Resolution Tribunal for Dormant Accounts in Switzerland. The Tribunal was established in 1997 to hear private claims against Swiss banks and was based on an independent audit begun in 1996 by the Volcker Commission that discovered more than 50,000 Swiss bank accounts worth more than $1 billion that had belonged to victims of the Nazi regime, accounts that had been hidden by Swiss banks for more than 50 years.[52] The Tribunal, of course, has not only a public aspect, but a private one. [See Chapter 9.]

[50] Bjorklund, Reconciling State Sovereignty and Investor Protection in Denial of Justice Claims, 45 *Virginia Journal of International Law* 809, 812 (2005); Updated U.S. Model BIT, 99 *American Journal of International Law* 259 (2005); K.J. Vandevelde, *Bilateral Investment Treaties: History, Policy, and Interpretation* 29 (2010).

[51] Lillich, Preface, *The Iran-United States Claims Tribunal 1981-1983 vii* (Lillich ed. 1984); W. Mapp, *The Iran-United States Claims Tribunal: The First Ten Years 1981-1991* (1993); Declaration of the Government of Algeria Concerning the Settlement of Claims by the Government of the United States of America and the Government of the Islamic Republic of Iran, arts. II, III, V, 20 *International Legal Materials* 230 (1981). There are some 771 cases listed in the consolidated table of cases from 1981 to 1990 in Volume 25 of the Tribunal's reports. See 25 *Iran-U.S. Claims Tribunal Reports xi-xxvii* (1992). See Stein, Jurisprudence and Jurists' Prudence: The Iranian-Forum Clause Decisions of the Iran-U.S. Claims Tribunal, 78 *American Journal of International Law* 1 (1984).

[52] Alford, The Claims Resolution Tribunal and Holocaust Claims Against Swiss Banks, 20 *Berkeley Journal of International Law* 250, 254-259 (2002).

B. INTERNATIONAL HUMAN RIGHTS LAW

The fashioning of an international law of human rights and the establishment of new international human rights organizations and tribunals have dated positivist notions about the relationship between individuals and international law. International human rights law posits the direct application of international law to individuals and in some instances gives individuals direct access to international legal machinery. These developments demonstrate that individuals, regardless of strict positivist doctrine, are now to be properly considered subjects not only of private, but also of public international law.[53]

1. *Human Rights and Natural Law*

The principle that law should protect the rights of individuals against the abuses of government is rooted in natural law. [See Chapter 3.] Human rights law can be dated at least back to John Locke's *Two Treatises of Government*, published in 1690. Locke believed that human rights, not governments, came first in the natural order of things:

> If Man in the State of Nature be so free, as has been said; If he be absolute Lord of his own Person and Possessions, equal to the greatest, and subject to no Body, why will he part with his Freedom? Why will he give up this Empire, and subject himself to the Dominion and Controul of any other Power? To which 'tis obvious to Answer, that though in the state of Nature he hath such a right, yet the Enjoyment of it is very uncertain, and constantly exposed to the Invasion of others. For all being Kings as much as he, every Man his Equal, and the greater part no strict Observers of Equity and Justice, the enjoyment of the property he has in this state is very unsafe, very unsecure. This makes him willing to quit a Condition, which however free, is full of fears and continual dangers: And 'tis not without reason, that he seeks out, and is willing to join

[53] L. Diaz-González, *Second Report on Relations Between States and International Organizations (Second Part of the Topic)*, U.N. Doc. A/CN.4/391 (1985).

> in Society with others who are already united, or have a mind to unite for the mutual *Preservation* of their Lives, Liberties and Estates.[54]

Locke's prose celebrated the rights of the English under the limited government won by the Glorious Revolution of 1688. The particular advantages of England's unwritten constitution, especially the separation and balance of powers among the executive, legislative, and judicial branches of government, were elaborated and popularized by the French political philosopher Montesquieu in *The Spirit of the Laws* in 1748.[55] In 1762, the revolutionary potential of human rights—"Man is born free; and everywhere he is in chains"—was proclaimed by Jean-Jacques Rousseau.[56] Democratic revolutions were soon to follow in America and throughout Europe.

On July 4, 1776, the American Declaration of Independence issued from Philadelphia. The intellectual influences of Locke, Montesquieu, and Rousseau on Thomas Jefferson's document were plain to see. In a ringing affirmation of human rights and the duty of governments to protect them, the delegates to the Continental Congress proclaimed:

> We hold these truths to be self-evident, that all men are created equal, that they are endowed by their Creator with certain unalienable Rights, that among these are Life, Liberty and the pursuit of Happiness. That to secure these rights, Governments are instituted among Men, deriving their just powers from the consent of the governed. That whenever any Form of Government becomes destructive of these ends, it is the Right of the People to alter or to abolish it, and to institute new Government, laying its foundation on such principles and organizing its powers in such form, as to them shall seem most likely to effect their Safety and Happiness.

In Europe and the United States, the last decades of the eighteenth century were a good time for affirmations of human rights. As the constitutions of the newly independent American states were drafted in

[54] J. Locke, *Two Treatises of Government* 395 (3d ed. 1698; P. Laslett rev. ed. 1963). Even earlier was England's *Magna Carta* of 1215, where barons compelled King John to accept fundamental rights, including the right to a trial of one's peers. www.nationalarchives.gov.uk (Dec. 12, 2025).

[55] Montesquieu, L'esprit des lois, *Oeuvres complètes* 527 (Editions du Seuil 1964).

[56] J.J. Rousseau, *The Social Contract* 3 (G.D.H. Cole ed. 1950).

1776, bills of rights enumerating specific rights were directly incorporated therein, even, as for Virginia, making up its first part.[57] The fashion of bills of rights spread to Europe. Jefferson wrote James Madison from Paris on January 12, 1789: "Everybody here is trying their hands at forming declarations of rights."[58] Jefferson continued to play his part, reading and critiquing Lafayette's draft of what, on August 27, 1789, a few weeks after the fall of the Bastille, would become the French National Assembly's Declaration of the Rights of Man and Citizen.[59] Its indebtedness to Rousseau's philosophy and Philadelphia's practice was widely acknowledged.[60] The French Declaration recognized and proclaimed "in the presence and under the auspices of the Supreme Being" a number of human rights, including the right to be free of arbitrary detention, the right to be presumed innocent until declared guilty, the right to freedom of religion, and the right to speak, write, and print freely.

On September 25, 1789, less than a month after the promulgation of the French Declaration, the first Congress of the new federal government of the United States of America proposed the first ten amendments to the United States Constitution.[61] These came into force following the tenth state ratification (Virginia's) on December 15, 1791, and make up the U.S. Bill of Rights.

Close in kinship, the American Declaration of Independence, the French Declaration of the Rights of Man and Citizen, and the U.S. Bill of Rights make up the eighteenth-century documentary foundation on which two centuries of legal protections of human rights have come to be built. Constitutional guarantees of human rights are now widespread. There has been reliance on the U.S. and French precedents even in countries outside the European tradition.[62] Moreover, there

[57] S.E. Morison, H.S. Commanger & W.E. Leuchtenburg, 1 *The Growth of the American Republic* 21 (6th ed. 1969).

[58] T. Jefferson, Letter of January 12, 1789, to James Madison, 14 *The Papers of Thomas Jefferson* 436, 437 (J.P. Boyd ed. 1958).

[59] T. Jefferson, Letter of June 3, 1789, to Rabaut de St. Etienne, 15 *The Papers of Thomas Jefferson* 166 (J.P. Boyd ed. 1958). One of Jefferson's biographers has commented that his influence on Lafayette's declaration of rights "was probably greater than appears in any formal record." D. Malone, *Jefferson and the Rights of Man* 223 (1951).

[60] L. Madelin, *La révolution* 84-86 (1911).

[61] B. Schwartz, *The Bill of Rights: A Documentary History* (1971).

[62] See, for example, the discussion of the constitutions of India and Japan in Hazard, The General Principles of Law, 52 *American Journal of International Law* 91, 92 (1958).

are strong human rights traditions in cultures outside of the European tradition, for example, in Islamic law[63] and, indeed, across the globe.[64] One study showed that 82 percent of the national constitutions drafted between 1788 and 1948 and 93 percent of the constitutions drafted between 1949 and 1975 provided some sort of human rights and fundamental freedoms.[65] Most national constitutions explicitly protect human rights.[66] Though the record of observing these guarantees has varied from country to country and from time to time, domestic constitutional protections of human rights have become in a little more than 200 years a legal commonplace.

2. *The Nuremberg Trial and Universal Human Rights Law*

Until relatively recently, there were no guarantees of human rights at the level of international law comparable to those sometimes available in municipal law. As we saw above, the prevalent philosophy of international law in the nineteenth and early twentieth centuries, legal positivism, maintained that international law was a law for states alone. Hence, it was thought to be antithetical for there to be international legal rights that individuals could assert against states, especially against their own governments. The traditional positivist doctrine was restated as late as 1955 in Lauterpacht's revision of Oppenheim's classic international law treatise:

> Since the Law of Nations is primarily a law between States, States are, to that extent, the only subjects of the Law of Nations. . . . But what is the normal position of individuals in International Law, if they are not

[63] M.A. Baderin, *International Human Rights in Islamic Law* (2003).

[64] C.G. Weeramantry, *Universalizing International Law* (2004).

[65] H. van Maarseveen & G. van der Tang, *Written Constitutions: A Computerized Comparative Study* 191-195 (1978). Some specific rights were more often guaranteed than others. For example, in constitutions drafted between 1949 and 1975, the right to a fair trial was protected in 91 percent, the right to freedom of expression in 87 percent, the right to liberty of person in 65 percent, the right against torture or against cruel, inhuman, or degrading treatment or punishment in 53 percent, and the right to equal access to public service in 30 percent. Id. at 195-198.

[66] *Constitutions of the Countries of the World* (A.P. Blaustein & G.H. Flanz eds. 1977).

> regularly subjects thereof? The answer can only be that, generally speaking, they are *objects* of the Law of Nations.[67]

The turning point in the modern history of the relationship between individuals and international law came in the August 8, 1945, decision of the Allies in World War II—the United States, the Soviet Union, Great Britain, and France—to try individual Nazis before the International Military Tribunal at Nuremberg for violations of international law. The decision had been mooted by the power of the victors in World War I to try the German Kaiser, Wilhelm II, for war crimes, but it was decided not to do so. Rather, the Kaiser found sanctuary in the Netherlands.[68] It was a different story after World War II. As the brutal practices of the Axis powers enraged public opinion, jurists developed a legal philosophy that held individuals accountable for war crimes.[69] The 1945 Allied agreement on the trial of individual war criminals put this into positive law. It read in part:

> The following acts, or any of them, are crimes coming within the jurisdiction of the Tribunal for which there shall be individual responsibility:
>
> (a) Crimes Against Peace: namely, planning, preparation, initiation or waging of a war of aggression, or a war in violation of international treaties, agreements or assurances, or participation in a common plan or conspiracy for the accomplishment of any of the foregoing;
>
> (b) War Crimes: namely, violations of the laws or customs of war. Such violations shall include, but not be limited to, murder, ill-treatment or deportation to slave labor or for any other purpose of civilian population of or in occupied territory, murder or ill-treatment of prisoners of war or persons on the seas, killing of hostages, plunder of public or private property, wanton destruction of cities, towns or villages, or devastation not justified by military necessity;
>
> (c) Crimes Against Humanity: namely, murder, extermination, enslavement, deportation, and other inhumane acts committed against any civilian population, before or during the war, or persecutions on political, racial or religious grounds in execution of or in connection

[67] L. Oppenheim, 1 *International Law* 636, 639 (8th ed. H. Lauterpacht 1955).

[68] See W.A. Schabas, *The Trial of the Kaiser* (2018).

[69] M. Lachs, *War Crimes* (1945).

> with any crime within the jurisdiction of the Tribunal, whether or not in violation of the domestic law of the country where perpetrated.[70]

In 1946, the International Military Tribunal at Nuremberg met to try, not the German state, but individual German officials. The Nuremberg Trial of the Nazis revealed a terrible record of human rights violations. Plainly, sovereign states, even arguably "civilized" states, could not always be trusted to delegate the levers of political and legal control to responsible parties. The Court reported:

> [M]ass murders and cruelties were not committed solely for the purpose of stamping out opposition or resistance to the German occupying forces. In Poland and the Soviet Union these crimes were part of a plan to get rid of whole native populations by expulsion and annihilation, in order that their territory could be used for colonization by Germans. Hitler had written in *Mein Kampf* on these lines, and the plan was clearly stated by Himmler in July 1942, when he wrote:
>
>> It is not our task to Germanize the East in the old sense, that is to teach the people there the German language and the German law, but to see to it that only people of purely Germanic blood live in the East.
>
> In August 1942 the policy for the Eastern Territories as laid down by Bormann was summarized by a subordinate of Rosenberg as follows:
>
>> The Slavs are to work for us. In so far as we do not need them, they may die
>
> Part of the "final solution" was the gathering of Jews from all German occupied Europe in concentration camps. Their physical condition was the test of life or death. All who were fit to work were used as slave laborers in the concentration camps; all who were not fit to work were destroyed in gas chambers and their bodies burnt. Certain concentration camps such as Treblinka and Auschwitz were set aside for this main purpose. With regard to Auschwitz, the Tribunal heard the evidence of Hoess, the Commandant of the camp from May 1st 1940 to December 1st 1943. He estimated that in the camp of Auschwitz alone in that time, 2,500,000 persons were exterminated, and that a further 500,000 died from disease and starvation.[71]

[70] Agreement for the Prosecution and Punishment of the Major War Criminals of the European Axis, art. 6, 59 Stat. 1544, 1547-1548 (1945).

[71] The Judgment of the International Military Tribunal at Nuremberg, 6 F.R.D. 69, 119, 129 (1946).

At Nuremberg and in other war trials, thousands of individuals were tried and convicted; hundreds were executed.[72] The Nuremberg Trial was meant to establish plainly and forcefully that the rules of public international law should and do apply to individuals. The Nuremberg Tribunal held that "[c]rimes against international law are committed by men, not by abstract entities, and only by punishing individuals who commit such crimes can the provisions of international law be enforced."[73] Nuremberg was also intended to demonstrate that the protection of human rights was too important a matter to be left entirely to states,[74] a proposition already enunciated in the Preamble and Article 55 of the Charter of the United Nations:

> We the Peoples of the United Nations [are] determined . . . to reaffirm faith in fundamental human rights. . . .
>
> [T]he United Nations shall promote: . . . universal respect for, and observance of, human rights and fundamental freedoms for all without distinction as to race, sex, language, or religion.[75]

Persuaded that the lessons of Nuremberg should not be forgotten and that human rights should be guaranteed by explicit provisions of international law, the General Assembly of the United Nations in 1948 voted the precepts of the Universal Declaration of Human Rights.[76] The Declaration set forth many rights, for example, the rights to "life, liberty and the security of person," to "equal protection of the law," to fair trials, to "own property," and to "freedom of thought, conscience and religion."[77] Like other General Assembly resolutions, however, the

[72] E. Davidson, *The Trial of the Germans* 1-38 (1972); for the Tokyo Trial of Japanese individuals after World War II, see N. Boister & R. Cryer, *The Tokyo International Military Tribunal: A Reappraisal* (2008).

[73] 6 F.R.D. 69, 110 (1946).

[74] Meron & Galbraith, Nuremberg and Its Legacy, *International Law Stories* 13 (J.E. Noyes, L.A. Dickinson, M.W. Janis & C.M. Vázquez eds., 2d ed. 2025).

[75] Charter of the United Nations, 59 Stat. 1031, T.S. No. 993, 3 Bevans 1153 (signed at San Francisco June 26, 1945; entered into force October 24, 1945).

[76] See Sadat, Shattering the Nuremberg Consensus: U.S. Rendition Policy and International Criminal Law, *Yale Journal of International Affairs*, Winter 2008, at 65, 66-67; U.N.G.A. Res. 217A (III), U.N. Doc. A/810, at 71 (December 10, 1948) [hereinafter cited as "U.N. Declaration"].

[77] U.N. Declaration, supra, arts. 3, 7, 10, 17, 18.

Universal Declaration does not in and of itself constitute a binding international obligation [see Chapter 3], though it may be cited as an evidence of a customary international law of human rights,[78] and some feel that by now it is itself part of customary international law.[79] In any case, as President Reagan noted in 1983, "the Universal Declaration remains an international standard against which the human rights practices of all governments can be measured."[80]

Besides the Universal Declaration, the United Nations has drafted more than 30 human rights conventions and issued as many human rights declarations and resolutions.[81] These and other treaties and evidences of customary international human rights law[82] now mount up in an impressive array. The central problem has become not so much finding a universal law of human rights (most agree that one now exists), but enforcing that law.[83] Of course, states may, if they

[78] See, e.g., Filartiga v. Peña-Irala, 630 F.2d 876, 882 (2d Cir. 1980).

[79] R.B. Lillich, H. Hannum, S.J. Anaya & D.L. Shelton, *International Human Rights: Problems of Law, Policy, and Practice* 135-164 (4th ed. 2006) [hereinafter cited as "Lillich"].

[80] Proclamation of Bill of Rights Day, Human Rights Day and Week, December 9, 1983, in U.S. Department of State, Selected Documents No. 22 (December 1983).

[81] These include the 1948 Convention on the Prevention and Punishment of the Crime of Genocide, the 1951 Convention Relating to the Status of Refugees, the 1953 Convention on the Political Rights of Women, the 1954 Convention Relating to the Status of Stateless Persons, the 1966 International Covenant on Economic, Social, and Cultural Rights, the 1966 International Covenant on Civil and Political Rights, the 1975 Declaration on Protection from Torture, the 1981 Declaration on the Elimination of All Forms of Intolerance and of Discrimination Based on Religion or Belief, the 1984 Convention against Torture and Other Cruel, Inhuman or Degrading Treatment or Punishment, the 1989 Convention on the Rights of the Child, and the 1990 International Convention on the Protection of the Rights of All Migrant Workers and Their Families. *Basic Documents on Human Rights* 31-242 (I. Brownlie 3d ed. 1992). There is a voluminous literature respecting the UN human rights conventions. See, for example, S. Joseph, J. Schultz & M. Castern, *The International Covenant on Civil and Political Rights* (2000); *The United Nations and Human Rights: A Critical Appraisal* (F. Mégret & P. Alston 2d ed. 2020); and T. Meron, *Human Rights Law-Making in the United Nations* (1986).

[82] See L.B. Sohn & T. Buergenthal, *International Protection of Human Rights* (1973).

[83] Buergenthal, The Normative and International Evolution of International Human Rights, 19 *Human Rights Quarterly* 703 (1997).

choose, apply international human rights law in their own municipal courts. [See Chapter 4.] The larger and more troubling question is what can be done in terms of international legal process. There are many examples of international human rights machinery—for example, the largely political processes available and often criticized in the United Nations.[84] Here three of the more prominent formal international legal processes are explored: European human rights law and the European Court of Human Rights, Inter-American human rights law and the Inter-American Court of Human Rights, and international criminal tribunals, especially the International Criminal Court.

3. European Human Rights Law

The atrocities perpetrated by the Nazis and their collaborators during the German occupation of Europe in the Second World War made an important impact on European self-perceptions. For centuries, Europeans had prided themselves on being more "civilized" than other peoples. The calamities of World War II shattered such self-confidence. Though the United Nations had adopted the Universal Declaration of Human Rights, many believed that Europe was morally obliged to go a step further, and groups promoting European union made the protection of individual human rights a high post-war priority. In 1948, the Hague Congress of the International Committee of the Movements for European Unity resolved that a European Charter of Human Rights be enacted,[85] and in 1949, the leaders of post-war Europe met to create a new

[84] See Sohn, Human Rights: Their Implementation and Supervision by the United Nations, 2 *Human Rights in International Law: Legal and Policy Issues* 369, 373 (T. Meron ed. 1984); *The Future of UN Human Rights Treaty Monitoring* (P. Alston & J. Crawford eds. 2000); U.S. Human Rights Record Assessed in UN Rights Council's Universal Periodic Review Process, 105 *American Journal of International Law* 139 (2011); Freedman & Mchangama, Expanding or Diluting Human Rights?: The Proliferation of United Nations Special Procedures Mandates, 38 *Human Rights Quarterly* 164 (2018); Cumming-Bruce & Ramzy, U.N. Report on Human Rights Abuses in Xinijian May Be Delayed Yet Again, *N.Y.* Times, Aug. 26, 2022, at A4; Shany, *Mellet v. Ireland:* Constitutional Limits on Abortion Before the Human Rights Committee, *International Law Stories* 135 (J.N. Noyes, L.A. Dickinson, M.W. Janis & Carlos M. Vázquez eds., 2d ed. 2025).

[85] R. Beddard, *Human Rights and Europe* 17-18 (1980).

regional international organization, the Council of Europe. Although the Council had other aims—rebuilding a devastated continent, uniting against Soviet aggression that had already consumed most of Eastern Europe, laying the groundwork for European political union[86]—the principal achievement of the founders of the Council of Europe was and remains the establishment of the foremost international legal system for the protection of human rights.[87]

At the first session of the Council of Europe's Consultative Assembly in 1949, Britain's Winston Churchill argued that universal legal prohibitions against violations of human rights, such as those set forth in the United Nations' Universal Declaration, ought to be enforced by regional international organizations and that a "European Court" be established before which violations of human rights "might be brought to the judgment of the civilised world."[88] The specter of the concentration camps was on the mind of another delegate, the former French Minister of Justice, Pierre-Henri Teitgen, who also called for a European court of human rights:

> Democracies do not become Nazi countries in one day. Evil progresses cunningly, with a minority operating, as it were, to remove the levers of control. One by one, freedoms are suppressed, in one sphere after another. Public opinion and the entire national conscience are asphyxiated. And then, when everything is in order, the "Führer" is installed and the evolution continues even to the oven of the crematorium.
>
> It is necessary to intervene before it is too late. A conscience must exist somewhere which will sound the alarm to the mind of a nation menaced by their progressive corruption, to warn them of the peril and to show them that they are progressing down a long road which leads far, sometimes even to Buchenwald or Dachau.
>
> An international court, within the Council of Europe, and a system of supervision and guarantees, could be the conscience of which we all

[86] These other tasks were eventually more successfully addressed by other means: The Marshall Plan rebuilt Europe's economies, see J.M. Jones, *The Fifteen Weeks: An Inside Account of the Genesis of the Marshall Plan* (2000); the North Atlantic Treaty Organization took on responsibility for Western Europe's defense, see A.J. May, *Europe Since 1939* 480-482 (1966 ed.); and the European Common Market, eventually the European Union, became the vehicle for European integration. [See Chapter 9.]

[87] M.W. Janis, R.S. Kay & A.W. Bradley, *European Human Rights Law* (3d ed. 2008) [hereinafter cited as "Janis, Kay & Bradley"].

[88] Council of Europe, 1 *Collected Edition of the Travaux Prèparatoires* 34 (1975).

> have need, and of which other countries [probably referring to Germany which was not then a Council member] have perhaps a special need.[89]

It was not only the reminder of Nazi Germany that motivated the founders of European human rights law. After the Communist seizure of power in the Eastern European states, the Western European leaders "were acutely aware of the challenge of Communism . . . ; it was the danger of dictatorship that made them conscious of the value of democracy."[90] As Sean MacBride, the Irish Minister for External Affairs, declared:

> The present struggle is one which is largely being fought in the minds and consciences of mankind. In this struggle, I have always felt that we lacked a clearly defined charter which set out unambiguously the rights which we democrats guaranteed to our people.[91]

A formal proposal for a European-wide organization ensuring the protection of human rights emanated from the Council's Assembly on August 19, 1949, and a draft Convention was prepared by a government-appointed Committee of Experts in February and March of 1950.[92] The European Convention for the Protection of Human Rights and Fundamental Freedoms was signed in Rome on November 4, 1950.[93] The first ratification was that by the United Kingdom in 1951, and on September 3, 1953, when nine more states had followed suit, the Convention came into force. As of December 2025, 46 European countries had ratified or subsequently acceded to the Convention: Albania, Andorra, Armenia, Austria, Azerbaijan, Belgium, Bosnia-Herzegovina, Bulgaria, Croatia, Cyprus, the Czech Republic, Denmark, Estonia, Finland, France, Georgia, Germany, Greece, Hungary, Iceland, Ireland, Italy, Latvia, Liechtenstein, Lithuania, Luxembourg, Malta, Moldova, Monaco, Montenegro, the Netherlands, North Macedonia, Norway,

[89] Id. at 292.

[90] A.H. Robertson, *Human Rights in Europe* 4 (2d ed. 1977).

[91] Quoted, id. at 5.

[92] Janis, Kay & Bradley, supra, at 12-19.

[93] European Convention for the Protection of Human Rights and Fundamental Freedoms, 213 U.N.T.S. 221, E.T.S. 5, U.K.T.S. 71 (1953) (signed at Rome November 4, 1950; entered into force September 3, 1953; not in force for the United States) [hereinafter cited as "European Human Rights Convention"].

Poland, Portugal, Romania, San Marino, Serbia, Slovakia, Slovenia, Spain, Sweden, Switzerland, Turkey, Ukraine, and the United Kingdom.[94]

The European Human Rights Convention and its subsequently adopted protocols assure a great many specific rights to everyone (even nationals of non-parties) within the jurisdiction of the 46 consenting European states.[95] The substantive rights listed include the "right to life,"[96] the right not to "be subjected to torture or to inhuman or degrading treatment or punishment,"[97] the "right to liberty and security of person,"[98] the "right to a fair and public hearing" in civil and criminal adjudications,[99] the right to be free from the application of *ex post facto* laws,[100] the right to respect for "private and family life,"[101] the "right to freedom of thought, conscience and religion,"[102] the "right to freedom of expression,"[103] the "right to freedom of peaceful assembly,"[104] and the "right to marry and to found a family."[105]

However, what makes the European Convention on Human Rights truly a distinctive contribution to modern international law is not so much its enumeration of substantive rights, but its establishment of an effective form of international legal machinery to enforce those rights.[106] The institutions of European human rights law are what deserve our more particular attention. As Britain's Lord McNair put

[94] Council of Europe, *States Parties to the Convention,* www.coe.int (Dec. 12, 2025). Following its invasion of Ukraine, Russia was expelled by the Council of Europe in 2022. There were always doubts about how well Russia fit within the system, see Janis, Russia and the 'Legality' of Strasbourg Law, 8 *European Journal of International Law* 93 (1997) [hereinafter cited as Janis, 'Legality'].

[95] European Human Rights Convention, supra, art. 1.

[96] Id., art. 2.

[97] Id., art. 3.

[98] Id., art. 5.

[99] Id., art. 6.

[100] Id., art. 7.

[101] Id., art. 8.

[102] Id., art. 9.

[103] Id., art. 10.

[104] Id., art. 11.

[105] Id., art. 12. On the substantive rights under the European Convention, see Janis, Kay & Bradley, supra, at 119-826; *Jacobs, White & Ovey: The European Convention on Human Rights* (B. Rainey, E. Wicks & C. Ovey eds. 7th ed. 2017).

[106] Frowein, European Integration Through Fundamental Rights, 18 *Journal of Law Reform* 5-7 (1984) [hereinafter cited as "Frowein"].

it in his speech formally inaugurating the European Court of Human Rights in 1959:

> The constitutions of many countries guarantee to individuals, whether their own nationals or not, certain elementary rights and freedoms which our generation regards as being the minimum required to ensure the dignity and decency of human life. Unfortunately, experience has shown that these constitutional guarantees, when remaining purely national, are not always strong enough to secure these objects, and are liable to be overridden by Governments or their officials or agents either by neglect or mistake, or by a ruthless determination to achieve their aims and policies regardless of the rights of individuals. Thus, a conflict can arise between an individual and a Government in which, if I may use the words of an English mediaeval chronicler, "There is too great might on the one side and un-might on the other."[107]

"To ensure the observance of the engagements undertaken by the High Contracting Parties," the Convention establishes the European Court of Human Rights.[108] After more than 40 years, Protocol No. 11 to the Convention merged what was, until then, the European Commission of Human Rights and the original Court into a single new Court responsible for both the Commission's and the old Court's traditional functions.[109] Although it is sometimes necessary to describe the Strasbourg system's work in historical terms, it is important to keep in mind that, beginning at the end of 1998, many of the Commission's activities, no matter how similarly they are executed, were assumed by the new Court and in 1999, the Commission itself was phased out.[110]

Pursuant to Article 33 of the Convention, and similar to Article 36 of the Statute of the International Court of Justice, states are authorized to go to the Court regarding "any alleged breach of the provisions of the Convention by another High Contracting Party."[111] Note that Article 33 of the European Human Rights Convention is broader than

[107] A.D. McNair, *Lord McNair: Selected Papers and Bibliography* 387 (1974).

[108] European Human Rights Convention, supra, art. 19.

[109] Protocol No. 11 to the Convention for the Protection of Human Rights and Fundamental Freedoms, Restructuring the Control Machinery Established Thereby, Council of Europe, H(94)5, 11 May 1994 [hereinafter cited as "Protocol No. 11"].

[110] On the merger of the Commission and the Court, see Janis, Kay & Bradley, supra, at 24-27.

[111] European Human Rights Convention, supra, art. 33.

the comparable provision in the ICJ Statute: Article 33 provides that any contracting state may complain about any other contracting state. There is no *Nottebohm* or *Barcelona Traction* requirement that an individual be protected only by the individual's national state. This liberality figured in the most important set of inter-state cases that have been heard, viz., the claims brought in 1967 by Denmark, Norway, Sweden, and the Netherlands against the Greek government on behalf of Greek nationals under the military regime.[112]

Furthermore, and radically dissimilar from the states-only provisions of the International Court's Statute, the Convention also permits that private parties may themselves apply to the Court for relief. This vital aspect of the Convention is now found in Article 34:

> The Court may receive applications from any person, non-governmental organization or group of individuals claiming to be the victim of a violation by one of the High Contracting Parties of the rights set forth in this Convention or the protocols thereto. The High Contracting Parties undertake not to hinder in any way the effective exercise of this right.[113]

Before 1998, what is now Article 34 was only optional, but, one by one, the members of the Council of Europe recognized the right of individual petition. The Commission, which became legally competent to receive interstate applications in 1953, could accept individual petitions in 1955.[114] By 1994, all 30 states then party to the European Convention had agreed to recognize the admissibility of private complaints.[115] The acceptance of the individual right of petition had become so general that Protocol No. 11 deleted the old option.[116]

Over more than 70 years, the Strasbourg legal system has become formal and well developed. Suffice it to say here that three of the former Commission's most important roles—filtering out a few complaints to investigate from the many submitted, attempting to mediate friendly settlements between individuals and governments, and preparing

[112] See 12 *Yearbook of the European Convention on Human Rights: The Greek Case* (1969).

[113] European Human Rights Convention, supra, art. 34.

[114] European Commission of Human Rights, *Stock-Taking on the European Convention on Human Rights: The First Thirty Years: 1954 Until 1984* 1 (1984).

[115] European Convention on Human Rights and Additional Protocols: Chart of Signatures and Ratifications as of 28 July 1994, 15 *Human Rights Law Journal* 114-115 (1994).

[116] Protocol No. 11, supra.

reports about alleged violations of the Convention—are now assumed by the new merged Court.[117] Although there was doubt that the new Court would command the respect paid to the old Commission and the old Court,[118] it is clear that the majority of European states were of the opinion that, given the expansion of both the case load and the membership of the Strasbourg system, it was imperative to replace the two-tiered Commission/Court structure with a single Court.[119]

Pursuant to the revised Convention, there is now one judge for (and usually from) each state party to the Convention, who, elected by the Parliamentary Assembly of the Council of Europe, sits for nine-year terms and may not be re-elected.[120] The judges meet in Single Judge formations, Committees of three, Chambers of five, and Grand Chambers of 17; generally, the Single Judge formations handle questions of admissibility, while Committees and Chambers are the ordinary, and Grand Chambers the extraordinary, courts of judgment.[121] It is widely acknowledged that the political independence of Strasbourg's judges has contributed greatly to the effectiveness of the Court, making the European Court of Human Rights, along with the European Court of Justice [see Chapter 9], one of the most effective international legal tribunals.[122]

Traditionally, only the states party to the Convention and the Commission had the right to bring cases to the Court.[123] States could refer cases to the Court so long as they were the national state of an individual petitioner, were themselves the petitioner, or were the state against which the complaint had been lodged.[124] Pursuant to old Article

[117] Janis, Kay & Bradley, supra, at 24-68. The vital and often highly discretionary role of the Strasbourg machinery should not be underestimated. In 1991, for example, the Commission opened some 5,550 provisional files, formally registered 1,648 applications, and declared only 217 applications admissible. European Commission on Human Rights, *Survey of Activities and Statistics 1991* 21 (1992).

[118] See Schermers, The Eleventh Protocol to the European Convention on Human Rights, 19 *European Law Review* 367 (1994).

[119] Council of Europe, *Explanatory Report to Protocol No. 11 to the European Convention on Human Rights*, Doc. H(94)5 (1994).

[120] A. Nussberger, *The European Court of Human Rights* 41 (2020) [hereinafter cited as "Nussberger"].

[121] Id. at 56-61.

[122] Helfer & Slaughter, Why States Create International Tribunals, 93 *California Law Review* 899, 903, 919, 955 (2005).

[123] European Human Rights Convention, as it then was, in M.W. Janis, R.S. Kay & A.W. Bradley, *European Human Rights Law: Text and Materials* 468-482 (1st ed. 1995).

[124] Id., art. 48.

46 of the Convention, "[a]ny of the High Contracting Parties may at any time declare that it recognises as compulsory *ipso facto* and without special agreement the jurisdiction of the Court in all matters concerning the interpretation and application of the present Convention."[125] By 1994, all 30 states then party to the European Convention had submitted to Article 46's compulsory jurisdiction.[126]

Although individuals could not themselves bring cases to the Court, private parties were most usually the actual initiators of suits before the Commission. Furthermore, individuals were allowed to have their own attorneys argue before the Court once either the Commission or a state brought the case to the Court. In its first judgment, the *Lawless* case, the Court rejected Ireland's arguments that the precedent of the International Court prohibiting individuals from independently submitting their observations should be followed:

> [T]he Court must bear in mind its duty to safeguard the interests of the individual, who may not be a Party to any court proceedings [but] nevertheless the whole of the proceedings in the Court, as laid down by the Convention and the Rules of Court, are upon issues which concern the Applicant [and] accordingly, it is in the interests of the proper administration of justice that the Court should have knowledge of and, if need be, take into consideration, the Applicant's point of view.[127]

The Court may not only decide whether the Convention has been violated; it may also award damages, which the Convention terms "just satisfaction." Article 41 provides:

> If the Court finds that there has been a violation of the Convention or the protocols thereto, and if the internal law of the High Contracting Party allows only partial reparation to be made, the Court shall, if necessary, afford just satisfaction to the injured party.[128]

Article 44 reads that "[t]he judgment of the Court shall be final."[129] In the *Ringeisen* case in 1972, the Court rejected Austria's assertion that

[125] Id., art. 46(1).

[126] Council of Europe, *Chart of Signatures and Ratifications, as of 9 September 1994.*

[127] European Court of Human Rights, Judgment of November 14, 1960, ser. A, no. 1, at 15.

[128] European Human Rights Convention, supra, art. 41.

[129] Id. at art. 44(1).

because the Court's judgments were final, claimants had to bring a new case if they were to seek Article 41 redress:

> [Article 44's] sole object is to make the Court's judgment not subject to any appeal to another authority.
>
> It would be a formalistic attitude alien to international law to maintain that the Court may not apply Article [41] save on condition that it either rules on the matter by the same judgment which found a violation or that this judgment has expressly kept the case open.[130]

After making its judgment on the merits, the Court has routinely postponed ruling on just satisfaction, permitting the state involved to settle on compensation or other redress with a private claimant. Sometimes, of course, no out-of-court settlement has been possible, and the parties have returned to the Court for an Article 41 ruling.

The "High Contracting Parties [are] to abide by the decision of the Court in any case to which they are parties," and although execution of the Court's decisions is entrusted to the Council of Europe,[131] states have with only rare exceptions voluntarily complied with the Court's judgments. Such compliance may involve payments to the injured party as well as amendment of national law. In its first 96 cases, to September 1985, the Court awarded "just satisfaction" in 38 instances. These ranged from 100 Dutch guilders (about $40) in the *Engle* case to 1,150,000 Swedish crowns (about $160,000) in the *Spörrong* case.[132] Since then, the amount demanded as just satisfaction soared to almost 2 billion euros in the 2011 *Yukos* award.[133] The Court has even in unusual circumstances awarded punitive damages, for example, 25,000 euros against Iceland for an unfair trial in *Sigurdsson* in 2003.[134]

Although the European Convention on Human Rights was signed in 1950 and entered into force in 1953, for 20 years it was, in the words of Jochen Frowein, a vice president of the former Commission, "a sleeping

[130] European Court of Human Rights, Judgment of June 22, 1972 (Article 50), ser. A, no. 15, at 7.

[131] European Human Rights Convention, supra, art. 46.

[132] European Court of Human Rights, Information Document Issued by the Registrar of the Court, at 9 (September 23, 1985).

[133] Nussberger, supra, at 163, referring to *OAO Neftyanaya Kompaniy Yukos v. Russia* (just satisfaction), 20 September 2011.

[134] Sigurdsson v. Iceland, European Court of Human Rights, Judgment of July 10, 2003, 40 *European Human Rights Reports* 15.

beauty, frequently referred to but without much impact."[135] Only by the 1970s had enough countries accepted the right of individual petition that a significant case load for the former Commission developed. Private claimants have brought the European human rights legal system alive. Between 1955 and 1997, there were only 13 state petitions filed with the Commission, but there were 39,034 private claims.[136] All but two of the more than 300 decisions and judgments of the European Court of Human Rights from 1959 to 1992 were in cases where individuals were the original petitioners. Comparing the business of the European Court of Human Rights to that of the International Court, one must be struck by how much it is the access of private claimants to the European human rights system that explains the difference in case load. Unlike the work of the International Court, which has remained more or less static for almost 100 years [see Chapter 5], the business of the European Court of Human Rights is rapidly growing. While there were only 10 European Court judgments and decisions in all of the 1960s, there were 26 cases in the 1970s, 169 in the 1980s, 809 in the 1990s, and more than 17,000 judgments in the first 15 years of the 2000s, about 1,100 judgments a year, more than 500 times the average annual case load of the ICJ.[137]

What makes European human rights law special is not only its impressive case load, but also its effectiveness. These two features may well be related. The fact that states have, on the whole, complied with the reports of the Commission and the decisions of the Court may well have encouraged potential litigants to petition Strasbourg for redress. The effectiveness of the European Court of Human Rights is remarkable. There is in European human rights law no compulsory machinery comparable to that available in a municipal legal system. The obligatory part of the European Human Rights Convention has been simply Article 46(1), which reads: "The High Contracting Parties undertake to abide by the final judgment of the Court in any case to which they are parties."[138] Monitoring and ensuring compliance is the responsibility

[135] Frowein, supra, at 8.

[136] 1997 *Yearbook of the European Convention on Human Rights* 76-79 (1998).

[137] European Court of Human Rights, *Overview 1959-2014* 3, 4. www.echr.coe.int (June 16, 2015). The Single Judge Formation has enabled a slight reduction in the number of annual cases, lately around 900 each year. Council of Europe, *Overview ECHR 1959-2019*, www.coe.org (Oct. 30, 2020).

[138] European Human Rights Convention, supra, art. 46(1).

of the largely ineffectual Committee of Ministers of the Council of Europe as set out in Article 46(2): "The final judgment of the Court shall be transmitted to the Committee of Ministers, which shall supervise its execution."[139]

If the Court finds that the internal law of a state violates the Convention, then the state is obliged to alter that law. The Court, however, will not instruct the state on how the change in municipal law is to be made, nor will the Court attempt to reform related aspects of municipal law. As the Court ruled in the *Marckx* case in 1979: "It is for the respondent State, and the respondent State alone, to take the measures it considers appropriate to assure that its domestic law is coherent and consistent."[140]

The Court has been increasingly willing to find states in violation of the Convention. In its early decisions, the Court seemed anxious to reassure its member states that it would be sensitive to their concerns and traditions. For example, in 1961, in its first substantive decision, the *Lawless* case, the Court decided that although Ireland would have otherwise violated Articles 5 and 6 of the Convention by detaining an IRA suspect for five months without trial, the state was permitted to derogate from the strict rules of the Convention because it was justified under the Convention's Article 15 in declaring a "public emergency threatening the life of the nation" and taking extraordinary measures.[141] While decisions such as *Lawless* might have reassured states, they did little to encourage individual petitions. It was only in 1968, 18 years after the signing of the European Convention on Human Rights and almost 10 years after the Court became competent to hear cases, that a decision, *Neumeister*, was rendered against a member state. The Court held that Austria's detention without trial for 26 months of a businessman accused of tax fraud violated Article 5's guarantees to a trial within a reasonable time or to a release pending trial.[142] Even more encouraging to private litigants have been the very recent judgments of the Court. Many of the Strasbourg judges seem more ready now than

[139] Id., art. 46(2).

[140] European Court of Human Rights, Judgment of June 13, 1979, ser. A, no. 31, at 20.

[141] European Court of Human Rights, Judgment of July 1, 1961, ser. A, no. 3, at 54-63.

[142] European Court of Human Rights, Judgment of June 27, 1968, ser. A, no. 8.

ever before to upset member states with decisions that stretch the language of the Convention.[143]

Probably the most famous judgment of the Court, the *Sunday Times* case, is also in the view of some critics one of its most arrogant.[144] *Sunday Times* concerned an injunction that the British attorney-general sought and obtained from the English courts to restrain the Sunday Times newspaper from publishing an article about legal proceedings brought on behalf of children born with physical defects resulting from the drug thalidomide, which had been taken by their mothers while pregnant. The defendant was Distillers Company, the British manufacturer and distributor of the drug. English law concerning the thalidomide children's right to recover from Distillers was unclear, and the legal proceedings and negotiations between the thalidomide children and Distillers dragged on into 1972, some 11 and 12 years after the children had been born and during which time the children needed and were sometimes not receiving expensive care. The Sunday Times article sought to pressure Distillers, more on moral than on legal grounds, into quickly reaching a generous out-of-court settlement.

Whether the British government had a right to enjoin the Sunday Times from publishing the disputed thalidomide article was exhaustively litigated in three English courts. A three-judge Queen's Bench Division panel unanimously decided in 1972 that publication should be enjoined on the grounds that the article would be a contempt of court because it interfered with Distillers' freedom of action in the litigation.[145] Three judges of the Court of Appeals reversed in 1973, holding, in the words of Lord Denning, that the thalidomide proceedings in court had "gone soundly to sleep."[146] Finally, in 1974, five judges of Britain's highest court, the House of Lords, found unanimously that an injunction should issue. Lord Reid wrote: "There has long been and there still is in this country a strong and generally held feeling that trial by newspaper is wrong and should be prevented."[147]

[143] Janis, Kay & Bradley, supra, at 74-89; C.C. Morrisson, *The Dynamics of Development in the European Human Rights System* 19 (1981) [hereinafter cited as "Morrisson"].

[144] European Court of Human Rights, Judgment of April 26, 1979, ser. A, no. 30; see Mann, Contempt of Court in the House of Lords and the European Court of Human Rights, 95 *Law Quarterly Review* 348 (1979).

[145] [1973] Q.B. 710, 711.

[146] [1973] Q.B. 710, 735, 738.

[147] [1974] A.C. 273, 300.

In most countries, legal proceedings of the kind in the *Sunday Times* case would, of course, have gone no further than the country's highest court. However, having accepted both the right of individual petition to the Commission and the jurisdiction of the European Court of Human Rights, the United Kingdom was subject to international human rights legal process. The Sunday Times brought the case to the European Commission, which in 1977 decided 8 to 5 that the British government had infringed the Sunday Times' right to freedom of expression under Article 10 of the Convention.[148] The Commission then referred the case to the Court, which in 1979 decided 11 to 9 in favor of the Sunday Times, the majority concluding "that the interference [the enjoining of the article] complained of did not correspond to a social need sufficiently pressing to outweigh the public interest in freedom of expression within the meaning of the Convention."[149]

For present purposes, who weighed rightly or wrongly is immaterial. Note only how close the issue was. Eight English judges (three at the trial level and five in the House of Lords), five European commissioners, and nine European judges felt that the balance tilted toward granting the injunction. Three English judges (in the Court of Appeals), eight European commissioners, and 11 European judges thought that the balance tilted toward freedom of the press and letting the Sunday Times publish. Thus, of the 44 judges and commissioners who considered the case, half went one way and half the other. Reasonable men and women could and did differ. As a matter of English law, the decision of the House of Lords was final, but the Lords' decision itself became part of the government activity about which the Sunday Times complained before the European Commission. Narrowly, both the Commission and the Court found against the United Kingdom. In international law, the United Kingdom was required to respect the judgment of the European Court, and when the European Court subsequently ruled that the British government was obliged to pay the Sunday Times, the United Kingdom complied with the judgment.[150]

[148] European Commission of Human Rights, Report of May 18, 1977, ser. B, no. 28, at 11, 77.

[149] European Court of Human Rights, Judgment of April 26, 1979, ser. A, no. 30, at 42.

[150] European Court of Human Rights, Judgment of November 6, 1980 (Article 50), ser. A, no. 38, at 19. The record of just satisfaction by the United Kingdom is at 24 *Yearbook of the European Convention on Human Rights* 476-480 (1981).

B. International Human Rights Law

It is important to note what a great departure the *Sunday Times* case was for the Court. Only three years before, in the 1976 *Handyside* case, the Court had decided by a lopsided 13 to 1 vote that the United Kingdom had not violated the Convention when it censored *The Little Red Schoolbook*, a book aimed at children, and prosecuted its British publisher for obscenity.[151] In *Handyside*, the Court held that a state had a certain "margin of appreciation" in deciding what to censor and that "[b]y reason of their direct and continuous contact with the vital forces of their countries, State authorities are in principle in a better position than the international judge to give an opinion" on moral requirements.[152] The complexion of the Court had changed in *Sunday Times*, and the seven new judges appointed since *Handyside* voted 5 to 2 for the newspaper, effectively providing a new majority in a judgment symbolic of the increasing activism of the Court.[153]

Decisions such as *Sunday Times* are important landmarks in the development of international law. They show international law at its most potent, giving individuals effective international remedies even against their own states and even in close cases. *Sunday Times* and like cases also pose challenges to state sovereignty. The whole system of European human rights law would be threatened if an important member of the Convention, such as Great Britain, should withdraw from the Strasbourg system.[154] What the Court must do is continually and carefully balance the scales between asserting its authority on the one side and avoiding too dangerous confrontations with national governments on the other. Indeed, there still remain some fields, for example, religious freedom, where the Court is reluctant to tread, and in others, for example, protecting asylum seekers, where the Court may have ventured too far.[155]

[151] European Court of Human Rights, Judgment of December 7, 1976, ser. A, no. 24.

[152] Id. at 22.

[153] Morrisson, supra, at 109.

[154] Brexit, British withdrawal from the European Union [see Chapter 9], has led to calls for the United Kingdom to also leave the Strasbourg Court. See O'Cinneide, Brexit and Human Rights, *Complexity's Embrace: The International Law Implications of Brexit* 297 (O. Fitzgerald & E. Lein eds. 2018).

[155] Janis, The Shadow of Westphalia: Majoritarian Religions and Strasbourg Law, 4 *Oxford Journal of Law & Religion* 75 (2015); The ECHR: Rights and Flights, *The Economist*, Apr. 27, 2024, at 45; Human Rights: Taking Back Control: Tightening How Courts Interpret International Law Could Work, *The Economist*, Nov. 22, 2025, at 50.

European human rights law, successful though it is, faces new challenges. Not only did the system "deepen" in the 1970s and 1980s by a greater penetration of Strasbourg law into the municipal legal systems of the Western member states, but it was "widened" by the inclusion, since 1990, of the Central and Eastern European former Communist states, more than doubling the system's membership from 22 to 47 nations.[156] This was no accident. The West actively promoted human rights as a solvent to dissolve the hold of the Soviet Union on the Communist bloc.[157] It would have been politically impossible for Western Europe to deny the newly sovereign states of Central and Eastern Europe membership in the Council of Europe and in the Strasbourg legal system.

It was decided in February 1996 to admit Russia to membership in the Council of Europe and, in 1997, to the European Convention on Human Rights. Russian accession, as well as that of perhaps some of the other new states, raised at least three new kinds of problems for Strasbourg. First, it is clear that the Russian legal system was not presently in compliance with the minimum standards of European human rights law.[158] Second, given the challenges to the rule of law in Russia, the number of complaints from Russia for Strasbourg would be considerable and that Strasbourg judgments would not be effectively implemented. Third, and in a way most troubling, there would be a strong temptation for the Strasbourg institutions to fashion a two-tier legal order, allowing lower than normal expectations for Russia. The threat of such a two-tier system is that the perceived "legality" of European human rights law is endangered, particularly from what, following H.L.A. Hart, one might call Europe's "internal point of view" undermining the law-like quality of Strasbourg law.[159]

Remarkably, for an international court, especially for an international court of human rights, the European Court of Human Rights has become a victim of its own success. As described in 2006 by Judge Wildhaber, then

[156] Id. at 22-23.

[157] S.B. Snyder, *Human Rights and the End of the Cold War* (2011).

[158] This was the widely accepted conclusion of a special study commissioned by the Council of Europe. Council of Europe, Parliamentary Assembly, Bureau of the Assembly, *Report of the Conformity of the Legal Order of the Russian Federation with Council of Europe Standards*, October 7, 1994, AS/Bur/Russia (1994). For the continuing troubles with Russia as a member of the Strasbourg system, see Kirchner, Interim Measures in Inter-State Proceedings Before the European Court of Human Rights: *Ukraine v. Russia*, 3 *University of Baltimore Journal of International Law* 33 (2014).

[159] H.L.A. Hart, *The Concept of Law* 90 (2d ed. 1994); Janis, 'Legality,' supra.

President of the Court, the "Court receives around 900 letters per day and some 250 international telephone calls. . . . [It has] some 81,000 pending applications."[160] Most every observer of the Strasbourg system agrees that the Court needs to find better ways to choose truly important cases from among the thousands of applications it receives each year and to produce a more coherent and consistent jurisprudence.[161] Moreover, it needs to address "major structural problems" leading to "unacceptable delays of implementation" of judgments not only in Russia, as above, but also in Italy, Turkey, Ukraine, and the United Kingdom.[162]

Despite these difficulties, there is no doubt that the European Court of Human Rights has made a significant contribution to international human rights law. In 2018, the Court issued a remarkable 1,014 judgments, dwarfing the work of every other human rights tribunal.[163] It is the foremost international institutional proponent of human rights law. In the words of Angelika Nussberger, for nine years the German judge on the Court:

> The Court has shown over many decades that it is a unique—and successful experiment. It was needed in the 1950s to help Europe start anew; it was needed in the 1990s to bring together East and West and to build up a new European identity; and it is needed now, more than ever, to turn Europe away from the road to "unfreedom" on which parts of it seem willing to embark.[164]

4. Inter-American Human Rights Law

It would be an attractive prospect to contemplate European human rights law as a model for other regions of the world. Outside of Western

[160] Wildhaber, The European Court of Human Rights: The Past, the Present, the Future, 22 *American University International Law Review* 521, 527 (2007).

[161] Janis, Kay & Bradley, supra, at 878-885.

[162] Parliamentary Assembly, Council of Europe, *Implementation of Judgments of the European Court of Human Rights*, Doc. 11020 (Sept. 18, 2006), at 1; see Janis, Kay & Bradley, supra, at 885-897. For modern techniques that address both the systemic and structural cases overloading the Strasbourg Court, see J. Czepek, The Application of the Pilot Judgment Procedure and Other Forms of Handling Large-Scale Dysfunctions in the Case Law of the European Court of Human Rights, 20 *International Community Law Review* 347 (2018).

[163] European Court of Human Rights, *Analysis of Statistics 2018*, at 4-7 (2019).

[164] Nussberger, supra, at 202.

Europe, saving some developments in Africa,[165] there has been real regional human rights progress only in the Americas. Inter-American human rights law is set in two overlapping frameworks, one based on the Charter of the Organization of American States (the "OAS" and the "OAS Charter"),[166] the other established by the 1969 American Convention on Human Rights.[167] The OAS, founded in 1890 as the International Union of American Republics and then in 1912 renamed the Pan American Union,[168] is presently founded on the 1948 Charter of the Organization of American States, which entered into force in 1951.[169] The OAS is composed of 35 member states, including the United States and all other independent American countries, 22 of which, not including the United States, have also, as of December 2025, ratified the American Convention on Human Rights.[170]

The original OAS Charter contained very little about human rights, only proclaiming "the fundamental rights of the individual without distinction as to race, nationality, creed, or sex,"[171] and had no institutional mechanisms to protect human rights. In 1960, however, the OAS established the Inter-American Commission on Human Rights (the "Inter-American Commission"), which was given limited powers to promote respect for the human rights embodied in the 1948 American Declaration of the Rights and Duties of Man,[172] theretofore a non-binding resolution of the OAS.[173] The American Declaration, like

[165] See M. Evans & R. Murray, *The African Charter on Human Rights and Peoples' Rights: The System in Practice, 1986-2006* (2d ed. 2008); and discussion below.

[166] 2 U.S.T. 2394, T.I.A.S. No. 2361, 119 U.N.T.S. 3 (signed at Bogota April 30, 1948; entered into force December 13, 1951); as amended, 21 U.S.T. 607, T.I.A.S. No. 6847 [hereinafter cited as "OAS Charter"].

[167] O.A.S. Treaty Series No. 36, at 1, reprinted in 9 *International Legal Materials* 673 (1970) (opened for signature in San José, Costa Rica November 22, 1969; entered into force July 18, 1978; not in force for the United States) [hereinafter cited as "American Human Rights Convention"]; Buergenthal, The Inter-American System for the Protection of Human Rights, 2 *Human Rights in International Law: Legal and Policy Issues* 439 (T. Meron ed. 1984) [hereinafter cited as "Buergenthal"].

[168] F.L. Kirgis, *International Organizations in Their Legal Setting* 19 (1977).

[169] OAS Charter, supra.

[170] www.oas.org (Dec. 14, 2025).

[171] OAS Charter, supra, art. 3(j).

[172] OAS Res. XXX, O.A.S. Off. Rec. OEA/Ser.L/V/I.4 (1945), as revised (1965) [hereinafter cited as "American Declaration"].

[173] Buergenthal, supra, at 471-472.

the European Convention on Human Rights, enumerates substantive rights, for example, the "right to life, liberty and the security of his person," the right to be "equal before the law," the "right freely to profess a religious faith,"[174] but, unlike the European Convention, does not itself provide for enforcement machinery. In 1970, the OAS Charter was amended by the 1967 Protocol of Buenos Aires.[175] The Protocol transformed the OAS Charter by strengthening the position of the Inter-American Commission and further institutionalizing the implementation of the American Declaration.[176] Since its 1970 amendment, the OAS Charter has provided that the Commission's function is "to promote the observance and protection of human rights and to serve as a consultative organ of the Organization in these matters."[177]

The second and more elaborate system of Inter-American human rights law has been generated by the 1969 American Convention on Human Rights,[178] which entered into force in 1978, and is modeled on the European Human Rights Convention. It contains a list of substantive rights,[179] and provides for the Inter-American Commission (which it shares with the OAS Charter system) and establishes an Inter-American Court of Human Rights (the "Inter-American Court").[180] The Inter-American Commission was reconstituted in 1979, with a new Statute approved by the OAS.[181] The Commission, composed of seven members who are to "represent all the member countries" of the OAS and are elected by the OAS General Assembly for four-year once-renewable terms, is charged to "develop an awareness of human rights among the peoples of America," to make reports, and to take actions on petitions.[182] "Any person or group of persons, or any non-governmental entity legally recognized in one or more member states of the Organization, may lodge petitions with the [Inter-American] Commission containing denunciations or complaints of violation of

[174] American Declaration, supra, arts. I, II, III.

[175] 21 U.S.T. 607, T.I.A.S. No. 6847.

[176] Buergenthal, supra, at 474-475.

[177] OAS Charter, supra, arts. 51(e), 112.

[178] American Human Rights Convention, supra.

[179] Id., arts. 3-25.

[180] Id., art. 33. S. Davidson, *The Inter-American Court of Human Rights* (1992).

[181] Organization of American States, *Annual Report of the Inter-American Commission on Human Rights 1984-1985* 5 (1985) [hereinafter cited as "1984-1985 Annual Report"].

[182] American Human Rights Convention, supra, arts. 34-37, 41.

[the] Convention by a State Party."[183] Additionally, states may recognize the competence of the Inter-American Commission "to receive and examine communications in which a State Party alleges that another State Party has committed a violation of a human right set forth in [the] Convention," a competence recognized, as of 2020, by ten states.[184] To be admissible, petitions from individuals or communications from states must be submitted after exhaustion of domestic remedies, must be lodged within six months of a final domestic decision, and must not be the subject of a petition or communication pending before another international procedure. The Inter-American Commission may investigate the case, must try to reach a friendly settlement, and must issue a report.[185]

The work of the Commission is not inconsiderable. In 2019, for example, the Inter-American Commission reported on the merits of 62 individual cases.[186] Yet in many cases the Commission receives little cooperation from governments, and the end result may be merely resolutions of the Commission and perhaps of the OAS Assembly condemning governmental acts.[187] Although the Commission's reports and resolutions may have some political effect, they fall far short of the efficacy shown in the European system.

The Inter-American Court of Human Rights is composed of seven judges, elected by the states parties to the American Convention to six-year once-renewable terms. Human Rights Judges were first elected to the Court, which sits in San José, Costa Rica, in May 1979.[188] As of October 2020, the judges were nationals of Argentina, Chile, Colombia, Costa Rica, Ecuador, Mexico, and Uruguay.[189]

[183] Id., art. 44.

[184] Id., art. 45. See www.corteidh.or.cr (Oct. 31, 2020).

[185] American Human Rights Convention, supra, arts. 46-51.

[186] Organization of American States, *2019 Annual Report of the Inter-American Commission on Human Rights* 59-60.

[187] See the cases in Inter-American Commission of Human Rights, *Ten Years of Activities 1971-1981* 99-311 (1982).

[188] American Human Rights Convention, supra, arts. 52-54; Lillich, supra, at 739-740; A.H. Robertson & J.G. Merrills, *Human Rights in the World* 177-179 (3d ed. 1989). On the Court generally, see S. Davidson, *The Inter-American Court of Human Rights* (1992).

[189] www.corteidh.or.cr (Oct. 31, 2020).

"Only the States Parties and the Commission shall have the right to submit a case to the Court."[190] States may submit to the contentious jurisdiction of the Inter-American Court, and as of April 2015, some 23 countries—Argentina, Barbados, Bolivia, Brazil, Chile, Colombia, Costa Rica, Dominica, the Dominican Republic, Ecuador, El Salvador, Grenada, Guatemala, Haiti, Honduras, Jamaica, Mexico, Nicaragua, Panama, Paraguay, Peru, Surinam, and Uruguay had done so.[191]

In 1981, the Inter-American Court heard its first contentious case, *Gallardo*,[192] in which it refused to take jurisdiction in a case involving the death of a Costa Rican citizen in a Costa Rican prison, because the matter had not been first submitted to the Inter-American Commission.[193] In 1986, the Commission submitted its first case to the Court. In *Velásquez Rodríguez*, an individual petition complained that Honduras maintained army death squads that caused the "disappearance" of opponents of the government.[194] The Inter-American Court of Human Rights heard argument in 1988 and on July 29 of that year found Honduras guilty of violating the "disappeared" Velásquez Rodríguez's rights under Articles 4 (right to life), 5 (right to humane treatment), and 7 (right to personal liberty) of the American Convention on Human Rights. The Court ruled, *inter alia*, that:

> The context in which the disappearance of Manfredo Velásquez occurred and the lack of knowledge seven years later about his fate create a reasonable presumption that he was killed. Even if there is a minimal margin of doubt in this respect, it must be presumed that his fate was decided by authorities who systematically executed detainees without trial and concealed their bodies in order to avoid punishment.[195]

[190] American Human Rights Convention, supra, art. 61(1).

[191] www.corteidh.or.cr (Apr. 12, 2015).

[192] No. G 101/81, Organization of American States, *Annual Report of the Inter-American Court of Human Rights 1982* 12 (1982).

[193] Id. at 17-18. The Inter-American Commission found no violation of the American Human Rights Convention, and the Court struck *Gallardo* from its docket in 1983. Organization of American States, *Annual Report of the Inter-American Court of Human Rights* 40-42 (1984) [hereinafter cited as "1984 Inter-American Court Report"].

[194] Velásquez Rodríguez, Inter-American Court of Human Rights, Judgment of July 29, 1988, reprinted in 28 *International Legal Materials* 291 (1989) [hereinafter cited as "Velásquez Rodríguez"], excerpted in Lillich, supra, at 338-345. See LeMoyne, In Human Rights Court, Honduras Is First to Face Death Squad Trial, *N.Y. Times*, Jan. 19, 1988, at A1.

[195] Velásquez Rodríguez, supra, at 328, 329-330.

In the words of Dean Claudio Grossman, formerly President of the Inter-American Commission on Human Rights, *Velásquez Rodríguez* was the "departure point for much of the Court's future jurisprudence."[196] Note, for example, the comparable proceedings against Argentina in *Garrido and Baigorria*, which in 1998 culminated in a Court order that Argentina pay reparations for disappearances after the military takeover in 1976.[197]

Another area of distinction for the Inter-American Court has been the recognition of collective rights. Going beyond the usual focus of international human rights courts on individual rights, the Inter-American Court in a 2015 case against Suriname supported claims of two indigenous groups of deprivation of collective property and denial of judicial protection. Suriname had sold mining concessions in traditional tribal territory without securing tribal consent.[198] In addition to its contentious jurisdiction, the Inter-American Court also has an advisory jurisdiction as set out in Article 64 of the American Human Rights Convention.[199] OAS states, whether or not they are parties to the American Convention, may request advisory opinions, as may some OAS organs.[200]

Whether Inter-American human rights law will develop apace with the progress of European human rights law is open to considerable question. Perhaps the gap between the two may be narrowing. Although it used to be that human rights abuses in the Americas were so much more dire than those in Western Europe, it may be that just as the situation in the Americas is improving, the European system with its broader membership now includes more trouble spots. Moreover, the case load of the Inter-American Court is increasing and, though it by no means matches the explosion of cases in the European Court of Human Rights, it more than rivals the work of the International Court

[196] Grossman, The *Velásquez Rodríguez* Case: The Development of the Inter-American Human Rights System, *International Law Stories* 77, 79 (J.E. Noyes, L.A. Dickinson & M.W. Janis eds. 2007) [hereinafter cited as "Grossman"].

[197] *Garrido and Baigorria* Case (Reparations), Inter-American Court of Human Rights, Judgment of Aug. 27, 1998, excerpted in Lillich, supra, at 773-779. For the Argentina disappearances generally, see id. at 731-779.

[198] Lixinski, Case of the Kalina and Lokono Peoples v. Suriname, Inter-American Court of Human Rights, November 25, 2015, 111 *American Journal of International Law* 147 (2017).

[199] American Human Rights Convention, supra, art. 64.

[200] 1984 Inter-American Court Report, supra, at 5-6.

of Justice. In 2014, for example, the Inter-American Court of Human Rights issued 16 judgments and seven orders.[201] Altogether, by 2025, the Court had decided 566 judgments and rendered 32 advisory opinions,[202] a very respectable total for any international court. However, the efficacy of the Inter-American Court seems to be much less than that of the European Court of Human Rights.[203]

Sadly, an important potential member of the American Human Rights Convention and subscriber to the contentious jurisdiction of the Court, the United States, has so far refused to ratify or to subscribe. This was so even during the Carter administration (1977-1981), the period when the United States most actively promoted international human rights.[204] Given the present attitude of the United States to the International Court of Justice [see Chapter 5], and the International Criminal Court [see below], it seems highly unlikely that the United States will soon contemplate active participation in yet another international tribunal.

Much less developed than either European human rights law or Inter-American human rights law is the regional international human rights law system in Africa. There the most important court is based on the African Charter on Human Rights and Peoples' Rights.[205] The

[201] *2017 Report of the Inter-American Court of Human Rights* 52.

[202] www.corteidh.or.cr (Dec.14, 2025).

[203] See Huneeus, Courts Resisting Courts: Lessons from the Inter-American Court's Struggle to Enforce Human Rights, 44 *Cornell International Law Journal* 493 (2011); Antoniazzi, Advisory Opinion OC-26/20, Denunciation of the American Convention on Human Rights Organizations and the Charter of the Organization of American States and Consequences for State Human Rights Organizations, 116 *American Journal of International Law* 409 (2022). A more optimistic perspective is to be found in Sikkink, Latin America's Protagonist Role in Human Rights, 12 *International Journal on Human Rights* 207 (2015).

[204] Margaret Thatcher, then the British Prime Minister, observed: "Ironically, therefore, President Carter found that he could only take [human rights] action against countries linked to the West, not against countries that were hostile and strong enough to ignore him." M. Thatcher, *The Autobiography* 211 (1995). This may be too strong a critique. Without the support of the Carter administration, it is doubtful that the Alien Tort Statute would be reinvigorated in the *Filartiga* case in 1980 [see Chapter 4].

[205] See F. Viljoen, *International Human Rights Law in Africa* (2d ed. 2012); M. Evans & R. Murray, *The African Charter on Human Rights and Peoples' Rights: The System in Practice, 1986-2006* (2d ed. 2008). Other African human rights tribunals are explored in Viljoen & Louw, State Compliance with the Recommendations of the African Commission on Human and Peoples' Rights: 1994-2004, 101 *American Journal of*

African Court of Human Rights and Peoples' Rights was constituted in 2004, and is composed of 11 judges sitting in Arusha, Tanzania.[206] The Court's competence to hear cases brought by individuals and NGOs is recognized by only eight of more than 40 African states.[207] It rendered its first judgment in 2013.[208] A second judgment, partially protecting a journalist fined and imprisoned for defamation of a government official, was rendered in 2014.[209] However, the African Human Rights Court, along with four other African international human rights law tribunals, had by 2015 made only some 113 judgments finding a violation of human rights law in 33 years.[210] According to one observer, even with these, "state compliance rates are poor."[211] This compares unfavorably with the European Human Rights Court and even with the Inter-American system. In practice, much crucial African human rights adjudication takes place before the International Criminal Court in The Hague, introduced below.

5. The International Criminal Courts

The Nuremberg Tribunal was an early venture as an international criminal court, but when it proved too difficult politically to fashion a permanent international criminal court at the universal level of the United Nations, the impetus shifted to Europe and the creation of the first and still the most influential regional international human rights system. There have now been more than 70 years of practice before the European Court of Human Rights in Strasbourg and, spreading from

---

International Law 1 (2007); and Alter, Helfer & McAllister, A New International Human Rights Court for West Africa: The ECOWAS Community Court of Justice, 107 *American Journal of International Law* 737 (2013).

[206] www.african-court.org (Dec. 15, 2025).

[207] Ibid.

[208] Court's First Judgment on the Merits Includes Comparative Law Aspects/ Restrictions on the Right to Vote Unlawful, Tanganyika Law Society et al. v. Tanzania, 33 *Human Rights Law Journal* 18 (2013).

[209] Shelton, Konaté v. Burkina Faso, App. No. 004/2013, African Court of Human and Peoples' Rights, December 5, 2014. 109 *American Journal of International Law* 630 (2015).

[210] Abebe, Does International Human Rights Law in Africa Make a Difference?, 56 *Virginia Journal of International Law* 527, 532 (2017).

[211] Ibid.

Europe, more than 40 years for the Inter-American Court of Human Rights in San Jose.

Remarkably enough, the end of the Cold War thawed out the long-frozen idea of a permanent universal international criminal court. On July 17, 1998, more than 100 countries, though not including the United States, agreed to the Rome Treaty and created what has been characterized as "a kind of global Nuremberg tribunal": the International Criminal Court (the ICC), more thoroughly explored below.[212] The establishment of the ICC closely followed the establishment of two *ad hoc* international criminal tribunals by the U.N. Security Council: in 1993 the International Criminal Tribunal for the Former Yugoslavia (ICTY),[213] and in 1994 for Rwanda.[214] New *ad hoc* international criminal tribunals have also been ventured for Sierra Leone and Cambodia.[215] Among the *ad hoc* international criminal courts, it is certainly the ICTY that has been most important.[216] The ICTY, which concluded its work in 2017, has been termed "pivotal" in developing international criminal law.[217]

Underpinning all the international criminal courts are at least four ambitions.[218] First is the wish that those who have violated international

[212] Stanley, U.S. Dissents, but Accord Is Reached on War-Criminal Court, *N.Y. Times*, July 18, 1998, at A3. See Hall, The Sixth Session of the UN Preparatory Committee on the Establishment of an International Criminal Court, 92 *American Journal of International Law* 548 (1998); Sadat & Carden, The New International Criminal Court: An Uneasy Revolution, 88 *Georgetown Law Journal* 381 (2000).

[213] Murphy, Progress and Jurisprudence of the International Criminal Tribunal for the Former Yugoslavia, 93 *American Journal of International Law* 57 (1999); G. Boas, *The Milošević Trial: Lessons for the Conduct of Complex International Criminal Proceedings* (2007).

[214] See Magnarella, Expanding the Frontiers of Humanitarian Law: The International Criminal Tribunal for Rwanda, 9 *Florida Journal of International Law* 421 (1994); T. Cruvillier & C. Voss, *The Court of Remorse: Inside the International Criminal Tribunal for Rwanda* (2010).

[215] For the Special Court for Sierra Leone, see *The Sierra Leone Special Court and Its Legacy* (C.J. Jalloh ed. 2014). For Cambodia's Khmer Rouge Tribunal, see Widhya, Keynote Address by the Permanent Representative of the Kingdom of Cambodia to the United Nations, 21 *Connecticut Journal of International Law* 239 (2006); Cambodia Tribunal Monitor, www.cambodiatribunal.org.

[216] A. Swart, A. Zabar & G. Sluiter, *The Legacy of the International Criminal Court for Yugoslavia in the Hague* (2011).

[217] Bowcott, Yugoslavia War Crimes Tribunal Draws to Close: Ninety People Sentenced During 24 Years of Inquiry: Court's End Marks Shift in International Justice, *The Guardian*, Dec. 21, 2017, at 26.

[218] Janis, The Utility of International Criminal Courts, 12 *Connecticut Journal of International Law* 161, 163 (1997).

human rights law be punished. As one of the earliest proponents of the ICTY, Professor Bassiouni, argued, given the atrocities committed, such courts are needed simply for "dispensing justice and punishing war criminals."[219] Second is the hope that individuals and governments will be deterred from violating human rights if they know that they will be held accountable, for example, "in Yugoslavia and elsewhere [if they] envisage 'final solutions' to their conflicts with ethnic and religious minorities."[220] Third is the goal that a record be kept to ensure that the conscience of humanity will not forget the wrongs that have been committed, that "a society simply cannot forget."[221] Fourth is the belief that progress by one human rights system can promote developments in another. As Nuremberg inspired Strasbourg, and Strasbourg inspired San José and Arusha, so all in turn have inspired the new *ad hoc* tribunals and the new permanent international criminal court.

The tale of the international criminal courts fits into two different stories, the first this chapter's account of the development of international human rights law, the second the story of the relationship between the United States and international law. Turning for a moment to the second story, we have already discussed the formal legal doctrines promoting the incorporation of treaties and the law of nations into the domestic law of the United States, doctrines that have made a considerable positive impact on the municipal laws of other states [see Chapter 4], as well as addressing more historical topics, such as the important contributions of the United States to the development of public international arbitration [see Chapter 5], the International Court of Justice [see Chapter 5], and the United Nations [see Chapter 7]. We have also touched on the sometime negativity of the United States toward international law and organization, for example, the opposition of the United States to the judgments of the ICJ in the *Nicaragua* and *Consular Convention* cases [see Chapter 5], the

[219] Bassiouni, The Former Yugoslavia: Investigating Violations of International Humanitarian Law and Establishing an International Criminal Tribunal, 18 *Fordham International Law Journal* 1191, 1201 (1995).

[220] Meron, The Case for War Crimes Trials in Yugoslavia, 72 *Foreign Affairs*, Summer 1993, at 122-123. Professor Drumbl has critiqued traditional notions of retributive justice and deterrence in international criminal law. M.A. Drumbl, *Atrocity, Punishment, and International Law* (2007).

[221] Goldstone, The United Nations' War Crimes Tribunals: An Assessment, 12 *Connecticut Journal of International Law* 227, 230 (1997).

refusal of the United States to join either the League of Nations or the Permanent Court of International Justice, institutions largely the creation of U.S. diplomatic promotions [see Chapters 7 and 5], the Bush administration's doctrine of preemptive war in the face of U.N. Charter Article 2(4) [see Chapter 6], apparent U.S. violations of the laws of war at Abu Ghraib and Guantánamo [see Chapter 6], and the attack of the Trump administration on the system of international law of trade, largely a U.S. post-war creation [see Chapter 9].

These instances of U.S. recalcitrance respecting international law and organization, examples of a more general national ambivalence about participation in international relations sometimes denominated as American "isolationism" or "exceptionalism,"[222] are replicated by the position of the United States *vis-à-vis* the International Criminal Court (ICC). United States opposition to the 1998 Rome Treaty surfaced during the Clinton administration both during the Treaty's negotiation and in 1998, when the President initially refused to sign the agreement. The problem's focus was and remains the insistence of the United States on exemptions for U.S. military personnel from the jurisdiction of the ICC, an insistence met with equally strong opposition from most other states.[223] The deadline for signing the Rome Treaty was December 31, 2000. Within a few hours of the deadline, President Clinton signed, but the United States did not ratify, the agreement, indicating that the United States could not accept the provisions for the ICC as they then stood.[224] Since then, the Rome Treaty came into force on July 1, 2002, following ratification by more than the necessary 60 states.[225] Just before the Rome Treaty entered into force, the Bush administration

[222] For discussions of American exceptionalism and isolationism and the impact on U.S. policy respecting international law, see Rubenfeld, The Two World Orders, in What Good Is International Law?, *Wilson Quarterly* (Autumn 2003), at 22; Koh, On American Exceptionalism, 55 *Stanford Law Review* 1479 (2003); J.A. Rabkin, *Law Without Nations?: Why Constitutional Government Requires Sovereign States* (2005); M.W. Janis, *America and the Law of Nations 1776-1939* (2010); and Janis, The United States and International Law: The United Nations Finds a Home, 56 *Villanova Law Review* 523 (2011).

[223] Efforts to Obtain Immunity from ICC for U.S. Peacekeepers, 96 *American Journal of International Law* 725 (2002); U.S. Efforts to Secure Immunity from ICC for U.S. Nationals, 97 *American Journal of International Law* 710 (2003).

[224] Schense & Washburn, The United States and the International Criminal Court, 35 *International Lawyer* 614, 614-622 (2001).

[225] War Crimes Tribunal Ratified, www.msnbc.com (Apr. 11, 2002).

repudiated the Clinton administration's signature: "[T]he United States does not intend to become a party to the treaty."[226] Over time, fears about the ICC have not abated. The Obama administration, like its predecessors, opposed the exposure of U.S. troops to ICC prosecution. The Trump administration has been even more hostile. Personalizing its opposition, in 2019, the United States revoked the U.S. visa of the ICC chief prosecutor, objecting to her effort to launch an investigation into U.S. military operations in Afghanistan, a proposal later blocked by the ICC's Pre-Trial Chamber.[227] In 2020, the Trump administration took further personal steps against the ICC prosecutor, imposing economic sanctions against her by freezing her bank account at the U.N. Federal Credit Union.[228]

Meanwhile, the ICC has struggled. Though the Rome Treaty was, as of January 2025, ratified by 125, and through 2014, more than $1 billion was spent on the Court, only a few trials have been completed.[229] Despite the fact that as of 2017, the ICC had secured only four convictions from its first 32 trials, the ICC's chief prosecutor, Fatou Bensouda, called this surprising statistic "fair," citing the "complex nature of the investigation" and the length of time of the proceedings.[230] Another problem is focus. Most of the ICC's investigations target Africa, putting "the ICC's reputation as a truly international tribunal [into] question."[231] In March 2016, a chamber of the ICC issued only the fourth judgment of the Court. In the *Bemba* case, a political and military leader in the Democratic Republic of the Congo was convicted of war crimes—murder, rape, and pillage—committed by his subordinates

[226] U.S. Notification of Intent Not to Become a Party to the Rome Statute, 96 *American Journal of International Law* 724 (2002).

[227] Galbraith, Contemporary Practice of the United States Relating to International Law, 113 *American Journal of International Law* 600, 625 (2019).

[228] Verma, Allies Balk at U.S. Sanctions on Rights Lawyer, *N.Y. Times*, Oct. 19, 2020.

[229] Kaye, Who's Afraid of the International Criminal Court?, *Foreign Affairs* (May/June 2011), at 1, 2; https://treaties.un.org (Feb. 18, 2019); ICC Assembly of States Parties, Updated Forecast of the Court on Its Budget Implementation for 2014, ICC-ASP/13/42 (Dec. 5, 2014); M.W. Janis, J.E. Noyes & L. N. Sadat, *International Law Cases and Commentary 7th ed.* 567 (2025).

[230] The International Criminal Count on Trial: A Conversation with Fatou Bensouda, 96 *Foreign Affairs*, No. 1, at 48, 50 (2015).

[231] Ibid. For a procedural decision, well short of a judgment, of the ICC, see Situation in the Democratic Republic of the Congo in the Case of the Prosecutor v. Thomas Lubanga Dyilo, Decision on the Confirmation of Charges, International Criminal Court, Pre-Trial Chamber I, ICC-01/04-01/06, Jan. 29, 2007.

in 2002 and 2003.[232] Not long after, in September 2016, in *Al Mahdi*, the Court convicted the leader of an armed group in Mali for war crimes—intentionally attacking protected cultural objects.[233] Given the weakness of the African regional human rights systems, perhaps the African focus of the ICC makes sense, but with ten out of eleven ongoing ICC proceedings involving Africa, there has been a movement among African governments to abandon the ICC.[234]

As of February 2019, there were just seven judgments of the ICC, not a good total for almost 20 years.[235] The ICC's questionable record seems to be one of the reasons why the ICC judges have not received the higher pay they have demanded.[236] Where the ICC has been most active, in Africa, it is criticized for failing to deal with the worst offenders and then for failing to secure convictions when it does act.[237] Now that it tries to broaden its geographical reach with possible suits against the United Kingdom, Israel, Saudi Arabia, and the United States, the ICC risks undermining its Western support.[238] Long frozen in theory, the ICC now shivers in practice.

[232] McDermott, Prosecutor v. Bemba, Judgment Pursuant to Article 74 of the Statute, International Criminal Court, March 21, 2016, 110 *American Journal of International Law* 526 (2016).

[233] Bishop-Burney, Prosecutor v. Ahmad Al Faqi Al Mahdi, International Criminal Court, Trial Chambers, September 27, 2016, 111 *American Journal of International Law* 126 (2017).

[234] Magliveras, The Withdrawal of the African States from the ICC: Good, Bad or Irrelevant, 66 *Netherlands International Law Review* 419, 421, 423 (2019). See Ssekandi & Tesfay, Engendered Discontent: The International Criminal Court in Africa, 18 *Georgetown Journal of International Affairs* 77 (2017).

[235] www.icc-cpi.int/pages/cases.aspx (Feb. 24, 2019).

[236] Simons, At The Hague, Judges Wrangle Over Awkward Questions About Their Paychecks, *N.Y. Times*, Jan. 21, 2019, at A6.

[237] The International Criminal Court: A Day of Reckoning Nears, *The Economist*, Feb. 15, 2020, at 42; International Law and Disorder: The World's Rules-Based Order is Cracking, *The Economist*, Jan. 2, 2024, at 49.

[238] Ibid. See La Foigia & Wang, Saudi Strikes in Yemen Put U.S. at Risk of War Crime Charges, *N.Y. Times*, Sept. 17, 2020, at 1, 12-13.

CHAPTER 9

International Law and the International Economy

The realm of international economic relations constitutes the principal field of international affairs where legal rules and processes are effectively employed. In practice, most lawyers who style themselves *international lawyers* do so because of some link to one or another form of international economic activity. It has long been recognized that this is a field where international rules apply to nationals, including corporations, as well as to nations. [See Chapter 8.] International economic law is vast, and to fully describe its rules and process is well beyond this book's introductory ambit. Yet to leave international economic law untouched would be to create a faulty impression of the modern character of international law as a whole. As a way of avoiding either extreme, therefore, this chapter briefly introduces, first, some parts of the law relating to international commerce and trade, then, second and third, two especially interesting and important forms of modern international economic legal process: the European Union and international commercial arbitration.

A. THE TRANSNATIONAL LAW OF COMMERCE AND TRADE

States have long used their laws and authority as means to affect the natural course of international trade. Nowadays, most every country has a wide variety of legal rules especially designed to facilitate or frustrate the international flow of goods, services, labor, and capital. Furthermore, many a municipal economic law not particularly designed for an international purpose is often nonetheless applied to international transactions.

Since national laws are normally drafted with a state's own economic, social, and political interests in mind, it is not unusual for the application of any country's laws to an international economic transaction to conflict with the interests of other states and, sometimes, with the interests of the international economy in general. There is, therefore, a large body of international economic law and organization devoted to the moderation and coordination of the particular international economic regulatory activities of the many states, a problem area also addressed by international conflict of laws, the topic of Chapter 10.

Altogether, national and international laws and processes relating to the international economy are sometimes styled "transnational law," a term employed in 1956 by the American jurist Philip Jessup to encompass "all law which regulates actions or events that transcend national frontiers."[1] Although Jessup intended this new term to apply to a broad spectrum of international activities, in practice "transnational law" has been used most often and helpfully in describing the laws that have to do with "international business transactions," itself a term frequently employed to cover the same field.[2]

1. *International Commercial Law*

The immense and ordinary flow of international commerce is a distinguishing feature of the modern world: U.S. wheat sold to Russia; Japanese automobiles sold to the United States; British whiskey sold to Japan; Costa Rican coffee sold to Britain; Saudi Arabian oil sold to Costa Rica; Russian gold sold to Saudi Arabia. Each day these and countless

[1] P. Jessup, *Transnational Law* 2 (1956). On Jessup, see Schacter, Philip Jessup's Life and Ideals, 80 *American Journal of International Law* 878 (1986).

[2] On the one hand: D.F. Vagts, W.S. Dodge, H. Buxbaum & H.H. Koh, *Transnational Business Problems* (7th ed. 2024); and M.W. Dowdle, *Transnational Law: A Framework for Analysis* (2022). On the other hand: D.C.K. Chow & T.J. Schoenbaum, *International Business Transactions* (4th ed. 2020); and R.H. Folsom, M. Van Alstine, M. Ramsey & M.P. Schaefer, *International Business Transactions* (14th ed. 2024).

other international sales transactions are affected by one or another form of merchant's contract providing, at least, for the quantity and quality of goods to be supplied and for the price to be paid. Such contractual arrangements for the international sale of goods are set in a legal context we know generally as international or transnational commercial law, itself a blend of national and international rules.

Modern international commercial law is rooted in the ancient *lex mercatoria*, the "law merchant," a medieval body of customary legal rules that was used in international commercial transactions to supplement the then often incomplete commercial law of states. The law merchant developed in the Italian city-states in the eleventh and twelfth centuries and then spread to other principal trading centers.[3] Before the rise of the modern state system, the *lex mercatoria* was common at least to the nations of Europe.[4] Frequently, *lex mercatoria* was applied in the merchants' own courts, known in England as "piepowder courts," which operated rather along the lines of modern private international arbitration.[5] By 1622, an English author could write of "a customary Law approved by the authoritie of all Kingdomes and Commonweales and not a Law established by the Soveraigntie of any Prince."[6]

However, it would go too far to suppose that the medieval *lex mercatoria* has somehow been passed down *en bloc* to the modern international commercial world.[7] This would be unlikely for no other reason than that the old *lex mercatoria* was never set forth in anything like a uniform or codified way. Alongside some settled rules were simply a number of local arrangements whereby merchants could settle their

[3] Berman, The Law of International Commercial Transactions, 2 *Emory Journal of International Dispute Resolution* 235 (1988); Von Caemmerer, The Influence of the Law of International Trade on the Development and Character of the Commercial Law in the Civil Law Countries, *The Sources of the Law of International Trade* 88 (Schmitthoff ed. 1964) [hereinafter cited as "Von Caemmerer"].

[4] F. Pollock & F.W. Maitland, 1 *The History of English Law* 467 (Milsom 2d ed. 1968).

[5] Davis, Market Courts and *Lex Mercatoria* in Late Medieval England, in *Medieval Merchants and Money: Essays in Honour of James L. Bolton* 271 (Allen & Davies eds. 2016); Hurst, Wanted - An International Law of Piepowder, 6 *British Yearbook of International Law* 61 (1925).

[6] Honnold, The Influence of the Law of International Trade on the Development and Character of English and American Commercial Law, *The Sources of the Law of International Trade* 70-71 (Schmitthoff ed. 1964) [hereinafter cited as "Honnold"].

[7] F. De Ly, *International Business Law and* Lex Mercatoria 15-20 (1992).

own disputes with their own law and without the interference of the King or other civil authorities.[8]

The medieval *lex mercatoria* was at first absorbed and then largely replaced by national commercial law, but vestiges of it still remain. For example, municipal courts sometimes defer to longstanding rules of international commerce, rules that may set somewhat different standards than those prescribed by national laws. In a well-known English case, a judge in the House of Lords ruled "that delivery of the bill of lading when the goods are at sea can be treated as delivery of the goods themselves, this law being so old that I think it is quite unnecessary to refer to authority for it."[9]

A modern *lex mercatoria* is also said by some to be evidenced by the occasional inclination of courts and arbitral tribunals, municipal and international, to reciprocally rely on each other's decisions so as to create a consistent pattern of international commercial jurisprudence. For example, it may be that consistent norms generated by International Chamber of Commerce arbitration have helped formulate a common law of international business transactions. Moreover, it seems that international arbitrators are especially keen to rely on the new *lex mercatoria*, at least in part because it gives them added discretion and relieves them of having to rely overly on foreign law with which they may be unfamiliar.[10]

During the seventeenth and eighteenth centuries, the newly emerging sovereign states of Europe subjected more and more commercial litigation to the jurisdiction of their national courts. At first, though the courts might be national, the law applied was often international.[11] As an English judge held in 1666, "the law of merchants is the law of the land, and the custome is good enough generally for any man, without naming him merchant."[12] In the nineteenth century, and as states drafted their own national commercial codes, positivist legal doctrine rejected the very possibility of an international *lex mercatoria*. [See Chapter 8.] Positivists postulated that all commercial contracts, even international commercial contracts, were necessarily

[8] Honnold, supra, at 71.

[9] E. Clemens Horst Company v. Biddell Brothers, [1912] A.C. 18, 22-23.

[10] G. Cuniberti, Three Theories of *Lex Mercatoria*, 52 *Columbia Journal of Transnational Law* 369, 410-430 (2014).

[11] Von Caemmerer, supra, at 88-90.

[12] Woodward v. Rowe, 2 Keb. 132, 84 Eng. Rep. 84 (1666).

governed by national, not international, rules. As the Permanent Court of International Justice opined in the *Serbian Loans* case, "Any contract which is not a contract between States in their capacity as subjects of international law is based on the municipal law of some state."[13]

By now, most every country has its own body of commercial rules, for example, the Uniform Commercial Code in the United States, the Sale of Goods Act in Great Britain, and the Code de Commerce in France. Though there are a wide variety of different commercial laws, there are some consistent patterns. As one observer noted, "it is a remarkable fact . . . that the law of international trade shows a striking similarity in all national legal systems."[14] In many transactions touching on two states, it may indeed be possible to work out a body of "transnational legal principles underlying both of the domestic systems involved."[15]

Nonetheless, despite the vital role that municipal commercial law plays,[16] it is often worthwhile for parties involved in international commercial transactions to turn to transnational commercial law. This can be sorted into three types: common international standards, model laws, and treaties.[17] An example of international standards is the incorporation by reference of uniform terms into international sales contracts, for example, the so-called Incoterms, for such concepts as "CIF" ("Cost, Insurance, and Freight") and "FOB" ("Free on Board").[18] Another example of international standards are the U.N. Guiding Principles on Business and Human Rights, which, according to some, have added a "significant human rights punch to private law of contracts, the new *lex mercatoria*, whose global reach and enforceability can

[13] 1929 P.C.I.J. Reports, ser. A, nos. 20-21, at 41.

[14] Schmitthoff, The Law of International Trade, Its Growth, Formulation and Operation, *The Sources of the Law of International Trade* 3 (Schmitthoff ed. 1964).

[15] E. Langen, *Transnational Commercial Law ix* (1973).

[16] Calliess, The Making of Transnational Contract Law, 14 *Indiana Journal of Global Legal Studies* 469 (2007); Commercial Law: Ruling the World: Globalisations Brings Business to London's Courts, and Creates New Competition, *The Economist*, Apr. 24, 2021, at 47.

[17] Cranston, Theorizing Transnational Commercial Law, 42 *Texas International Law Journal* 597, 598 (2007).

[18] International Chamber of Commerce, *Incoterms 2020* (2020 ed.); International Trade Administration, U.S. Department of Commerce, *Know Your Incoterms*, www.trade.gov/know-your-incoterms (accessed Dec. 19, 2025).

affect workplace conditions, the welfare of communities and environmental practices worldwide."[19]

As for model laws and international instruments, the League of Nations and the United Nations have long been active in efforts to unify the field.[20] The United Nations, for example, established the United Nations Commission on International Trade Law (UNCITRAL) to promote the progressive harmonization and unification of the law of private international trade.[21] UNCITRAL convened the 1980 Vienna Conference, which drafted the United Nations Convention on Contracts for the International Sale of Goods.[22] The Vienna Sales Convention generates useful rules compromising differences relating, *inter alia*, to the revocation and acceptance of offers and the passing of risk.[23] The Convention came into force in 1988 and, as of December 2025, had been ratified by 97 states, including Argentina, Australia, Austria, Belgium, Brazil, Canada, Chile, China, Egypt, Finland, France, Germany, Italy, Japan, Mexico, the Netherlands, Norway, Russia, Singapore, Spain, Sweden, Switzerland, Syria, the United States, and Zambia.[24] By now, the Vienna Sales Convention has generated an impressive body of case law and commentary.[25]

[19] Ruggie & Sherman, Adding Human Rights Punch to the New *Lex Mercatoria*: The Impact of the UN Guiding Principles on Business and Human Rights on Commercial Law Practice, 2015 *Journal of International Dispute Settlement* 455, 456.

[20] See David, The International Unification of Private Law, 2 *International Encyclopedia of Comparative* Law, ch. 5 at 124-126 (1971) [hereinafter cited as "David"].

[21] Id. at 125.

[22] T.I.A.S. (done at Vienna April 11, 1980; entered into force January 1, 1988); U.N. Doc. A/CONF. 97/18 (April 10, 1980); also published in 19 *International Legal Materials* 668 (1980) and *The Convention for the International Sale of Goods: A Handbook of Basic Materials* (Magraw & Kathrein eds. 2d ed. 1990) [hereinafter cited as "U.N. International Sales Convention"]; see M.J. Bonnell, The CISG, European Contract Law and the Development of a World Contract Law, 56 *American Journal of Comparative Law* 1 (2008).

[23] UN International Sales Convention, supra, arts. 16, 19, 66-70; for the rules of the Convention generally, see J. Honnold, *Uniform Law for International Sales Under the 1980 U.N. Convention* (2d ed. 1991); A.H. Kritzer, *Guide to Practical Applications of the United Nations Convention on Contracts for the International Sale of Goods* (1989).

[24] www.cisg-online.org (accessed on Dec. 18, 2025).

[25] See J.A. Spanogle & P. Winship, *International Sales Law* (2d ed. 2011); I. Schwenzer & P. Hachem, The CISG—Successes and Pitfalls, 57 *American Journal of Comparative Law* 457 (2009).

Besides UNCITRAL, a number of other international organizations, public and private, have been involved in unifying or codifying international private law. UNIDROIT, or as it is more formally known, the Rome International Institute for the Unification of Private Law, was established under the League of Nations in 1926. Based in Rome with 63 member states, UNIDROIT has made important contributions to the unification of international commercial law.[26] Its drafts on arbitration helped the United Nations develop the 1958 New York Convention on the Recognition and Enforcement of Foreign Arbitral Awards.[27] The Hague Conference on Private International Law has generated a number of important conventions,[28] for example, those relating to judicial procedures. [See Chapter 10.] The Hague Conference conventions have made influential impacts upon many municipal legal systems.[29] Also worthy of note is the work of the International Maritime Committee and the International Chamber of Commerce. All of these institutions contribute to the development of modern international commercial law, sometimes promoting harmonization by binding law, other times by generating soft law.[30] [See Chapter 3.]

2. *International Trade Law*

Besides providing laws to govern merchants' international contracts, states have long been in the business of using their legal systems to promote, protect, and facilitate and at times to frustrate international trade.[31] The most fundamental sort of national law regulating

[26] Novy, The Role of the UNIDROIT in the Unification of International Commercial Law with a Specific Focus on the Principles of International Commercial Contracts, 5 *Czech Yearbook of International Law* 341 (2014).

[27] David, supra, at 133-140. See Chapter 10.

[28] Id. at 141-150.

[29] See Symposium: The Hague Conference on Private International Law, 40 *Netherlands International Law Review* 1 (1993).

[30] H.D. Gabriel, The Advantages of Soft Law in International Commercial Law: The Role of Unidroit, Uncitral, and the Hague Conference, 34 *Brooklyn Journal of International Law* 655 (2009); R. Sorieul, E. Hatcher & C. Emery, Possible Future Work by Uncitral in the Field of Contract Law: Preliminary Thoughts from the Secretariat, 58 *Villanova Law Review* 491 (2013).

[31] A. Sykes, *The Law and Economics of International Trade Agreements* (2023); for some of the history see H. Pirenne, *Early Democracies in the Low Countries* 20-21, 68-69 (Saunders trans. 1963).

international trade is the tariff. Very simply, a tariff is a levy payable to a state at the place of import of a foreign good. It is a duty that not only swells state coffers (its traditional rationale), but also increases the cost of the foreign product to consumers and thereby stimulates sales of competing domestic products (the tariff's more usual modern justification). Besides tariffs, quotas (which restrict the quantity of foreign goods that may be imported) and other protectionist devices achieve the same aim of protecting national markets from foreign competition.

Although tariffs and similar protectionist measures help some domestic producers, they tend to hurt consumers who have to pay higher prices; they also hurt those sectors of the national economy, dependent upon exports, that face retaliatory measures taken by foreign states. Unmoderated, restrictive trade regulation may lead to beggar-thy-neighbor economic wars, such as the one that precipitated the Great Depression of the 1930s. So, though protectionist sentiment may be strong in any nation, the interests of producers threatened by foreign imports are often more than balanced by the interests of consumers and exporters who benefit by relatively free international trade.[32] So, for example, in the United States the share of gross domestic product composed of imports and exports more than doubled between 1970 and 2004 from 12 to 24 percent.[33] Exports alone reached a high of 13.7 percent of GDP in 2014, and, though they declined to 12.1 percent in 2018, still account for a significant share of U.S. production.[34]

To reduce the impact of protectionist trade measures, countries have long concluded international agreements providing reciprocally for the favorable treatment of each other's merchants. Indeed, one of the principal missions of the United States' first diplomats was to negotiate as many treaties of friendship, commerce, and navigation ("FCN treaties") as they could.[35] Some parts of one of these early agreements, the 1794 Jay Treaty of Amity, Commerce, and Navigation, originally negotiated with England, are still in force between the United States

[32] J.H. Jackson, W.J. Davey & A.O. Sykes, *Legal Problems of International Economic Relations* 7-37 (4th ed. 2002) [hereinafter cited as "Jackson, Davey & Sykes"].

[33] D.W. Drezner, *U.S. Trade Strategy* 4 (2006).

[34] https://fred.stlouisfed.org/series/B020RE1Q156NBEA (accessed June 8, 2023).

[35] D. Malone, *Jefferson and the Rights of Man* 3, 21-27 (1951).

and Canada. Its Article 14 illustrates the kinds of favorable treatment states have traditionally extended to each other:

> The people and Inhabitants of the Two Countries respectively, shall have liberty, freely and securely, and without hindrance and molestation, to come with their Ships and Cargoes to the Lands, Countries, Cities, Ports, Places and Rivers within the Dominions and Territories aforesaid, to enter into the same, to resort there, and to remain and reside there, without any limitation of Time: also to hire and possess, Houses and warehouses for the purposes of their Commerce; and generally the Merchants and Traders on each side, shall enjoy the most complete protection and Security for their Commerce; but subject always, as to what respects this article, to the Laws and Statutes of the Two Countries respectively.[36]

Though bilateral investment treaties have become much more common, the United States is still a party to more than 40 FCN treaties.[37] The one between the United States and France, for example, assures "full legal and judicial protection" to each other's nationals and companies, and extends "national treatment," that is, treatment "upon terms no less favorable than the treatment therein accorded, in like situations, to the nationals and companies, as the case may be, of such other High Contracting Party" with respect to "access to the courts of justice," "engaging in all types of commercial, industrial, financial and other activities for gain," "leasing, utilizing and occupying real property," and "obtaining and maintaining patents."[38] Similar sorts of protections are to be found nowadays not only in FCN treaties but also in bilateral investment treaties, so-called BITs.[39]

[36] 12 Bevans 13, 8 Stat. 116, T.S. No. 105 (signed at London November 19, 1794; entered into force October 28, 1795). For the Jay Treaty's impact on international adjudication, see Chapter 5.

[37] See U.S. Department of State, *Treaties in Force 2018* 1-520; Coyle & Yackee, Reviving the Treaty of Friendship: Enforcing International Investment Law in U.S. Courts, 49 *Arizona State Law Journal* 61 (2018).

[38] Convention of Establishment, Protocol, and Declaration Between the United States and France, arts. I, III(1), V(1), VII(1), VIII(1), XIV(1), 11 U.S.T. 2398, T.I.A.S. No. 4625, 401 U.N.T.S. 75 (signed at Paris November 25, 1959; entered into force December 21, 1960).

[39] Vandevelde, U.S. Bilateral Investment Treaties: The Second Wave, 14 *Michigan Journal of International Law* 621 (1993). See, e.g., the 1993 United States-Argentine

FCN treaties often figure in litigation before municipal courts. In Sumitomo Shoji America, Inc. v. Avagliano, the U.S. Supreme Court decided that a wholly owned U.S. subsidiary of a Japanese corporation was to be treated as a U.S. national and not as a Japanese national specially protected by the FCN treaty between the United States and Japan.[40] In Wickes v. Olympic Airways, the U.S. Sixth Circuit held that the FCN treaty between the United States and Greece did not permit a Greek government-owned airline to discriminate in favor of Greeks in its hiring for other than high-level managerial personnel.[41] In BG Group, PLC v. Republic of Argentina, the Supreme Court set a modest standard of judicial review for decisions made by international arbitral tribunals respecting investment treaties involving foreign sovereigns.[42]

Other sorts of bilateral treaties facilitate international economic cooperation of a more specific character. One commentator has usefully catalogued the varieties of non-FCN bilateral commercial treaties: sectoral trade agreements (such as those for specific commodities, payments, and clearing agreements); investment promotion and protection treaties; and industrial, scientific/technical, and economic cooperation agreements.[43]

Alongside the many bilateral economic treaties are the important multilateral agreements made in the setting of the General Agreement on Trade and Tariffs (GATT). Drafted first in Geneva in 1947, GATT was originally intended to be only one part of the structure of an International Trade Organization. The more comprehensive organization did not materialize until 1994 as the World Trade Organization (WTO).[44] This long left GATT alone, originally devised as a temporary agreement, as the principal international means for regulating

---

BIT in Nash, Contemporary Practice of the United States Relating to International Law: Bilateral Investment Treaties: United States–Argentina, 87 *American Journal of International Law* 433 (1993); New BIT Model Followed in New Treaty with Uruguay, 99 *American Journal of International Law* 259 (2005).

[40] 457 U.S. 176 (1982).

[41] 745 F.2d 363 (6th Cir. 1984).

[42] 572 U.S. 25 (2014).

[43] Herrmann, Commercial Treaties, 8 *Encyclopedia of Public International Law* 85, 89-91 (1985).

[44] Marrakesh Agreement Establishing the World Trade Organization (WTO) (done at Marrakesh April 15, 1994; entered into force January 1, 1995). The revised GATT is now an annex to the WTO Agreement.

international trade.[45] More than a single treaty, GATT is a complex set of more than 100 agreements revised on a periodic basis. Its aim is the moderation of national foreign trade policies to ensure, as much as possible, the unencumbered flow of international commerce. GATT includes schedules that, in great detail, set reciprocal tariffs and rules that restrain states from implementing non-tariff barriers. Today the GATT treaty functions within the context of the WTO.[46]

An important change from the old 1947 GATT-based international trade system to the 1994 WTO is the institution of a formal dispute settlement procedure pursuant to the WTO's Dispute Settlement Understanding agreement (DSU).[47] The creation of this legalistic process adds to the proliferation of international courts [see Chapter 5], the WTO panels and Appellate Body joining the international adjudicative ranks alongside the International Court of Justice [see Chapter 5], the International Tribunal for the Law of the Sea [see Chapter 7], the European Court of Human Rights [see Chapter 8], the Inter-American Court of Human Rights [see Chapter 8], the International Criminal Tribunals for the former Yugoslavia and Rwanda [see Chapter 8], the permanent International Criminal Court [see Chapter 8], and the European Court of Justice [see below].

As settling trade disputes became less diplomatic and more "judicialized," more cases found their way to the DSU. In the words of two commentators: "Nowhere else has international conflict resolution by judges emerged more forcefully or developed more rapidly" than in the WTO.[48] Other observers, counting 330 WTO dispute settlement

[45] Jackson, Davey & Sykes, supra, at 208-218.

[46] J.H. Jackson, *The World Trading System: Law and Policy of International Economic Relations* 58-59 (1997). For more on the negotiations leading to the WTO, see J.H. Jackson, *Restructuring the GATT System* (1990).

[47] Brewster, Shadow Unilateralism: Enforcing International Trade Law at the WTO, 30 *University of Pennsylvania Journal of International Law* 1133 (2009); Goldstein & Steinberg, The Law and Politics of International Trade Delegation: Negotiate or Litigate?: Effects of WTO Judicial Delegation on U.S. Trade Politics, 71 *Law & Contemporary Problems* 257 (2008).

[48] Esserman & Howse, The WTO on Trial, 82 *Foreign Affairs* (January/February 2003), at 130-131. See the annual review of WTO cases, beginning Bhala & Gantz, WTO Case Review 2000, 18 *Arizona Journal of International & Comparative Law* 1 (2001), to Bhala et al., WTO Case Review, 34 *Arizona Journal of International & Comparative Law* 281, 284-285 (2017).

cases in the decade since 1995, remark: "Members have, in general, implemented the recommendations and rulings made by the panels and by the Appellate Body, including the United States, the most frequent WTO litigant appearing as claimant 80 times and as respondent in 88 cases."[49] WTO case law made an important contribution to the general development of international law.[50]

U.S. participation in international trade dispute settlement has, however, greatly diminished in the last few years. The nationalistic economic policies of the Trump administration are very much at odds with the multilateral trading system established and supported by the United States since 1945.[51] The United States has refused to appoint new members to the WTO Appellate Body, effectively, as of 2020, halting the operations of that institution.[52] A similar shift characterizes the new international economic policy of Great Britain, another traditional supporter of free trade and multilateralism. The Conservative government of the United Kingdom has withdrawn from the European Union in a so-called Brexit, an act applauded by the Trump administration.[53] Whether populist opponents of economic multilateralism will succeed in reversing the course of the post-war international economic system is an important international political, as well as legal, question.

Nationalistic threats to arbitration of international trade disputes extend to regional trade organizations, such as those of the European Union discussed below, of the European Free Trade Association for

[49] Kreps & Arend, Why States Follow the Rules: Toward a Positional Theory of Adherence to International Legal Regimes, 16 *Duke Journal of Comparative & International Law* 331, 384 (2006). These numbers have increased. As of 2026, the United States has been a WTO claimant in 124 cases, a respondent in 165 cases, and a third party in 185 cases, https://www.wto.org/english/tratop_e/dispu_e/dispu_by_country_e.htm (April 14, 2026).

[50] Pauwelyn, The Role of Public International Law in the WTO: How Far Can We Go?, 95 *American Journal of International Law* 535 (2001); Cameron & Gray, Principles of International Law in the WTO Dispute Settlement Body, 50 *International & Comparative Law Quarterly* 248, 248-250 (2001).

[51] Chow, The Revival of Economic Nationalism and the Global Trading System, 40 *Cardozo Law Review* 2133 (2019).

[52] Galbraith, U.S. Refusal to Appoint Members Renders WTO Appellate Body Unable to Hear New Appeals, 114 *American Journal of International Law* 518 (2020); The Great Regression: The International Economic Order is Breaking Down. Critics Will Miss Globalization When It Is Gone, *The Economist*, May 11, 2024, at 13.

[53] McCorriston & Sheldon, Economic Nationalism: U.S. Trade Policy vs. Brexit, 14 *Ohio State Business Law Journal* 64 (2020).

some of the European states outside the European Union,[54] for the Trade Agreement among Canada, Mexico, and the United States,[55] and of the Caribbean Community and its Caribbean Court of Justice[56]—all have international dispute settlement mechanisms at risk. Admittedly, judicialization of trade disputes is not without its pitfalls, e.g., private corporate impairment of national sovereignty and governmental control.[57]

Within the broad ambit of the law of the international economy range a legion of subjects too vast to be any more than merely counted here. Each constitutes a legal specialty of considerable complexity, importance, and employment. There are, for example, international financial and securities law,[58] international antitrust law,[59] international tax law,[60] and international investment law.[61] Each of these specialties employ thousands of international lawyers.

[54] Fredericksen, The EFTA Court 15 Years On, 59 *International & Comparative Law Quarterly* 731 (2010)

[55] Brower, Investor-State Disputes Under NAFTA: The Empire Strikes Back, 40 *Columbia Journal of Transnational Law* 43 (2001); Hillman, Conflicts Between Dispute Settlement Mechanisms in Regional Trade Agreements and the WTO—What Should the WTO Do?, 42 *Cornell International Law Journal* 193 (2009).

[56] Barry, Caribbean Court of Justice Original Jurisdiction, 103 *American Journal of International Law* 561 (2009).

[57] Weisman, Trade Pact Seen as Door for Suits Against U.S., *N.Y. Times*, Mar. 26, 2015, at B1; Bird-Pollan, The Sovereign Right to Tax: How Bilateral Investment Treaties Threaten Sovereignty, 32 *Notre Dame Journal of Legal Ethics & Public Policy* 107 (2018).

[58] See H.S. Scott & A. Gelpern, *International Finance: Transactions, Policy, and Regulations* (24th ed. 2023); Stevenson & Williams, United States Legal Aspects of International Securities Transactions, 3 *A Lawyer's Guide to International Business Transactions* (Surrey & Wallace eds. 1980); The IMF: Nightmare on 19th Street: A Bastion of the Post-War Economic Order Faces an Almighty Identity Crisis, *The Economist*, Apr. 8, 2023, at 59).

[59] See *World Antitrust Law and Practice* (J.J. Garrett ed. 1997); B.E. Hawk, *United States, Common Market and International Antitrust: A Comparative Guide* (2d ed. 1986).

[60] See D.R. Tillinghast, *Tax Aspects of International Transactions* (2d ed. 1984); R. Mason, The Transformation of International Tax, 114 *American Journal of International Law* 353 (2020).

[61] See T.F. Clasen, *Foreign Trade and Investment: A Legal Guide* (1987); A.F. Lowenfeld, *International Private Investment* (2d ed. 1982).

B. EUROPEAN UNION LAW

One of the most developed forms of international economic law is that generated by European economic integration. This brief introduction to what is now known as the law of the European Union (EU) highlights a few aspects of the system that are useful for our general study of international law: the origin and nature of the EU, the nature and work of the European Court of Justice (ECJ), and whether EU law is really a form of international law at all.

1. *The European Union*

The very nomenclature is notoriously confusing. What was originally the "European Economic Community" (EEC) and often called the "European Common Market" was for a time the "European Communities," then became the "European Community," and is now the "European Union."[62] The problem is due in some measure to the EU's "highly convoluted structure," which has been gracefully termed "more of a *bricoleur's* amateurism than a brick layer's strive for perfection and attention to detail."[63] The confusion of the nomenclature is made only worse when we remember that there is yet another international institutional structure for Europe, the Council of Europe, with its own Assembly, Commission, and Court. [See Chapter 8.]

The European Economic Community, a regional international organization established by the Treaty of Rome of March 25, 1957,[64] an agreement that came into force on January 1, 1958, included six original member states: Belgium, France, the Federal Republic of Germany,

[62] See J.D. Dinnage & J.F. Murphy, *The Constitutional Law of the European Union* 3, https://european-union.europa.eu (accessed June 8, 2023).

[63] Curtin, The Constitutional Structure of the Union: A Europe of Bits and Pieces, 30 *Common Market Law Review* 17, 22-26 (1993).

[64] Treaty Establishing the European Economic Community, U.K.T.S. 15 (1979) (with authoritative English language text), 298 U.N.T.S. 11 (concluded at Rome March 25, 1957; entered into force January 1, 1958 as amended; not in force for the United States). The 1957 EEC Treaty is the second of eight foundational treaties spanning 50 years from the European Coal and Steel Community Treaty in 1951, to the Treaty of Lisbon of 2007, which constitute today's European Union.

Italy, Luxembourg, and the Netherlands. For many years called the "Common Market" or simply "the Six," on July 1, 1967, the EEC was formally merged with the European Coal and Steel Community and the European Atomic Energy Community into what is now termed the European Community.[65] The denomination "the Six" is by now long out of date inasmuch as Denmark, Ireland, and the United Kingdom joined the Community in 1973, Greece in 1981, Spain and Portugal in 1986, Austria, Finland, and Sweden in 1995, Cyprus, Czech Republic, Estonia, Hungary, Latvia, Lithuania, Malta, Poland, Slovakia, and Slovenia in 2004, Bulgaria and Romania in 2007, and Croatia in 2013. In all, there were 28 EU member states as of 2020, when the United Kingdom chose to leave in its Brexit, leaving 27 member states. However, other countries, including Turkey and many Central and Eastern European states formerly part of the Soviet bloc, may someday join and further swell the number of member states.

The aspirations for European unity that helped prompt the organization of the Council of Europe in 1949 [see Chapter 8] provided much the same stimulus to the formation of the Common Market eight years later. To a considerable extent, the EEC can be viewed as a second try at European integration after it became plain that the Council of Europe (which included the United Kingdom, then as now hesitant about real and effective European integration) was not destined to become an effective vehicle for achieving European union. The idea behind the EEC was to start again, this time proceeding with a limited membership and a restricted agenda. The functional theory of European integration subscribed to by many of the founders of the Common Market hypothesized that if European economic integration could first be achieved, then political and military union would likely follow.

The founders of the EEC looked to several historical precedents, especially the experiences of the United States and Germany, where economic integration marched hand in hand with political union. The founders were also motivated by political considerations of the day, especially desires to bring peace to Europe and especially to end decades of bloody antagonism between France and Germany,[66] provide a common front against Soviet expansion in Europe, and offer a new

[65] J.-V. Louis, *The Community Legal Order* 9 (1980) [hereinafter cited as "Louis"].

[66] Monnet, A Ferment of Change, *The Common Market: Progress and Controversy* 40, 41-45 (Krause ed. 1964); The EU: 1713 Edition: How the Ideas of an 18th-Century French Abbott Still Dominate the EU Today, *The Economist*, Aug. 21, 2021, at p. 44.

global role for Western Europe after the dissolution of Europe's colonial empires.[67] Furthermore, there was the straightforward economic goal of reaping the benefits of a more efficient European-wide market for goods and services, labor, and capital. Set against all these potential gains were several fears: that the Common Market would make too great an inroad into national sovereign powers, that the new system would be dominated by one or the other of Germany or France, that the Soviet Union would feel threatened, and that the neutral states of Europe, especially Austria and Finland, would be politically and economically isolated by its establishment.

The EEC Treaty reflected a balancing of these hopes and fears. In Article 2, the Treaty set forth basic economic, political, and social objectives, promoting the EU's four fundamental freedoms—the free movement of goods, people, capital, and services:[68]

> The Community shall have as its task, by establishing a common market and an economic and monetary union and by implementing common policies . . . to promote throughout the Community a harmonious, balanced and sustainable development of economic activities, a high level of employment and of social protection, equality between men and women, sustainable and non-inflationary growth, a high degree of competitiveness and convergence of economic performance, a high level of protection and improvement of the quality of the environment, the raising of the standard of living and quality of life, and economic and social cohesion and solidarity among Member States.[69]

As well as setting out substantive international economic law, the EU's treaties have a constitutional role and establish Community institutions, principally four bodies: the Parliament, the Council, the Commission, and the Court of Justice. The Parliament consists "of representatives of the peoples of the States brought together in the Community" and has been, since 1979, a directly elected parliamentary body. As of 2025, there were 720 elected members, the largest contingents, 96 and 81, from Germany and France, the smallest, only six, from Cyprus, Malta, and Luxembourg.

[67] E. Benoit, *Europe at Sixes and Sevens* 1-4 (1961).
[68] C. Barnard, *The Substantive Law of the EU: The Four Freedoms* (6th ed. 2019).
[69] EEC Treaty, supra, art. 2.

B. European Union Law

The Council consists of representatives of the sovereign states party to the Union and is principally responsible for making Community law in the form of regulations, directives, and decisions. In many cases it operates pursuant to a qualified majority. Since 2014, any proposal made by the Commission or the EU's High Representative for Foreign Affairs and Security to the Council must have the support of 55 percent of member states and the member states in favor must represent at least 65 percent of the total EU population.[70] The Commission, based in Brussels, is the executive body of the Union and is composed of 27 members and a staff of over 32,000, making it one of the largest international bureaucracies in the world.[71] The EU's European Investment Bank is "the biggest multilateral financial institution in the world" with 3,400 on its Luxembourg-based staff.[72]

Whether or not the European Union moves much beyond its present mostly economic focus remains open to doubt. The EU's proposed Constitutional Treaty of 2004 was abandoned after it was rejected by public referenda in France and the Netherlands.[73] As one commentator observed, the "Constitution's rejection by founding members of the EU does not in itself spell the end of the union, but it both reflects and deepens a profound crisis in the process of European unification."[74] On December 1, 2009, the Treaty of Lisbon formally replaced the European Community with the European Union and the Treaty establishing the European Community became the Treaty on the Functioning of the European Union.[75] The Treaty of Lisbon created new posts: a President of the European Council and a High Representative of the Union for Foreign Affairs and Security Policy.[76] Despite the Lisbon Treaty, there

[70] www.eur-lex.europa.eu/summary/glossary/qualified_majority.html (June 8, 2023).

[71] www.europa.eu (Sept. 26, 2020).

[72] www.eib.org/en/index.htm (June 8, 2023).

[73] Treaty Establishing a Constitution for Europe, [2004] OJ C316/1. See P. Craig & G. de Burca, *E.U. Law: Text, Cases, and Materials* 31-36 (4th ed. 2008) [hereinafter cited as "Craig & de Burca"].

[74] Cohen-Tangui, The End of Europe?, 84 *Foreign Affairs* 55 (2005).

[75] General Secretariat of the Council of the EU, Information Note: Treaty of Lisbon, www.europa.eu (June 9, 2011).

[76] Ibid.

was a fierce debate about the fate of the EU as it faced political and economic crises in the midst of a global recession.[77]

Nowhere, perhaps, has there been more skepticism about the European Union than in the United Kingdom, always deeply divided about the wisdom of the "European Project." As noted above, British obstructionism after the foundation of the Council of Europe in 1949 led six core nations—France, Germany, Italy, the Netherlands, Belgium, and Luxembourg—to found the British-free European Coal and Steel Community in 1951, and the European Economic Community in 1957, in order to promote more decisive European integration. By the 1960s, many in Great Britain concluded that British hopes of prospering without economically integrating with Europe were less likely than before. In the nineteenth century, Great Britain was probably the richest nation, its wealth generated by a huge colonial empire including India, Ireland, Canada, the British Caribbean, South Africa, British West and East Africa, Singapore, Hong Kong, Malaysia, Australia, and New Zealand.[78] The British Empire is now mostly all lost and with it much of the foundation for British economic well-being. Joining with Europe was the great hope of some. However, two attempts by Great Britain in 1963 and 1967 to join the EEC were both vetoed by France's Charles de Gaulle, who feared that Britain would never be a reliable partner. Once de Gaulle left office, British European hopes were realized and the United Kingdom finally joined the EEC in 1973. For more than 40 years, the British, albeit never as enthusiastic as most other Europeans, were important participants in the Common Market/EU.[79]

However, considerable British opposition to Europe remained, nourished in part by nostalgia for Britain's lost empire and also by populist concern about Britain's faltering greatness and threats to its sovereignty. In 2013, British prime minister David Cameron promised a popular referendum on the European Union in an attempt to close the breach in his Conservative Party between business interests, largely pro-EU, and populist groups, largely anti-EU. When the referendum was held in 2016, British participation in the EU was voted down, roughly

[77] Farrell & Quiggin, How to Save the Euro and the EU, 90 *Foreign Affairs* 96 (2011).

[78] *The Oxford History of the British Empire: The Nineteenth Century* (A. Porter ed. 1999).

[79] An immense English-language literature on EU law emerged. One of the classic teaching texts is Craig & de Burca, supra.

by a 52 to 48 margin.[80] After almost four years of parliamentary and diplomatic haggling, the new Conservative British prime minister, Boris Johnson, finally had legislation in hand to officially withdraw the United Kingdom from the European Union ("Brexit") on February 1, 2020. Brexit has, of course, very important political and economic implications for Great Britain and for Europe, but it also opened up many unanswered questions of international law, as Britain needed to negotiate hundreds of trade agreements.[81] Of these, the most important will be a new agreement with the EU. Though many uncertainties lie ahead, "one thing is certain: Brexit and its aftermath will produce more, rather than less, international law."[82]

2. *The European Court of Justice*

For our purposes the most important institution of the Community is the European Court of Justice (the Court), since 2009, along with the General Court (EGC), part of the Court of Justice of the European Union. The Court was given its mandate in Article 220: to "ensure that in the interpretation and application of this Treaty the law is observed,"[83] an injunction that the Court has interpreted to refer not only to EU law, but to general principles of law and international law as well.[84]

The Court, which sits in Luxembourg, is composed of 27 judges, one from each state belonging to the Community; and is assisted by 11 advocates-general.[85] The role of the advocates-general may be more familiar to civil than to common lawyers; generally, the advocates-general

[80] A. Glencross, *Why the UK Voted for Brexit: David Cameron's Great Miscalculation* (2016).

[81] Larik, Brexit, the EU-UK Withdrawal Agreement, and Global Treaty (Re-) Negotiations, 114 *American Journal of International Law* 443 (2020).

[82] Id. at 462. Under the new Labour government, the UK has been inching back to the European Union. One step is a new agreement in 2025 re-instating the student exchange program, Erasmus. Young People from All Backgrounds to Get Opportunity to Study Abroad as UK-EU Deal Unlocks Erasmus, www.gov.uk (Dec. 17, 2025), (accessed Dec. 22, 2025).

[83] EC Treaty, supra, art. 220 (ex 164).

[84] D. Wyatt & A. Dashwood, *The Substantive Law of the EEC* 47-52 (1980).

[85] www.europa.eu/european-union/about-eu/institutions-bodies/court-justice_en (accessed Dec. 22, 2025).

act as a sort of *amicus*, giving friendly non-partisan advice to the Court. The opinions of the advocates-general are usually printed alongside the judgments and opinions of the Court and may be of useful persuasive value in understanding the law of the Community.

The jurisdiction of the European Court of Justice, though complex, is perhaps most easily understood by assigning its various aspects to three heads: cases brought by states, cases brought by EU institutions, and cases involving private litigants. First, states may come to the Court to complain about breaches of the Treaty of Rome allegedly made either by other states or by EU institutions. Jurisdiction for state-versus-state disputes was found in Articles 227 and 239:

> A Member State which considers that another Member State has failed to fulfil an obligation under this Treaty may bring the matter before the Court of Justice.[86]
>
> The Court of Justice shall have jurisdiction in any dispute between Member States which relates to the subject matter of this Treaty if the dispute is submitted to it under a special agreement between the parties.[87]

Article 230 provided for cases brought by states against the EU's institutions:

> The Court of Justice shall review the legality of acts adopted jointly by the European Parliament and the Council, of acts of the Council, of the Commission and of the ECB, other than recommendations or opinions, and of acts of the European Parliament intended to produce legal effects vis-à-vis third parties.[88]

Second, as Article 230 above provided, the institutions of the EU were also permitted to go to the Court to complain about each other's acts. In addition, pursuant to Article 226: The Court may hear complaints from the Commission when the Commission considers "that a Member State has failed to fulfill an obligation under [the] Treaty."[89]

Third, and most interesting among the heads of jurisdiction of the Luxembourg Court, was the Court's jurisdiction with respect to cases

[86] EC Treaty, supra, art. 227 (ex 170).
[87] Id., art. 239 (ex 170).
[88] Id., art. 230 (ex 173).
[89] Id., art. 226 (ex 169).

brought by or against private parties, the kind of jurisdiction that is forbidden to the International Court of Justice, but has proved so popular for the European Court of Human Rights. Article 226 also provided for litigation initiated by individuals and corporations.

Private parties could also be involved in litigation referred to the European Court of Justice for its advisory opinion pursuant to the Treaty of Rome's Article 234:

> The Court of Justice shall have jurisdiction to give preliminary rulings concerning:
>
> (a) the interpretation of this Treaty;
>
> (b) the validity and interpretation of acts of the institutions of the Community and of the ECB;
>
> (c) the interpretation of the statutes of bodies established by an act of the Council, where those statutes so provide.
>
> Where such a question is raised before any court or tribunal of a Member State, that court or tribunal may, if it considers that a decision on the question is necessary to enable it to give judgment, request the Court of Justice to give a ruling thereon.
>
> Where any such question is raised in a case pending before a court or tribunal of a Member State, against whose decision there is no judicial remedy under national law, that court or tribunal shall bring the matter before the Court of Justice.[90]

Proposals had long been made that an EU court of first instance be created to reduce the workload of the European Court of Justice, especially with regard to staff cases; indeed, the establishment of just such a lower first instance court was approved in principle as early as 1974.[91] However, not until 1988 was what became the EGC finally approved, and only in 1989 did the EGC commence its proceedings.[92] There must be at least two EGC judges from each of the 27 member states.[93] The EGC's jurisdiction extends to (1) direct actions brought by natural or legal persons against acts of or failures to act by Community institutions, (2) actions by member states against the Commission, (3) acts by

[90] Id., art. 234 (ex 177).

[91] L.N. Brown & F.G. Jacobs, *The Court of Justice of the European Communities* 64-69 (3d ed. 1989).

[92] J. Steiner, *Textbook on EEC Law* 19 (3d ed. 1992).

[93] https://curia.europa.eu (June 23, 2020).

member states against the Council respecting state aid and dumping, (4) actions for compensation for damages caused by the Community, (5) actions based on Community contracts explicitly vesting jurisdiction in the CFI, (6) actions respecting Community intellectual property, and (7) disputes between the institutions of the European Union and their staff concerning employment relations and the social security system. EGC decisions generally may be appealed to the ECJ.[94]

The contrast between the actual practice of the European Court of Justice and the state-oriented posture of international law positivist doctrine is striking. [See Chapter 8.] The European Court of Justice is a busy international court. In terms of its case load, it is far more active than the International Court of Justice. [See Chapter 5.] On a regular basis, it hears cases brought by and involving private litigants and determines the rights and obligations of private parties based on the regional international legal rules embodied in the Treaty of Rome and promulgated by the EU's political and administrative organs. Furthermore, as is examined below, private parties may rely on these provisions of regional international law in national as well as in international litigation. There is probably no part of international law so routinely integrated with domestic law as European economic law is with the municipal law of the EU member states.

A landmark case, early in ECJ jurisprudence, that helped establish the place of private litigants before the European Court was Van Gend en Loos v. Nederlandse Tariefcommissie.[95] A Dutch company, Van Gend, imported a plastic product from the Federal Republic of Germany into the Netherlands in 1960, two years after the Treaty of Rome had come into force. Although the product had been subject to a three percent import duty in 1958, because of a reclassification by Dutch authorities an eight percent duty was newly applied in 1960. The company complained that the imposition of this higher duty violated Article 12 of the EC Treaty, which provides: "Member States shall refrain from introducing between themselves any new customs duties on imports or exports or any charges having equivalent effect, and from increasing those which they already apply in their trade with each other."

[94] Craig & de Burca, supra, at 68-69.
[95] [1963] 2 *Common Market Law Reports* 105.

Van Gend unsuccessfully appealed the application of the higher duty to a Dutch Inspector of Import and Excise Duties and then appealed to the Netherlands Tariff Court. The Tariff Court, before deciding the case, used its permissive power under what is now Article 234 of the Treaty of Rome to ask a preliminary question: "Whether Article 12 of the E.E.C. Treaty has an effect within the territory of a member-State, in other words, whether on the basis of this Article, citizens of the member-States can enforce individual rights which the court of the member-State should protect."[96] The ECJ's answer went to the heart of two of the central issues of international law generally and of EU law in particular: How and when are rules of international law incorporated into municipal law? How and when may individuals rely on international legal rules? [See Chapter 4.] The ECJ used the *Van Gend* case as the occasion for announcing legal principles broadly supporting the direct incorporation of EU law into the municipal legal systems of the member states and the direct availability of these rules to private parties. In a widely cited passage, the Court held as follows:

> [T]he Community constitutes a new legal order in international law, for whose benefit the States have limited their sovereign rights, albeit within limited fields, and the subjects of which comprise not only the member-States but also their nationals. Community law, therefore, apart from legislation by the member-States, not only imposes obligations on individuals but also confers on them legal rights.[97]

Thus, EU law may be self-executing or, as is sometimes the expression in European economic law, have "direct effect." [For the doctrine of self-execution in U.S. law, see Chapter 4.] EU law may in appropriate circumstances be relied upon by individuals and by corporations in domestic litigation even though the national legislature may not have enacted the rule into national law. So, for example, in *Van Gend* the Court held:

> The text of Article 12 sets out a clear and unconditional prohibition, which is not a duty to act but a duty not to act. This duty is imposed without any power in the States to subordinate its application to a positive act of internal law. The prohibition is perfectly suited by its nature to

[96] Id. at 108.
[97] Id. at 129.

> produce direct effects in the legal relations between the member-States and their citizens.
>
> The carrying out of Article 12 does not require legislative intervention by the States. The fact that the Article designates the member-States as subject to the duty to abstain does not imply that their nationals may not be the beneficiaries of the duty.[98]

Given that EU law may be self-executing and have direct effect within national legal systems, questions then arise as to the exact relation between EU law and national law. The usual proposition in international law is that the applicable rules concerning the incorporation of international law into municipal law and those concerning the relation between international law and municipal law are norms of national constitutional law. [See Chapter 4.] Thus, although countries may be bound at a state-to-state level by rules of international law, these self-same international legal rules are effective in municipal courts only when so authorized by national constitutional provisions.

A somewhat different result, however, obtains with respect to European economic law. This difference was made plain in the ECJ's judgment in Costa v. Ente Nazionale per l'Energia Elettrica.[99] The *Costa* case was brought to an Italian municipal court by a shareholder of a private electricity company that had been nationalized by the Italian government. The shareholder, Costa, refused to pay a small electricity bill charged by the public successor to the nationalized private company. Among the many reasons the shareholder gave in defending his refusal to pay, was that the Italian nationalization violated several provisions of the Treaty of Rome. The trial judge referred several questions both to the Italian Constitutional Court and, in accordance with what is now Article 234, to the European Court of Justice.

The opinion of the Italian Constitutional Court issued first. It declared that according to Italian constitutional law, treaty obligations, including obligations under the EEC treaty, had the same status as enactments of the Italian legislature. The constitutional rule in Italy was that the treaty or enactment last in time prevailed in case of a conflict. The Italian Constitutional Court held that since the Italian nationalization was subsequent in time to the Treaty of Rome, there was no point in referring the case to the European Court of Justice, since the

[98] Id. at 130.

[99] [1964] *Common Market Law Reports* 425.

subsequent Italian law must take precedence in an Italian court regardless of Italy's international obligations.[100]

Next came the holding of the ECJ, which refused to accept the Italian court's reasoning. To do so would mean that the direct effect of EU law would be different in different countries: What might have direct effect in Germany because of a provision of German constitutional law might not have direct effect in Italy because of different provisions in Italian constitutional law. In *Costa* the ECJ restated the propositions of *Van Gend* respecting the direct effect of the Treaty of Rome and went further to prescribe a certain supremacy for EU law:

> As opposed to other international treaties, the Treaty instituting the EEC has created its own order which was integrated with the national order of the member-States the moment the Treaty came into force; as such, it is binding upon them. In fact, by creating a Community of unlimited duration, having its own institutions, its own personality and its own capacity in law, apart from having international standing and more particularly, real powers resulting from a limitation of competence or a transfer of powers from the States to the Community, the member-States, albeit within limited spheres, have restricted their sovereign rights and created a body of law applicable both to their nationals and to themselves. The reception, within the laws of each member-State, of provisions having a Community source, and more particularly of the terms and of the spirit of the Treaty, has as a corollary, the impossibility, for the member-State, to give preference to a unilateral and subsequent measure against a legal order accepted by them on a basis of reciprocity.[101]

The importance of the ECJ's position in cases like *Van Gend* and *Costa* is plain. The Court views state sovereignty as divisible and delegable. It is entirely possible for the EU member states to give up a portion of their sovereignty to an international institution. Indeed, according to the ECJ, this is precisely what the EU member states did in consenting to the Treaty of Rome. Within the areas of their competences, the Community, EU law, and the ECJ have priority as against nation-states, national laws, and national courts.[102] No other international institution, no other international law, no other international court has such

[100] Id. at 435-436.
[101] Id. at 455.
[102] Louis, supra, at 13-18.

supremacy. A commentator observed: "The Luxembourg-based court often resembles the Wizard of Oz in reverse: a mighty institution determined to portray itself as a puny one. . . . Governments may grumble about [ECJ] decisions, but they obey them."[103]

3. European Union Law as International Law

It is commonly acknowledged that the European Court of Justice has gone so far in strengthening its own position and that of the European Community in general that by now EU law has become something like a federal law for Europe.[104] Does EU law, nevertheless, remain part of international law? Some argue that EU law now so differs from traditional international law that it should be counted a "well-developed 'legal system,'" really more municipal than international law.[105] Others reckon that, despite some federal features, EU law is at best a hybrid that displays characteristics of both international and municipal law.[106] Still others view EU law as part of "an extremely complex process of constitution-making for a political institution whose character does not fit within our familiar categories."[107]

The debate about the true nature of EU law has important implications for our notions about international law in general. The objection sometimes made that EU law cannot be international law because EU law is directly applicable to individuals as well as to states rests on the doubtful foundation of narrow legal positivism that insists that only states may be subjects of international law. [See Chapter 8.] In practice, however, the law of nations and international law have long accepted individuals as their subjects in some circumstances. The applicability

[103] The Wizards of Luxembourg: The European Court of Justice Gets Used to Life in the Spotlight, *The Economist*, May 23, 2020, at 26.

[104] Stein, Lawyers, Judges, and the Making of a Transnational Constitution, 75 *American Journal of International Law* 1 (1981); Eeckhout, The Growing Influence of European Law, 33 *Fordham International Law Journal* 1490 (2010).

[105] Jones, The Legal Nature of the European Community: A Jurisprudential Analysis Using H.L.A. Hart's *Model of Law and a Legal System*, 17 *Cornell International Law Journal* 1, 5 (1984).

[106] Bridge, American Analogues in the Law of the European Community, 11 *Anglo-American Law Review* 130, 151-152 (1982).

[107] Pernice, The Treaty of Lisbon: Multilevel Constitutionalism in Action, 15 *Columbia Journal of European Law* 349, 351 (2009).

and availability of EU law to individuals is really more an example of the inclusiveness of international law than they are a proof of any basic dissimilarity between EU law and international law.[108]

A more serious objection to EU law as a form of international law is that rarely in general international law are there law-generating, law-adjudicating, or law-enforcing institutions comparable to those of the EU. For example, in distinguishing international law from municipal law, H.L.A. Hart noted that international law lacks "the formal structure of . . . a legislature, courts with compulsory jurisdiction and officially organized sanctions."[109] Hart felt that without these institutions, international law more resembles a form of primitive law than it does municipal law.[110] Judged in terms of their formal structures, EU institutions are certainly much more developed than are most institutions on the plane of general international law. Does this make EU law not international law?

It is clear "that the Union is not a state in a classical sense for it has no territory of its own except as defined in the Treaties for the purpose of their application, no population which is not a citizenry of the Member States . . . , while its 'government' has no powers except those defined by Treaty."[111] It is a political fact of life that states, like the United Kingdom, can withdraw from the European Union with an ease much unlike the restraints on secession in any national federation. So EU law cannot be municipal law as we would normally know it. It may, however, be reasonable to measure EU law and indeed any legal system, international or municipal, by the degree to which it has settled or formal structures responsible for and capable of making, adjudicating, and enforcing legal rules. In this structural sense, EU law may be usefully regarded as a variety of international law, but one with highly developed formal institutions, so developed that they are indeed very much like those of a national legal system.

[108] See Janis, Individuals as Subjects of International Law, 17 *Cornell International Law Journal* 61, 69-71 (1984).

[109] H.L.A. Hart, *The Concept of Law* 226 (1961).

[110] Id. at 209.

[111] D. Lasok & J.W. Bridge, *Law and Institutions of the European Union* 27 (6th ed. 1994).

C. INTERNATIONAL COMMERCIAL ARBITRATION

1. *The Character of International Commercial Arbitration*

Among the most useful and distinctive legal processes of international law are the many international arbitral tribunals employed to resolve international economic disputes. These international commercial arbitral tribunals are distinguished from tribunals of public international arbitration, which are established by states to settle political differences. [See Chapter 5.] René David defines this commercial form of legal process as "a device whereby the settlement of a question, which is of interest for two or more persons, is entrusted to one or more other persons—the arbitrator or arbitrators—who derive their powers from a private agreement, not from the authorities of a State, and who are to proceed and decide the case on the basis of such an agreement."[112]

There are thousands of international commercial arbitrations every year. The International Chamber of Commerce alone, for example, has administered more than 23,000 international commercial arbitrations since the foundation of its Court of Arbitration in 1923.[113] Although most international commercial arbitrations involve only private parties, states are increasingly sued. It has been reported that there are about 300 claims filed each year in international commercial arbitrations against states.[114] International commercial arbitration is often entrusted to permanent arbitral institutes, sometimes private and other times state sponsored, which are in the regular business of establishing and facilitating international commercial arbitration. The administrative services of these permanent arbitral institutes are only to be had

[112] R. David, *Arbitration in International Trade* 5 (1985) [hereinafter cited as "David, Arbitration"]. On international commercial arbitration generally, see T. Várady, J.J. Barceló III & A.T. von Mehren, *International Commercial Arbitration: A Transnational Perspective* (3d ed. 2006) [hereinafter cited as "Várady"]; M.L. Moses, *The Principles and Practice of International Commercial Arbitration* (3d ed. 2017); M. Schinazi, The *Three Ages* of *International Commercial* Arbitration (2021).

[113] International Court of Arbitration, 2018 *ICC Dispute Resolution Bulletin* 52.

[114] G. Born, A New Generation of International Adjudication, 61 *Duke Law Journal* 775, 860 (2012).

for a fee, and such payments, along with the necessary sums rendered to arbitrators and advocates, make for a profit-oriented environment. The various centers, cities, and states offering arbitral institutes are in hot competition for the favor of those businesses interested in employing arbitrators rather than judges to settle their international commercial disputes.

Despite the essentially private character of the proceedings, it is important to note that international commercial arbitrations are usually decided on the basis of law and not by employing general notions of equity or fairness. Furthermore, arbitral agreements and the decisions of arbitral tribunals are routinely recognized and enforced in municipal courts.[115] Much of the real effectiveness of private international arbitration emanates from this link to national legal systems [see Chapter 10]. Even in disputes involving recalcitrant sovereign states, like Argentina and Russia, municipal courts have been crucial in enforcement actions.[116]

International commercial arbitration is normally viewed as an alternative to municipal litigation, offering certain advantages over domestic courts. Though one of these advantages is often perceived to be the relative speed and inexpensiveness of arbitration, arbitration may in fact be neither quicker nor cheaper than adjudication. More important in practice is the neutrality that arbitration offers. It may be fairer and mutually more convenient for parties to an international business transaction to arbitrate their disputes in a third country, rather than to turn to formal judicial proceedings in one or another of their own nations. In sending litigants to ICC arbitration in Paris pursuant to a contract's choice-of-forum clause, Justice Stewart for the Supreme Court in Scherk v. Alberto-Culver Co. wrote:

> A contractual provision specifying in advance the forum in which disputes shall be litigated and the law to be applied is, therefore, an almost indispensable precondition to achievement of the orderliness

[115] See Beatson, International Arbitration, Public Policy Considerations, and Conflicts of Law: The Perspectives of Reviewing and Enforcing Courts, 33 *Arbitration International* 175 (2017).

[116] See Hold-Outs Upheld: A Court Ruling Against Argentina Has Implications for Other Governments, *The Economist*, Nov. 3, 2012, at 74; Now Try Collecting: In Business Disputes Taken to Arbitration, Winning Is Just the Start, *The Economist*, Aug. 2, 2014, www.economist.com (Apr. 15, 2015).

> and predictability essential to any international business transaction. Furthermore, such a provision obviates the danger that a dispute under the agreement might be submitted to a forum hostile to the interests of one of the parties or unfamiliar with the problem area involved.[117]

Another advantage of arbitration is the control that parties may exercise over arbitral as opposed to judicial proceedings. In arbitration, parties are usually permitted to have a say in the selection of their arbitrators, and since arbitrators, unlike municipal judges, need not necessarily be lawyers, the parties may be able to choose arbitrators who have special expertise or competence with respect to the matter at hand. Parties may also each be able to choose arbitrators especially familiar with their own law, business, or country. The parties are also usually permitted to settle on a place and a language for arbitration that are mutually convenient and familiar. An arbitration, unlike an adjudication, may have many of its procedural rules set by the parties. Finally, and this is sometimes very important, arbitral proceedings, unlike judicial proceedings, may at the request of the parties often be kept secret.[118]

2. *International Chamber of Commerce Arbitration*

The best-known international commercial arbitral institute is that operated by the International Chamber of Commerce (ICC) in Paris. A description of its work will serve as an introduction to international commercial arbitration in general. The ICC is a private non-governmental organization that speaks for business before international agencies, promotes the harmonization of international trade practices and terminology, and provides specialized services to facilitate international commerce.[119] One of the ICC's specialized services is its Court of Arbitration, which since its establishment in 1922 has handled more than 17,000 international

[117] 417 U.S. 506, 516 (1974).

[118] On the continuing support of the U.S. Supreme Court for international arbitration, see Sanchez, ASIL Insight: Recent Developments in U.S. International Arbitration Law: Will Congress Take on the Supreme Court?, https://www.asil.org/insights/volume/14/issue/35/recent-developments-us-international-arbitration-law-will-congress-take (Nov. 30, 2010).

[119] International Chamber of Commerce, Introduction to Arbitration, www.iccwbo.org (Aug. 29, 2011).

commercial arbitrations, lately about 400 cases each year, more than any other organization.[120] In 2017, for example, the ICC rendered 512 awards and received 810 requests for arbitration.[121]

Despite its name, the ICC Court of Arbitration is not a court that hears and decides cases, but an administrative organization. Its function is to oversee *ad hoc* arbitral tribunals that are set up by private agreement to decide specific cases. For a fee based on the sum in dispute, the ICC provides an administrative structure to facilitate private international arbitration.

Since the ICC is a private institution with neither compulsory process nor mandatory jurisdiction, parties wishing to submit their disputes to ICC arbitration must explicitly agree to employ the organization. The ICC's standard arbitration clause recommended for parties wishing to specify ICC arbitration in their contracts is as follows:

> All disputes arising in connection with the present contract shall be finally settled under the Rules of Conciliation and Arbitration of the International Chamber of Commerce by one or more arbitrators appointed in accordance with the said Rules.[122]

[120] W.L. Craig, W.W. Park & J. Paulsson, *International Chamber of Commerce Arbitration* §1.02 (2d ed. 1990) [hereinafter cited as "Craig, Park & Paulsson"]. International Chamber of Commerce, Arbitration Today, www.iccwbo.org (Aug. 29, 2011). More than 200 ICC awards are to be found excerpted in the three volumes of *ICC Arbitral Awards: 1974-1985* (S. Jarvin & Y. Derains eds. 1990), *1986-1990* (S. Jarvin, Y. Derains & J.-J. Arnaldez eds. 1994), and *1991-1995* (J.-J. Arnaldez, Y. Derains & D. Hascher eds. 1997).

[121] International Court of Arbitration, 2018 *ICC Dispute Resolution Bulletin.*

[122] International Chamber of Commerce, *Rules for the ICC Court of Arbitration* 6 (1980). There are similar clauses suggested for other languages:

> Tous différends découlant du présent contrat seront tranchés définitivement suivant le Règlement de Conciliation et d'Arbitrage de la Chambre de Commerce Internationale par un ou plusieurs arbitres nommés conformément à ce Règlement.
>
> Alle aus dem gegenwärtigen Vertrage sich ergebenden Streitigkeiten werden nach der Vergleichs und Schiedsgerichtsordnung der Internationalen Handelskammer von einem oder mehreren gemäss dieser Ordnung ernannten Schiedsrichtern endgültig entschieden.
>
> Todas las desavencias que deriven de este contrato serán resueltas definitivamente de acuerdo con el Reglamento de Conciliación y Arbitraje de la Cámara de Comercio Internacional por uno más árbitros nombrados conforme a este Reglamento.

Of course, parties may supplement the standard clause with provisions relating to, *inter alia*, the appointment of arbitrators, the place and language of arbitration, and the enforcement of the arbitral award.[123] A party wishing to arbitrate sends a Request for arbitration to the Secretariat of the ICC Court of Arbitration in Paris. Pleadings, much as in a regular court case, follow. The procedural rules are those set by the ICC as modified by agreement between the parties and as supplemented and enforced by the national legal system of the place of the proceeding.

Though the ICC Court of Arbitration formally appoints arbitrators, the parties are entitled to nominate one or three arbitrators as they wish. The ICC Court of Arbitration also has the power to appoint arbitrators if the parties cannot agree or if one party, properly within the jurisdiction of the arbitration, refuses to nominate an arbitrator. In choosing arbitrators, the parties or the ICC Court of Arbitration may seek to find individuals with a special expertise concerning the subject matter of the dispute or with a good acquaintance of the applicable law. They may also look to judges, lawyers, or law professors who are already familiar with international arbitration in general. Normally, if the ICC Court is to choose a sole arbitrator or a third arbitrator on a three-person panel, it will choose a national of a country other than that of either of the parties.

The arbitral proceedings are conducted by the *ad hoc* arbitral panel, but are supervised to a degree by the ICC Court of Arbitration. Although an arbitrator may be named by one of the parties, he must be independent of the parties. It is possible for an arbitrator to be challenged for bias by a party, in which case the ICC Court of Arbitration decides the challenge. Parties may, of course, be represented by counsel of their own choosing. There is no special bar admitted to practice before the ICC, and lawyers admitted in many jurisdictions appear.[124]

International commercial arbitration may be subject to a considerable amount of judicial supervision in the country in which the arbitration takes place. Since parties agreeing to arbitration may want

[123] See Park, Arbitration of International Contract Disputes, 39 *Business Lawyer* 1783, 1796 (1984). Suggestions for more detailed arbitration clauses are to be found in Ulmer, Drafting the International Arbitration Clause, 20 *International Lawyer* 1335 (1986).

[124] Craig, Park & Paulsson, supra, §§10.01-10.07, 27.01-27.05, 1.01.

to avoid the costs and delays of judicial proceedings, there is often a decision to choose a place for arbitration where the municipal courts will not overly interfere with the arbitration. In order to encourage private international arbitration within their territories, countries like Great Britain have passed legislation insulating international commercial arbitration from the ordinary scrutiny of local judges.[125]

The parties, by submitting to ICC arbitration, agree to respect the award of the arbitrators, which is deemed to be made at the place of the arbitral proceedings. An ICC arbitration, like any international commercial arbitration, must rely on either the good will of the parties or municipal enforcement procedures. In some situations, it is more readily possible to recognize and enforce a private international arbitral award than it is to recognize and enforce a judgment of a foreign court [see Chapter 10].

3. Other International Arbitral Centers

The "emergence of a global legal profession, united by participation in a form of dispute processing that transcends national legal systems," is owed in no small measure to the "club" of lawyers from many countries that built up around the ICC in Paris in the 1950s and 1960s. Today, the club has expanded both geographically and numerically, no longer being the domain of "gentlemen missionaries for arbitration."[126] There are now a great many international arbitral centers, public and private, hotly in pursuit of the profitable practice of international commercial arbitration. It was estimated in 2014 that increasing international arbitral proceedings by only 10 to 20 percent in New York City would add as much as $400 million to the revenues of city law firms.[127]

[125] Hacking, The "Stated Case" Abolished: The United Kingdom Arbitration Act of 1979, 14 *International Lawyer* 95 (1980); Park, Judicial Supervision of Transnational Commercial Arbitration: The English Arbitration Act of 1979, 21 *Harvard International Law Journal* 87 (1980); Várady, supra, at 38-58.

[126] American Bar Foundation, *Forty Years of Research: 1952-1992* 5 (1993). See J. Kleinheisterkamp, *International Commercial Arbitration in Latin America* (2005); Brower & Sharpe, International Arbitration and the Arab World, 97 *American Journal of International Law* 643 (2003).

[127] E. Olson, Cities Compete to Be the Arena for Global Legal Disputes, *N.Y. Times*, Sept. 12, 2014, at B5. Regarding China's efforts to become a center of international commercial arbitration, see China Courts the World, *The Economist*, June 8, 2019, at 42.

An important example of a state-sponsored international commercial arbitral organization is the International Centre for Settlement of Investment Disputes (ICSID), which is the arbitral arm of the World Bank in Washington. ICSID was founded by the Convention on the Settlement of Investment Disputes Between States and Nationals of Other States.[128] As of February 2026, there are 165 member states.[129] Although it took more than a decade for ICSID to hear 20 cases, nowadays ICSID hears about 25 cases each year.[130] By 2019, ICSID had rendered 297 awards.[131] One of the world's largest claims, more than $7 billion, was pending before ICSID in 2011, in an arbitration brought by Exxon Mobil against Venezuela, but the U.S. Court of Appeals for the Second Circuit blocked Exxon from enforcing the award.[132]

ICSID was established to facilitate private investment in the developing countries by providing a neutral forum for dispute settlement between private investors and foreign states. Such a neutral forum is useful because a private investor may be reluctant to entrust dispute settlement to the municipal courts of a foreign country for fear that the judges and laws may unduly favor the host country's government. Equally, a foreign government may be loath to submit itself to the jurisdiction of the courts of the private investor's own country. The ICSID Convention provides as follows:

> The jurisdiction of the Centre shall extend to any legal dispute arising directly out of an investment, between a Contracting State (or any constituent subdivision or agency of a Contracting State designated to the Centre by that State) and a national of another Contracting State, which the parties to the dispute consent in writing to submit to the Centre.

[128] 17 U.S.T. 1270, T.I.A.S. No. 6090, 575 U.N.T.S. 159 (done at Washington March 18, 1965; entered into force October 14, 1966) [hereinafter cited as "ICSID Convention"]. See Kinnear, The Role of ICSID in International Economic Law, 26 *Journal of International Economic Law* 35 (2023).

[129] icsid.worldbank.org/about/member-states/database-of-member-states (Feb. 21, 2026).

[130] Parra, The Development of the Regulations and Rules of the International Centre for Settlement of Investment Disputes, 41 *International Lawyer* 52-56 (2007).

[131] International Centre for Settlement of Investment Disputes, 2019 *The ICSID Caseload Statistics* 18, https://icsid.worldbank.org/resources/publications/icsid-caseload-statistics (Jan. 21, 2021).

[132] Curriden, Holding Chavez over a Barrel: Exxon Mobil's Dispute with Venezuela Has Global Implications, *ABA Journal*, April 2011, at 18; reuters.com/article/us-exxon-mobil-venezuela-idUSKBN19W1SU (Feb. 28, 2019).

> When the parties have given their consent, no party may withdraw its consent unilaterally.[133]

ICSID recommends that investment contracts include the following basic clause to establish ICSID's jurisdiction:

> The parties hereto hereby consent to submit to the International Centre for Settlement of Investment Disputes any dispute in relation to or arising out of this Agreement for Settlement by conciliation/arbitration pursuant to the Convention on the Settlement of Investment Disputes between States and Nationals of Other States.[134]

ICSID may either conciliate or arbitrate a dispute. There are standing panels of conciliators and arbitrators, some appointed by the contracting states, others chosen by the President of the World Bank. In any case, the parties agree among themselves as to which persons from these panels shall conciliate or arbitrate their dispute, or, if there is no agreement, each party may name one of three conciliation commissioners or arbitrators. Conciliation commissions and arbitral tribunals are judges of their own competence and proceed according to the Convention and rules of procedure elaborated by ICSID.[135]

In the United States, the principal private arbitral organization, the American Arbitration Association (AAA), is second only to the ICC in the number of international arbitrations it administers.[136] The AAA suggests the following standard arbitration clause:

> Any controversy or claim arising out of or relating to this contract, or the breach thereof, shall be settled by arbitration in accordance with the Commercial Arbitration Rules of the American Arbitration Association, and judgment upon the award rendered by the Arbitrator(s) may be entered in any Court having jurisdiction thereof.[137]

Besides the AAA, many other national arbitral institutes are in place to facilitate the settlement of international commercial disputes.

[133] ICSID Convention, supra, art. 25(1).

[134] International Centre for Settlement of Investment Disputes, *ICSID Model Clauses* 5 (July 7, 1981).

[135] ICSID Convention, supra, arts. 5, 12-16, 28-31, 36-40, 32-33, 41, 44.

[136] Craig, Park & Paulsson, supra, §1.02; *Business International*, Oct. 12, 1979, at 326-327. See *International Commercial Arbitration in New York* (McClendon & Goodman eds. 1986).

[137] AAA, *Commercial Arbitration Rules* 2 (April 1, 1981).

These include arbitral organizations in Australia, Austria, Bulgaria, the People's Republic of China, Germany, Hong Kong, Hungary, India, Japan, South Korea, Malaysia, the Netherlands, Norway, Romania, Spain, Sweden, Switzerland, and the United Kingdom.[138] Typically, these other national institutes have a rather smaller international case load than either the ICC or the AAA. The London Court of International Arbitration, for example, handles an international case load that is less than ten percent of that of the ICC.[139]

In addition to the general-purpose arbitration offered by the ICC and other national institutes, specialized arbitration services are provided by various specific trade groups. There are, for example, special institutes or sets of rules for trade in grain, coffee, cocoa, sugar, and metals, as well as several institutes or sets of rules for maritime disputes.[140] Such specialized arbitration is legion in world practice. It has been estimated that most of the roughly 10,000 arbitrations in the United Kingdom in 1978 involved international maritime and commodity disputes.[141]

Some international commercial arbitrations do not involve any formal arbitral institute, but are entirely *ad hoc* proceedings constituted specially by the parties, albeit often making reference to some set of procedural rules, for example, those promulgated by UNCITRAL.[142] States may especially prefer non-institutionalized arbitrations so as not to compromise their authority by recognizing institutional arbitral agencies.[143] Indeed, *ad hoc* international commercial administration may prove especially attractive to authoritarian governments not ordinarily inclined to the rule of law; third-party dispute settlement may prove necessary to attract foreign investment and some governments may prefer it to empowering the state's own judicial machinery.[144]

[138] C.M. Schmitthoff, *International Commercial Arbitration*, Vol. II (looseleaf) [hereinafter cited as "Schmitthoff"].

[139] Craig, Park & Paulsson, supra, §1.02.

[140] Schmitthoff, supra, Vol. III.

[141] David, Arbitration, supra, at 34.

[142] United Nations Commission on International Trade Law, UNCITRAL Arbitration Rules, U.N. Doc. A/CN.9/IX/CRP.1 (April 28, 1976), reprinted in 15 *International Legal Materials* 702 (1976). For the decision of an *ad hoc* arbitral tribunal pursuant to the UNCITRAL rules, see Wintershall A.G. v. Qatar, 28 *International Legal Materials* 795 (1989).

[143] David, Arbitration, supra, at 35-36.

[144] Massoud, International Arbitration and Judicial Politics in Authoritarian States, 39 *Law and Social Inquiry* 1 (2014).

CHAPTER 10

International Conflict of Laws

International law addresses not only the political and economic relations of nations, but also the interface between municipal legal systems. In civil law countries, this interface is studied under the rubric of *private international law* even though what is largely at issue are the international relations of courts, legislatures, and executives, surely a matter of public concern. In the United States, the subject's more usual appellation is *conflict of laws*, but it must be remembered that the relevant laws and processes have a great deal to do with conflict avoidance and international judicial cooperation.

However styled, these rules have an important part to play in municipal as well as in international fora. As the U.S. Supreme Court explained in Hilton v. Guyot:

> International law, in its widest and most comprehensive sense,—including not only questions of right between nations, governed by what has been appropriately called the law of nations, but also questions arising under what is usually called private international law, or the conflict of laws . . . is part of our law, and must be ascertained and administered by the courts of justice as often as such questions are presented in litigation. . . .[1]

[1] 159 U.S. 113, 163 (1895).

A. PRINCIPLES OF JURISDICTION

In international law, the term *jurisdiction* is usually taken to denote the legal power or competence of states to exercise governmental functions. Different kinds of governmental functions are signaled by different adjectival references. We refer to legislative or prescriptive jurisdiction when we talk about the authority of states to make and apply laws, to executive or administrative jurisdiction when we contemplate the power of states to enforce laws, and to judicial or adjudicatory jurisdiction when we think about the competence of courts to bring parties before them and to render authoritative judgments. Problems about jurisdiction figure quite generally in international relations. Governments must often decide how far to assert their governmental functions and when to resist the exercise of jurisdictional authority by other states.

1. The Territorial Principle

International law knows several principles justifying a state's assertion of jurisdiction. Among these, the principle of the territorial jurisdiction of states is probably the most important. The principle of territorial jurisdiction stems from the most essential attributes of state sovereignty: a distinct and delineated territory, a known and loyal population, and a government capable of acting independently both at home and abroad.

Modern international law and relations are often dated from the Peace of Westphalia of 1648, the settlement that brought a close to the bloody Thirty Years' War. Perhaps the most important result of that conflict was the determination of European states, reflected in a pair of laboriously detailed treaties, that the princes of Europe were to be recognized as securely ensconced as sovereign authorities in their respective territories.[2] At least since that date, the principles of the territorial

[2] The two treaties making up the Peace of Westphalia, viz., the October 14, 1648 Treaties of Peace between Sweden and the Holy Roman Empire and between France and the Empire, are to be found in 1 *Consolidated Treaties Series* 119-356. See Chapter 6.

sovereignty and the jurisdiction of states have been two of the most fundamental principles of international law.

Early in the history of the United States, in *The Schooner Exchange*, the Supreme Court affirmed the principle of the "full and absolute territorial jurisdiction . . . of every sovereign."[3] In U.S. jurisprudence, the territorial principle was given its greatest scope late in the nineteenth and early in the twentieth centuries. Then it was even maintained that no sovereign state had the legal competence to assert its jurisdictional authority, be it to apply, enforce, or adjudicate the law, outside of its own territory.

A classic U.S. court judgment imposing strict territorial limits on state jurisdiction is American Banana Co. v. United Fruit Co., in 1909.[4] There, Justice Holmes refused to apply U.S. federal antitrust law to the allegedly monopolistic activities overseas of one U.S. company injuring another in the U.S. domestic market:

> [T]he general and almost universal rule is that the character of an act as lawful or unlawful must be determined wholly by the law of the country where the act is done. . . . For another jurisdiction, if it should happen to lay hold of the actor, to treat him according to its own notions rather than those of the place where he did the acts, not only would be unjust, but would be an interference with the authority of another sovereign, contrary to the comity of nations, which the other state concerned justly might resent.[5]

Holmes did not, and indeed did not need to, say if the strict territorial rule was international or municipal in character or derivation. His implication was that the principle of exclusive territorial jurisdiction had a place in both legal systems. Holmes considered the territorial principle to be virtually unassailable: "The very meaning of sovereignty is that the decree of the sovereign makes law."[6]

Today the principle of territorial jurisdiction is universally accepted, though no longer is it thought of as constituting the exclusive basis

[3] 11 U.S. (7 Cranch) 116, 137 (1812).

[4] 213 U.S. 347 (1909).

[5] Id. at 356.

[6] Id. at 358. For more on the emergence of the trade in bananas, see S. May & G. Plaza, *The United Fruit Company in Latin America* (1958). An emphasis on territorialism and sovereignty in *American Banana* also reflects the policy preferences supporting the act of state doctrine, see below.

for the assertion of state jurisdictional authority. Rather, territoriality is seen as one of several foundations of jurisdiction, albeit the most fundamental. In the United States, the *Restatement of Foreign Relations Law of the United States (Second)* gave the territorial principle pride of place.[7] Similarly, the Restatement (Fourth) gives a state jurisdiction with respect to "persons, property, and conduct within its territory"[8]

If international law or municipal law restricted the jurisdiction of states solely to their own territories, the topic of jurisdiction would be relatively simple. However, there are several other recognized categories of jurisdiction that are *extraterritorial*, so called because they make claims to jurisdiction outside the territory of the state. Any exercise of extraterritorial jurisdiction by its very nature overlaps the territorial jurisdiction of another state; thus, a conflict of jurisdictions automatically ensues.

2. *The Nationality Principle*

The most fundamental principle of extraterritorial jurisdiction is nationality. As early as the first authoritative commentator on jurisdiction, the Italian jurist Bartolus, himself a confirmed territorialist, it has been admitted that a state's laws may be applied extraterritorially to its citizens, individuals or corporations, wherever they may be found.[9] Thus, a person or a company located or doing business in a foreign country may be subject not only to the territorial jurisdiction of the foreign state, but also to the jurisdiction of its national government.

Nationality is an accepted basis for jurisdiction in U.S. courts. In Blackmer v. United States, a U.S. citizen implicated in the Teapot Dome

[7] American Law Institute, *Restatement (Second) of the Foreign Relations Law of the United States* §17 (1965) [hereinafter cited as "Restatement (Second)"].

[8] American Law Institute, *Restatement of the Law Fourth: The Foreign Relations Law of the United States: Selected Topics in Treaties, Jurisdiction, and Sovereign Immunity* 142 [hereinafter cited as "Restatement (Fourth)"]. For an analysis of the Restatements (Second) and (Third) with respect to jurisdiction, see Olmstead, Jurisdiction, 14 *Yale Journal of International Law* 468 (1989). For an analysis of the treatment of jurisdiction in the Restatement (Fourth), see Dodge, Jurisdiction in the Fourth Restatement of Foreign Relations Law, 18 *Yearbook of Private International Law* 143 (2016/2017).

[9] *Bartolus on the Conflict of Laws* 51 (Beale trans. 1914).

scandals of the 1920s fled to France, where he was served with process by U.S. officials and ordered to return to the United States to testify in a criminal trial. Though he argued that he was immune from the jurisdiction of the United States while he resided in France, the Supreme Court held differently:

> [Blackmer] continued to owe allegiance to the United States. By virtue of the obligations of citizenship, the United States retained its authority over him, and he was bound by its laws made applicable to him in a foreign country. Thus, although resident abroad, the petitioner remained subject to the taxing power of the United States. . . . For disobedience to its laws through conduct abroad he was subject to punishment in the courts of the United States. . . . Nor can it be doubted that the United States possesses the power inherent in its sovereignty to require the return to this country of a citizen, resident elsewhere, whenever the public interest requires it, and to penalize him in case of refusal.[10]

The Restatement (Fourth) provides that a state has jurisdiction with respect to its nationals both within and outside its territory.[11] As the Supreme Court held in 1952 in Steele v. Bulova Watch Co.: "Congress in prescribing standards of conduct for American citizens may project the impact of its laws beyond the territorial boundaries of the United States."[12] The extraterritorial jurisdiction of a state over its nationals may in some circumstances be asserted by a component state of a federal union.[13] Jurisdiction based on nationality has traditionally been found in French law: "A French national may be brought before a French court for responsibilities incurred by him in a foreign country even due a foreigner."[14] Nationality jurisdiction may well become more significant in English law, long a bastion of territorial jurisdiction.[15]

[10] 284 U.S. 421, 436-437 (1932).

[11] Restatement (Fourth), supra, at 148.

[12] 344 U.S. 280, 282 (1952).

[13] Skiriotes v. Florida, 313 U.S. 69, 77 (1941).

[14] "Un Français pourra être traduit devant un tribunal de France, pour des obligations par lui contractées en pays étranger, même avec un étranger." Code Civil, art. 15.

[15] Arnell, The Case for Nationality-Based Jurisdiction, 50 *International & Comparative Law Quarterly* 955 (2001).

3. *The Effects Principle*

A much more controversial form of extraterritorial jurisdiction is the so-called effects principle. Extraterritorial though it may be in practice, in theory the effects principle is grounded on the principle of territorial jurisdiction. The premise is that a state has jurisdiction over extraterritorial conduct when that conduct has an effect within its territory. Effects jurisdiction is sometimes called *objective jurisdiction*, since it is the object of conduct that is its realm. It is thus distinguished from *subjective jurisdiction*, another term for territorial jurisdiction, where what is encompassed is the subject or the actor responsible for conduct.

The effects principle received one of its most notable enunciations in the *Lotus* case, where the Permanent Court of International Justice was asked to decide whether Turkey had violated "the principles of international law" by asserting criminal jurisdiction over a French officer who had been navigating a private French vessel when it collided with and sank a Turkish ship on the high seas. [See Chapter 3.] The issue was one of extraterritoriality because the Frenchman had at all times during the collision been on French territory, that is, aboard the French ship, although damage had been inflicted upon Turkish territory, that is, on the Turkish ship. The *Lotus* court adopted a strictly positivist view of international law, seeing it as a law entirely generated by the positive acts of states and emanating "from their own free will as expressed in conventions or by usages generally accepted as expressing principles of law."[16] The Permanent Court searched for "a rule of international law limiting the freedom of States to extend the criminal jurisdiction of their courts to a situation uniting the circumstances of the present case" and, finding none, ruled that Turkey had not acted improperly either in seizing the French officer or in trying him for violating Turkish law while outside Turkish territory.[17]

A pivotal U.S. case involving the effects principle is United States v. Aluminum Co. of America, which concerned the practices of aluminum companies accused of violating U.S. antitrust law. A Canadian firm, Aluminum Limited, participated in a cartel based in Switzerland that, *inter alia*, restricted imports to the United States. Should the Canadian company be caught within the web of U.S. law for its overseas acts?

[16] 1927 P.C.I.J. Reports, ser. A, no. 10, at 18.
[17] Id. at 21-33.

The court held that since the companies in the cartel had intended to affect U.S. commerce and since there had indeed been an effect on U.S. imports, Limited's activities were properly within the regulatory reach, that is, the legislative jurisdiction, of the United States.[18] The basis for the extraterritorial application of U.S. law was explained to be the rule that "any state may impose liabilities, even upon persons not within its allegiance, for conduct outside its borders that has consequences within its borders which the state reprehends; and these liabilities other states will ordinarily recognize."[19] The Supreme Court itself adopted the effects principle in Continental Ore v. Union Carbide in 1962.[20]

There is, however, a presumption of statutory interpretation that U.S. statutes are not to be applied extraterritorially unless Congress so intends. As Justice Scalia emphasized in 2010 in Morrison v. Nat'l Australian Bank Ltd., there is a "longstanding principle of American law 'that legislation of Congress, unless a contrary intent appears, is meant to apply only within the territorial jurisdiction of the United States.' "[21] Congress may, of course, legislate an extraterritorial assertion of U.S. law that is deemed substantive rather than jurisdictional.[22]

The Restatement (Fourth) reads that a state has jurisdiction with respect to "conduct outside its territory that has a substantial effect within its territory."[23] The United States has been sometimes criticized as employing extraterritorial effects jurisdiction too extensively.[24] However, the United States is not alone in asserting jurisdiction based on extraterritorial conduct causing a territorial effect. As long ago as

[18] 148 F.2d 416, 442-448 (2d Cir. 1945).

[19] Id. at 443.

[20] 370 U.S. 690 (1962). A roughly similar factual scenario to *Aluminum* was deemed to warrant an exercise of territorial, not effects, jurisdiction by the European Court of Justice in 1988, in the *Wood Pulp* case, [1988] *European Court Reports* 5193.

[21] 561 U.S. 247, 255 (2010); see M.I. Steinberg & K. Flanagan, Transnational Dealings—*Morrison* Continues to Make Waves, 46 *International Lawyer* 829 (2012); and Dodge, The Presumption Against Extraterritoriality in Two Steps, 110 *American Journal of International Law Unbound* 45 (2016).

[22] The Seventh Circuit ruled that the 1982 Foreign Trade Antitrust Improvement Act should be read as adding an extraterritorial element of a claim to the Sherman Antitrust Act. Minn-Chem, Inc. v. Agrium Inc., 683 F.3d 845 (7th Cir. 2012) (en banc), *cert. dismissed,* 82 U.S.L.W. 3070 (U.S. July 2013) (No. 12-650).

[23] Restatement (Fourth), supra, at 148.

[24] See, e.g., Stern, Can the United States Set Rules for the World?: A French View, 31 *Journal of World Trade,* No. 4, at 5 (1997).

1935, a Harvard-conducted comparative survey found that "national legislation and jurisprudence have developed the so-called objective territorial principle which establishes the jurisdiction of the State to prosecute and punish for crime commenced without the State but consummated within its territory." The survey touched not only on the *Lotus* case and U.S. examples, but also on practice drawn from Great Britain, Argentina, Mexico, Norway, Denmark, Brazil, France, and Germany.[25] "Objections" to the Restatements' assertions of extraterritorial jurisdiction "have decreased as more states employ it."[26]

4. *Other Principles of Jurisdiction*

Besides nationality and effects, there have been suggested and accepted from time to time a variety of other foundations for a state's exercise of extraterritorial jurisdiction. Three should be mentioned here: the protective principle, the universality principle, and the passive personality principle. The protective principle provides that a state has jurisdiction to prescribe law with respect to extraterritorial conduct directed against crucial state interests, especially state security.[27] In United States v. Pizzarusso, the Second Circuit decided that an alien could be indicted and convicted under U.S. and international law for knowingly making false statements under oath in Canada on a U.S. visa application. The Court held that even though the United States had neither territorial nor nationality jurisdiction, the protective principle could be employed: State jurisdiction could be based on "conduct outside its territory that threatens its security as a state or the operation of its governmental functions, provided the conduct is generally recognized as a crime under the law of states that have reasonably developed legal systems."[28] The Court pointed out that "[s]tatutes imposing criminal

[25] Codification of International Law, Jurisdiction with Respect to Crime, Dickinson, Reporter, 29 *American Journal of International Law* (Supplement no. 1) 435, 487-494 (1935) [hereinafter cited as "Harvard Research"].

[26] Knox, A Presumption Against Extraterritoriality, 104 *American Journal of International Law* 351, 356-357 (2010).

[27] Restatement (Fourth), supra, at 148.

[28] 388 F.2d 8, 10 (2d Cir. 1968), *cert. denied*, 392 U.S. 936 (1968), citing Restatement (Second), supra, §33.

liability on aliens for committing perjury in United States Consulates in foreign countries have been in existence for over one hundred years."[29]

The universality principle determines "jurisdiction by reference to the custody of the person committing the offense."[30] The universality principle is perhaps best illustrated by the jurisdiction that every state traditionally has over pirates and slave traders,[31] and by the more modern jurisdiction that some states claim over those who commit crimes against human rights. In Filartiga v. Peña-Irala, the Second Circuit held that "the torturer has become—like the pirate and slave trader before him—*hostis humani generis*, an enemy of all mankind."[32] [See Chapter 8.] In Demjanjuk v. Petrovsky, the Sixth Circuit agreed that Israel had universal jurisdiction over a Nazi war criminal even though his crimes were committed before Israel was a state.[33] Belgium's Law Relative to Serious Violations of International Humanitarian Law, "widely recognized as the most far-reaching example of a state exercising 'universal jurisdiction,'" has prompted complaints, for example, against Chile's General Pinochet, Cuban President Castro, PLO leader Yasser Arafat, Israeli Prime Minister Sharon, and, in a charge repudiated by the United States, U.S. President George H.W. Bush.[34] Universal jurisdiction provides the foundation for much of modern international human rights law and, as such, is very controversial as applied both in municipal courts and in international tribunals.[35]

The passive personality principle "would allow jurisdiction over foreigners when their acts affect, not the national territory, but subjects

[29] Id. at 11.

[30] Harvard Research, supra, at 435; Addis, Imagining the International Community: The Constitutive Dimension of Universal Jurisdiction, 31 *Human Rights Quarterly* 129 (2009).

[31] United States v. Smith, 18 U.S. (5 Wheaton) 153, 161 (1820). For a critical view of universal jurisdiction over pirates, see A.P. Rubin, *The Law of Piracy* (2d ed. 1998). For the continuing problems posed by the slave trade, see Kapstein, The New Global Slave Trade, 85 *Foreign Affairs* (Nov./Dec. 2006), at 103.

[32] 630 F.2d 876, 890 (2d Cir. 1980).

[33] 776 F.2d 571, 582-583 (6th Cir. 1985), *cert. denied*, 475 U.S. 1016 (1986).

[34] U.S. Reaction to Belgian Universal Jurisdiction Law, 97 *American Journal of International Law* 984 (2003).

[35] See Addis, Imagining the International Community: The Constitutive Dimension of Universal Jurisdiction, 31 *Human Rights Quarterly* 129 (2009), and Hovell, The Authority of Universal Jurisdiction, 29 *European Journal of International Law* 427 (2018).

of the state asserting jurisdiction, wherever they may be."[36] The passive personality principle is embodied, for example, in the French civil code where French courts are given jurisdiction over persons anywhere who are legally responsible to French nationals even with respect to obligations incurred outside France.[37]

B. JUDICIAL CONFLICTS AND COOPERATION

The various forms of extraterritorial jurisdiction ensure that there will be frequent conflicts of state jurisdiction—legislative, executive, and adjudicatory. As a hypothetical example, a Canadian injuring a Frenchman in the United States while engaged in a conspiracy to counterfeit English currency could trigger the territorial jurisdiction of the United States, the nationality jurisdiction of Canada, the protective jurisdiction of England, and the passive personality jurisdiction of France. In practice, there are countless such cases of concurrent jurisdiction, situations where two or more states claim jurisdiction over the same actors and transactions.

Rarely are such cases of international jurisdictional conflict entrusted to any sort of international dispute settlement procedure. Typically, their resolution depends upon cooperation between the nation-states involved and upon the restraint and sense of accommodation displayed by municipal courts. It is generally agreed that there are principles of international comity that should guide states and judges in moderating assertions of jurisdiction. More controversial is the proposition that there are some definite limits that international law sets upon the jurisdiction of states.[38]

[36] D.P. O'Connell, 2 *International Law* 901 (1965 ed.).

[37] "L'étranger . . . pourra être traduit devant les tribunaux de France, pour les obligations par lui contractées en pays étranger envers des Français." Code Civil, art. 14. The passive personality principle was used against France in the *Lotus Case.* See Chapter 3.

[38] Though public and private international law share much of the same history, "two branches of the same tree," most countries look predominantly to national sources for their conflicts rules. DeBoer, Living Apart Together: The Relationship

B. Judicial Conflicts and Cooperation

In any case, national courts have long accommodated foreign legal systems by recognizing and enforcing foreign judgments and awards and otherwise assisting foreign courts. Such *ad hoc* cooperation is sometimes facilitated by international agreements.

1. Comity, Constitutional Limits, and *Forum Non Conveniens*

Potential and actual conflicts among the jurisdictional reaches of national legal systems are often avoided or moderated simply by a certain deference shown by one nation's courts to the courts and laws of another state, a deference denoted as *comity*. In the United States, the classic statement of the principle of comity is to be found in Hilton v. Guyot:

> "Comity," in the legal sense, is neither a matter of absolute obligation, on the one hand, nor of mere courtesy and good will, upon the other. But it is the recognition which one nation allows within its territory to the legislative, executive, or judicial acts of another nation, having due regard both to international duty and convenience, and to the rights of its own citizens, or of other persons who are under the protection of its laws.[39]

Comity is the foundation on which has been built structures for the recognition and enforcement by national courts of the judgments of foreign courts and of the awards of foreign arbitral tribunals. Just as important, comity underlies rules calling for the application in certain circumstances of foreign law by municipal courts, an exercise frequently repeated using ordinary municipal choice-of-law principles. For example, in Lauritzen v. Larsen, the Supreme Court in 1953 had to decide whether to apply Danish or American law to a Danish seaman's claim against a Danish ship owner for injuries sustained in Cuba; the seaman had joined the ship in New York. In holding that Danish law should apply, the Court reasoned as follows:

Between Public and Private International Law, 57 *Netherlands International Law Review* 183, 204-207 (2010).

[39] 159 U.S. 113, 163-164 (1895).

> International or maritime law in such matters as this . . . aims at stability and order through usages which considerations of comity, reciprocity and long-range interest have developed to define the domain which each nation will claim as its own. Maritime law, like our municipal law, has attempted to avoid or resolve conflicts between competing laws by ascertaining and valuing points of contact between the transaction and the states or governments whose competing laws are involved. The criteria, in general, appear to be arrived at from weighing of the significance of one or more connecting factors between the shipping transaction regulated and the national interest served by the assertion of authority.[40]

In maritime cases involving foreign seamen and foreign vessels, the Court has "made clear its reluctance to intrude domestic labor law willy-nilly into the complex of considerations affecting foreign trade, absent a clear congressional mandate to do so."[41] Such restraint in applying forum law to matters properly within the regulatory reach of other states may sometimes even be shown in cases where the foreign law offends the sensibilities of the forum court.[42]

Comity, too, is shown when a judge decides not to hear a case over which the court has jurisdiction, but which is, for one reason or another, better suited to be decided by a foreign tribunal. For example, in The Bremen v. Zapata Off-Shore Co., the U.S. Supreme Court chose to enforce a choice-of-forum clause and sent a Texas company to litigation in London over a dispute with a German corporation about the towage of an ocean-going oil drilling rig, a judgment that marked a "turning point" in U.S. law.[43] Chief Justice Burger, for the Supreme Court, wrote:

> Here we see an American company with special expertise contracting with a foreign company to tow a complex machine thousands of miles across seas and oceans. The expansion of American business and industry will hardly be encouraged if, notwithstanding solemn contracts, we

[40] 345 U.S. 571, 582 (1953).

[41] Windward Shipping v. American Radio Ass'n, 415 U.S. 104, 110 (1974); see G. Gilmore & C.L. Black, *The Law of Admiralty* 471-484 (2d ed. 1975); Davies, Maritime Liens and Choice of Law, 42 *Tulane Maritime Law Journal* 269 (2018).

[42] Banco Nacional de Cuba v. Sabbatino, 376 U.S. 398 (1964); Dougherty v. Equitable Life Assurance Soc., 266 N.Y. 71 (1934).

[43] Buxbaum, The Interpretation and Effect of Permissive Forum Selection Clauses Under U.S. Law, 66 *American Journal of Comparative Law Supplement* 127, 129 (2018).

> insist on a parochial concept that all disputes must be resolved under our laws and in our courts. . . . We cannot have trade and commerce in world markets and international waters exclusively on our terms, governed by our laws, and resolved in our courts.[44]

Comity, especially in circumstances involving concurrent adjudicatory jurisdiction, is a matter often left up to the *ad hoc* discretion of the courts. Insofar as a judge prefers to hear a dispute him or herself and not to defer to a foreign court, comity may provide little help in effectively allocating judicial business. When there is a judicial sentiment that foreign courts are unreliable or that foreign justice or foreign law is unfair, comity breaks down altogether. In Smith Kline & French Laboratories v. Bloch, England's Lord Denning, far from deferring to an ongoing legal process in the United States, enjoined a British national from suing in Pennsylvania:

> As a moth is drawn to the light, so is a litigant drawn to the United States. If he can only get his case into their courts, he stands to win a fortune. At no cost to himself, and at no risk of having to pay anything to the other side. The lawyers there will conduct the case "on spec" as we say, or on a "contingency fee" as they say. The lawyers will charge the litigant nothing for their services but instead they will take 40 per cent of the damages, if they win the case in court, or out of court on a settlement. If they lose, the litigant will have nothing to pay to the other side. The courts in the United States have no such costs deterrent as we have. There is also in the United States a right to trial by jury. These are prone to award fabulous damages. They are notoriously sympathetic and know that the lawyers will take their 40 per cent before the plaintiff gets anything. All this means that the defendant can be readily forced into a settlement. The plaintiff holds all the cards.[45]

Similarly, but less dramatically, the U.S. Court of Appeals for the District of Columbia Circuit held in the *Laker Airways* case in 1984:

> [T]here are limitations to the application of comity. When the foreign act is inherently inconsistent with the policies underlying comity, domestic recognition could tend either to legitimize the aberration or to encourage retaliation, undercutting the realization of the goals served

[44] 407 U.S. 1, 8-9 (1972).
[45] [1983] 2 All E.R. 72, 74.

> by comity. No nation is under an unremitting obligation to enforce foreign interests which are fundamentally prejudicial to those of the domestic forum.[46]

In *Laker*, the courts of the United Kingdom and the United States were locked in a judicial battle very much unmoderated by comity and were for several years unable to decide where Laker's complaints about its competitors allegedly conspiring to put it out of business should be litigated. There were even conflicting restraining orders issued: U.S. courts prohibited the defendant from proceeding in England,[47] and English courts prohibited Laker from suing in the United States.[48] The embarrassing judicial standoff was finally broken when the House of Lords, England's highest court, obligingly dissolved the English judicial injunction against Laker.[49]

In the *Laker* case, the breakdown in comity was accentuated by the British government, which issued an order pursuant to what is called a "blocking statute," in that instance the Protection of Trading Interests Act. The Act permits the British government to prohibit compliance with foreign judicial or administrative proceedings if they are deemed to damage or be a threat to damage the trading interests of the United Kingdom. The Act was especially directed at what the British view as overly aggressive extraterritorial application of U.S. antitrust law, and it even includes a provision permitting British persons or companies to recover in British courts the treble damages collected in some U.S. antitrust actions.[50]

A confusing treatment of comity was provided by the U.S. Supreme Court in 1993, in *Hartford Fire.* The question was whether U.S. antitrust law applied to activities of London reinsurers who allegedly promoted an illegal restriction (under U.S. law) to the terms of commercial

[46] Laker Airways v. Sabena, Belgian World Airlines, 731 F.2d 909, 937 (D.C. Cir. 1984).

[47] Laker Airways Ltd. v. Pan American World Airways, 559 F. Supp. 1124 (D.D.C. 1983).

[48] British Airways v. Laker Airways, [1983] 3 All E.R. 396, reprinted in 23 *International Legal Materials* 568 (1984).

[49] British Airways Bd. v. Laker Airways Ltd., [1984] 3 All E.R. 39, reprinted in 23 *International Legal Materials* 727, 741 (1984).

[50] 1980, ch. 11, reprinted in 21 *International Legal Materials* 834 (1982); see Lowe, Blocking Extraterritorial Jurisdiction: The British Protection of Trading Interests Act, 1980, 75 *American Journal of International Law* 257 (1981).

general liability insurance policies available in the United States. In his opinion for the Court, Justice Souter held that "even assuming that in a proper case a court may decline to exercise Sherman Act jurisdiction over foreign conduct . . . , international comity would not counsel against exercising jurisdiction in the circumstances alleged here."[51] Justice Souter argued that he did not have to engage in a comity analysis, deciding to defer or not to the United Kingdom, its law or courts. In his view there was no "true conflict between domestic and foreign law" since, though British law permitted the activities allegedly made illegal by the United States, Britain did not order the London reinsurers to violate U.S. antitrust law.[52] In dissent and rather more persuasively, Justice Scalia felt that more attention had to be paid to comity, that the relevant notions of comity here concerned "international choice-of-law principles," and that, following Restatement (Third), "a nation having some 'basis' for jurisdiction to prescribe law should nonetheless refrain from exercising that jurisdiction 'with respect to a person or activity having connections with another state when the exercise of such jurisdiction is unreasonable.' "[53] Professor Dam has lamented that *Hartford Fire* generated "a murky and unsatisfactory doctrinal squabble between the Souter majority and the Scalia minority over the terminology and principles to be used in determining the extraterritorial applicability of a statute."[54] Lamentably, it can also be observed that the majority view in *Hartford Fire* joins those in *Alvarez-Machain* [see Chapter 4] and *Breard* [see Chapter 5] as examples of the Supreme Court taking rather less account of the sensibilities of other countries than perhaps it ought. The Supreme Court's squabbling over the role of comity in interpreting the extraterritorial effect of statutes emerged once more in 2005 in *Spector*, where the Court again "splintered" on the doctrine.[55] Comity seems better served by the Supreme Court elsewhere, e.g., *The Paquete Habana* [see Chapter 3], *Foster & Elam* [see Chapter 4], *Lauritzen* above,

[51] Hartford Fire Insurance Co. v. California, 509 U.S. 764, 798 (1993).

[52] Ibid.

[53] Id. at 818.

[54] Dam, Extraterritoriality in an Age of Globalization: The *Hartford Fire* Case, 1993 *Supreme Court Review* 289.

[55] Spector v. Norwegian Cruise Line Ltd., 545 U.S. 119 (2005). See Hollis, Application of U.S. Law to Foreign-Flag Cruise Ships—Interpreting Statutes to Avoid Conflicts with International Law, 99 *American Journal of International Law* 881, 887 (2005).

Bremen above, and *Piper* below. There is still a vital role that comity can play in moderating conflicting extensions of national jurisdiction.[56]

To avoid cases of conflicts over extraterritorial jurisdiction, some assertions of state law that might offend foreign nations have been held to violate basic tenets of federalism. For example, see *Zschernig, Crosby,* and *Garamendi,* all discussed in Chapter 4.[57] The Constitution's supremacy clause forbids the states from applying their law to a case if a treaty of the United States applies.[58] There may even sometimes be a federal common law rule such as the act of state doctrine, which in an international field is held to be preemptive.[59]

Furthermore, U.S. constitutional law sets for its component states a "significant contacts" test for choice-of-law or legislative jurisdiction[60] and a "minimum contacts" test for adjudicatory jurisdiction.[61] However, although such constitutional law sometimes prevents a state of the United States from extending its laws[62] or from adjudicating a matter[63] because "significant contacts" or "minimum contacts" are too slight, such rules by their very non-exclusive nature may prove inadequate for deciding which of several states, foreign or domestic, should have prescriptive or adjudicatory jurisdiction when more than one state satisfies the constitutional tests, i.e., when there is concurrent jurisdiction.

To settle such cases of concurrent jurisdiction and to avoid offending the interests of foreign states and defendants, U.S. courts have increasingly employed the doctrine of *forum non conveniens. Forum non conveniens* is neither a rule of constitutional compulsion nor, strictly speaking, a jurisdictional principle. It comes into play only once it has

[56] Ginsburg & Talady, The Enduring Vitality of Comity in a Globalized World, 24 *George Mason Law Review* 1069 (2017); Dodge, International Comity in American Law, 115 *Columbia Law Review* 2071 (2015).

[57] Zschernig v. Miller, 389 U.S. 429 (1968); Crosby v. National Trade Council, 530 U.S. 363 (2000); American Insurance Association v. Garamendi, 539 U.S. 396 (2002).

[58] Ware v. Hylton, 3 U.S. (3 Dallas) 199 (1796).

[59] Banco Nacional de Cuba v. Sabbatino, 376 U.S. 398 (1964).

[60] Allstate Ins. Co. v. Hague, 449 U.S. 302 (1981).

[61] International Shoe Co. v. Washington, 326 U.S. 310 (1945).

[62] Phillips Petroleum Co. v. Shutts, 472 U.S. 797 (1985).

[63] World-Wide Volkswagen Corp. v. Woodson, 444 U.S. 286 (1980). In Helicópteros Nacionales de Colombia v. Hall, 466 U.S. 408 (1984), the Supreme Court held that, in a case arising out of a helicopter crash in Peru, Texas could not assert adjudicatory jurisdiction over a Colombian corporation that bought helicopters in Texas and sent personnel to the state for training.

been determined that a U.S. court has judicial jurisdiction. *Forum non conveniens* is a judge-made principle of common law that permits a court at its discretion to refuse to adjudicate a case properly within its jurisdiction on the grounds that the court is not sufficiently a "convenient" court or that another state's or country's court would be a fairer place to hear the case. The determination is made by looking not only at the relative merits of adjudicating the dispute in one or another court, but also at the relative rights of the parties. *Forum non conveniens* is defined by the Restatement (Second) of Conflict of Laws as follows: "A state will not exercise jurisdiction if it is a seriously inconvenient forum for the trial of the action provided that a more appropriate forum is available to the plaintiff."[64] The Foreign Relations Law Restatement (Fourth) has similar wording: "Under the federal doctrine of *forum non conveniens,* a federal court may dismiss a case if: (a) there is an available and adequate alternative forum; and (b) despite the deference owed to the plaintiff's choice of forum, the balance of private and public interests favors dismissal."[65]

Forum non conveniens is a relatively recent doctrinal development in the United States and received its crucial impetus only in 1947.[66] Nowadays, the doctrine has become increasingly useful as U.S. extraterritorial jurisdiction has been expanded. As more and more cases are deemed to fall within the legislative and judicial jurisdiction of the United States, courts fashioned the doctrine as a means by which to defer to foreign states and foreign courts. In practice, *forum non conveniens* has become the most important means employed in U.S. courts for exercising comity in cases of conflicting jurisdictional regimes.[67]

Key to the modern *forum non conveniens* doctrine is the judgment of the U.S. Supreme Court in Piper Aircraft Co. v. Reyno.[68] California

[64] American Law Institute, *Restatement of the Law (Second) Conflict of Laws* §84 (1969).

[65] Restatement (Fourth), supra, at 243.

[66] See Gulf Oil Corp. v. Gilbert, 330 U.S. 501 (1947); Koster v. (American) Lumbermens Mutual Casualty Co., 330 U.S. 518 (1947); Barrett, The Doctrine of *Forum Non Conveniens,* 35 *California Law Review* 380 (1947).

[67] Texas was one of the few U.S. state jurisdictions where the courts had refused to adopt the modern U.S. federal approach to *forum non conveniens.* See Albright, In Personam Jurisdiction: A Confused and Inappropriate Substitute for Forum Non Conveniens, 71 *Texas Law Review* 351 (1992). However, in 1993, the Texas legislature enacted a statute permitting Texas courts to employ the doctrine. See Weintraub, International Litigation and Forum Non Conveniens, 29 *Texas International Law Review* 321 (1994); Teitz, *Transnational Litigation* 123-125 (1996).

[68] 454 U.S. 235 (1981).

lawyers representing Scottish heirs to Scottish citizens killed in the crash of a Scottish aircraft made their California legal secretary, Gaynell Reyno, the personal representative of the estates of the Scottish decedents. Reyno then sued the U.S. manufacturers of the plane and of the plane's engine in California state court. Defendants removed the action to a federal district court in California, transferred the case to a federal district court in Pennsylvania where the plane had been manufactured, and finally asked the Pennsylvania federal court to dismiss the action on the grounds of *forum non conveniens* to permit the case to be tried in Scotland.

Reyno objected that litigating in Scotland would defeat one of her principal objects in bringing the suit to the United States, viz., securing more favorable U.S. substantive law. The Supreme Court held, however, that "[t]he possibility of a change in substantive law should ordinarily not be given conclusive or even substantial weight in the *forum non conveniens* inquiry." The Court felt that the essence of making the decision was answering the question of convenience. One of the benefits of dismissing on the grounds of *forum non conveniens* was not having to make complicated choice-of-law determinations, a benefit that would be entirely lost if the court, before the facts were proved, had to determine which laws would apply in a U.S. court and which in a foreign court. The Court refused to say that unfavorable choice of law should never be a consideration, but where, as in *Piper*, it could not be said that using Scottish law would violate the "interests of justice," it was not enough that plaintiff might simply win a smaller damage award.[69]

Looking to the factual pattern in *Piper*, the Supreme Court observed that since the real parties in interest, the Scottish heirs, were not located in the United States, there was little reason to assume that the choice of U.S. courts was made to suit plaintiff's real convenience. Furthermore, much of the relevant evidence and many of the crucial witnesses were located in Great Britain. The Supreme Court decided that the *forum non conveniens* determination should be made at "the sound discretion of the trial court," balancing "all relevant public and private interest factors," and held that the trial court had not abused its discretion by finding that Scotland, which had "a very strong interest" in trying the litigation, should be the place of trial.[70]

[69] Id. at 247, 250-255.
[70] Id. at 255-258.

B. Judicial Conflicts and Cooperation

In In re Union Carbide Corporation Gas Plant Disaster at Bhopal, India, the U.S. Second Circuit affirmed the decision of the federal court for the Southern District of New York that India was the proper forum for litigation involving the deaths of more than 2,000 persons and injuries to more than 200,000, the worst industrial accident in history. Weighing the private interest factors, the circuit court held:

> [T]he plant has been constructed and managed by Indians in India. . . . The vast majority of material witnesses and documentary proof bearing on causation of and liability for the accident is located in India, not the United States. . . . The records are almost entirely in Hindi or other Indian languages, understandable to an Indian court without translation. The witnesses for the most part do not speak English but Indian languages. . . . These witnesses could be required to appear in an Indian court but not in a court of the United States.[71]

Similarly, the public interest factors tilted toward India:

> [P]laintiffs have conceded that in view of India's strong interest and its greater contacts with the plant, its operation, its employees, and the victims of the accident, the law of India, as the place where the tort occurred, will undoubtedly govern.[72]

In 2007, in *Sinochem*, the Supreme Court unanimously reaffirmed the importance of giving the trial court broad discretion to dismiss cases on the grounds of *forum non conveniens*. Rejecting the Third Circuit's decision that the trial court had to determine first that it had jurisdiction before dismissing an international case on the grounds of *forum non conveniens*, Justice Ginsburg wrote:

> This is a textbook case for immediate *forum non conveniens* dismissal. The District Court's subject-matter jurisdiction presented an issue of first impression in the Third Circuit, and was considered at some length by the courts below. Discovery concerning personal jurisdiction would have

[71] 809 F.2d 195, 200-201 (2d Cir. 1987), *cert. denied*, 484 U.S. 871 (1987).

[72] Id. at 201. For further developments in the *Bhopal* Case, see Janis, The Doctrine of Forum Non Conveniens and the *Bhopal* Case, 34 *Netherlands International Law Review* 192 (1984); Bhopal litigation drags on in India. The Bhopal Disaster: The Slow Pursuit of Justice, *The Economist*, June 26, 2010, at 43; The Bhopal Gas Leak: An Unending Nightmare, *The Economist*, Dec. 5, 2024, at 29.

burdened Sinochem with expense and delay. And all to scant purpose: The District Court inevitably would dismiss the case without reaching the merits, given its well-considered *forum non conveniens* appraisal. Judicial economy is disserved by continuing litigation in the Eastern District of Pennsylvania given the proceedings long launched in China. And the gravamen of Malaysia International's complaint—misrepresentations to the Guangzhou Admiralty Court in the course of securing arrest of the vessel in China—is an issue best left for determination by the Chinese courts.[73]

2. *International Legal Limits to State Jurisdiction*

What sort of limits, if any, international law sets on the jurisdiction of states is a controversial question. Most civil law systems view jurisdictional rules as purely municipal law. Jurists from such systems characterize the "'international' element of this so-called private international law [as consisting] of ubiquitous and recurrent problems much more than of a body of secured general principles."[74] Common lawyers are somewhat more ready to admit true international rules into the body of conflict of laws.[75] Wheaton's classic Anglo-American nineteenth-century international law text argued, in language similar to Justice Holmes' holding in *American Banana*, that no state had the right to extend its legislative or judicial power into the territory of a foreign state except with the consent of the foreign state.[76] A principal International Court case dealing with extraterritorial jurisdiction, *Lotus*,[77] can be read both ways on this question. On the one hand, it offers the explicit assumption that international legal limits to state jurisdiction are not to be presumed. On the other hand, *Lotus* seems to suppose that, in some

[73] Sinochem Int'l Co. Ltd. v. Malaysia Int'l Shipping Corp., 549 U.S. 422, 435-436 (2007). A commentator has remarked that the "broader significance" of *Sinochem* is its "style of reasoning"; the Court's "pragmatic approach to transnational litigation" enhances judicial economy and reduces inconvenience. Whytock, U.S. Supreme Court Decides Forum Non Conveniens Case, *ASIL Insight*, Vol. 11, issue 10 (Apr. 5, 2007), www.asil.org/insights (Mar. 7, 2019).

[74] Kahn-Freund, General Problems of Private International Law, 143 *Hague Recueil* 139, 148 (1974).

[75] See Hilton v. Guyot, 159 U.S. 113, 163 (1895).

[76] H. Wheaton, *Elements of International Law with a Sketch of the History of the Science* 98-129 (1st ed. 1836).

[77] 1927 P.C.I.J. Reports, ser. A., no. 10.

circumstances, it is possible for the jurisdiction of states to be limited by international legal rules so long as such rules have been plainly consented to by states.[78]

Running through the decided cases of the United States and those of other countries is the presumption that state jurisdiction is determined by the states themselves, albeit tempered by their own notions of comity. Set against this are mostly doctrinal assertions that there are international legal limits to the jurisdiction of states. In the United States, the debate about international legal limits to the jurisdiction of states is often framed in terms of the Restatements. Section 40 of the Restatement (Second) dealt with "Limitations on Exercise of Enforcement Jurisdiction" and read rather like a statement of comity:

> Where two states have jurisdiction to prescribe and enforce rules of law and the rules they may prescribe require inconsistent conduct upon the part of a person, each state is required by international law to consider, in good faith, moderating the exercise of its enforcement jurisdiction, in the light of such factors as
>
> (a) vital national interests of each of the states,
>
> (b) the extent and the nature of the hardship that inconsistent enforcement actions would impose upon the person,
>
> (c) the extent to which the required conduct is to take place in the territory of the other state,
>
> (d) the nationality of the person, and
>
> (e) the extent to which enforcement by action of either state can reasonably be expected to achieve compliance with the rule prescribed by that state.[79]

The Restatement (Third), however, went much further. It did not simply require states to "consider" balancing factors in cases of conflicts of jurisdiction. Rather, the Restatement (Third) provided that even when a basis for jurisdiction exists, a state may not exercise prescriptive jurisdiction when the exercise of such jurisdiction would be "unreasonable."[80] Whether the exercise of jurisdiction is reasonable or not is to be "determined by evaluating all relevant factors," some of which include the place of the activity and of its effect; nationality; its

[78] See Guilfoyle, SS Lotus (France v. Turkey) (1927), *Landmark Cases in Public International Law* 89 (Bjorge & Miles eds. 2017).

[79] Restatement (Second), supra.

[80] American Law Institute, *Restatement (Third) of the Foreign Relations Law of the United States* §403(1) (1987).

importance to the regulating state; the existence of justified expectations; its importance to the international political, legal, or economic systems; consistency with international traditions; interests of other states; and the likelihood of conflict with other states.[81] If the exercise of jurisdiction by two states would not be unreasonable, then the Restatement (Third) read that each state should evaluate both states' interests in exercising jurisdiction and one state should defer to the other state if it deems that other state's interest to be greater than its own.[82]

The Restatement (Third) was unsupported by precedent when it asserted that reasonableness is a limit imposed by international law.[83] The principal case on which the Restatement (Third) relied was Timberlane Lumber Co. v. Bank of America.[84] However, the *Timberlane* case explicitly held that the balancing of interests test for the assertion of extraterritorial jurisdiction was "not defined by international law"; instead, it relied, *inter alia*, on the comity principle of Section 40 of the Restatement (Second).[85] *Timberlane*, which dealt with the extraterritorial application of U.S. antitrust law, asked

> [w]hether the interests of, and links to, the United States—including the magnitude of the effect on American foreign commerce—are sufficiently strong, vis-à-vis those of other nations, to justify an assertion of extraterritorial authority.[86] . . .
>
> The elements to be weighed include the degree of conflict with foreign law or policy, the nationality or allegiance of the parties and the locations or principal places of business of corporations, the extent to which enforcement by either state can be expected to achieve compliance, the relative significance of effects on the United States as compared with those elsewhere, the extent to which there is explicit purpose to harm or affect American commerce, the foreseeability of such effect,

[81] Id. §403(2).

[82] Id. §403(3).

[83] Section 403 was the most hotly controversial part of the entire revision of the Restatement. See the summary of the final debate on the section, Annual Meeting of American Law Institute, 54 U.S.L.W. 2593, 2595 (1986); Houck, Restatement of the Foreign Relations Law of the United States (Revised): Issues and Resolutions, 20 *International Lawyer* 1361, 1368-1372 (1986).

[84] 549 F.2d 597 (9th Cir. 1976).

[85] Id. at 609, 613.

[86] Id. at 613.

and the relative importance to the violations charged of conduct within the United States as compared with conduct abroad.[87]

While it might well be that the incorporation of a balancing test into international law would be a useful development, it was too early to agree that U.S. foreign relations law imposes an international legal requirement to weigh jurisdictional interests. It is more accurate to report that a balance of interests limit to extraterritorial jurisdiction is a feature of some, though not all, U.S. cases and that it seems that the limit is perceived as one stemming from notions of comity.[88] The Restatement (Fourth) returned to the more reasonable comity point of view: "In exercising jurisdiction to prescribe the United States takes account of the legitimate interests of other nations as a matter of prescriptive comity."[89]

Other countries have been even less inclined than the United States to gauge state jurisdiction on a measure of balancing of interests. F.A. Mann, a leading British international lawyer, claimed that there was no support for such an approach anywhere but in the United States and that "it should be firmly rejected"; he put the basic principle of international law quite simply: "The State has the right to exercise jurisdiction within the limits of its sovereignty, but is not entitled to encroach upon the sovereignty of other States."[90] Believing that sovereignty is fundamentally territorial in character, Mann, reflecting British laws and lawyers in general, is suspicious of many extraterritorial assertions, especially those of the United States.[91] Professor Brilmayer has put international legal limits alongside the U.S. Constitution and the judicial discretion of comity as "considerations" that U.S. courts take into account when evaluating U.S. extraterritorial assertions.[92]

[87] Id. at 614.

[88] For a more sympathetic view of the Restatement (Third) with respect to international legal limits on extraterritorial jurisdiction, see A.F. Lowenfeld, *International Litigation and Arbitration* 46-68 (1993).

[89] Restatement (Fourth), supra, at 148.

[90] Mann, The Doctrine of International Jurisdiction Revisited After Twenty Years, 186 *Hague Recueil* 9, 20 (1984).

[91] Id. at 20-98.

[92] Brilmayer, The Extraterritorial Application of American Law: A Methodological and Constitutional Approach, 50 *Law and Contemporary Problems* 11, 14-16 (Summer 1987).

Perhaps the best accounting of the status of international legal limits to state jurisdiction was rendered by Judge Fitzmaurice in *Barcelona Traction*:

> [I]nternational law does not impose hard and fast rules on States delimiting spheres of national jurisdiction . . . but leaves to States a wide discretion in the matter. It does however (a) postulate the *existence* of limits—though in any given case it may be for the tribunal to indicate what these are for the purposes of that case; and (b) involve for every State an obligation to exercise moderation and restraint as to the extent of the jurisdiction assumed by its courts in cases having a foreign element, and to avoid undue encroachment on a jurisdiction more properly appertaining to, or more appropriately exercisable by, another State.[93]

3. Foreign Judgments and Awards

Whether it be termed law or discretion, international law or municipal law, the doctrine of comity takes on its most concrete form in the policy of states, in certain circumstances, to recognize and enforce foreign judgments and awards and to compel (or at least not to frustrate) foreign judicial and arbitral proceedings. The comity displayed toward foreign judgments, awards, and proceedings not only promotes international cooperation, but also serves justice and fair play by ensuring that disputes are tried only once and that successful litigants have judicial and arbitral decisions in their favor respected in other states.

With respect to the recognition and enforcement of foreign judgments and awards, the full faith and credit clause, Article 4(1) of the U.S. Constitution, dictates a virtually unassailable principle of recognition and enforcement of U.S. sister state court judgments.[94] No such mandate, however, supports judgments running between the United States and foreign countries. Rather, the recognition and enforcement of foreign judgments and awards is, like other areas governed by comity, a matter where courts are given considerable discretion in deciding whether a foreign judgment or award will be recognized or enforced. The reigning U.S. precedent is again provided by Hilton v. Guyot:

[93] 1970 I.C.J. Reports 3, 105.

[94] See Fauntleroy v. Lum, 210 U.S. 230 (1908).

> [W]here there has been opportunity for a full and fair trial abroad before a court of competent jurisdiction, conducting the trial upon regular proceedings, after due citation or voluntary appearance of the defendant, and under a system of jurisprudence likely to secure an impartial administration of justice between the citizens of its own country and those of other countries, and there is nothing to show either prejudice in the court, or in the system of laws under which it was sitting, or fraud in procuring the judgment, or any other special reason why the comity of this nation should not allow it full effect, the merits of the case should not, in an action brought in this country upon the judgment, be tried afresh, as on a new trial or an appeal, upon the mere assertion of the party that the judgment was erroneous in law or in fact.[95]

As *Hilton* held, U.S. courts may choose not to recognize and enforce a foreign judgment if the foreign proceedings were irregular or if the foreign court did not have proper personal jurisdiction over the defendant. If, however, the foreign proceedings appear to have been fair, then the U.S. court will not usually allow fact or law to be relitigated, but will simply recognize and enforce the foreign judgment in this country. So in Somportex Limited v. Philadelphia Chewing Gum Corp., when American defendants refused to appear to argue in an English contract action, even though by jurisdictional principles common to both England and the United States they were properly subject to the adjudicatory jurisdiction of the English courts, the U.S. courts recognized and enforced the foreign judgment without permitting defendants to dispute either the facts or the law of the case.[96] It may be, though, that the U.S. court will require a degree of reciprocity before recognizing and enforcing a foreign decree. Indeed, France's failure to provide reciprocal treatment to U.S. judgments defeated the enforcement action in *Hilton*.[97]

Although this area seems ripe for international agreement, the United States is party to no convention on the recognition and enforcement of foreign judgments. Indeed, such a proposed treaty between the United States and the United Kingdom foundered on British fears of

[95] 159 U.S. 113, 202-203 (1895).

[96] 453 F.2d 435 (3d Cir. 1971), *cert. denied*, 405 U.S. 1017 (1972).

[97] Hilton v. Guyot, 159 U.S. 113, 210-228 (1895). The requirement of reciprocity is not, however, federally mandated, and states may and do differ from the *Hilton* case in this respect; see Johnston v. Compagnie Générale Transatlantique, 242 N.Y. 381 (1926).

extensive U.S. extraterritorial jurisdiction. A draft universal judgments convention was concluded at The Hague in 2018, but it is doubtful that, even if ratified by others, such a treaty would ultimately number the United States among its members.[98] The European Union, however, has concluded the Brussels Convention on Jurisdiction and the Enforcement of Judgments in Civil and Commercial Matters, which provides for the recognition and enforcement of judgments among member states while protecting against more exorbitant jurisdictional reaches.[99]

Though not a party to any treaty for the recognition and enforcement of foreign court judgments, the United States is a party to the 1958 New York Convention on the Recognition and Enforcement of Foreign Arbitral Awards.[100] Furthermore, on October 9, 1986, the Senate gave its advice and consent to the ratification of the 1975 Inter-American Convention on International Commercial Arbitration, a regional agreement intended to overcome the longstanding reluctance of many Latin American countries to recognize international arbitration.[101] Thus, as of December 2025, with respect to the 176 countries party to the New York Convention and the 19 countries party to the Inter-American Convention, the United States is bound by international law to compel foreign arbitration and to recognize and enforce many foreign arbitral awards, though there is no such compulsion with respect to their judicial proceedings or decisions.[102]

[98] Maier, A Hague Conference Judgments Convention and United States Courts: A Problem and a Possibility, 61 *Albany Law Review* 1207 (1998); Weintraub, How Substantial Is Our Need for a Judgments-Recognition Convention and What Should We Bargain Away to Get It?, 24 *Brooklyn Journal of International Law* 167 (1998).

[99] See Bartlett, Full Faith and Credit Comes to the Common Market: An Analysis of the Provisions of the Convention on Jurisdiction and Enforcement of Judgments in Civil and Commercial Matters, 24 *International & Comparative Law Quarterly* 44 (1975).

[100] 21 U.S.T. 2517, T.I.A.S. No. 6997, 330 U.N.T.S. 3 (done at New York June 10, 1958; entered into force June 7, 1959; for the United States December 29, 1970).

[101] OAS/Ser. A/20 (SEPF) (done at Panama January 30, 1975; entered into force June 16, 1976; for the United States October 27, 1990); 14 *International Legal Materials* 336; American Arbitration Association, 10 *Lawyers' Arbitration Letter*, No. 4, at 1-6 (December 1986); Lowry, The United States Joins the Inter-American Arbitration Convention, 7 *Journal of International Arbitration*, No. 3, at 83 (1990).

[102] www.newyorkconvention.org (accessed Dec. 30, 2025); www.oas.org (accessed Dec. 30, 2025). Even non-contracting states may sometimes enjoy the benefits of the New York Convention, see Graving, How Non-Contracting States to the "Universal"

B. Judicial Conflicts and Cooperation

The Supreme Court has displayed a distinct preference for international arbitration. In Scherk v. Alberto-Culver Co., an American defendant was sent to international arbitration in Paris:

> A contractual provision specifying in advance the forum in which disputes shall be litigated and the law to be applied is, therefore, an almost indispensable precondition to achievement of the orderliness and predictability essential to any international business transaction. . . . A parochial refusal by the courts of one country to enforce an international arbitration agreement would not only frustrate these purposes, but would invite unseemly and mutually destructive jockeying by the parties to secure tactical litigation advantages. . . . [It would] damage the fabric of international commerce and trade, and imperil the willingness and ability of businessmen to enter into international commercial agreements.[103]

Although *Scherk* chose not to reach the issue of whether the New York Convention required arbitration, the Court concluded that the Convention "confirmed" its contractual analysis and demonstrated national and international policy "to encourage the recognition and enforcement of commercial arbitration agreements in international contracts and to unify the standards by which agreements to arbitrate are observed and arbitral awards are enforced in the signatory countries."[104]

In Mitsubishi Motors Corporation v. Soler Chrysler-Plymouth, Inc., the Supreme Court relied on the New York Convention in sending a Puerto Rican automobile dealer to arbitration in Japan.[105] As in *Scherk*, the objection was raised that some of the law involved, in this case U.S. antitrust law, called for the exclusive jurisdiction of the U.S. courts. The Court held that if "international arbitral institutions . . . are to take a central place in the international legal order, national courts will need to 'shake off the old judicial hostility to arbitration,' and also their customary and understandable unwillingness to cede jurisdiction of a claim arising under domestic law to a foreign or

New York Arbitration Convention Enjoy Third-Party Benefits but Not Third-Party Rights, 14 *Journal of International Arbitration*, No. 3, at 167 (1997).

[103] 417 U.S. 506, 516-517 (1974).

[104] Id. at 520-521.

[105] 473 U.S. 614 (1985).

transnational tribunal." It was remarked that the national courts would have an opportunity to ensure that U.S. antitrust law was adequately addressed "at the award enforcement stage," the New York Convention explicitly providing that a country may refuse to enforce an award if enforcement "would be contrary to the public policy of that country."[106] Of course, if Soler or another defendant had assets outside the United States, Mitsubishi or another plaintiff need not necessarily bring the arbitral award to the United States for enforcement.

4. *Judicial Assistance and Extradition*

Judges have traditionally been willing, under proper circumstances, to render assistance to foreign courts, especially to help them serve process and to obtain evidence in their territory.[107] Usually such cooperation follows receipt of a letter rogatory, also called a letter of request, wherein the foreign court asks the court to do or permit some judicial act within its territory. These traditional cooperative procedures have been strengthened by the Hague Conventions on the Service Abroad of Judicial and Extrajudicial Documents in Civil or Commercial Matters and on the Taking of Evidence Abroad in Civil or Commercial Matters.[108] The relationship between these Hague Conventions and municipal law has posed difficulties for the courts in practice.[109]

In Volkswagenwerk Aktiengesellschaft v. Schlunk, for example, the Supreme Court held that the Hague Service Convention provided "mandatory" language respecting service of process abroad for both state and federal courts, but that the definition of what was "service

[106] Id. at 638, citing Kulukundis Shipping Co. v. Amtorg Trading Corp., 126 F.2d 978, 985 (2d Cir. 1942), and the Convention's art. V(2)(b).

[107] E.F. Scoles, P. Hay, P.J. Borchers & S.C. Symeonides, *Conflict of Laws* 518-543 (4th ed. 2004).

[108] 20 U.S.T. 361, T.I.A.S. No. 6638, 658 U.N.T.S. 163 (done at The Hague November 15, 1965; entered into force February 10, 1969), reproduced in 28 U.S.C.A., following Rule 4 of the Federal Rules of Civil Procedure; 23 U.S.T. 2555, T.I.A.S. No. 7444, 847 U.N.T.S. 231 (done at The Hague March 18, 1970; entered into force October 7, 1972), reproduced in 28 U.S.C.A., following §1781.

[109] See Reisenfeld, Service of United States Process Abroad: A Practical Guide to Service Under the Hague Service Convention and the Federal Rules of Civil Procedure, 24 *International Lawyer* 55 (1990); Sadoff, The Hague Evidence Convention: Problems at Home of Obtaining Foreign Evidence, 20 *International Lawyer* 659 (1986).

abroad" was a matter that the Convention left to the relevant internal law, in this case the law of the state of Illinois:

> The Convention does not prescribe a standard, so we almost necessarily must refer to the internal law of the forum state. If the internal law of the forum state defines the applicable method of serving process as requiring the transmittal of documents abroad, then the Hague Service Convention applies.[110]

There are bilateral treaties that facilitate judicial cooperation. The United States-Swiss Treaty on Mutual Assistance in Criminal Matters,[111] which though it does not require assistance if a state's "sovereignty, security or similar essential interests" are threatened, has been frequently employed with respect to U.S. securities law investigations.[112] The Swiss courts have, for example, provided the Securities and Exchange Commission with information about the identities of Swiss bank customers accused of violating the antifraud provisions of U.S. securities law.[113]

However, cooperation in criminal matters does not extend to the domestic application of foreign criminal law. As Chief Justice Marshall held in *The Antelope*: "The Courts of no country execute the penal laws of another."[114] So courts routinely refuse to permit prosecutions under foreign criminal law and may deny the application of other foreign public law if that law is "penal" in an international law sense, that is, if it concerns "an offense committed against the State, and which, by the

[110] 486 U.S. 694, 699, 700 (1988). Justice Brennan, writing for three Justices concurring, felt that, though there was not "service abroad" in this case, the definition of "service abroad" should be found in the Convention; otherwise, different internal definitions would undermine the Treaty. Id. at 708-716. For the majority, Justice O'Connor argued that "parties that comply with the Convention ultimately may find it easier to enforce their judgments abroad." Id. at 706.

[111] 27 U.S.T. 2019, T.I.A.S. No. 8302, 1052 U.N.T.S. 61 (signed at Bern May 25, 1973; entered into force January 23, 1977).

[112] Id., art. 3(1)(a); see Raifman, The Effect of the U.S.-Swiss Agreement on Swiss Banking Secrecy and Insider Trading, 15 *Georgetown Journal of Law & Policy in International Business* 565 (1983).

[113] See Leich, Contemporary Practice of the United States Relating to International Law, 79 *American Journal of International Law* 722, 727-728 (1985).

[114] 23 U.S. (10 Wheat.) 66, 123 (1825); see Janis, The Recognition and Enforcement of Foreign Law: *The Antelope*'s Penal Law Exception, 20 *International Lawyer* 303 (1986).

English and American constitutions, the executive of the State has the power to pardon."[115]

Instead, courts may as a matter of comity or, if obliged by treaty, must extradite persons to foreign countries so they may be tried there for criminal offenses. Treaties providing for extradition are an ancient feature of international relations.[116] The United States is party to more than 100 extradition treaties and receives more than 300 requests for extradition each year.[117] Unfortunately, the decision of the Supreme Court in *Alvarez-Machain*[118] casts a shadow over such treaties in general. [See Chapter 4.]

Generally, extradition treaties provide that a state is obligated to extradite persons to another state when the other state shows that the person is sought for trial for a crime allegedly committed within the jurisdiction of that state or for punishment for a crime committed in that state after conviction and flight from that state.[119] The obligation to extradite is normally subject to a number of exceptions, including an inadequate showing that the accused has committed the offense, a previous trial for the same offense, that the offense is not a crime in both the requesting and the requested state, that the period of limitations has run in either state, and when the offense is shown to be political in nature.[120]

Of all the exceptions, the one respecting political offenses has been the most controversial in practice. An early English rule, much relied upon by U.S. courts, is elaborated in *Castioni*:

> [I]t must at least be shewn that the act is done in furtherance of, done with the intention of assistance, as a sort of overt act in the course of

[115] Huntington v. Attrill, 146 U.S. 657, 667 (1892); see Leflar, Extrastate Enforcement of Penal and Governmental Claims, 46 *Harvard Law Review* 193 (1932). For an interesting challenge to the rule, see Dodge, Breaking the Public Law Taboo, 43 *Harvard International Law Journal* 161 (2002).

[116] G. Gilbert, *Aspects of Extradition Law* 9-11 (1991); Vieira, L'évolution récente de l'extradition dans le continent américain, 185 *Hague Recueil* 151, 170-171 (1984).

[117] M.C. Bassiouni, *International Extradition: United States Law and Practice iv* (4th ed. 2002) [hereinafter cited as "Bassiouni"].

[118] 504 U.S. 655 (1992).

[119] Restatement (Third), supra, at §475.

[120] Id. §476.

> acting in a political matter, a political rising, or a dispute between two parties in the State as to which is to have the government in its hands.[121]

The definition of what constitutes a "political rising" may not be an easy matter. For example, on the one hand, in Eain v. Wilkes, the Seventh Circuit held that a member of the Palestine Liberation Organization could be extradited to Israel to stand trial for a bombing in an Israeli marketplace. The court found that the act was aimed at undermining the social foundation of the government and was thus anarchistic and not entitled to protection as a political offense.[122] On the other hand, in *Matter of Mackin*, the Second Circuit upheld a magistrate's decision that a member of the Irish Republican Army could not be extradited to the United Kingdom because the crimes of which he was accused, for example, the attempted murder of a British soldier in Belfast, were incidental to a political uprising in Northern Ireland and thus were political offenses.[123] In Quinn v. Robinson, the Ninth Circuit held that the murder of a police constable in London by an IRA member did not fall within the exception because though there was a political uprising in Northern Ireland, acts in support of the uprising should not be protected if they were "exported" to another country.[124]

Faced with terrorist acts against civilian populations, albeit for political ends, governments have begun considering narrowing the political offense exception. The United States and the United Kingdom have signed and ratified a Supplementary Treaty to their 1972 Extradition Treaty.[125] The Supplementary Treaty excludes a number of offenses from being "regarded as an offense of a political character," including offenses within the scope of certain treaties, for example, those protecting aviation, and certain crimes such as murder, manslaughter, malicious wounding or inflicting grievous bodily harm, kidnapping, the taking of a hostage, and the causing of an explosion likely to

[121] [1891] 1 Q.B. 149, 156. See Recent Decisions: The Political Offense Exception to Extradition: A 19th Century British Standard in 20th Century American Courts, 59 *Notre Dame Law Review* 1005 (1984).

[122] 641 F.2d 504, 520-523 (7th Cir. 1981), *cert. denied,* 454 U.S. 894 (1981).

[123] 668 F.2d 122 (2d Cir. 1981).

[124] 783 F.2d 776, 813-814 (9th Cir. 1986), *cert. denied,* 479 U.S. 882 (1986).

[125] See the President's Letter of Transmittal, July 17, 1985, reprinted in 24 *International Legal Materials* 1104 (1985); the 1972 Treaty is at 28 U.S.T. 227; T.I.A.S. No. 8468 (signed at London June 8, 1972; entered into force January 21, 1977).

endanger or cause serious damage to property or the making of such an explosion.[126]

If there is no treaty regulating extradition between two countries, courts employ principles of reciprocity and comity to decide whether to extradite. National legislation may also provide some guidance. In any case, extradition without a treaty is a matter governed by no very definite rules of international law and may well be subject to considerable judicial discretion.[127]

C. IMMUNITIES TO JURISDICTION

1. *Foreign Sovereign Immunity*

The doctrine of foreign sovereign immunity shields foreign sovereigns from the jurisdictional reach of municipal courts on the theory that to implead the foreign sovereign could upset the friendly relations of the states.[128] It has been reported that questions relating to jurisdictional immunities figure more before national courts than do any other questions of international law.[129] Foreign sovereign immunities is a field

[126] Supplementary Extradition Treaty Between the United States of America and the United Kingdom (signed at Washington June 25, 1985), art. 1, reprinted in 24 *International Legal Materials* 1105 (1985). A critique of the Supplementary Treaty is to be found in Blakesley, The Evisceration of the Political Offense Exception to Extradition, 15 *Denver Journal of International Law & Politics* 109 (1986). On the history and character of the political offense exception, see Bassiouni, supra, at 594-675. On changes to the U.S./U.K. Extradition Treaty, see New U.S./E.U. and U.S./U.K. Extradition Treaties, 98 *American Journal of International Law* 848 (2004); Senate Approves U.K. Extradition Treaty and Other Bilateral and Multilateral Treaties, Attaches Reservations and Understandings, 101 *American Journal of International Law* 199 (2007).

[127] Bassiouni, supra, at 47-48.

[128] See E. Chukueneke Okeke, *Jurisdictional Immunities of States and International Organizations* (2018) [hereinafter cited as "Chukueneke Okeke"].

[129] Bouchez, The Nature and Scope of State Immunity from Jurisdiction and Execution, 10 *Netherlands Yearbook of International Law* 3, 4 (1979). Between 1999 and 2008, there was a 70 percent increase in reported U.S. foreign sovereign immunity cases. Portnoy et al., The Foreign Sovereign Immunities Act: 2008 Year in Review, 16 *Law and Business Review of the Americas* 179, 180 (2010). There is a more recent survey of case law in Crowell & Moring LLP, The Foreign Sovereign Immunities Act: 2014

where national courts play a most important role in shaping international law.[130]

In the United States, the doctrine of foreign sovereign immunity was first authoritatively rendered by Chief Justice John Marshall in 1812 in The Schooner Exchange v. M'Faddon.[131] A French warship, the *Balaou,* was forced by bad weather to enter the port of Philadelphia where it was libeled by U.S. citizens who alleged that the ship was in reality *The Schooner Exchange,* a merchant vessel wrongfully seized and confiscated on the high seas by the French government. Marshall held that though "[t]he jurisdiction of the nation within its own territory is necessarily exclusive and absolute,"[132] such theoretically absolute territorial jurisdiction had to be limited in practice with respect to foreign sovereigns:

> One sovereign being in no respect amenable to another, and being bound by obligations of the highest character not to degrade the dignity of his nation, by placing himself or its sovereign rights within the jurisdiction of another, can be supposed to enter a foreign territory only under an express license, or in the confidence that the immunities belonging to his independent sovereign station, though not expressly stipulated, are reserved by implication, and will be extended to him.[133]

As for foreign sovereigns, so for their warships: It was "a principle of public law, that national ships of war, entering the port of a friendly power open for their reception, are to be considered as exempted by the consent of that power from its jurisdiction."[134]

Affording a foreign sovereign immunity does not deny plaintiffs all redress; it only forecloses their national courts. Claimants may always turn to the foreign sovereign's judicial system or avail themselves of

---

Year in Review, 21 *Law and Business Review of the Americas* 141 (2016). For the doctrine in general, see Chukueneke Okeke, supra.

[130] See Roberts, Comparative International Law?: The Role of National Courts in Creating and Enforcing International Law, 60 *International & Comparative Law Quarterly* 57 (2011). This may not always be a good thing, see Damrosch, Changing International Law of Sovereign Immunity Through National Decisions, 44 *Vanderbilt Journal of Transnational Law* 1185 (2011).

[131] 11 U.S. (7 Cranch) 116 (1812).

[132] Id. at 136.

[133] Id. at 137.

[134] Id. at 145-146.

diplomatic channels. Indeed, diplomacy in *The Schooner Exchange* case finally led to a measure of compensation.[135]

The Foreign Sovereign Immunities Act of 1976 (FSIA) codifies what had been in the United States an area of common law. The FSIA provides that "[s]ubject to existing international agreements to which the United States is a party at the time of enactment of this Act a foreign state shall be immune from the jurisdiction of the courts of the United States and of the States except as provided [in the Act]."[136] A "foreign state" is defined to include "an agency or instrumentality of a foreign state," which in turn is defined as including separate legal entities that are either "an organ of a foreign state or political subdivision thereof, or a majority of whose shares or other ownership interest is owned by a foreign state or political subdivision thereof" and "which is neither a citizen of a State of the United States . . . nor created under the laws of any third country."[137]

Before the passage of the FSIA, the granting of immunity was often decided on the basis of a formal suggestion made by the Department of State. One of the principal objects of the FSIA was to relieve the State Department of the burden and possible diplomatic repercussions of determining whether immunity should be afforded.[138] The FSIA now provides that claims of foreign states to immunity are to be decided by the courts.[139] The FSIA, however, does not preclude the State Department from filing with a court its suggestions about the granting of sovereign immunity. In its first such intervention since the enactment of the FSIA in 1976, the State Department argued successfully in Jackson v. People's Republic of China that the FSIA should not be applied retroactively to permit American bondholders to sue the People's Republic of China in the United States on 1911 Imperial Chinese Government railway bonds.[140]

[135] Reeves, A Note on Exchange v. M'Faddon, 18 *American Journal of International Law* 320 (1924).

[136] Pub. L. No. 94-583, 90 Stat. 2891, as amended, Pub. L. No. 100-669 (1988), 28 U.S.C. §1604 [hereinafter cited as "FSIA"].

[137] Id. §1603(a), (b).

[138] Statement of C.N. Brower, Legal Adviser to the Department of State, *Hearings on Immunities of Foreign States,* House of Representatives, Committee on the Judiciary, Serial No. 10, June 7, 1973, at 14-28.

[139] FSIA, supra, §1602.

[140] 596 F. Supp. 386 (N.D. Ala. 1984), *aff'd,* 794 F.2d 1490 (11th Cir. 1986), *cert. denied,* 480 U.S. 917 (1987).

C. Immunities to Jurisdiction

The most important exception to the rule of foreign sovereign immunity exposes a foreign sovereign to suit when the foreign government engages in commercial rather than public activities. The commercial activities exception is based on the notion that, though a state's acts may sometimes be those of a sovereign, *acta imperii*, they are at other times those of a merchant, *acta gestionis*. As states in the nineteenth and twentieth centuries increasingly engaged in business pursuits, it seemed unfair to shield such commercial activities from litigation in the national courts of foreign countries.

The commercial activities exception, also known as the restrictive theory of foreign sovereign immunity, was relatively late in arriving in the United States. For many years, the U.S. rule was the principle of absolute sovereign immunity. Jurisdiction over the commercial activities of foreign states, such as merchant shipping, was regularly rejected by the U.S. courts.[141] The restrictive theory was adopted in the United States in 1952 when in the Tate letter, the Acting Legal Adviser to the State Department communicated his opinion to the Justice Department that because many countries had adopted or were contemplating adopting the restrictive theory and because "the widespread and increasing practice on the part of governments of engaging in commercial activities makes necessary a practice which will enable persons doing business with them to have their rights determined in the courts," the United States should no longer afford absolute immunity to foreign states.[142] Although perhaps not bound in law to follow such advice from the Executive Branch, U.S. courts did in fact change course and begin to hear and decide cases brought against foreign sovereigns for their commercial activities.[143]

Like the doctrine of foreign sovereign immunity in general, the restrictive theory has moved from its common law foundations into U.S. statute. Section 1605 of the FSIA establishes a foreign state's commercial activities as one of a number of exceptions to Section 1604's presumptive grant of immunity to foreign states and to their political subdivisions, agencies, and instrumentalities:

> A foreign state shall not be immune from the jurisdiction of courts of the United States or of the States in any case . . . in which the action is

[141] Berizzi Brothers Co. v. The Pesaro, 271 U.S. 562 (1926).

[142] Letter of Acting Legal Adviser, Jack B. Tate, to Department of Justice, May 19, 1952, 26 *Department of State Bulletin* 984, 985 (1952).

[143] Victory Transport, Inc. v. Comisaria General de Abastecimientos y Transportes, 336 F.2d 354 (2d Cir. 1964), *cert. denied*, 381 U.S. 934 (1965).

> based upon a commercial activity carried on in the United States by the foreign state; or upon an act performed in the United States in connection with a commercial activity of the foreign state elsewhere; or upon an act outside the territory of the United States in connection with a commercial activity of the foreign state elsewhere and that act causes a direct effect in the United States.[144]

The FSIA provides only slight guidance as to what is or is not commercial activity:

> A "commercial activity" means either a regular course of commercial conduct or a particular commercial transaction or act. The commercial character of an activity shall be determined by reference to the nature of the course of conduct or particular transaction or act, rather than by reference to its purpose.[145]

Thus, what constitutes commercial activity in any particular case is more a question of judicial precedent and discretion than it is one of statutory direction.[146]

The FSIA codifies several other exceptions to foreign state immunity of which the most important, next to the commercial activities exception, is the exception relating to waivers, that is, permitting suit in any case "in which the foreign state has waived its immunity either explicitly or by implication, notwithstanding any withdrawal of the waiver which the foreign state may purport to effect except in accordance with the terms of the waiver."[147] Explicit waivers are to be found in treaties among states as well as in negotiated agreements with private parties. For example, the Treaty of Friendship, Commerce, and Navigation Between the United States and Japan provides:

[144] FSIA, supra, §1605(a)(2).

[145] Id. §1603(d).

[146] See Texas Trading & Milling Corp. v. Federal Republic of Nigeria, 647 F.2d 300, 310 (2d Cir. 1981), *cert. denied,* 454 U.S. 1148 (1982), deciding that the purchase of cement by the government of Nigeria was "in the nature of a private contract for the purchase of goods. Its purpose—to build roads, army barracks, whatever—is irrelevant." In Republic of Argentina v. Weltover, Inc., 504 U.S. 607 (1992), a unanimous Supreme Court decided that the commercial activities exception permitted private bondholders to sue Argentina when it unilaterally rescheduled repayment of government bonds. See Pizzurro, Republic of Argentina v. Weltover, Inc., 86 *American Journal of International Law* 820 (1992).

[147] FSIA, supra, §1605(a)(1).

C. Immunities to Jurisdiction

> No enterprise of either party, including corporations, associations, and government agencies and instrumentalities, which is publicly owned or controlled shall, if it engages in commercial, industrial, shipping or other business activities within the territories of the other party, claim or enjoy, either for itself or for its property, immunity therein from taxation, suit, execution of judgment or other liability to which privately owned and controlled enterprises are subject therein.[148]

Typical of public/private waivers are those negotiated by private purchasers of foreign government bonds, such as the one described in a prospectus for the sale of Norwegian government securities:

> Norway will irrevocably waive any immunity from jurisdiction to which it might otherwise be entitled in any action arising out of or based on the Notes which may be instituted by any holder of a Note in any State or Federal court in New York City or in any competent court in Norway.[149]

As might be imagined, implicit waivers usually prove more troublesome for the courts than do explicit waivers. Typical factual patterns often involve agreements to arbitrate. It is a basic principle of U.S. law that agreements to arbitrate (whether involving a foreign state or not) imply a submission to the adjudicatory jurisdiction of the courts so as to enable the courts to compel arbitration and to enforce any arbitral award. The landmark case comes from New York:

> Defendants' agreement without reservation to arbitrate in London according to the English statute necessarily implied a submission to the procedure whereby that law is there enforced. Otherwise the inference must be drawn that they never intended to abide by their pledge.[150]

The implicit waiver exception with respect to arbitral agreements was significantly bolstered in 1988, with amendments to the FSIA. A new exception to the jurisdictional immunities of foreign states was added for cases

[148] Art. 18(2), 4 U.S.T. 2063, T.I.A.S. No. 2863, 206 U.N.T.S. 143 (signed at Tokyo April 2, 1953; entered into force October 30, 1953).

[149] Prospectus for $125,000,000 Kingdom of Norway 8⅛ Percent Notes Due January 15, 1983, at 38 (Securities and Exchange Commission Registration No. 2-60522, January 12, 1978).

[150] Gilbert v. Burnstine, 255 N.Y. 348, 354, 174 N.E. 706 (1931).

> in which the action is brought, either to enforce an agreement made by the foreign State with or for the benefit of a private party to submit to arbitration all or any differences which have arisen or which may arise between the parties with respect to a defined legal relationship, whether contractual or not, concerning a subject matter capable of settlement by arbitration under the laws of the United States, or to confirm an award made pursuant to such an agreement to arbitrate if [one of several conditions respecting a relationship to the United States is met].[151]

Of course, there may still be implicit waiver questions concerning agreements not meeting the standards of the new arbitral exception as well as concerning implicit waivers read from provisions contractually implying submission to U.S. or state municipal litigation.[152]

In the United States, besides the exceptions to a state's sovereign immunity for commercial activities and for its waivers, the FSIA provides an exception for cases involving property "taken in violation of international law," or for property acquired by succession or gift or for property that is immovable and located in the United States. The Act also excepts personal injury claims such as those likely to occur in automobile accidents. There is no immunity in admiralty suits where a "maritime lien is based upon a commercial activity of the foreign state." A new exception was added by the Antiterrorism and Effective Death Penalty Act of 1996 to cover cases "in which money damages are sought against a foreign state for personal injury or death that was caused by an act of torture, extrajudicial killing, aircraft sabotage, hostage taking, or the provision of material support or resources" for such acts.[153]

Despite the greater specificity of the FSIA, ambiguities about foreign state immunities still precipitate litigation. In *Dole Food* in 2003, the Supreme Court interpreted the FSIA not to provide protection to several companies that asserted they were instrumentalities of Israel.

[151] FSIA, supra, §1605(a)(6).

[152] For example, in Joseph v. Office of the Consulate General of Nigeria, 830 F.2d 1018 (9th Cir. 1987), the court found there had been an implicit waiver of sovereign immunity by Nigeria when it signed a lease agreement providing, *inter alia*, "[i]n the event that any action shall be commenced by either party hereto arising out of, or concerning this lease or any right or obligation derived therefrom, then in addition to all other relief at law or equity, the prevailing party shall be entitled to recover attorney's fees as fixed by the court." The court concluded that the agreement "contemplates participation of the United States courts in disputes between Joseph and her tenants."

[153] FSIA, supra, §1605(a)(3), (4); §1605(a)(5); §1605(b); §1605(a)(7).

Justice Kennedy held that the "State of Israel did not have direct ownership in either of the Dead Sea companies at any time pertinent to this suit. Rather, these companies were, at various times, separated from the State of Israel by one or more intermediate corporate ties."[154] *Altmann* in 2004 involved the return of art works taken by the Nazis during World War II. Justice Stevens interpreted the FSIA as to apply to conduct before the statute's enactment.[155] In *Permanent Mission of India to the United Nations*, Justice Thomas for the Supreme Court held that city tax liens were entitled to the FSIA exception to immunity respecting "rights in immovable property in the United States."[156] In 2010, the Supreme Court unanimously held in Samantor v. Yousuf that a foreign government official was not shielded by the FSIA for alleged torture under the Alien Tort Statute or the Torture Victims Protection Act, but held open the possibility that immunity might be provided by the common law.[157] In 2018, the Supreme Court protected ancient tablets held at the University of Chicago on loan from Iraq from attachment in a terrorism suit.[158] In 2019, in *Jam*, the Supreme Court held 7-1 that

[154] Dole Food Co. v. Patrickson, 538 U.S. 468, 473 (2003). Professor Vázquez notes that *Dole Food* "significantly narrows the scope of the FSIA." Vázquez, Addendum to "New Supreme Court Term Includes Issues of Foreign Sovereign Immunity," American Society of International Law, *ASIL Insights* (May 2003).

[155] Republic of Austria v. Altmann, 541 U.S. 677 (2004). Professor Brower observes that *Altmann*, by viewing sovereign immunity as a matter of comity rather than legal obligation, "may reinforce the perception of a waning commitment to international law throughout the United States and its three branches of government." Brower, United States Supreme Court: Republic of Austria v. Maria V. Altmann, 99 *American Journal of International Law* 236, 242 (2005).

[156] Permanent Mission of India to the United Nations v. City of New York, 551 U.S. 193 (2007). Professor Greenawalt laments that the Court's "majority opinion is noteworthy for its limited reliance on international and foreign legal sources to inform its interpretation of the FSIA and for its lack of deference to the contrary expressed views of the Executive Branch." Greenawalt, Foreign Sovereign Immunities Act: Supreme Court Upholds New York City Action for Tax Liens, American Society of International Law, *ASIL Insights* (August 2007).

[157] 560 U.S. 305 (2010). See Stephens, The Modern Common Law of Foreign Official Immunity, 79 *Fordham Law Review* 2669 (2011); Totten, The Adjudication of Foreign Official Immunity Determination in the United States Post-*Samantar*: A Circuit Split and Its Implications, 26 *Duke Journal of Comparative & International Law* 517 (2016).

[158] Rubin v. Islamic Republic of Iran, 583 U.S. 202 (2018). See Galbraith, Contemporary Practice of the United States Relating to International Law, 112 *American Journal of International Law* 486, 469 (2019).

for an international organization headquartered in the United States, the FSIA, rather than earlier sovereign immunity case law, governed liability.[159]

2. *The Act of State Doctrine*

Though not itself strictly speaking a rule of immunity, the act of state doctrine, embodying a special deference sometimes shown by national courts toward the public acts of foreign states done within their own territories, is closely linked to the doctrine of sovereign immunity in practice. In the United States, the act of state doctrine was first enunciated in Underhill v. Hernandez.[160] A U.S. citizen asked the U.S. courts to award him damages for his detention by Venezuelan armed forces. The Supreme Court refused.

> Every sovereign State is bound to respect the independence of every other sovereign State, and the courts of one country will not sit in judgment on the acts of the government of another done within its own territory. Redress of grievances by reason of such acts must be obtained through the means open to be availed of by sovereign powers as between themselves.[161]

Although in *Underhill* an immunity notion might equally well have been employed to protect the Venezuelan government and its agents from the scrutiny of the U.S. court, over time, the act of state doctrine has evolved into a doctrine with quite a different foundation than that of foreign sovereign immunity. Instead of looking to the limits of the jurisdiction of national courts as does the foreign sovereign immunity doctrine, the act of state doctrine is fundamentally concerned with the prescriptive jurisdiction of the foreign state. Thus, instead of operating as a jurisdictional principle, the act of state doctrine functions rather like a choice-of-law rule. The result may be viewed as a court's

[159] Jam v. Int'l Fin. Corp., 139 S. Ct. 759 (2019). See Federal Republic of Germany v. Phillip, 592 U.S. 169 (2021), where takings in Nazi Germany against its own citizens was held to be domestic and not international and subject to an FSIA exception.

[160] 168 U.S. 250 (1897).

[161] Id. at 252.

acceptance of the legitimacy of a foreign state's territorial prescriptions, untested either by international or domestic standards.[162]

In practice, this means that the act of state doctrine, unlike the doctrine of foreign sovereign immunity, may be employed by private as well as by public litigants. So, for example, in another classic act of state case, Oetjen v. Central Leather Co., a U.S. leather company was able to rely on the act of state doctrine to defeat a claim that property in its possession had been illegally seized by the Mexican government:

> The principle that the conduct of one independent government cannot be successfully questioned in the courts of another is as applicable to a case involving the title to property brought within the custody of a court, such as we have here, as it was held to be to the cases cited, in which claims for damages were based upon acts done in a foreign country, for it rests at last upon the highest considerations of international comity and expediency. To permit the validity of the acts of one sovereign State to be re-examined and perhaps condemned by the courts of another would very certainly "imperil the amicable relations between governments and vex the peace of nations."[163]

Despite their doctrinal differences, the act of state doctrine and the rules of foreign sovereign immunity are functionally similar insofar as both defer to foreign sovereigns and compel domestic claimants to appeal to foreign courts or submit to the vagaries of diplomacy to protect their interests. As the court in *Oetjen* remarked: "The remedy of the former owner, or of the purchaser from him, of the property in controversy, if either has any remedy, must be found in the courts of Mexico or through the diplomatic agencies of the political department of our Government."[164]

The high water mark for the act of state doctrine came in Banco Nacional de Cuba v. Sabbatino.[165] The case concerned the expropriation by the Cuban government of a Cuban sugar company, C.A.V., owned by U.S. nationals. The question for the U.S. courts was whether proceeds for some sugar sold by C.A.V. should be paid over to the Cuban national bank acting as representative for the Cuban government or

[162] See generally Restatement (Third), supra, §443.
[163] 246 U.S. 297, 303-304 (1918).
[164] Id. at 304.
[165] 376 U.S. 398 (1964).

rightfully belonged to Sabbatino, who was the New York-appointed receiver of C.A.V.'s assets in New York, and, in effect, was acting for the expropriated U.S. owners. Pursuant to Cuban law, the sugar proceeds were the property of the Cuban government, but Sabbatino argued that the U.S. courts should apply international legal minimum standards requiring adequate compensation for expropriated property, rather than accept the Cuban confiscation as legitimate.

The lower federal courts agreed to look to international law and held that the Cuban expropriation was illegal, but the Supreme Court reversed.

> [T]he Judicial Branch will not examine the validity of a taking of property within its own territory by a foreign sovereign government, extant and recognized by this country at the time of suit, in the absence of a treaty or other unambiguous agreement regarding controlling legal principles, even if the complaint alleges that the taking violates customary international law.[166]

The Supreme Court held that the act of state doctrine was compelled neither "by the inherent nature of sovereign authority" nor "by some principle of international law," but emerged from "the proper distribution of functions between the judicial and political branches of the Government on matters bearing upon foreign affairs."[167] The Court felt judges needed to be especially restrained when they dealt with "aspects of international law [which] touch much more sharply on national nerves than do others."[168] Since "[t]here are few if any issues in international law today on which opinion seems to be so divided as the limitations on a state's power to expropriate the property of aliens," the Court saw itself better off leaving the question of securing Cuban compensation for expropriated property to the Executive Branch of the government.[169]

[166] Id. at 428.

[167] Id. at 421, 427-428.

[168] Id. at 428.

[169] Id. at 428-437. Some date the act of state doctrine to *Sabbatino* rather than *Underhill.* See Henderson, The American Act of State Doctrine, 47 *Georgia Journal of International Law* 507 (2016).

Congress reacted swiftly and with hostility to the *Sabbatino* decision. In 1964, the Foreign Assistance Act was amended to read, in part, as follows:

> [N]o court in the United States shall decline on the ground of the federal act of state doctrine to make a determination on the merits giving effect to the principles of international law in a case in which a claim of title or other right to property is asserted by any party including a foreign state (or a party claiming through such state) based upon (or traced through) a confiscation or other taking after January 1, 1959, by an act of that state in violation of the principles of international law, including the principles of compensation and the other standards set out in this subsection: *Provided*, That this subparagraph shall not be applicable (1) in any case in which an act of a foreign state is not contrary to international law or with respect to a claim of title or other right to property acquired pursuant to an irrevocable letter of credit of not more than 180 days duration issued in good faith prior to the time of the confiscation or other taking, or (2) in any case with respect to which the President determines that application of the act of state doctrine is required in that particular case by the foreign policy interests of the United States and a suggestion to this effect is filed on his behalf in that case with the court.[170]

The applicable "principles of international law" are "speedy compensation for such property in convertible foreign exchange, equivalent to the full value thereof as required by international law."[171]

Since the Sabbatino Amendment, it has been a downhill road for the act of state doctrine in judicial practice. In the *Sabbatino* case itself, on remand, the district court applied the Sabbatino Amendment and, following the judgment of the court of appeals already reversed on other grounds by the Supreme Court, held that Cuba's expropriation of C.A.V. violated international law.[172] The court of appeals affirmed, and the Supreme Court refused to hear the case again.[173]

In its next pronouncement on the act of state doctrine, First National City Bank v. Banco Nacional de Cuba,[174] the Supreme Court

[170] 22 U.S.C. §2370(e)(2).

[171] 22 U.S.C. §2370(e)(1).

[172] Banco Nacional de Cuba v. Farr, 243 F. Supp. 957 (S.D.N.Y. 1965).

[173] 383 F.2d 166 (2d Cir. 1967), *cert. denied*, 390 U.S. 956 (1968).

[174] 406 U.S. 759 (1972).

in four separate opinions avoided relying on the congressional amendment "reversing" *Sabbatino*, but nonetheless refused to apply the doctrine. Instead, Justice Rehnquist, writing for himself and two other of the five Justices in the majority, endorsed the so-called *Bernstein* exception, as formulated by the Second Circuit Court of Appeals, Bernstein v. Van Heyghen Freres, S.A.,[175] a case where the executive department had advised the courts that it did not want the act of state doctrine applied. Per Justice Rehnquist in *First National City Bank*:

> The act of state doctrine is grounded on judicial concern that application of customary principles of law to judge the acts of a foreign sovereign might frustrate the conduct of foreign relations by the political branches of the government. We conclude that where the Executive Branch, charged as it is with primary responsibility for the conduct of foreign affairs, expressly represents to the Court that application of the act of state doctrine would not advance the interests of American foreign policy, that doctrine should not be applied by the courts.[176]

Neither Justice Douglas nor Justice Powell, who joined the majority in abandoning the act of state doctrine in *First National City Bank*, chose to rely on the *Bernstein* exception. Justice Brennan, however, writing for the four dissenting Justices felt that the act of state doctrine was fundamentally grounded on the idea that certain issues were political questions beyond the competence of the judiciary regardless of what advice the courts received from the President: "The Executive Branch, however extensive its powers in the area of foreign affairs, cannot by simple stipulation change a political question into a cognizable claim."[177]

In *First National City Bank*, Justice Rehnquist sought to blend the act of state doctrine back into the doctrine of foreign sovereign immunity.

> The separate lines of cases enunciating both the act of state and sovereign immunity doctrines have a common source in the case of The Schooner Exchange v. M'Faddon. There Chief Justice Marshall stated the general principle of sovereign immunity: sovereigns are not presumed without explicit declaration to have opened their tribunals to suits against

[175] 163 F.2d 246 (2d Cir. 1947).
[176] 406 U.S. 759, 767-768 (1972).
[177] Id. at 788-789.

> other sovereigns. Yet the policy considerations at the root of this fundamental principle are in large part also the underpinnings of the act of state doctrine. . . . [B]oth the act of state and sovereign immunity doctrines are judicially created to effectuate general notions of comity among nations and among the respective branches of the Federal Government.[178]

The blending of the act of state doctrine into foreign sovereign immunity went even further in Alfred Dunhill of London v. Cuba, where Justice White refused to accord act of state treatment to the repudiation of debts owed by Cuban-nationalized cigar companies.

> Repudiation of a commercial debt cannot, consistent with [the] restrictive approach to sovereign immunity, be treated as an act of state; for if it were, foreign governments, by merely repudiating the debt before or after its adjudication, would enjoy an immunity which our Government would not extend them under prevailing sovereign immunity principles in this country. This would undermine the policy supporting the restrictive view of immunity, which is to assure those engaging in commercial transactions with foreign sovereignties that their rights will be determined in the courts whenever possible.[179]

The courts have held that the act of state doctrine protects the sovereignty of foreign states, and when a foreign sovereign merely provides its machinery of justice to private litigants, the doctrine does not come into play. So, for example, if "the allegedly 'sovereign' acts of [a state] consisted of judicial proceedings which were initiated by . . . a private party and [not by the state] itself," then the act of state doctrine is inapplicable.[180] Similarly, a state's sovereignty is not infringed by a U.S. court's review of the legality at U.S. law of an extraterritorial act of a private party if that act is only authorized or permitted, rather than compelled, by a foreign state.[181]

In W.S. Kirkpatrick and Co. v. Environmental Tectonics Corp. International, the Supreme Court refused yet again to apply the act of state doctrine, in this instance raised by a U.S. company defending itself

[178] Id. at 762.

[179] 425 U.S. 682, 698-699 (1976).

[180] Timberlane Lumber Co. v. Bank of America, 549 F.2d 597, 608 (9th Cir. 1976).

[181] Continental Ore Co. v. Union Carbide & Carbon Corp., 370 U.S. 690, 706 (1962).

in a civil complaint. Kirkpatrick had pleaded guilty in a criminal investigation under the Foreign Corrupt Practices Act, admitting that it had bribed Nigerian officials to win a contested contract to build an aeromedical center at a Nigerian air force base. Kirkpatrick defended itself against a civil claim brought against it by a U.S. competitor for the contract on the grounds, *inter alia*, that if U.S. courts heard the case, it would embarrass the Nigerian government. Writing for the Court, Justice Scalia held:

> The short of the matter is this: Courts in the United States have the power, and ordinarily the obligation, to decide cases and controversies properly presented to them. The act of state doctrine does not establish an exception for cases and controversies that may embarrass foreign governments, but merely requires that, in the process of deciding, the acts of foreign sovereigns taken within their own jurisdictions shall be deemed valid. That doctrine has no application to the present case because the validity of no foreign sovereign act is at issue.[182]

The future of the act of state doctrine is much debated. Critics complain that, when employed, the doctrine is "bizarre" because it "requires a United States court to direct a United States citizen to turn over property in the United States to a foreign state, pursuant to an act of that state that violates international law."[183] At best, perhaps, "*Sabbatino*'s holding is modest."[184] In 1988, Congress made a rule that the act of state doctrine could not be used to prevent "[e]nforcement of arbitral agreements, confirmation of arbitral awards, and execution upon judgments based on orders confirming such awards."[185]

However, the doctrine is not dead yet. The Restatement (Fourth) provides, respecting the act of state doctrine: "In the absence of a treaty or other unambiguous agreement regarding controlling legal principles, courts in the United States will assume the validity of an official act of a foreign sovereign performed within its own territory."[186] For

[182] 493 U.S. 400, 409-410 (1990).

[183] Halberstam, Sabbatino Resurrected: The Act of State Doctrine in the Revised Restatement of U.S. Foreign Relations Law, 79 *American Journal of International Law* 68, 76 (1985).

[184] Childress, When Erie Goes International, 105 *Northwestern University Law Review* 1531, 1569 (2011).

[185] Pub. L. No. 100-669, §1, 102 Stat. 3969 (November 16, 1988).

[186] Restatement (Fourth), supra, at §303. For a discussion of the similar provision in the Restatement (Third), see Leigh, *Sabbatino*'s Silver Anniversary and the Restatement: No Cause for a Celebration, 24 *International Lawyer* 1 (1990).

example, in 1992, in United States v. Merit, the Ninth Circuit, adhering to the act of state doctrine, refused to examine whether South Africa had followed its own extradition laws.[187] So, it seems that, though the influence of the doctrine has certainly receded since the *Sabbatino* case,[188] act of state still plays a useful role in reminding courts of the legislative interests of foreign states and of the need to attempt to coordinate conflicting laws with a view to comity among nations.[189]

3. Diplomatic and Consular Immunities

As the International Court reminded Iran in the *Diplomatic and Consular Staff* case, "there is no more fundamental prerequisite for the conduct of relations between States than the inviolability of diplomatic envoys and embassies."[190] The international legal rules protecting foreign diplomats from the jurisdiction of the receiving state are some of the oldest in history and, despite Iran's recent example, some of the most generally well respected.[191] Long a part of customary international law, diplomatic immunities are now in large measure codified in treaty form.

The 1961 Vienna Convention on Diplomatic Relations[192] has been ratified by most states and constitutes one of the most widely accepted international conventions. Its universal appeal betokens the fact that

[187] 926 F.2d 917, 921 (9th Cir. 1992), *cert. denied*, 506 U.S. 1072 (1992). In Society of Lloyd's v. Siemon-Netto, 457 F.3d 94 (D.C. Cir. 2006), the D.C. Circuit held that the act of state doctrine prevented a U.S. court from considering whether a U.K. statute was an unlawful delegation of power under English law. Id. at 102-103.

[188] See Kashef v. BNP Paribas S.A., 925 F.3d 53 (2d Cir. 2019), where the Second Circuit refused to apply the doctrine, holding that alleged acts of genocide were not shielded from U.S. judicial scrutiny when "both Sudan's own laws and a universal international consensus prohibit us from deeming genocide an 'official act' of Sudan, or for that matter, of any state." Id. at 60.

[189] For a survey of the acts of state doctrine in modern English law, see Perreau-Saussine, British Acts of State in English Courts, 78 *British Year Book of International Law 2007* 176 (2008).

[190] 1979 I.C.J. Reports 7, 19.

[191] *Satow's Guide to Diplomatic Practice* 106 et seq. (Gore-Booth ed. 5th ed. 1979).

[192] 23 U.S.T. 3227, T.I.A.S. No. 7502, 500 U.N.T.S. 95 (done at Vienna April 18, 1961; entered into force April 24, 1964; for the United States December 13, 1972) [hereinafter cited as "Diplomatic Relations Convention"].

the protection of diplomats is a matter of common concern to states from widely differing traditions. Its central provision is Article 29:

> The person of a diplomatic agent shall be inviolable. He shall not be liable to any form of arrest or detention. The receiving State shall treat him with due respect and shall take all appropriate steps to prevent any attack on his person, freedom or dignity.

The same principle figured in one of the earliest U.S. cases applying the law of nations. In Respublica v. De Longchamps, the Court held that "[t]he person of a public minister is sacred and inviolable. Whoever offers any violence to him, not only affronts the Sovereign he represents, but also hurts the common safety and well-being of nations; he is guilty of a crime against the whole world."[193]

From the principle of the inviolability of foreign diplomats follows the other incidents of diplomatic immunity. Foreign missions are inviolable, and the "agents of the receiving State may not enter them, except with the consent of the head of the mission."[194] The archives and documents of the mission are inviolable.[195] "The private residence of a diplomatic agent shall enjoy the same inviolability and protection as the premises of the mission."[196] A diplomatic agent is immune from all criminal jurisdiction of the receiving state, as well as from its civil jurisdiction except as it concerns certain real property, questions of succession, and "an action relating to any professional or commercial activity exercised by the diplomatic agent in the receiving State outside his official functions."[197]

Consuls are concerned with the international economic relations of states, rather than with their political relations. Consuls have not traditionally been accorded the same immunities as diplomats.[198] Only two consular immunities are generally recognized in customary international law: the inviolability of consular archives and the immunity of consuls for their official acts.[199] The 1963 Vienna Convention on

[193] 1 U.S. (1 Dallas) 111, 116 (1784).

[194] Diplomatic Relations Convention, supra, art. 22(1).

[195] Id., art. 24.

[196] Id., art. 30(1).

[197] Id., art. 31(1)(c).

[198] B. Sen, *A Diplomat's Handbook of International Law and Practice* 243 (3d ed. 1988) [hereinafter cited as "Sen"].

[199] Id. at 285.

Consular Relations[200] codifies such consular immunities, but in accordance with tradition does not accord consuls immunity when they act in their personal capacities. Thus, consuls, unlike diplomats, are not immune from either the civil or the criminal jurisdiction of domestic courts when they act outside their official roles.[201] The International Court of Justice has held the United States in violation of the Consular Relations Convention in a number of cases—*Breard, LaGrand,* and *Avena*—where foreign nationals were not advised of their treaty right to request consular assistance in criminal prosecutions. [See Chapter 5.]

[200] 21 U.S.T. 77, T.I.A.S. No. 6820, 596 U.N.T.S. 261 (done at Vienna April 24, 1963; entered into force March 19, 1967; for the United States December 24, 1969).

[201] Sen, supra, at 290-292. The alleged violation of the Vienna Convention on Consular Relations by the United States is at issue in the *Breard* case before the ICJ, see Chapter 5, and Aceves, The Vienna Convention on Consular Relations: A Study of Rights, Wrongs, and Remedies, 31 *Vanderbilt Journal of Transnational Law* 257 (1998).

Table of Cases

I. INTERNATIONAL TRIBUNALS

A. The International Court

B. The European Court of Human Rights

C. The European Court of Justice

D. Inter-American Court of Human Rights

E. International Military Tribunal at Nuremburg

F. International Tribunal for the Former Yugoslavia

G. International Arbitral Tribunals

H. International Criminal Court

I. International Tribunal for the Law of the Sea

J. African Court of Human Rights and Peoples' Rights

II. MUNICIPAL TRIBUNALS

A. United States

B. United Kingdom & Commonwealth

C. Other Municipal Courts

Index

Index

Index

Index

www.ingramcontent.com/pod-product-compliance
Lightning Source LLC
LaVergne TN
LVHW080006210926
848481LV00011B/2955

* 9 7 9 8 8 9 2 0 7 5 3 8 1 *